The 1902 Pittsburgh Pirates

ALSO BY RONALD T. WALDO
AND FROM MCFARLAND

*Honus Wagner and His Pittsburgh Pirates:
Scenes from a Golden Era* (2015)

*Pennant Hopes Dashed by the Homer in the Gloamin':
The Story of How the 1938 Pittsburgh Pirates
Blew the National League Pennant* (2013)

*The Battling Bucs of 1925: How the Pittsburgh Pirates
Pulled Off the Greatest Comeback in World Series History* (2012)

Hazen "Kiki" Cuyler: A Baseball Biography (2012)

*Fred Clarke: A Biography of the Baseball
Hall of Fame Player-Manager* (2011)

The 1902 Pittsburgh Pirates
Treachery and Triumph

RONALD T. WALDO

McFarland & Company, Inc., Publishers
Jefferson, North Carolina

LIBRARY OF CONGRESS CATALOGUING-IN-PUBLICATION DATA

Waldo, Ronald T., 1961–
　　The 1902 Pittsburgh Pirates : treachery and triumph / Ronald T. Waldo.
　　　p.　　cm.
　　Includes bibliographical references and index.

　　ISBN 978-0-7864-7832-3 (softcover : acid free paper) ∞
　　ISBN 978-1-4766-1506-6 (ebook)

　　1. Pittsburg Pirates (Baseball team)—History—20th century.　I. Title.

GV875.P5W34   2015
796.357'640974886—dc23   2015013288

BRITISH LIBRARY CATALOGUING DATA ARE AVAILABLE

© 2015 Ronald T. Waldo. All rights reserved

No part of this book may be reproduced or transmitted in any form or by any means, electronic or mechanical, including photocopying or recording, or by any information storage and retrieval system, without permission in writing from the publisher.

On the cover: Clarence "Ginger" Beaumont, Kitty Bransfield, Jesse Tannehill and stadium Exposition Park, Pittsburgh (National Baseball Hall of Fame Library, Cooperstown, New York)

Printed in the United States of America

McFarland & Company, Inc., Publishers
　Box 611, Jefferson, North Carolina 28640
　　www.mcfarlandpub.com

Acknowledgments

This book, like the five that preceded it, was a labor of love. And the hundreds of hours that go into the research and writing of such a project can make it seem at times like a solitary affair. It is not. All along the way, people stepped forward to offer help of all kinds, some of it indispensable.

As always, I would like to extend thanks to the fine people at the Baseball Hall of Fame, and specifically to photo archivists Jenny Ambrose and Pat Kelly. As has been the case with all of my books, Jenny immediately responded to my queries, and Pat found the perfect photos to accompany the story I was hoping to tell. I commend them both for their professionalism and attention to detail.

I would also like to posthumously offer thanks to friend Lenny Langlois. Lenny always enjoyed reading my historical baseball perspectives, while I loved consuming his viewpoints about the current state of baseball, through the eyes of someone who once played the game. While I only knew Lenny for a couple of years, I would like to offer my gracious thanks for his positive influence, and hope he is commiserating with and getting a chance to pitch against some of the game's greats on baseball's eternal diamond.

Most importantly, I would like to extend a sincere thank you to friend and fellow baseball writer Kathryn Gill, who supplied inspiration at various stages. At times during long days working on this book project, I would take a break to read Kathryn's work, and on many occasions her writings about baseball rejuvenated me and got the creative juices flowing once again. Her passion, devotion and dedication to the game of baseball are both irrefutable and refreshing. Kudos to Kathryn for representing baseball so honorably.

I have to believe if Kathryn had been alive in 1902 while one of the greatest teams in baseball history was frolicking about Exposition Park wreaking havoc on the rest of the National League, she would have been connected to baseball in some fashion. I suspect Kathryn would have been a baseball scribe, passionately covering her beloved New York Highlanders once they entered the baseball scene in 1903, or possibly a pioneer years before Helene Hathaway Britton by owning that American League squad. I wholeheartedly believe that players like Fred Clarke and Honus Wagner from that golden baseball era who loved the game would have been proud to call Kathryn Gill their friend, just as I am today.

Table of Contents

Acknowledgments v
Preface 1

1. Player Influx Catapults Pittsburgh into a Pennant Contender 5
2. Williams Jumps to the Americans, Pirates Win the Pennant 25
3. Barney Dreyfuss Battles Fellow National League Magnates 46
4. Pittsburgh Breaks Out of the Gate in Splendid Fashion 68
5. Executive Discipline Fails to Derail the Pirates Train 88
6. Honus Wagner and Jack O'Connor Heading to St. Louis? 109
7. Jack Chesbro Becomes the National League's Top Pitcher 129
8. Pirates Rooters Demand a Shift to the American League 149
9. Ban Johnson Lures Pirates Stars to the American League 169
10. Jack Chesbro and Jesse Tannehill Issue an Ultimatum to Dreyfuss 190
11. Pittsburgh Breaks Record as Tommy Leach Fight Intensifies 211
12. Pirates Win Third Consecutive Pennant Despite Loss of Stars 232

Appendices
    A: 1902 Pittsburgh Pirates Roster 255
    B: 1902 Pittsburgh Pirates Statistics 257
Chapter Notes 259
Bibliography 282
Index 285

Preface

Throughout its rich history, the game of baseball has gone through many changes and seen numerous alterations to its rules, strategies and long-standing institutions. Major league baseball has also experienced many transformations to its organizational structure as franchises have come and gone, while modifications to the game's top associations have been frequent. One such change occurred following the 1899 season as National League owners decided that contraction and consolidation should rule the day and usher in a new era of baseball that would be more profitable in the twentieth century. The twelve-team National League aggregation that had been established in 1892 changed to an entity containing eight franchises for the 1900 campaign as teams in Louisville, Washington, Cleveland and Baltimore were eliminated.

For many years, baseball fans from the blue collar, industrial city of Pittsburgh, Pennsylvania, had passionately rooted for their favorite team, even though these Pirates rooters experienced disappointment year after year. Pennants and championships were not part of the vocabulary in this town whose mills produced the vital steel that allowed America to grow. The closest Pittsburgh came to tasting pennant glory during the 1890s occurred when the Pirates finished in second place in the National League in 1893. After Pittsburgh secured a seventh-place finish in 1899, the prospects for improvement in 1900 finally looked promising due to the National League's contraction strategy.

Whether it was a stroke of good luck or just the result of conscientious negotiating between two baseball magnates, the Pirates franchise received a huge boost in December 1899, when players from the Louisville Colonels squad were traded to Pittsburgh. Louisville owner Barney Dreyfuss and Pittsburgh baseball magnate William Kerr hammered out an agreement that changed the Smoky City's baseball landscape forever. After the acquisition of

Fred Clarke, Honus Wagner, Tommy Leach and Deacon Phillippe, people connected to baseball now considered Pittsburgh a legitimate title contender whereas they had snickered in the past at such a suggestion.

Those Pirates rooters who had always believed that a National League pennant was a possibility were vindicated when this deal brought in star players and added Barney Dreyfuss to the team's ownership group. The Pittsburgh Pirates quickly became baseball's dominant team and were the first true baseball dynasty of the twentieth century, as pennants commemorating National League titles for 1901, 1902 and 1903 flew at the team's home diamond at Exposition Park. Nestled in Allegheny City on the North Side near downtown Pittsburgh, Exposition Park was the scene of baseball history in an area whose rich heritage is well known. Businessman H. J. Heinz and steel moguls Henry Phipps and Andrew Carnegie each resided in Allegheny at one time. Painter Mary Cassatt, writer Mary Roberts Rinehart, General George Robinson and actress Lois Weber were also born in this municipality where some of the early chapters regarding baseball history were written at Exposition Park.

While the 1903 Pittsburgh Pirates participated in the first modern World Series against the Boston Americans, it was the 1902 squad that defined that franchise during its glorious, three-year stretch dominating the National League. Cut from the same cloth as hard-working people from the city's steel mills and factories, players on that 1902 Pittsburgh Pirates squad put everything on the line each day as they aspired to become one of the greatest teams in baseball history. The end result was a record-breaking campaign which saw that team establish a National League record for victories in a season. By reaching such lofty standards, the 1902 Pittsburgh Pirates also confirmed their legitimacy in any future debates regarding the greatest teams in baseball history.

This book looks closely at that phenomenal season and all of the key events, elements and accomplishments surrounding the 1902 Pittsburgh Pirates. Besides examining the 1902 Pirates team and season, the book also takes a close look at how this squad developed after the Louisville consolidation, and at some of the major problems that confronted Barney Dreyfuss during his first two seasons as the team's owner. Given all of the maneuvers and obstructions perpetrated by less than honorable league colleagues as Dreyfuss attempted to hold on to his highly competitive team, the ultimate reward achieved in 1902 seems that much sweeter from a historical perspective.

As expected, standard bearers of the Pittsburgh Pirates legacy such as Fred Clarke, Honus Wagner and Deacon Phillippe play a huge role in the story of the 1902 season. While these three men always seem to be in the middle of any discussion of that era of Pirates history, other players demand our attention. Jesse Tannehill, Jack Chesbro, Jack O'Connor and Lefty Davis are four excellent examples. On the 1902 team, at least, these players were every bit as important as their more famous counterparts.

When I undertook the task of writing a book about this particular Pirates team, I had my own ideas regarding their greatness and place in baseball history. As I worked on this project and finally completed the book, I found I had a much deeper appreciation for this team due to one major factor. Players on the 1902 Pittsburgh Pirates squad knew they were a great team and made sure opposing teams were aware of this fact. The 1902 Pittsburgh Pirates possessed a swagger that bordered on arrogance at times, which I found to be one of the key ingredients to their success. While this self-assurance served them well, it was the overinflated egos of some players that also led to that team's demise during the summer of 1902, when American League agents secured a few of these men who crossed a line due to believing their own hype.

The 1902 season was the last year that the National and American leagues operated as separate organizations battling for the largest piece of the baseball pie. The war between these two factions finally ended when a peace accord was reached in January 1903. With each league co-existing equally, the first modern World Series was played in 1903 and every following season after that except two. In 1904, the New York Giants refused to play the Boston Americans in a post-season series, while the 1994 World Series was cancelled due to a players' strike. Five teams in Pittsburgh Pirates history have won World Series: 1909, 1925, 1960, 1971 and 1979.

It seems fitting that the record-setting 1902 Pirates won the National League pennant during the final season of a sometimes forgotten baseball era. There is no denying that Fred Clarke's 1902 squad was just as good, if not better, than those five units that claimed world championships for the city of Pittsburgh. It also does not stretch one's baseball intelligence to claim confidently that the 1902 Pittsburgh Pirates were one of the greatest teams in baseball history.

1

Player Influx Catapults Pittsburgh into a Pennant Contender

During the late 1890s, baseball's unique dichotomy was unmistakable for both those men who played the game and faithful fans who rooted for their favorite squad among the National League's 12 teams. As the nineteenth century came to an end, baseball's major league structure had definitely become a two-class system. The identical, good baseball teams consistently finished near the top, while the horrible squads that pulled up the rear each year never changed. In 1896, the pennant-winning Baltimore Orioles outdistanced second-place Cleveland by nine-and-a-half games. The Boston Beaneaters squeaked past Baltimore to claim the title in 1897 and then secured their second consecutive championship one year later when they tied a National League record with 102 wins in 1898. The Brooklyn Superbas bucked the league trend in 1899 after they went from being a second-division dweller one year earlier to championship status when their 101–47 record was good enough to distance second-place Boston by eight games.

While Baltimore and Boston were baseball's dominant teams as the nineteenth century concluded, lower ranking aggregations like the Washington Nationals, Louisville Colonels and Pittsburgh Pirates were still anxiously awaiting an opportunity to drink sweet nectar from the championship chalice. The Cleveland Spiders had fallen on hard times in 1899 as they posted an abysmal 20–134 record three years after they had finished in second place. As a new century dawned, the prospect of improvement for three of the league's bottom-feeder franchises was bleak. A plan was in the works among magnates of the National League to pare the organization down to eight teams for the 1900 campaign. Early rumors indicated that Washington, Cleveland, Baltimore and Louisville were the franchises most likely to be purged.

Louisville team secretary Harry Pulliam alerted Colonels president Barney Dreyfuss to the possibility that their club might be eliminated. Pulliam's foresight in recognizing the inevitable before the contraction process moved out of the discussion stage proved to be a stroke of genius. Pulliam recommended to Dreyfuss that he attempt to pull as much monetary capital together as possible while also striking up friendships with owners from clubs that would be remaining in the National League. This strategy paid immediate dividends for Dreyfuss during a meeting with Cincinnati owner John T. Brush at French Lick, Indiana. Brush stated he had picked up a $5,000 option on the Pittsburgh franchise by backing former Pirates manager W. H. Watkins in his bid to join team ownership. Brush asked Dreyfuss if he wanted to pick up the option since he no longer could follow through with the deal. Dreyfuss, anxious to remain in baseball with the prospect of his Louisville franchise being eliminated, expressed interest in Brush's proposal. After a meeting with some people in Louisville, Dreyfuss agreed to Brush's proposition.[1]

Dreyfuss, accompanied by Watkins, immediately made a trip to Pittsburgh to confer with Pirates owner William W. Kerr. Kerr informed Dreyfuss that Watkins' option had expired. Undeterred by the disappointing news, Dreyfuss convinced Kerr to allow him to assume sole control of Watkins' option.[2] Now that the Louisville owner had his foot in the door, he began negotiations with Kerr to solidify his position within the Pittsburgh Pirates' ownership hierarchy. After some discussions, Dreyfuss believed he had reached an agreement with Kerr that was satisfactory to both parties. Dreyfuss intended to make a trip to Pittsburgh on November 3 in order to pay Kerr the option price of $70,000 that would allow him to become a partner in the Pirates' ownership group.[3] When Dreyfuss reached the Smoky City, joy and hope were replaced with disappointment and disgust when Kerr decided to kill the deal.[4]

"I am sorry that I cannot leave the sum of money I have with me in Pittsburgh," said Dreyfuss. "But Mr. Kerr does not want it, and I guess I'll take it home. I brought it on to pay off the balance on the purchase of the club. Mr. Kerr, however, would not give me a guarantee that there was more than 850 shares of stock issued, or that the club debts exceeded $586. He admitted that if he were the buyer in such a deal he would want such a guarantee. He said my agreement as drawn was all right, but still he wouldn't sign anything. So the deal is off."[5]

Pirates baseball fans in the Smoky City who actually followed the reports regarding this potential shift in ownership probably did not give the story

1. Player Influx Catapults Pittsburgh into a Pennant Contender

another thought once Dreyfuss left Pittsburgh following his rejection by Kerr. It was likely that even diehard baseball rooters in the Smoky City expressed little interest when they read a story in *The Pittsburgh Press* on December 7, 1899, which claimed that Dreyfuss had once again opened negotiations with Kerr to purchase a piece of the Pirates. The article stated that Louisville's president was negotiating with Kerr, along with owners from the Chicago and New York clubs, to secure a deal which gave him the most advantageous outcome. When cornered by the Pittsburgh baseball scribes, Dreyfuss expressed hope that the Louisville club would be sold by Monday, December 11.[6]

While stories regarding initial discussions between Dreyfuss and Kerr probably had bored the average Pirates fan who was not interested in purchase prices and stock options, new information regarding an agreement likely piqued the curiosity of savvy rooters. It was reported that Dreyfuss was offered stock valued at $15,000 in exchange for Louisville players such as Fred Clarke, Deacon Phillippe, Rube Waddell and Honus Wagner.[7] When Smoky City inhabitants opened up their newspapers two days later on December 9, the front page was filled with stories covering the local area's news. Excitement was the buzzword at Pittsburgh's Union Station when it was reported that two children on a train coming from Chicago possibly had smallpox. Tension and panic were relieved when city physician Dr. R. T. Taylor examined the children once the train reached Pittsburgh and discovered they had chicken-pox.[8]

Another article on the front page covered the collapse of an old brick building at 543–545 Penn Avenue that injured pork packer David E. Francis.[9] When readers finally turned to the newspaper's sports section, they were informed that a deal had been struck between William Kerr and Barney Dreyfuss one day earlier which brought the former Louisville owner into the fold as a member of the Pittsburgh Pirates' ownership amalgamation. Dreyfuss gave out a statement to the press regarding how the deal came together while explaining the secrecy which all parties maintained throughout these negotiations.[10]

> It was not known to many, but I came here two weeks ago, and practically closed the deal with Mr. Kerr. We understood each other thoroughly at that time and as I severed my connection with the Louisville club on October 31, I really acted as an agent of Capt. Kerr and P. L. Auten.
>
> It would have been fatal to our plans if any information regarding them had leaked out at the time and I did everything possible to preserve the secret. My talk with Mr. Kerr was over early in the afternoon, and as the train for Louisville did not leave until 9:30 p.m. I did not know how to put in the time. I met a friend and he kindly gave me an invitation to stay in his office until 8 o'clock. I went to the station by the way of side streets and walked beyond the sheds until

the train started, jumping aboard when it reached me. I was thankful that my presence was not discovered. I was authorized by Messrs. Kerr and Auten to present to the stockholders of the Louisville club the proposition which was consummated yesterday.

The Louisville club had its meeting last Monday night and appointed a committee with power to act. Harry Pulliam was chairman and as all the stockholders had discussed the plan for days before the meeting, the appointment of the committee was practically an acceptance of Pittsburgh's offer. At yesterday's conference here all that remained to be done was the signing of papers and this was done a few minutes after we got together at the Seventh Avenue hotel.[11]

This transaction was viewed as a blockbuster deal. Called one of the biggest baseball deals in the history of the National Game by *The Sporting News,* Pittsburgh's organization received an immediate infusion of baseball talent that was unprecedented. The Pirates obtained pitchers Rube Waddell, Deacon Phillippe, Bert Cunningham, Patsy Flaherty and Walt Woods, catchers Tacks Latimer and Chief Zimmer, first baseman Mike Kelley, second baseman Claude Ritchey, third baseman Tommy Leach and outfielders Fred Clarke and Honus Wagner. The four players turned over to Louisville were pitcher Jack Chesbro, catcher George Fox, second baseman John O'Brien and infielder Art Madison.[12] Stockholders of the Louisville club also received $25,000, part of which was contributed by Dreyfuss, according to Louisville's Harry Pulliam.[13]

This historic deal was consummated at Kerr's office in the Arbuckle Building. Fellow owner Phil L. Auten was also present representing the Pirates, while Dreyfuss and Harry Pulliam were at the meeting on behalf of the Louisville franchise. Louisville manager and captain Fred Clarke, considered the greatest all-round outfielder in the National League, also accompanied his bosses during this crucial excursion to the Smoky City. After the transaction was finalized between both sides, Dreyfuss announced that Clarke immediately would assume Pittsburgh's managerial responsibilities.[14] Before Clarke left the Smoky City to be with his wife, Annette, and daughter Helen, in Winfield, Kansas, for Christmas, he gave an assessment of his expectations regarding the 1900 baseball campaign.[15]

"I am more than pleased with the deal, for I have long desired to play in Pittsburgh," said Clarke. "Other members of the Louisville team who are included in this deal will, I know, be delighted with the announcement that they are to become Pirates. Yes, I consider myself most fortunate—in fact, I cannot recall an instance where a manager of a National League club had so much excellent material from which to select a team. I do not anticipate any trouble when it comes to the task of placing the men, and if nothing happens

1. Player Influx Catapults Pittsburgh into a Pennant Contender   9

I am satisfied that the Pittsburgh Club next season will become one of the strongest ever known in the National League.[16]

"Mr. Dreyfuss has promised to send me a list of the players and when that arrives at Winfield I will lose myself on the ranch and spend a week or so studying the paper, so that when I return to Pittsburgh I will have some idea how the team will be on the field. In the meantime any announcement as to the make-up will be unauthorized and mere guess work."[17]

Fred Clarke's résumé as Louisville's manager certainly was far from what he had achieved as a player since entering the league in 1894. While Clarke had solid seasons at the plate in 1895 (.347), 1897 (.390) and 1899 (.340), the best he could do running the Colonels since taking over as their skipper in 1897 was a 75–77 record with a ninth-place finish in 1899. This actually was the best record Louisville had posted since the National League became a 12-team aggregation in 1892. During that eight-year period, the Colonels finished in last place three times. The success of the Pittsburgh Pirates franchise was only slightly better in the 1890s. In 1899, the Pirates finished seventh with a mark of 76–73. Even though Pittsburgh did not land in the basement from 1892 through 1899, they occupied the National League's second division every season except in 1893, when they finished second, and in 1892 and 1896 when they crept out of the bottom half into sixth place.

Separately, Pittsburgh and Louisville had way too many gaping holes on their rosters to receive serious pennant contender consideration as the nineteenth century ended. This scenario changed once the deal between Barney Dreyfuss, William Kerr and Phil Auten was finalized on December 8, 1899. On paper, the immediate infusion of Louisville's talented, top-flight players quickly turned Pittsburgh from an also-ran into a National League pennant contender. Former Colonels players like Fred Clarke, Honus Wagner, Rube Waddell, Claude Ritchey and Tommy Leach were expected to mesh nicely with a small nucleus of Pirates stars that included Sam Leever, Jesse Tannehill, Clarence Beaumont and Jimmy Williams.

On December 13, 1899, the annual meeting of the Pittsburgh Baseball Club was held in Atlantic City, New Jersey. During this yearly summit, Barney Dreyfuss was elected as president of the club for 1900. Phil Auten was named the team's vice-president, William W. Kerr was selected as the team treasurer and Dreyfuss' friend from Louisville, Harry Pulliam, assumed the title of secretary.[18] While Kerr's responsibilities were being reduced from his former position as president, this did not mean the new role as team treasurer meant his only responsibility was to hand out checks on the first and 15th of each month.[19]

"Well, you bet I am taking an interest in the game," Kerr told a reporter, "but of course having turned the reins over to Mr. Dreyfuss I am now doing a thinking part, preferring to let Barney do the talking. Candidly, I do not know what the circuit committee has done, nor do I have any idea what it intends doing, but I do know that no matter how all this wrangling and talking turns out the Pittsburgh club will be found transacting business at the old stand. I have not given much attention to the rumors about a rival league, perhaps for the reason that no one has yet threatened to place an opposition team in this city. Of course I would like to see the National League membership reduced to eight clubs, but I do not at this time see how this is to be brought about. Our team? Well, my boy, just keep an eye on Manager Fred Clarke when the season opens and he will show you a few baseball tricks that will be new to the great patrons of the game in this city. Let 'em come on with eight, 12, 14 or 16 clubs—it won't make any difference to me. Not a bit! We will treat 'em all alike."[20]

Kerr's gushing enthusiasm regarding Fred Clarke was not misguided as Pittsburgh's baseball patrons attempted to learn more about the squad's new players. While many Smoky City fans were ecstatic that local lads like Carnegie's John Peter "Honus" Wagner and George Edward "Rube" Waddell of Bradford were now members of the Pirates, many viewed the acquisition of Clarke to be a major coup. One of the best players in the National League, though still learning the nuances of strategic maneuvers as a field general, Clarke was a shrewd tactician with the bat. During a trip to Chicago in January, Clarke explained why he was so proficient in the matter of placing hits.[21]

"I can place the ball about where I want," Clarke confidently declared, "but I can't tell whether I am going to send out a fly or a grounder. It is possible to control your hit as to general direction, sending the ball into any fields, but impossible to make it a fly or a grounder hit at will. To be successful a batter has to study his pitcher, and this is just as essential as it is for the pitcher to study the batter."[22]

Many Pirates fans believed Fred Clarke, the player, would continue to accomplish spectacular feats for Pittsburgh in 1900. These same rooters were not as effusive in their praise when the subject of Fred Clarke, the manager, was discussed. One noteworthy fan from the Smoky City was not even convinced that Clarke was better than the man he replaced. "Fred Clarke is a great player, but as a manager I do not think he outclasses Patsy Donovan," stated the well posted rooter. "In fact Patsy has many advantages over the Colonel. McGraw is in a class by himself, and as a leader ranks next to Hanlon. It is ridiculous to talk about other managers being 'just as good.'"[23]

1. Player Influx Catapults Pittsburgh into a Pennant Contender 11

Outfielder Patsy Donovan had been a favorite of the Pittsburgh fans ever since he joined the Pirates during the 1892 season. He also managed the Corsairs on two occasions, pulling down duty as Kerr's and Auten's pilot in 1897 and 1899. When Clarke was named as the Pirates' new skipper after Barney Dreyfuss worked out the deal to join Pittsburgh's ownership group, Donovan's status with the team could best be described as tenuous. Not wanting any obstacles that could pose a problem in 1900 where Donovan might have second-guessed some of Clarke's managerial decisions, the star outfielder was sold to the St. Louis Cardinals for $1,000 in January.

Donovan's shift to St. Louis was not the only move that Clarke and Dreyfuss made, tweaking the Pirates roster before the team left for spring training in March. Pitcher Tully Sparks was sold to the Philadelphia Phillies in February. Hurler Bill Hoffer was released in March and first baseman Mike Kelley quickly followed him out the door when Dreyfuss peddled the former Colonel to Indianapolis of the American Association for cash. When the National League officially eliminated Louisville, Cleveland, Baltimore and Washington from the circuit, Jack Chesbro, George Fox, John O'Brien and Art Madison were sent back to Pittsburgh in March before the Colonels shut down operations. Fox, O'Brien and Madison were disposed of with expediency, while Chesbro's continued employment in the National League hinged upon his ability to show Clarke and Dreyfuss more ability than he exhibited in 1899 when he went 6–9 with an ERA of 4.11.

Chesbro wasted no time signing a contract for the 1900 season, when his baseball rights were once again assumed by the Pirates. Two previous holdouts also followed Chesbro into the Buccaneer fold as pitcher Sam Leever and outfielder Tom O'Brien, who had played for the New York Giants in 1899, attached their signatures to Pirates contracts. One month earlier Leever, a former schoolmaster who went 21–23 in 1899, stated that he would rather train to become a more proficient trap shooter in an Ohio country school rather than sign a contract at the terms suggested by Dreyfuss.[24] In February, Leever had returned his contract unsigned with a letter which articulated the schoolmaster's wish to discuss a few points with the Pirates' owner before he came to terms. Dreyfuss, while baffled by Leever's stance, insinuated that negotiations between the two sides had no chance of becoming a reality.[25]

"For the life of me I cannot understand what Sam is driving at," remarked Dreyfuss. "He does not say that he will not sign for the salary offered—does not even hint that the terms of the contract are unsatisfactory. I don't know what he wants to argue, but I do know that he will not argue any points with me. He has been tendered a contract. If he does not like it, he can let it alone. It is all up to him. I have said my little say."[26]

The signings of Leever, Chesbro and O'Brien left former Louisville Colonels hurler Ellsworth Elmer "Bert" Cunningham as the Pirates' only remaining holdout. After having a career season for Louisville in 1898 when he went 28–15, the 34-year-old pitcher slumped a bit in 1899 as he posted a 17–17 record, buttressed by a 3.84 ERA. Baseball writers in Pittsburgh speculated that Cunningham had not signed because he might be nursing a grievance or was waiting to see if a Louisville entry which he possibly would be given a chance to manage was included in the new American League. Barney Dreyfuss readily admitted that he did not know why Cunningham had failed to forward his contract to Pirates headquarters.[27] Growing impatient with whatever Cunningham's problem was, Dreyfuss rendered the pitcher's reason for not signing a moot point when he sold Cunningham to the Chicago Orphans on March 9.

Cunningham's removal from Pittsburgh's roster finalized the group of players that manager Fred Clarke planned on taking to spring training. Preparing the Pirates for the 1900 baseball campaign began in Thomasville, Georgia, on March 15 when Clarke and his troops arrived to begin the important training session. Clarke got started one day later as he put the boys through a spirited practice on Friday morning. Leading by example, Clarke got in as much work as some of the squad's younger recruits. He was commended for immediately implementing his plans for spring training. Clarke's promptness in getting down to serious work indicated he could successfully handle the huge responsibility that had been placed on his shoulders.[28]

Clarke held training sessions in both the morning and afternoon on the second day of camp. His constant cry of "Save the arms" cascaded throughout the field during the four hours of intense practice as Pittsburgh's manager cautioned youngsters who were a bit too exuberant for their own good loosening up in the warm sun. Dressing for dinner that evening was a painful affair for many tired players who had worked like slaves during the team's first training sessions.[29] While everything ran smoothly for Clarke on the baseball diamond during Pittsburgh's initial practices, the same could not be said regarding a crucial creature comfort during the team's stay in Thomasville.

When the Pirates arrived in Thomasville on March 15, the hotel which they had secured accommodations was overcrowded. Because no rooms were available, an adjoining church was prepared to serve as lodging for the Pittsburgh Pirates team. Despite conditions not being ideal, Fred Clarke stated that all of his players were comfortable and that no man had complained in

1. Player Influx Catapults Pittsburgh into a Pennant Contender   13

any way.³⁰ Young third baseman Tommy Leach, who roomed with Clarke during their stay in Thomasville and was very popular with his teammates, claimed he was a member of that happy group of Pirates, even though he was slated to be utility player in 1900.³¹

"Why, certainly I am satisfied with my position," said Leach. "Why shouldn't I be, when you work for such people as Mr. Dreyfuss and Harry Pulliam, not to mention Clarke? I would prefer to play on the team regularly, but as there are stars in all the positions now, I suppose I will have to wait my turn."³²

While the Pirates spent most of their time in Thomasville getting down to serious business, this did not preclude some incidents aimed at breaking the monotony and adding a mirthful twist to the trip. One such episode transpired at the church where Pittsburgh established its headquarters. The church had a huge bell in the steeple that was rung whenever a fire occurred. This was a piece of information that had not been forwarded to the Pittsburgh Pirates' entourage. One morning, veteran Bill "Pop" Schriver thought it would be a great idea to wake up his sleeping teammates by ringing the bell. Schriver went up into the steeple and pulled the rope a few times. After the bell bellowed out a few loud twangs, Thomasville erupted into a frenzy of activity and the fire department was dispatched to take care of the crisis. When it was discovered that this was only a false alarm, manager Fred Clarke had to convince the town's mayor not to impose the $10 fine that was customary in such cases.³³

When Clarke was not playing diplomat he was busy on the baseball diamond working diligently to mold his squad into a top-flight pennant contender. Pittsburgh's new manager was extremely confident that his team would be one of the National League's best clubs in 1900. "I don't claim that we are going to win the pennant," said Clarke during a training break, "but I will say that we have as likely a bunch as any fan ever looked on, and if we don't land the flag we will be knocking at the door and fighting to get in. It is a great team, and no mistake—the strongest I ever played with, and if we don't finish—well—where we finish, I will be greatly disappointed. The players all seem to have taken well to each other, and I expect and will demand absolute harmony."³⁴

A small group of baseball writers who watched the Pirates during their exhibition game tour did not seem to hold the same high opinion of the team as Clarke. Joe Campbell was the most outspoken member of this group. Campbell and his disciples suddenly developed an abnormal interest in the Pirates because the gentlemen believed Clarke's players were a headless horde of brainless players. Campbell offered a blistering montage of mistakes that proved Pittsburgh's players could not think. He cited an instance when Clarke did not know enough to run to first base after he hit the ball. Campbell also lamented the fact that shortstop Fred "Bones" Ely possibly could always field a grounder and throw it into center field as he did during an exhibition game. Campbell criticized second baseman Claude Ritchey for being prone to stand and hold the baseball instead of trying to complete a double play.[35]

No Pirates player was exempt from scrutiny as Campbell continued citing his scathing litany of mistakes claiming that Honus Wagner and Clarence Beaumont were liable to participate in a game of tag between themselves when the ball was smacked into the outfield. Campbell also claimed that third baseman Jimmy Williams did not possess enough common sense to run in on a bunt hit. He saved his most blatant critique for young first baseman Frank "Pop" Dillon. Campbell claimed that Dillon, who lacked confidence when he had to react quickly to a play in front of him, was prone to start on a tour of the base paths when an opponent placed a ball in play. While manager Fred Clarke realized it would take some time for this new aggregation of players to run like a well-oiled machine, he refuted Campbell's contention that Pittsburgh's players had defective top-pieces.[36]

"I have no fear of the players showing any form of weakness," Clarke wrote to baseball scribe Al. E. Gheny, "and I will venture the prediction that the thinking part will be taken care of in good shape. The boys will play the fine points of the game as well as any of them. We have a crowd of intelligent young men and one or two old ones who know a thing or two about the tricks of the trade, and before the season is very far advanced they will demonstrate to the satisfaction of the baseball world that certain baseball writers have made moon-faced monkeys of themselves.

"Our pitching staff will be one of the finest ever collected on one team. We have four men to work regularly and two or three corking good ones to fall back on in case of an emergency. Our infield will be decidedly strong. Dillon at first base is one of the best fielders in that position the game has ever known. He is a young man of more than ordinary intelligence and is not afraid to take a chance when it comes to turning a trick or working an inside play. In our practice work he has shown up finely with the stick and I am confident he will make good in that direction when the games count. He has a natural swing, and there is no reason in the world why he should not develop into one of the best batsmen in the country.

"Ritchey, Ely and Williams are all there, both in the field and at the bat. They work together beautifully. I do not know where the Pittsburgh Club could get two such outfielders as Wagner and Beaumont. They are strong throwers, good fielders, regular stickers and fast on the bases. It is too bad that our men cannot think, but I guess they will make up for that deficiency by their splendid all round work."³⁷

The opportunity to test Joe Campbell's and Fred Clarke's theories regarding the Pirates came as Pittsburgh opened the 1900 campaign on April 19 in St. Louis at League Park. All of the positive expectations and hype were deflated somewhat when Cy Young tossed a shutout and the Cardinals, with former Pirates manager Patsy Donovan at the helm, prevailed, 3–0. Clarke's opening day lineup had him, Clarence Beaumont and Honus Wagner in the outfield. The infield consisted of Jimmy Williams at third base, Fred Ely at short, Claude Ritchey second base and Pop Dillon playing first. Pitcher Sam Leever and catcher Chief Zimmer were Clarke's battery in this game that ushered in a new era of Pittsburgh Pirates baseball.

Smoky City fans who were expecting great things from this latest installment of the Pirates felt the same kind of disappointment and apathy that had plagued them for years, as Fred Clarke's team stumbled out of the gate. When April ended, the Pirates were mired in sixth place with a 4–6 record. Brainless play on the part of Clarke's troops was also prevalent during the season's early stages. Honus Wagner was caught napping on two occasions while occupying a base, and Clarence Beaumont and another player had been doubled up on fly balls to the outfield.³⁸ Pittsburgh's slow start was compounded by the fact that star third baseman Jimmy Williams hurt himself in Cincinnati when he lost a battle against League Park's hard, rocky infield. Although he was only expected to miss a few games, the loss of a player who led the Pirates in hitting with a .354 average in 1899 even for a short period of time hampered a team trying to find its way.³⁹

Barney Dreyfuss and Fred Clarke decided to tinker with the roster to jump-start the team. On April 30, veteran Duff "Dick" Cooley was purchased from the Philadelphia Phillies for $1,000 to give Pittsburgh an upgrade at first base. Pop Dillon's glaring deficiencies and inexperience at the initial sack resulted in his being farmed out to Detroit. While Cooley was expected to deliver better results at the plate than Dillon, who batted .111 over five games in 1900, things did not run smoothly for the veteran player. When Pittsburgh was in Chicago for a series against the Orphans, Dreyfuss arrived at the hotel one night and found that every player was in his room except for Cooley.⁴⁰

"Where is Dick Cooley?" Dreyfuss asked team secretary Harry Pulliam.

"I do not know," answered Pulliam.

"Well, I do," answered Dreyfuss. "I just saw him at the Auditorium with two women and a batting average of .115."⁴¹

Cooley's indiscretions were minor when compared to those of another member of the Pirates squad who kept Barney Dreyfuss, William Kerr and Fred Clarke on their toes due to his free-spirit nature. Southpaw hurler George Edward "Rube" Waddell possessed enormous raw talent that was overshadowed at times by his eccentric behavior. As the season progressed through May, the rumor that Waddell was likely to be traded to another team started gathering steam. Waddell had not shown any of the speed he exhibited in 1899 as his pitches were liberally swatted by opponents at various ballparks during the early stages of the 1900 campaign.[42] Making matters worse for Waddell was that his behavior had annoyed Pittsburgh management on more than one occasion.

One evening in early May when the Pirates were in town for a short home stand, Waddell was spotted serving beer and free lunches at a bar in the eastern section of Pittsburgh. He explained that he was helping out the proprietor of the establishment. When word of his moonlighting reached Barney Dreyfuss and William Kerr, the magnates threw up both hands, signaling surrender, and vowed to release the southpaw unless he severed his connection with this side-show silliness immediately. Waddell promised to be good if he was given a second chance. While Dreyfuss and Kerr showed more patience in respect to Waddell's idiosyncrasies, manager Fred Clarke's disgust became more apparent as his patience was stretched beyond its limits.[43]

Clarke was slowly tiring of Waddell's unpredictable behavior. On more than one occasion Waddell, distracted by other things such as playing marbles or baseball with local kids, failed to show up at the ballpark for a game when Pittsburgh played at home. Clarke cringed whenever Pawnee Bill's Wild West Show made an appearance in the Smoky City. He suspended Waddell when the southpaw hurler injured his wrist trying to curve a brick. A few days later, Waddell punctured his neck doing flip-flops while playing a pick-up baseball game during his short exile from the Pirates' squad.[44] Realizing that something had to be done with Waddell in order to maintain discipline, Clarke and Dreyfuss decided on July 25 to loan him to Connie Mack's Milwaukee team in the American League. After pitching a few games during his suspension for a semi-pro team in Punxsutawney, PA, Waddell agreed to join Mack's squad at a salary of $250 a month.[45]

Even though Cooley and Waddell tested the resolve of Pirates management in May, the team started to show more life on the baseball diamond. The Pirates went 16–10 during May to rise to fourth place with a 20–16 record. The Pirates made a crucial move on May 22 that helped solidify their catching weakness when Barney Dreyfuss purchased veteran Jack O'Connor from the St. Louis Cardinals. To acquire O'Connor, Dreyfuss had to outbid both Boston

1. Player Influx Catapults Pittsburgh into a Pennant Contender   17

and Chicago. The deal was deemed necessary because regular backstops Chief Zimmer and Pop Schriver had experienced trouble rounding into shape. Pirates fans were anxious to see if the energetic O'Connor's ginger could help assist the team in showing more life at times on the baseball field.[46]

    The deal to acquire O'Connor from St. Louis ended up being a bigger bargain for Dreyfuss than he had imagined. When Dreyfuss submitted an offer of $2,000 to secure O'Connor's services, Cardinals owner Frank de Haas Robison agreed to sell his catcher to Pittsburgh. O'Connor was released immediately was paid $300, and was advanced the same amount of money from Pittsburgh. Dreyfuss then received a telegram from Robison which stated that the offer of $1,000 for O'Connor was satisfactory. A few days after O'Connor joined the Pirates, Robison received a check from Dreyfuss for $1,300. St. Louis' owner immediately questioned Dreyfuss' intentions and demanded to know why the check was not for the full price of $2,000, with the $300 bonus that had been remitted.[47]

    Dreyfuss responded that St .Louis made the sale for $1,000. Robison became angry, insisting that the purchase price was $2,000, and mailed the check back to Dreyfuss. When Dreyfuss presented the telegram stating that Robison had accepted the offer of $1,000 for O'Connor, St. Louis' owner was flabbergasted. Someone in the Cardinals' front office obviously had made a mistake finalizing the paperwork regarding O'Connor's transfer to Pittsburgh.[48] The addition of an old war horse such as O'Connor to Pittsburgh's roster could not have come at a better time, since one of the team's star players was mired in the worst slump of his illustrious career. On May 28, left fielder Fred Clarke's batting average stood at a wretched .156.

    Unlike many other National League stars who saw their overall play plummet when a batting slump occurred, Clarke did not allow his struggles at the plate to affect the remainder of his game. He was as active as ever in the outfield, making catches that many of his contemporaries did not dare to attempt. If making such plays hurt his batting average, but helped Pittsburgh win games, Clarke was satisfied with the outcome. Pittsburgh's star left fielder always tried to get his hand on the baseball, even when the chance of snagging a fly ball was slim.[49] While Clarke's hustle and dedication could never be questioned, his overall health during the season's first two months certainly was causing the Pirates manager enormous problems. While the team was on a trip through the east, Clarke was forced to return to Pittsburgh on June 7 due to a kidney ailment and minor liver trouble.[50]

    Clarke's health issues were not considered serious. Pittsburgh's manager went to a resort in Cambridge Springs, Pennsylvania, to rest and recuperate.

He was expected to be sidelined for up to three weeks.[51] Barney Dreyfuss claimed that Clarke had constantly fretted over the work of his team. This caused a decline in his performance at the plate as his eyesight grew poorer with each passing day. While Clarke was on the disabled list, Tom O'Brien took over in left field and Duff Cooley assumed the managerial reins. O'Brien possessed great skill, but could not play the inside game as Clarke did. Cooley was an adequate replacement at best as team skipper, since he could not come close to earning the respect that Clarke had gained from Pittsburgh's players.[52]

A five-game losing streak while Clarke was resting in Cambridge Springs prompted Pittsburgh's manager to attempt a return to the lineup even though physicians had advised him to remain away from the game for a few more weeks. Clarke played left field during an 8–5 loss to Chicago at Exposition Park on June 16 and the following day when the Pirates lost to the Orphans, 8–1. The exertion of the first game, a long trip to Chicago Saturday night, and the excitement of Sunday's game took its toll physically on Clarke. He literally collapsed during the ninth inning. After the contest, Clarke was dejected as he informed Barney Dreyfuss and Harry Pulliam that he would have to quit baseball for an indefinite period of time. His teammates were despondent over the fact that their manager was ill.[53]

Clarke missed only three games as he remained on the sidelines for eight more days. He returned to the lineup on June 26 as the Pirates defeated Chicago at Exposition Park, 8–6. Pittsburgh proceeded to go 9–1 in their next ten games as Clarke seemed to be rejuvenated following the short break away from baseball. After the Pirates swept an Independence Day doubleheader from Boston at Exposition Park, they stood in third place with a 34–28 record which left them five games behind the defending champion Brooklyn Superbas. Just as it seemed that Pittsburgh was ready to overtake Brooklyn, Clarke's troops slipped into another funk. Mediocrity was the norm throughout the remainder of July as the Pirates' record stood at 43–38 when the month ended.

Distractions due to a player's personality and a critical injury contributed to Pittsburgh's malaise as Clarke and Dreyfuss attempted to get the Pirates' ship steered in the right direction. Persistent rumors that New York manager Buck Ewing wanted to acquire southpaw Jesse Tannehill dogged the team for weeks. Tannehill stated that he did not wish to leave Pittsburgh and would not shirk his responsibility when called upon.[54] This attitude on Tanny's part seemed to directly contradict news that leaked out near the end of June. There were some bad feelings between Pirates management and Tannehill due to the pitcher's indifference. As it turned out, he wanted to get away from the Smoky City. Ewing sold Tannehill on the virtues of becoming a Giant and told Dreyfuss he would be charitable and take the southpaw off Pittsburgh's hands since his arm was dead.[55]

Dreyfuss intended to leave Tannehill behind in Pittsburgh to think about his indiscretion as Pittsburgh opened a four-game series against Chicago on June 17. These plans changed when Sam Leever was unable to make the trip due to an injury. Facing the realization that he had better do something to appease Pirates management, Tannehill pitched one of his best games of the season when he defeated the Orphans, 8–1, on June 20. When Clarke took charge of the Pittsburgh squad, he had been warned that Tannehill might be a troublemaker. He laughed off the suggestion and stated he would treat every man fairly, and hoped he would receive the same kind of treatment

Shortly after the big deal between Louisville and Pittsburgh was finalized on December 8, 1899, Barney Dreyfuss announced that Fred Clarke would assume the Pirates' managerial duties. The first few months of the 1900 season were tough for Clarke, who was batting only .156 on May 28. The star outfielder was also forced to the sidelines in June with a kidney ailment (courtesy of the National Baseball Hall of Fame Library, Cooperstown, New York).

in return. The clever little southpaw's disposition certainly had changed for the worse during the past two years.[56] Salary issues seemed to consume Tannehill more than it had in the past.

While the problem surrounding star pitcher Jesse Tannehill seemed to be subsiding for the moment, an injury to third baseman Jimmy Williams added some suspense to Pittsburgh's plight in July. During a 23–8 loss at Exposition Park to the Philadelphia Phillies on July 13, Williams injured his leg during the first inning. He was on third base when Phillies catcher Ed McFarland snapped a throw to Harry Wolverton, trying to catch him napping. When Williams dove back into third, he caught his foot on the bag and rolled over, moaning in pain. He was surrounded by his teammates, who pulled his leg, slapped his calves, wiped his brow and got him back on his feet. Williams limped around for a few minutes and then hobbled off the field as Tommy Leach took his place.[57]

Despite a season filled with adversity, Pittsburgh remained within striking distance of Brooklyn in the National League standings. Even though the Pirates posted only a 13–10 record in August, they moved past the Philadelphia Phillies into second place. At one point, it was reported that Pittsburgh was playing the best article of ball being furnished in the National League.[58] Back to performing at the top of his game, manager Fred Clarke offered his evaluation of Pittsburgh's recent success.

"I am not making any boasts," said Clarke, "but I do not think anyone can attribute our good position in the race to luck. We have been playing consistently, and had not we been forced to take up our last Eastern trip with a patched up team I think we would now be several notches closer to that Brooklyn bunch."[59]

There was one group of rooters at Exposition Park that did not care whether skill or luck was guiding the Pirates in 1900. Some of these "sporty fellows" didn't always root for the home team. Exposition Park was riddled with gamblers who would place their wager the evening before a game was played or that afternoon in the ballpark. The owners of the Pittsburgh club were vehemently opposed to betting on Pirates games, but their jurisdiction did not extend beyond the ballpark. While open betting wasn't permitted in the grandstand, this rule did not prevent some men from quietly making wagers as large sums of money changed hands within the confines of Exposition Park.[60] Since so much cash was being risked, it came as no surprise that these bettors voiced their opinion vociferously when things were not going as planned. Brooklyn manager Ned Hanlon was shocked at how these vile patrons behaved with malicious intent when the Superbas played an August series at Exposition Park.

> It is an outrage the way some of these knockers abuse a team. Here is the Pittsburgh Club playing pennant ball, something Pittsburgh has been clamoring for, for a long time, but just because the team downs us two out of three, some dishonest fellow sets up the whine that the games are not on the square. I am glad to note that the majority of people to whom I have spoken are giving the Pirates the credit they deserve.[61]

The Pirates continued battling gallantly to wrestle the top spot away from Brooklyn. Fred Clarke's squad saved their best baseball for the stretch drive as Pittsburgh posted an 18–9 record in September. After September 25, the Pirates were only one game out of first place and a mere ten percentage points

1. Player Influx Catapults Pittsburgh into a Pennant Contender

behind Hanlon's Superbas.[62] Pittsburgh was able to make a run for the pennant even though some of their players were forced to the sidelines. Third baseman Jimmy Williams was pulled from the starting lineup due to a nagging ankle injury.[63] Honus Wagner, who was doing phenomenal work for the Pirates, was summoned to Pittsburgh during a long eastern swing due to the death of his mother, Katheryn Wagner, on September 10.[64] While Pittsburgh continued surging despite these setbacks, their long-term pennant aspirations were dealt a serious blow when Fred Clarke injured his leg in a game at Exposition Park against St. Louis on September 20.[65]

A deep, dark pall overcame the hopes and dreams of Exposition Park's diehard patrons as Clarke walked off the baseball diamond. Clarke's absence was not noticeable at first as the Pirates forged onward and Tom McCreery did fine work as a replacement in left field.[66] Pittsburgh's manager returned to the lineup for two games against Cincinnati on September 26 and 27 before being sidelined once again. After being forced to leave the game in the first inning when he tried to play against St. Louis on October 6, Fred did not appear in another contest. Everything quickly came crashing down for the team when they fell into a slump and went 1–6 from September 24 through October 6. Brooklyn easily clinched the pennant even though Pittsburgh went 5–2 during the final week. When the Pirates returned home for their final series at Exposition Park after four games in St. Louis, Barney Dreyfuss accused some of his players of loafing even though Pittsburgh won three of the four contests against the Cardinals.[67]

Dreyfuss explained that he was very dissatisfied with some of his players' work in recent games. When there was a strong possibility that Pittsburgh might win the National League pennant, Dreyfuss had offered to give each member of the Pirates a $1,000 bonus if the team finished in first place and $500 if they landed in second. He seemed to be having a change of heart in respect to those men he believed had loafed while taking the bonus for granted. "It is the duty of the players to do their best all the time," said Dreyfuss. "The public pays to see baseball and not loafing matches. Tuesday's game could have been won if the boys had attended to business. Some of them who thought they had a cinch on a nice present will be mistaken."[68]

Even though Pittsburgh faded during the pennant race's home stretch, their 1900 season was an undisputable success. The Pirates finished in second place with a record of 79–60 and trailed the pennant-winning Brooklyn Superbas, who posted a mark of 82–54, by 4½ games. While the majority of Pittsburgh's rooters wanted to see a pennant flag fly at Exposition Park, they were delighted that this squad which had been dubbed the "Headless Wonders" by one baseball writer before the season finished in second place.⁶⁹ Pirates fans were also ecstatic over some of their favorite players' individual performances in 1900. Honus Wagner led the National League in hitting with a .381 average and also paced the circuit in doubles (45) and triples (22). Fred Clarke parlayed a resurgence at the plate during the second half to raise his average to .276 after a brutal start. Deacon Phillippe (20–13, 2.84 ERA) and Jesse Tannehill (20–6, 2.88 ERA) were Pittsburgh's aces. Rube Waddell, who returned to the Pirates in August, posted a league low ERA of 2.37 even though he went only 8–13.

In the spirit of competition and good sportsmanship, *The Pittsburgh Chronicle-Telegraph* brokered a post-season series between Pittsburgh and Brooklyn. The newspaper also offered a cup trophy designed by Hardy & Haynes to be awarded to the victorious team. The trophy, made entirely of silver and lined with gold, was made in the shape of a punch bowl and had an estimated value of $500.⁷⁰ When Pittsburgh's players realized at the 11th hour they had made a mistake trying to handle the logistical needs of this series, Harry Pulliam's services were requested so his solid pedigree in this area could be utilized. Pulliam immediately wired Ned Hanlon for information regarding his Brooklyn club and insisted upon having high-priced umpires Hank O'Day and Tim Hurst officiate the games.⁷¹

Nearly 4,000 fans were on hand at Exposition Park on October 15 as Brooklyn, behind the solid pitching of Joe McGinnity, defeated Pittsburgh in the best-of-five series' first game, 5–2.⁷² The Superbas captured Game Two one day later, 4–2, as wretched fielding on the part of Jimmy Williams, Tom O'Brien and Jack O'Connor sabotaged a strong performance by Sam Leever.⁷³ Pittsburgh finally placed a game in the win column on October 17 when Deacon Phillippe shut out the Superbas, 10–0. Tommy Leach was the game's star as he reached base five times, scored four runs and knocked in one teammate.⁷⁴ The Pirates' momentum was short-lived as Joe McGinnity showed Clarke and his players on October 18 why Brooklyn had won two consecutive National League pennants. McGinnity stifled Pittsburgh throughout the afternoon and claimed the series for Brooklyn with a 6–1 victory.⁷⁵

When the victorious Superbas returned to their lodgings at the Monongahela House after the final game, at the suggestion of Joe Kelley a unanimous vote was taken to award the cup trophy to McGinnity so it could be placed on display at his machine shop in Oklahoma.⁷⁶ The receipts from the four games, which totaled about $3,000, were divided equally among the players. Brooklyn was formally presented with *The Chronicle-Telegraph Trophy* on October 19, 1900, at Pittsburgh's Alvin Theater. The presentation occurred

1. Player Influx Catapults Pittsburgh into a Pennant Contender 23

after the first act of "Papa's Wife." Players from both squads watched as Mayor William J. Diehl presented Joe Kelley with the big silver cup while actress Anna Held stood nearby. After the night's festivities, McGinnity received the cup and was awarded a $100 bonus from the Brooklyn magnates.[77] Shortly after the cup series ended, Fred Clarke critiqued Pittsburgh's fine season.

> We lost the cup series on its merits and have no explanation to make. It is great satisfaction to know that we rank as the second team in the official standing at the close of the race. That is something for a one-year team to be proud of. Then again we made more money than any other club, so I am told. A number of new players will be added to our roster in 1901 and it will be a surprise to me if we do not do better in the next race than we did last year.[78]

Many baseball fans in Pittsburgh were left to ponder whether star southpaw Jesse Tannehill would be a member of the 1901 Pittsburgh Pirates. During the series with Brooklyn, Clarke used Sam Leever, Deacon Phillippe and Rube Waddell while Tannehill remained on the sidelines. Rumors abounded prior to the series that Clarke had no intention of using him and was prepared to remove him from the roster. It was also claimed that Pittsburgh's manager had no use for Waddell and considered him a nuisance. Clarke was known to have a quick temper and was not a man to be trifled with when it boiled over.[79] Another story pursued by the press claimed that Tannehill had refused to pitch during the series against Brooklyn. The southpaw pitcher wasted no time explaining his side of the story as rumors regarding this supposed temperamental behavior started gathering momentum.[80]

> If Dreyfuss and Clarke want to get rid of me I will go, providing a deal is satisfactory to me. Pittsburgh is the best town in the country to play in, and I have been treated handsomely there. Any ball player who has played in that city and wants to get away is a sucker. During the Cup Series with Brooklyn there was a statement published to the effect that I had refused to pitch any of the games. This is not true, because I was never asked to pitch.
> In justice to me I think that Manager Clarke should have denied the story at the time, but he did not see fit to do so. As far as a portion of the public souring on me is concerned that is all bosh. Nobody has soured on me save Dreyfuss and Clarke. So long as a pitcher wins a majority of his games the public is satisfied. I did that, and I can't see what kick there is coming against me or my work. I want it understood, however, that I will not go to any club, and a deal must be satisfactory to me before I consent to be transferred.[81]

Although Tannehill's status as a Pirate in 1900 was still unclear, there was no such ambivalence when it came to Fred Clarke. President Barney Dreyfuss wasted no time announcing that Pittsburgh's star left fielder and manager had signed a new contract that covered more than one season. "We did not want to have to bother with a contract with our manager every year," said Dreyfuss, "so just fixed it up with him for a number of years."[82]

Success on the baseball diamond made it imperative that Clarke's services be guaranteed for a number of seasons. Besides the Pirates' fine work against National League competition, the franchise had profited greatly on the business side in 1900. Although treasurer William Kerr declined to discuss how much money the Pittsburgh Pirates made, the figure was estimated to be not far below $70,000.[83] Baseball fans throughout the Smoky City reasoned that such financial prosperity meant the team's executives were coexisting in joyful bliss. The first report which indicated this was not the case came in November when it was reported that Frank Balliett likely would return to his post as team secretary in 1901, since Harry Pulliam was moving on to Chicago as an assistant to owner James A. Hart.[84] Pulliam immediately denied that he intended to join the Chicago organization, leading to speculation that William Kerr and Phil Auten planned on firing the team secretary but had not informed him of their intention.[85]

In early December, Pulliam demanded that an immediate vote be taken to elect a secretary for the Pittsburgh club.[86] While baseball fans were trying to make sense of the situation regarding Pulliam, they were blindsided in late December by the news that Kerr and Auten also wanted to depose Barney Dreyfuss as president of the Pittsburgh Pirates organization. It seemed that Dreyfuss' fellow owners wanted to remove the little magnate because "he had been a little out of line lately."[87] For the second year in a row, Barney Dreyfuss' existence in baseball was in jeopardy of being terminated. As had been the case following the 1899 campaign, Dreyfuss planned on fighting until the bitter end.

2

Williams Jumps to the Americans, Pirates Win the Pennant

Even though Pittsburgh battled for the National League pennant and finished the 1900 baseball campaign in second place behind Brooklyn, this highly successful showing did not seem to matter to magnates William Kerr and Phil Auten. The two longtime owners were committed to eliminating the two men from Louisville whose positive vision and baseball savvy had helped improve the team's fortunes during their first year running the club. Kerr and Auten appeared to be using the false premise that Harry Pulliam was going to join the Chicago Orphans organization as their justification for firing Pittsburgh's team secretary.[1] One of the issues they had with Barney Dreyfuss was his blistering reaction to the Pulliam situation. Dreyfuss, whose loyalty to his friend was indestructible, was not afraid to speak his mind about Pulliam's firing and never minced words when he offered an opinion about the matter or criticized his partners.[2]

While Kerr's patience regarding Dreyfuss' indiscreet comments was wearing thin, a second reason why he was considering a vote to elect a new team president rose to the surface. It was reported that Kerr was not happy because Dreyfuss was spending the off-season living in New York. He believed Dreyfuss should be in Pittsburgh at all times looking after the franchise's affairs. There was also the revelation by someone close to the situation that Dreyfuss was not fighting so much for the retention of Pulliam as team secretary, but to block Frank Balliet, who happened to be Phil Auten's nephew, from being elected to that post. On more than one occasion, Pulliam also indicated that it was Auten who seemed to be his main detractor while Kerr acquiesced to his partner's wishes and had not promoted the plan to fire him.[3] The inference that Dreyfuss was not concerned with Pulliam's plight lacked plausibility given Dreyfuss' response to a reporter's query during a December interview in New York.

"I could not feel worse if I were losing my own brother in a business venture," responded Dreyfuss when the reporter commented that he was losing a good man in Harry Pulliam. "He was worth fully $10,000 to the Pittsburgh club last year, and if I can help him any he will have a better thing in the future than he has had in the past. Harry is an ex-newspaper man, and got us more free advertising than anyone else could have possibly done. The fact that he is leaving Pittsburgh is no reflection on his ability. He knows baseball, is popular and will be a good man for some club. He will catch on all right and will make good wherever he goes. Baseball is like any other business, and it requires hustling to make it go. Pulliam is a hustler and deservedly popular with everybody. He knows how to boost the game intelligently, and his value will be appreciated after he is gone from Pittsburgh."[4]

Dreyfuss heaped laudatory praise upon his friend and colleague during this interview that appeared in *The Pittsburgh Press* on December 17, 1900, because Pulliam had decided to tender his resignation instead of waiting to be fired. When Pulliam visited Dreyfuss to inform him of his intentions, Dreyfuss wished him good luck, thanked Pulliam for the great work he had done, and slipped a personal check for $500 into his hand.[5] Pulliam decided to force Kerr's and Auten's hand in this sordid matter since he was unable to negotiate with any other teams in baseball while he continued to twist in the wind. By resigning from his post, he could turn his attention toward some potential available positions within the New York Giants or Chicago Orphans organizations.[6]

The acceptance of Pulliam's resignation on the part of Kerr and Auten helped set the rumor mill into motion regarding further upheaval within the Pittsburgh Pirates' management structure. While it was public knowledge that Dreyfuss' position as team president was in jeopardy, the tale that Brooklyn's Hughie Jennings would be brought to Pittsburgh to replace Fred Clarke as manager caught many Smoky City fans off-guard. The story perpetuated in Brooklyn claimed that Kerr and Auten regretted not buying Jennings' release two years earlier so he could manage the Pirates. Since Ned Hanlon's presence prevented Hughie from achieving his goal of piloting a major league club in Brooklyn, this tale suggested that while Philadelphia was not willing to pay the price for his release, Pittsburgh was eager to make a deal.[7] Before this story was afforded the opportunity to grow, Kerr quickly dismissed the idea that anyone other than Fred Clarke would be managing Pittsburgh in 1901. "You can state positively that Fred Clarke will be the manager of the Pittsburgh team at home and abroad," stated Kerr as he dismissed the rumors of Jennings being the Pirates' manager and first baseman in 1901.[8]

All of these stories and rumors certainly were disconcerting to loyal fans who believed a National League pennant was a strong possibility in 1901. Due to the team's success in 1900, many reasoned that William Kerr and Phil Auten were being disingenuous in wanting to eliminate the front office people connected to the Louisville merger one year ago. It was almost as if they were saying, "Thank you for the infusion of baseball talent, now keep your nose out of our business!" Although Barney Dreyfuss was the largest individual stockholder in the Pittsburgh franchise, Kerr and Auten controlled a majority block of 501 out of the 1,000 available shares. It was their intention to direct the policy of the organization in the future even though Pittsburgh made at least $40,000 in 1900 under Dreyfuss' steady stewardship.[9]

One of Kerr's main reasons for opposing Dreyfuss lost validity when the true story regarding why he was living in New York came to light. Dreyfuss decided to spend the winter in New York because the smoke and fog in Pittsburgh did not agree with him. The little magnate also had a personal reason for wintering in Gotham. One of his children was under the care of a specialist in New York, and due to the fact that Dreyfuss was deeply devoted to his wife and kids, he wanted to be near them during this time of crisis.[10] Following the yearly National League meeting in New York which was attended by executives of the Pirates' management hierarchy, Kerr and Fred Clarke returned to Pittsburgh while Dreyfuss did not accompany them.[11] While Clarke attended the meetings in New York, he sported a mustache. When he reached the Smoky City, Pittsburgh's manager was clean shaven as he talked to a reporter about his hunting activities since the baseball season ended.[12]

> Game? Why I left over 200 pieces at the town where I was hunting. Too much to carry. Level ground to shoot on, a good dog and a fine gun did it all. Yes, I have a chance to go after mountain lions along with Vice-President Roosevelt. I am invited to attend a shoot for the gay and festive partner in a portion of New Mexico, about three weeks hence. The party will have twenty dogs in a pack and if they don't get a few cats, then there are none in the locality they intend to visit. I hope to be there, but then a baseball man cannot tell this winter just what time he may be needed.[13]

Stories about the power struggle within Pittsburgh's ownership ranks and a hunting trip with the Vice-President of the United States were not the only morsels of information available for consumption by Pirates rooters. Third baseman Jimmy Williams exited the realm of bachelorhood when he married

Miss Nan Lee Smith of Sturgeon Street in Allegheny on November 21, 1900. The ceremony involving Williams and Miss Smith, one of Allegheny's most popular young women, was a private affair in which only immediate relatives were in attendance.[14] Williams' nuptials were the undeniable high point of his year following a disappointing, injury-plagued season for the Pirates. After hitting .354 and driving in 116 runs during his rookie campaign in 1899, Williams slumped to a .264 average in 1900, while his RBI total dropped to 68. He was so embarrassed over his performance that he believed a trade before the 1901 season would be in everyone's best interest.[15]

"I made a miserable showing here last season," said Williams, "and I think a change would do me good. I was treated royally by the club owners and the public, but for some reason I could not make good on the home ground and would like to get away."[16]

Williams' name quickly became attached to a trade rumor as New York pundits leaked a story that Pittsburgh planned on shipping the third baseman to the Giants for pugnacious first baseman Jack Doyle. While Pirates officials did not deny they were interested in Doyle, they quickly declared that Williams would not be swapped if a deal was consummated.[17] A December newspaper article stated that Pittsburgh attempted to trade pitcher Jack Chesbro and shortstop Fred "Bones" Ely to Boston for veteran shortstop Herman Long, but manager Frank Selee nixed the transaction and negotiations were called off.[18] A few days after this story appeared in *The Pittsburgh Press,* it was reported in the *Boston Globe* that Rube Waddell had been offered to the Beaneaters for $2,000.[19]

While it came as no surprise that Waddell's ticket out of Pittsburgh likely would be punched due to his peculiar behavior and unreliability, rumors surrounding Chesbro were a bit more puzzling to one Pittsburgh writer who could not understand the sudden desire to trade him.[20] Chesbro, who was purchased by Pittsburgh from Richmond of the Atlantic League in July of 1899, posted a solid record of 15–13 in 1900 after a rough rookie campaign one year earlier. While these stories about two young pitchers who each had one year of service pitching for Pittsburgh faded away, two rumors surrounding a veteran hurler raised some eyebrows among Pirates fans.

On two separate occasions, southpaw Jesse Tannehill's name was linked to a story regarding a deal with the Cincinnati Reds. Tannehill had started his career with the Reds in 1894 before Pittsburgh drafted him from Richmond (which was in the Virginia League at the time) on September 26, 1896. Tannehill quickly became the staff ace as he topped the 20-win mark in 1898 (25–13, 2.95 ERA), 1899 (24–14, 2.82 ERA) and 1900 (20–6, 2.88 ERA). The first report on December 22 surrounding a deal stated that Pittsburgh planned on swapping Tannehill to Cincinnati for southpaw pitcher Frank "Noodles" Hahn.[21] A week later, *The Sporting News* reported that treasurer William Kerr had written Reds owner John T. Brush about a trade involving Tannehill and Reds pitcher Ed Scott. It was intimated that Tannehill was on the trading block because manager Fred Clarke wanted to get rid of him.[22]

All of this speculation surrounding a Tannehill deal abruptly ended when Kerr told the *Cincinnati Enquirer* that he had no intention of parting with the southpaw.[23] Besides discussions regarding the possibility that he could be playing for another team in 1901, Tannehill's name was in the headlines throughout the final months of 1900. Shortly after the season ended, Tannehill and Pirates teammate Tom O'Brien joined a group of players from Brooklyn and New York that traveled by boat for a baseball excursion to Cuba. The team was slated to play games in Havana against four squads from the Cuban National League.[24] Even though the trip was rather uneventful for Tannehill, O'Brien became very ill while the ship traveled to Cuba.

Although southpaw Jesse Tannehill went 20–6 with a 2.88 ERA for Pittsburgh in 1900, he was linked to two trade rumors involving the Cincinnati Reds during the off-season. The temperamental pitcher also suffered a huge financial setback in November of 1900. Tannehill lost $1,000 in savings after the Newport Bank in Bellevue, Kentucky, where he had deposited the money, failed (courtesy of the National Baseball Hall of Fame Library, Cooperstown, New York).

One of O'Brien's teammates on this trip claimed that O'Brien was advised to drink sea water to combat seasickness. The fact that he drank three quarts of the salty water added to O'Brien's illness and prevented him from playing a game in Havana.[25] When he returned to the United States, O'Brien immediately entered the hospital. Upon the recommendation of his doctor, he boarded a train for the mountains of Arizona where it was hoped the climate would help him recover his health.[26] While Tannehill's health was not at risk when he returned from Cuba, his finances had suffered a severe blow in late

November. He lost over $1,000 in savings after the Newport Bank in Bellevue, Kentucky, where he had deposited the money, failed. Tannehill decided not to winter in his hometown across the river from Cincinnati so he could secure work in Pittsburgh during the off-season.[27]

While in Pittsburgh after Christmas, Tannehill made a proclamation that did not seem to make much sense given his recent financial calamity. While discussing the newly formed Protective Association of Baseball Players' battle to gain more rights in baseball, he called upon all loyal sons of the game to quit the field for a year. This comment certainly was not expected to impress the general public, who did not believe that players were baseball slaves as Tannehill suggested. The recent loss of coin in his treasury made this declaration about a players' strike and loafing for a year utter nonsense on his part.[28] Two days after Tannehill's comments appeared in print, union attorney Harry Taylor explained the position of those men he represented during an interview in Buffalo on December 28.

"These are expressions of approval from some of the best players in both the National and American Leagues," said Taylor as he displayed a stack of letters, "and you would be surprised if some of the names were mentioned, but that I will not do, for their letters I regard as confidential, and to give the writers' name would probably do them injury with the magnates at some future time. They appear to be of the same mind, however, and the sentiment of one and all appear to be that of fight for right and they say that they will give battle to the last to win their point. Every man brings me further evidence that the men will say that they will stay out of the game if some of their simple demands are not granted.

"Mind you, these communications are from stars, leaders in their profession, men without whose services the great game of baseball would be a farce and whose loss would cripple the magnates deeply, for the great multitude of fans would refuse to patronize the sport were they to be forced out. While I do not advocate or favor such a thing as a strike, it appears from the letters that the men do, and that I will have but little to say if such a course is found to be necessary; they will probably go on without me if I do not agree with them in such a matter."[29]

Of course, the question still remained whether Barney Dreyfuss would be at the helm running the Pittsburgh Pirates and dealing with this whole union issue. While William Kerr had questioned how the story ever got out that it was his and Phil Auten's intention to oust Dreyfuss as team president, there was no doubt that Dreyfuss likely would go because he vehemently opposed the decision to replace Harry Pulliam with Frank Balliet.[30] Shrewd maneuvering on Dreyfuss' part and some bungling by the Kerr-Auten faction helped give the little magnate a stay of execution regarding his baseball life. During a December meeting in Atlantic City to elect team officers, hesitance on the part of Kerr and Auten had given Dreyfuss an infusion of hope. Since the National League's ten-year agreement (the league's charter document from 1891 when they merged with the American Association) was about to expire and nothing had been resolved bringing about a new deal during meetings that were going on in New York, Kerr and Auten were reluctant to dismiss the popular Dreyfuss at that time.[31]

This failure by the anti–Dreyfuss faction to elect team officers in the meeting's regular order violated by-laws that had been established many years prior to this power struggle. Had Kerr and Auten conducted the vote, no court would have ruled against Dreyfuss' ouster since the contract regarding Dreyfuss' and Pulliam's continued front office employment predicated upon the club making a profit was a gentlemen's, verbal agreement.[32] In early January, Dreyfuss secured another victory during a second conference in Atlantic City. The majority stockholders allowed that summit to go by default when team president Dreyfuss was permitted to protest the meeting's legality. William Kerr readily admitted a mistake was made when they followed the advice of club attorney Judge Norman Rowe and allowed the meeting to be stopped. Upon reflection, he believed the stockholders should have transacted their business in spite of Dreyfuss' objection.[33]

D. I. Heyman, a lawyer representing Barney Dreyfuss' and Harry Pulliam's interests, was the man responsible for bringing this meeting to a swift conclusion. Heyman, who also held ten shares of stock in the team, claimed that according to the charter and by-laws of the Pittsburgh franchise, and the laws of New Jersey under which the club was incorporated, the meeting was illegal because notices about the proceedings had not been sent out 20 days in advance. Heyman also stated that the notices mailed out were not properly drawn and therefore not binding on anything that may be resolved at this conference. Dreyfuss ruled that the point was well taken and he ordered an immediate adjournment. This course of events only strengthened the resolve of Kerr and Auten in their effort to remove Dreyfuss from the presidency.[34]

Kerr and Auten held secret sessions in Pittsburgh to determine what their next course of action would be.[35] Further action came swiftly as Norman Rowe appeared before Justice Gilbert Collins of the New Jersey State Supreme Court in Trenton and requested that an order be issued to compel the directors of the Pittsburgh Athletic Association, the name under which the Pirates franchise was incorporated, to hold a meeting. Justice Collins decided that the proper remedy for this situation was for Rowe to apply to the full bench for an order to hold a meeting. This motion before all of the justices was scheduled on the court docket for February 19, 1901.[36] Prior to Rowe filing this motion with the New Jersey State Supreme Court, Kerr and Auten stated they would hold a meeting to banish Barney Dreyfuss no matter how the court ruled.[37]

Shortly after this latest setback for the anti–Dreyfuss faction, William Kerr decided silence was the best course of action going forward. Kerr asked friends to please excuse him for not wanting to mention the trouble and made up his mind that all future discussion could be debated by others in the newspapers.

> I could not tell you a news item if I tried all day. There has been nothing of any kind to turn up. I have had to content myself reading all about the doings of the American League and others.
> Clarke? Why the last time I heard from him I think he was in Des Moines. He said that he was ready to come on here any time and get to work for the club. He hoped that we would get a fine start for the season. Fred is all right and will be here in plenty of time to get matters in ship shape for the bruising bout.[38]

Barney Dreyfuss' astute tactics had kept Kerr and Auten playing defense since that first December meeting in Atlantic City. His various legal maneuvers allowed him to gain what he needed most, which was time. Dreyfuss wanted to do everything within his power to delay this proceeding so there would be enough time to find investors who could back him financially. Once the little magnate had everything lined up, he struck with cunning precision. Dreyfuss declared in early February that he would either sell his stock or buy that of his antagonists since he could no longer work with Kerr and Auten. Believing that Dreyfuss could not possibly consummate the deal, Dreyfuss' partners offered him an option regarding the controlling stock.[39]

With financial assistance from proprietor Oliver Hershman of *The Pittsburgh Press* and W. K. Schoepf, manager of the Consolidated Traction Company, Dreyfuss was able to purchase the block of stock owned by William Kerr and Phil Auten. On February 18, 1901, the deal was consummated where Dreyfuss and his investors paid $66,150 to buy out Kerr's and Auten's stock. After putting up $47,000 in cash and Louisville's top players in late December 1899, to grab 49 percent ownership in the Pirates, and then clearing a record profit of $43,000 for the franchise in 1900, Barney Dreyfuss was now the undisputed majority owner of the Pittsburgh organization. Since a

2. Williams Jumps to the Americans, Pirates Win the Pennant 33

resolution to this tenuous power struggle had finally been reached, the case scheduled to be heard by the New Jersey State Supreme Court in Trenton was dropped.[40]

When an election of club officers was finally held after Dreyfuss became majority owner, he was retained as Pittsburgh's team president. Schoepf was elected to the position of vice-president, and Harry Pulliam returned so he could assume the dual roles as secretary and treasurer.[41] During the final stages of this behind-the-scenes choreography by Dreyfuss before he pounced and wrestled the Pittsburgh franchise from Kerr and Auten, the Pirates lost a capable player due to a tragic set of circumstances. On February 3, 1901, outfielder and first baseman Tom O'Brien passed away in Phoenix, Arizona, from pneumonia. O'Brien, a native of the Pittsburgh suburb of Verona, never recovered from the illness he suffered in Cuba.[42]

Following O'Brien's untimely death, more information was released surrounding how dire his condition had been upon returning from Havana. Drinking salt water to combat seasickness had produced hemorrhages, likely due to some internal ruptures in his body. After O'Brien returned to the United States, he lost 40 pounds in three weeks. He initially seemed to be recovering his health when he went to Arizona, but typhoid-pneumonia attacked him, and he was unable to stave off the disease due to his weakened physical condition.[43] A few weeks after O'Brien's funeral, Barney Dreyfuss received a returned letter which was unopened and never delivered in Arizona that he had written to O'Brien two days before his death, advising O'Brien to remain idle for one season and to call upon him for any assistance he might need.[44]

Due to O'Brien's tragic death, Dreyfuss and Pirates manager Fred Clarke suddenly had a void to fill for a solid utility player. While O'Brien had seen some action at first base in 1900, he was not slated to start at that position in 1901. That task was going to fall on the shoulders of rookie William Edward "Kitty" Bransfield, whom the Pirates had purchased from Worcester of the Eastern League after he hit .369 in 1900.

The possibility that Bransfield or any other Pirate might not be playing baseball in 1901 was still a legitimate concern among team owners of the National League, who hoped to avert a possible player strike. A crucial meeting between both sides in New York was slated for the end of February. Chicago Orphans team president James Hart was determined to settle these issues so baseball's integrity could remain intact.[45]

Hart enlisted the help of Fred Clarke to assist in helping with this delicate matter. He believed Clarke would be perfect acting as an arbitrator as the players and magnates worked toward ironing out their differences. As a player, Clarke was personally popular with his teammates, while as manager and captain, he held the confidence of Barney Dreyfuss and other owners.[46] On the evening of February 26, a potential walkout was averted when representatives of the players and owners reached an agreement. Pittsburgh catcher Charles "Chief" Zimmer, who was the acting president of the Protective Association of Baseball Players, secured the concessions asked for by the players of the National League.[47]

The concessions focused mainly on players' rights. These new rules were approved by the league committee and immediately adopted as law. First, no owner would be permitted to sell, assign, exchange or in any way dispose of a player except by absolute and unconditional release. The only exception to this rule was if the proposed disposition of a player was submitted to him in writing and the player in question consented to being released. The second point was crucial since it stipulated that a player could not be suspended or fired by his club owner for refusing to agree to the proposed sale or transfer of his services.[48]

A few days after this agreement was reached, Barney Dreyfuss received a pile of contracts for the 1901 season from Zimmer. By Saturday, March 9, Dreyfuss had 15 players' signatures attached to contracts for the 1901 campaign. The only players who had not signed were Zimmer, Deacon Phillippe, Jack O'Connor and Clarence "Ginger" Beaumont. Each player was expected to be in line within a week as O'Connor was already training in Hot Springs, Arkansas, Beaumont stated he was eager to sign, and Phillippe had not been heard from in weeks since he was tramping about the wilderness in South Dakota.[49] One player who would not be joining the Pirates anytime soon was catcher Harry Smith. Dreyfuss had spent $500 the previous fall to purchase Smith from Connie Mack's Milwaukee team. When Mack took over Philadelphia's American League franchise for the 1901 season, he visited Smith at his home in Canton, Ohio, and signed him to play for the Athletics. On March 8, Dreyfuss instructed his lawyer to bring suit against Mack in court for alleged breach of contract.[50]

At the end of March, a man who was a teammate of Smith for a short time during 1900 became the first Pirates player to challenge team ownership according to the new concessions brokered by the Protective Association of Baseball Players. On March 30, 1901, it was reported that Rube Waddell had refused to be traded to the Boston Beaneaters. Waddell's refusal was the first case in baseball under this new rule that had been adopted at the February National League conference in New York. Even though Waddell did not belong to the union, he was still protected under these new guidelines. Waddell explained why he had no intention of leaving Pittsburgh.[51]

"I have been true to the Pittsburgh Club, and want it to stand by me," declared Waddell. "Six weeks ago Connie Mack visited Plano, Butler County, in search of me. I was out fox hunting, but Connie got my dad to drive him 14 miles through the mud to me. I refused all sorts of offers from Mack, and I told him I was never going to leave my friend Pulliam. Neither will I."[52]

Connie Mack's interest in Waddell and his deceitful deed in signing Harry Smith after he received a payment of $500 for selling the catcher to Barney Dreyfuss indicated that American League agents were serious about making overtures to steal players from the Pirates. Dreyfuss had been fairly lucky so far during the early stages of a war that was brewing between the established National League and the upstart American League. Philadelphia, Boston, Chicago and Brooklyn had been hit hardest as players like Nap Lajoie, Bill Bernhard, Chick Fraser, Jimmy Collins, Hugh Duffy, Clark Griffith, Sam Mertes, Lave Cross, Fielder Jones and Joe McGinnity had decided to jump to the American League.

While American League president Ban Johnson was in Detroit, he admitted that a deal with Dreyfuss not to raid his team was now null and void due to the Pittsburgh owner's criticism of tactics employed by the rival league.[53] Pirates third baseman Jimmy Williams had decided to get in some early training at Hot Springs, Arkansas, under the watchful eye of catcher Jack O'Connor. It was Williams' goal to round into top condition after an injury-prone season in 1900. He had benefitted from a daily regimen of exercise and Hot Springs' therapeutic mineral baths which allowed him to get almost down to his playing weight.[54] O'Connor left Williams on his own for a while so he could return to St. Louis and help a candidate who was running in the city's upcoming municipal election.[55] After O'Connor left the Arkansas resort, Baltimore Orioles manager John McGraw came to Hot Springs determined to sign Williams for the 1901 campaign.

Smooth talking by McGraw, a nice dinner and copious amounts of wine convinced Williams and Mike Donlin of the St. Louis Cardinals to switch leagues. It was announced at 11:45 on the evening of March 24 that Williams had signed a contract to play for Baltimore in the American League during the 1901 season. The contract called for him to make a yearly salary of $2,600, while he received a $500 bonus the minute he signed.[56] One day after Williams decided to leave the Pirates, his wife received a telegram from her husband stating that he was with McGraw. Mrs. Williams, a native of Allegheny where

Exposition Park was located, was devastated over the news that her husband had signed with Baltimore. She claimed Jimmy was delighted with the terms Pittsburgh had offered and started training early so he would be in top condition to play better baseball than he did last season.[57]

Making matters worse for Mrs. Williams was the fact she did not speak to her husband or know his whereabouts after he wired her that he would be returning to Pittsburgh shortly. McGraw kept Williams sequestered for two days as he took the player to Baltimore over the main line of the B&O Railroad. When the full squad of Pirates players reported to leave for Hot Springs for spring training on March 30, Williams, O'Connor and Claude Ritchey were the only absent members from Fred Clarke's brigade. Williams' status was in limbo since he was AWOL, O'Connor was still in St. Louis dealing with politics, and Ritchey was out of commission with the measles.[58] After having breakfast and unpacking baggage for two hours on April Fool's Day, Clarke ordered his men to report to the ballpark for a spirited training session. A clerk at the Eastman Hotel where the Pirates were staying gave a detailed account of the course of events which had led to John McGraw stealing Jimmy Williams from Pittsburgh.[59]

> The signing by McGraw of Williams and Donlin was really a bit of luck coupled with a large amount of Johnnie's well-known smooth con. Both players had come here to train, and had practically accepted the terms of their respective magnates. Mac told them a lot of nice things about what the American League was going to do to the National this summer, gave them a few good tips on the races, entertained them at an elegant dinner at the Arkansas Club, told them that they were both on teams that would likely force them to sit on the bench all summer as extra men, and then offered them the increase in their contracts that all ball players have been looking for, guaranteed them that they would be regulars on his Baltimore club, and then pulled out from the inside pocket of his dress coat and handed them a nice fountain pen with a gold point, told them to sign up and all would leave next day for Baltimore, it was easy for McGraw, and both signed.[60]

While the Pirates continued their preparations for the upcoming season in Hot Springs, Jimmy Williams returned to Pittsburgh on April 2 with his wife after the Allegheny girl, who was very loyal to the local club, had traveled to Baltimore to find her husband.[61] Two days after Williams arrived in the Smoky City, Barney Dreyfuss announced that the Pirates would not get involved in a bidding war for the third baseman. Dreyfuss stated that Williams would not be given one dollar more than the $2,400 which was offered when his contract was mailed to Williams' winter home of Denver in March.[62] Dreyfuss believed the Pirates had a double claim on Williams' services because of the option clause in his contract from 1900 and the fact that he accepted terms

2. Williams Jumps to the Americans, Pirates Win the Pennant

of the club for the 1901 campaign. When pressed by a Pittsburgh reporter who happened to run into him on April 3, Williams refused to make a statement but did answer a few questions.[63]

"I will see my attorney first," replied Williams when the reporter asked him to make a statement about the Baltimore matter.

"How about that $500 you are said to have received from McGraw at Hot Springs to sign a contract with the Baltimore Club?" asked the reporter.

"I did not get $500 from McGraw," responded Williams.

"Did you not sign a contract to play for McGraw?" countered the reporter.

"No, I did not," Williams answered.[64]

Barney Dreyfuss announced that the Pittsburgh club might consider filing suit against Williams and the American League's Baltimore organization. His lawyers were prepared to argue that Williams' contract in 1900 differed from the standard player document. That contract specifically provided that he would play for Pittsburgh in 1901, and it was further affirmed that Williams accepted a continuation of this contract in a letter which he wrote to Pirates officials.[65] Word quickly reached John McGraw that Williams possibly would be jumping back to Pittsburgh and was in daily conferences with Dreyfuss regarding a proper course of action. While worried, McGraw refused to believe that Williams would not be playing for Baltimore in 1901.[66] "I simply don't believe a word of it," said McGraw. "Williams signed a contract to play in this city and received $500 advance money. He simply can't go back on that, or there is no law in this land to protect people's property. I do not believe that Williams would do such a thing, and I shall reserve judgment until I discover the truth."[67]

Part of the problem regarding any possible court proceedings between Baltimore and Pittsburgh was Williams' confusion regarding the whole matter. As manager Fred Clarke put it, "To this day Williams doesn't know what sort of a contract he signed with Baltimore."[68] In respect to McGraw's premise that Dreyfuss and Williams were in conference daily, this assessment was inaccurate. Williams was forced to wait a few days in Pittsburgh while Dreyfuss recovered from an illness. When the two gentlemen finally did get together, Williams told Dreyfuss he was willing to stay with Pittsburgh if they protected him against any legal action initiated by the Baltimore organization. Dreyfuss' desire to retain his player's services was diminished when Williams could not provide an accurate statement regarding the nature of the paper he had signed.[69]

When Williams made the humiliating admission that he did not know what he had placed his signature on that fateful Sunday night, Dreyfuss determined that such uncertainty would present problems in a court of law.[70] Pittsburgh's owner decided not to fight for Williams' services, and the young infielder joined the Baltimore Orioles. After Williams left the Smoky City with his wife, Dreyfuss cleared up a few false rumors about what was discussed between the two parties.

> I do not believe the alleged interviews which made Williams say that I hounded him all the time he was here this week. Jimmy knows better than that. I saw him only twice while he was here. He did nearly all of the chasing and called at my office twice when I was not there. I saw him less than two hours during his visit, and any statement to the contrary is not true. All stories coming out of Baltimore must be taken with a peck or two of salt, if today's batch is a fair sample. There is not the slightest truth in the report that I offered Williams a big salary to return to Pittsburgh, the one club that has a moral right to his services. If Williams had proved loyal he would have received exactly the same salary that he got last year, and not a cent more. I could not have afforded to take him back at any terms. All the other players signed at my figure and they were glad to do so, and to have awarded disloyalty would have been unfair to them.[71]

Potential trepidation over Jimmy Williams' exit was alleviated by the fact that Dreyfuss and manager Fred Clarke had Tommy Leach waiting in the wings, ready to take over at third base. Leach had batted .213 in 51 games in a utility role for Pittsburgh in 1900. Purchased by the Louisville Colonels for $650 from Auburn of the New York State League in August of 1898, Leach played three games during the 1898 campaign. In 1899, he appeared in 106 games while splitting time between third base and shortstop and batted .288 for the Colonels. Based on his performance during Louisville's final National League season, Clarke was confident that Leach would be a more than capable replacement for Williams at third base.

> There is considerable speculation regarding third base. Now I want to say that Williams, when in form, is a great player, but last year he was far behind his form. He did not play his game, in short he was more or less a failure. Well, Leach will play a better game this year than Williams did last year and of this I am sure. Leach will certainly field much better than Jimmy did at any rate. This will make the team better both at first and at third bases and that will mean a great deal.[72]

One week later on April 19, as the Pirates squad sat idly in cool, cloudy, rainy Cincinnati after the season opener had been cancelled for two consecutive days, Clarke further assessed why Pittsburgh was a better team with Leach at third base rather than Williams. "No, we don't miss Williams," said Clarke. "He weighed over 200 pounds when he reported, and he could not possibly get into shape by this time. Leach, on the other hand, is in shape and is a reliable, hard-working player. Of course I would like to have kept Williams, but since he is gone I do not regret it."[73]

2. Williams Jumps to the Americans, Pirates Win the Pennant 39

Pittsburgh finally opened the 1901 campaign at League Park on Saturday, April 20. Sam Leever throttled the Reds as he tossed a complete game and defeated Cincinnati, 4–2. While the new National League rule of foul balls counting as strikes seemed to affect Pittsburgh more than Cincinnati, Fred Clarke's team prevailed in the end.[74] Rookie first baseman Kitty Bransfield made a fine debut for the Pirates as he stroked a single, smacked a triple and drove in one run. Cincinnati writer J. Ed Grillo heaped effusive praise upon Bransfield after watching him play his first game in a Pirates uniform.

> First baseman Bransfield, of the Pirates is a ball player from head to foot. He handles himself like an expert first baseman, and there does not seem to be the slightest question about his hitting ability. His hitting reminds one very much of Lajoie. He does not take a long swing, but just a short, snappy motion with the bat seems to send the ball. His triple in the sixth was a terrific drive to deep left, which would have been an easy home run on dry grounds. Unlike most youngsters, Bransfield knows how to field his position. He covers lots of ground and handles thrown balls perfectly. It is decidedly questionable if there is another man of his size in the game who can run as fast as he. He showed great speed on the bases Saturday.[75]

After this one-game series in Cincinnati, the Pirates traveled to St. Louis and were soundly thumped by the Cardinals, 10–4, on April 23. Even though Rube Waddell was highly ineffective against St. Louis, especially in the seventh frame before Jack Chesbro replaced him, Clarke cut the maligned southpaw some slack. Clarke was not ready to blame Waddell for this bad performance since he had been up against the same bad weather that had made the whole Pittsburgh squad stiff and slow. Clarke believed the time for criticism had not yet arrived since his players could not be expected to reach a high standard until the weather improved.[76] The Pirates finished their short, season-opening road trip on April 24 with a two-run ninth inning rally that gave them a 5–4 victory over St. Louis.

Bad weather continued to haunt the Pirates as they returned to Pittsburgh and prepared to play their home opener at Exposition Park on April 27. Team secretary Harry Pulliam was trying to decide whether the Saturday date would remain firm or if the opener would be moved to Monday, April 29, due to water on the field at Exposition Park. When the Pirates arrived in Pittsburgh, they accepted an offer from Father McDermott to play an exhibition game against Pittsburgh College (now Duquesne University) on the bluff the afternoon of April 26. While the Pirates got in some work playing this practice game, Patsy Donovan's Cardinals squad was permitted to use a baseball diamond at the Kennywood Amusement Park to get in some work.[77] The home opener went on without a hitch on April 27 as St. Louis battered Pittsburgh and Jesse Tannehill, 7–2.

Bad weather prevented Pittsburgh from hitting any kind of stride as they compiled a 3–3 record during April. While not being able to practice was becoming an inconvenience for Fred Clarke, an old problem was causing Pittsburgh's manager some unnecessary consternation. Rube Waddell had not been available to the team since he pitched in the exhibition game against Pittsburgh College. It seemed that he had decided to go to his home in Prospect and made numerous refreshment stops on his way. His father, John Waddell, brought Rube back to Exposition Park on May 1. Rube's father had always begged for patience with his son since he claimed screwy behavior ran in the family. Even though Barney Dreyfuss had always smiled during such conversations with John Waddell, Clarke could not be placated by this piece of information.[78]

Clarke decided to toss Waddell into the fray that afternoon against Chicago. His performance as his father watched from the stands was absolutely abysmal. Waddell showed no speed, no control, and was unable to snap off any devastating curve balls. In the first inning he gave up three hits, threw a wild pitch, and walked four men as Chicago sent nine batters to the plate before Clarke replaced him with Jack Chesbro. The following day, Waddell received a letter from a furniture company in Pittsburgh asking him if he would like to drive a delivery wagon for $50 a week if Pittsburgh decided to release him due to his poor pitching. The annual salary working for this company actually was more than the yearly stipend of $1,200 that Barney Dreyfuss paid Waddell. That night, Clarke stormed into Dreyfuss' office and insisted that Waddell be sent packing.[79]

"Sell him, release him, drop him off the Monongahela Bridge," demanded a seething Clarke. "Do anything you like, so long as you get him the hell off my ball team!"[80]

Dreyfuss quickly acquiesced to Clarke's wishes as he convinced Chicago Orphans manager Tom Loftus to take Waddell off his hands. When Clarke saw Loftus a half-hour after the deal had been finalized on Thursday, May 2, he laughed over the fact that someone else would now have to deal with Waddell's idiosyncrasies. Loftus smiled back and said, "Well, I bet a cigar that I get work out of him."[81] Pirates officials kept the transaction a secret from the press until Friday evening since an announcement earlier in the day might lead to possible complications in Waddell leaving his hometown.[82] Such caution proved prudent since Waddell was not at his boarding house on Thursday evening after Loftus arranged a meeting with the pitcher. Loftus and Dreyfuss walked through a driving rainstorm to Waddell's domicile and found only his wife, Mrs. Florence Waddell, there. While Dreyfuss stood outside, Mrs. Waddell informed Loftus that her husband had gone into the city to take care of some affairs.[83]

Loftus returned the following day, corralled Waddell, got his signature on a contract, and sent his new acquisition to Chicago on the early train.[84] There seemed to be a sense of happiness and relief among members of Pittsburgh's squad when it was announced that Waddell had been sold to Chicago. Every man declared that they never knew what kind of zany antic he might pull during a game. Jack O'Connor refused to work behind the plate when Waddell pitched, and while Jiggs Donahue was willing, he was unable to properly handle the task. This left only Chief Zimmer to take up the task, but the veteran catcher was not always available.[85] After Waddell's release, Pittsburgh's play perked up a bit as they went 6–1 against Chicago in Exposition Park and the Orphans' home park of West Side Grounds.

During the third game in Chicago on May 8, Fred Clarke was forced to leave in the fifth inning when he collided with Orphans third baseman Fred Raymer. As Clarke was rounding third, Raymer gave Pittsburgh's manager a hip check and sent him tumbling to the ground. Clarke experienced so much pain that he feared one of his ribs was broken. Pittsburgh's star outfielder was taken to Cook County Hospital where a thorough examination showed that although he was badly bruised, there was no fracture.[86] Many Pirates supporters believed that Raymer was guilty of a rough, cheap trick when he bumped Pittsburgh's manager. Silence about the matter on Clarke's part was not surprising. He believed it was not prudent to make a parlor game out of baseball. Once Clarke started running the bases, he usually did not take into account human obstacles that could prevent him from scoring. When a collision occurred and he got the worst of it, he never complained.[87]

Two days after Clarke was injured, Pittsburgh moved into the National League's top spot for the first time since 1896 with a 3–0 victory over Cincinnati at Exposition Park.[88] After this high point was reached on May 10, Pittsburgh slumped for the second year in a row with Clarke disabled. The Pirates went 2–7 before Clarke made his triumphant return on May 24 as his two hits and two runs scored helped Pittsburgh to a 6–4 victory over Boston.[89] Although Jesse Tannehill was an adequate replacement for Clarke in left field while he was injured, the Pirates always seemed to miss their captain's leadership when he could not play. Barney Dreyfuss felt that Clarke's presence in the lineup would have added a few more games into the win column during the recent eastern trip.

"Fred Clarke is getting along well," said Dreyfuss, "but he cannot throw a ball farther than about 50 feet because of his injured breast. Of course, he cannot slide. We would have won every game in the east except the one Chesbro pitched at Philadelphia if Fred Clarke had been in the contests."[90]

When May ended, Pittsburgh found itself in fourth place with a 16–14 record. They trailed the first-place New York Giants by two games. June got off to a raucous start at Exposition Park when Cincinnati defeated the Pirates, 4–3. Umpire Bert Cunningham, a former pitcher who had been released by Barney Dreyfuss in 1900 after he came to Pittsburgh in the big transaction involving Louisville, made numerous bad calls that infuriated Pittsburgh's players. Before the contest started, Cunningham told Tommy Leach that he intended to get even with the Pirates for his release a year ago.[91] The fans at Exposition Park showed their anger when he erroneously called catcher Chief Zimmer out on a pickoff play by Reds pitcher Doc Newton in the eighth inning. Rooters became incensed when Cunningham ordered Leach and Claude Ritchey from the game in the top of the ninth frame for remarks they made regarding the previous controversy.[92]

When Kitty Bransfield was called out at first base in the ninth inning after he laid down a beautiful bunt and seemed to beat the throw at first base by two steps, Cunningham's inadequate work that afternoon finally drove a group of patrons to violence. When the game ended, over 2,000 men and boys chased umpire Cunningham off the Exposition Park grounds. He probably would have suffered a serious injury if Fred Clarke and Honus Wagner had not hastened to the umpire's rescue and acted as his bodyguards. Two policemen usually would have restored order in minutes since there always was a contingent of officers at Exposition Park from the Allegheny headquarters. On this day, no officer lifted a finger to protect Cunningham. Patrons in the grandstand sympathized with the umpire. One fan shouted at the unruly mob, criticizing their barbaric behavior until he was hoarse.[93]

Minor problems such as this one with Cunningham did not deter Pittsburgh's resolve one bit. At the end of June, the Pirates set in first place with a record of 33–23. They led the second-place New York Giants by two games and the third-place trio of Brooklyn, Philadelphia and St. Louis by three. Pittsburgh continued to roll in July as they went 16–9 for the month to take a three game lead over the Philadelphia Phillies and St. Louis Cardinals. The Pirates excelled on the diamond even though third baseman Tommy Leach missed some time when he became ill during a long eastern trip in June and early July. After a short recuperation period at Cambridge Springs, Leach returned to Pittsburgh, ready to play when Fred Clarke needed him.[94] Clarke's name was also in the headlines when he established one of the 1901 campaign's top batting marks during a 9–2 victory over Cincinnati on July 23 at Exposition Park. He went 4-for-5 as he hit for the cycle and accounted for ten total bases.[95]

Even though Pittsburgh seemed to be making a case for being the National League pacesetters during the summer of 1901, this did not mean that Clarke and Barney Dreyfuss were resting on their laurels. Two transactions added some depth to the Pirates. On June 22, outfielder Alfonzo "Lefty" Davis was signed as a free agent after his release from the Brooklyn Superbas. On July 25, Dreyfuss and Clarke secured the services of southpaw hurler Eddie Doheny from the New York Giants. While both of these men had been deemed expendable by their former teams, Clarke felt Davis and Doheny would thrive in Pittsburgh. Davis' signing had a domino effect on Pittsburgh's lineup as Clarke searched for a way to get the speedster onto a baseball diamond more frequently. The logical progression for placing Davis in right field along with Clarke and Ginger Beaumont in Pittsburgh's outfield was to move Honus Wagner to the infield, where shortstop Fred "Bones" Ely was hitting an anemic .208.

Although Ely was a fan favorite in Pittsburgh, manager Fred Clarke had tired of the veteran's numerous injury complaints. The first solution to Clarke's problem was to play shortstop himself. This plan lasted one game after he had a horrendous, three-error performance. Youngster Lew Carr's work at shortstop was found to be lacking as the rookie lasted only nine games. Since Lefty Davis was now available to play right field for Pittsburgh, Clarke announced on July 23 that he planned on moving Honus Wagner to shortstop.[96] Two days after Clarke's proclamation, Ely was handed his unconditional release.[97] Wagner, who initially balked at the idea of playing shortstop, talked Clarke into shifting Leach there so he could play third base.[98]

While Clarke acceded to Wagner's wishes, he urged Leach to convince his star player from Carnegie that it would be in the team's best interest if Wagner played shortstop. Leach used two logical premises as he attempted to persuade Wagner to switch positions. Leach argued that Wagner could cover more ground at shortstop since he was a bigger man. He also used the sympathy ploy when he told Wagner that it made more sense for him to play the more strenuous shortstop position since Leach recently had suffered from heat stroke. After three days of imploring on Leach's part, Wagner finally agreed to switch. Honus Wagner made his major league debut at shortstop on July 27, 1901, as Pittsburgh defeated the St. Louis Cardinals, 7–4.[99]

Shortly after Fred Ely was released, it was revealed that the veteran shortstop had been working as an emissary for the American League, spreading their propaganda in the Pittsburgh Pirates clubhouse. This story may have remained a secret if Ely did not go around Pittsburgh complaining to various people from the daily newspapers when Pittsburgh dropped him. One of Ely's friends in the world of publishing did not hesitate in leaking this information to the general public. "Probably the principle cause for the release of Ely was the connection of his name with an American League team in this city next year," stated Ely's friend. "If the National and the American Leagues do not amalgamate or come to an amicable understanding at the close of this season it is certain that Pittsburgh will be represented in the opposition league next year and Ely is slated for manager."[100]

After spurning offers from Boston, Chicago, Cincinnati and New York of the National League, and Washington, Cleveland and Milwaukee of the Americans, Ely signed with Connie Mack's Philadelphia Athletics on August 3, 1901.[101] Shortly after Ely signed with the Athletics, various Philadelphia newspapers published stories claiming that Honus Wagner, Jesse Tannehill and Sam Leever would be playing for the American League in 1902. The validity of this prose certainly appeared questionable when the claim was made that Cincinnati's Ginger Beaumont would also jump. Factual accuracy was irrelevant since Beaumont obviously played for Pittsburgh. What these Philadelphia column crunchers did not know was that every Pirates player had signed a contract to play for Pittsburgh in 1902. These important documents, which had been locked up in a box at one of the safe deposit companies in Pittsburgh, were put on display for a few Smoky City reporters at the club's office in late August.[102]

Such distractions did not discourage Fred Clarke's players one bit as they remained focused on the goal of winning the National League pennant. When August ended, the Pirates found themselves clinging to a tight, 2½-game lead over the second-place Philadelphia Phillies. Pittsburgh's record stood at 62–41, while Philadelphia posted a mark of 63–47 and third-place Brooklyn remained close at 62–48. Any hope that the Phillies or Superbas had of overtaking the Pirates was extinguished as Clarke's brigade of swashbucklers blazed a path of destruction in September. Neither team could keep pace as Pittsburgh went 25–7 for the month and pushed their season record to 87–48.

Pittsburgh clinched the National League pennant in a manner befitting a championship caliber team when they defeated Brooklyn, 5–4, at Exposition Park on September 27 (revised statistics later showed that Pittsburgh had actually secured the pennant on September 26). Trailing the Superbas, 4–2, heading into the bottom of the eighth inning, Pittsburgh rallied to cop the flag. Lefty Davis led off the frame and brought the crowd to its feet when he drilled a low line drive to the fence in front of the left field bleachers. Davis probably would have rounded the bases with an inside-the-park homer if he did not trip rounding second base. He staggered to his feet and made it to third base with a triple. Fred Clarke drew a walk, but Brooklyn pitcher Frank Kitson redeemed himself a bit when he handled Ginger Beaumont's tap bunt and threw Davis out at the plate. Davis kept the rundown going long enough so Clarke could reach third base and Beaumont second.[103]

Honus Wagner stepped to the plate and promptly tied the baseball game when he blasted a double to center field that Brooklyn's Patrick "Cozy" Dolan had trouble handling. Clarke and Beaumont scored as Wagner stood at second base. Moments later, Kitty Bransfield gave Pittsburgh a 5–4 lead with a single to left that drove home Wagner with the winning run. Though Brooklyn put their first two runners on base in the top of the ninth inning when Charlie Irwin reached first on third baseman Jimmy Burke's error and Duke Farrell smacked a single, Deacon Phillippe shut the door and snuffed out any potential rally.[104] For the first time in their long history, the Pittsburgh Pirates were National League champions!

3

Barney Dreyfuss Battles Fellow National League Magnates

Pittsburgh's solid baseball during September closed the deal on a monumental season in the Smoky City. A 25–7 record for the month guaranteed Fred Clarke's boys total control of the 1901 pennant. When August ended, Philadelphia and Brooklyn were still within striking distance of overtaking the first-place Pirates. By the time Pittsburgh claimed the flag on September 27, their lead over the second-place Phillies had grown to ten games. Three days before the Pirates claimed the pennant, an article appeared in newspapers across the country stating that Pittsburgh's capturing of the championship bunting was a foregone conclusion. This story asserted that Pittsburgh was entitled to their current position in front of the pack. There was no fluke or luck involved as Fred Clarke and his players had earned this title through the sweat of their brow.[1]

The article noted that although it was predicted that Pittsburgh would not stand the strain of a tough pennant battle, they persevered and never displayed any symptoms of a weak heart or yellow character. The key ingredient to Pittsburgh's success was that their pitching staff was in good form throughout the entire 1901 baseball campaign. One aspect of the Pirates game that impressed many observers was the seriousness with which Clarke's team went about their work. Of course, while earnestness marked the play of Clarke's squad, at times this eagerness trumped sound judgment and led to ridiculous demonstrations of kicking over umpiring decisions.[2]

Fred Clarke's conduct in this respect was criticized, even though the writer readily admitted that captains and managers from other National League teams also engaged in such tactics. The perception regarding Clarke was that his penchant for running in from left field to growl at an umpire was

3. Barney Dreyfuss Battles Fellow National League Magnates 47

The 1901 Pittsburgh Pirates claimed the first National League pennant in franchise history. Pittsburgh finished the season with a record of 90–49 and outdistanced the second-place Philadelphia Phillies by 7½ games. *Front row, left to right*: Lefty Davis, Tommy Leach, Jesse Tannehill, Ginger Beaumont, Claude Ritchey. *Middle row*: Jimmy Burke, Ed Doheny, Fred Clarke, Jack O'Connor, Kitty Bransfield. *Rear row*: Jack Chesbro, Chief Zimmer, George Merritt, Deacon Phillippe, Ed Poole, Honus Wagner, George Yeager. Missing from photograph: Sam Leever (courtesy of the National Baseball Hall of Fame Library, Cooperstown, New York).

not befitting for a player of that stature. In respect to hard work and dedication, Clarke had few peers. When Pittsburgh moved into first place over the summer, Clarke was asked if he thought the pressure of setting the league pace was a source of worry for his players.[3] "No," Clarke replied. "Whether we are first or not we will go ahead and win as many games as we can. If we hold the lead all right; if we don't, we won't, that's all. But if it comes down to a tight finish between us and some other team we are confident at our ability to beat the other fellows out."[4]

Supreme confidence in their own ability was the key factor in Pittsburgh easily outdistancing their National League rivals. When the season closed on

October 6, the pennant-winning Pirates' record stood at 90–49. Second-place Philadelphia finished 83–57, 7½ games behind the champions from the Smoky City. A big celebration to honor the conquering champions occurred at Exposition Park on October 2 during Pittsburgh's final home game against Boston. Despite rain and a cool, stiff wind, a large crowd of loyal Pirates rooters showed up at Exposition Park to join in the celebration. Barney Dreyfuss exhibited the depth of his kindness by inviting newsboys throughout Pittsburgh to come and watch the day's festivities for free. A parade and procession on the grounds at Exposition Park preceded the presentation of a $500 loving cup to president Dreyfuss and his champion Pirates.[5]

A horse-drawn carriage containing the silver trophy stopped at home plate alongside a group of hansoms containing some of the most important railroad owners in the United States. These donors of the cup got out of their carriages and crowded around the trophy. Boston's players were lined up to the left of home plate, while Fred Clarke's team took up a position on the right. S. P. Woodside, president of the Railroad Club, presented Dreyfuss with the loving cup and made a brief speech that encapsulated the festive occasion.[6]

> Gentlemen of the Pittsburgh Baseball Club, it is with great pleasure and the highest appreciation of the honor conferred on me, that I come before you today as the spokesman for such a representative body of railroad men as have joined together to render to you a testimonial of their regard and esteem.
> After a long period of time you have placed Pittsburgh once more in the proud position of leaders in one of the most manly and elevating athletic sports. To do this you have responded to every call of duty promptly and cheerfully! You have fought an uphill fight, have not been daunted by accidents or reverses, and have conducted yourselves in such manner as to earn and receive the approbation and respect not only of the men of this smoky burg, but of the boys as well. Many of your names and records are as well known and, I dare say, better appreciated, by some, at least, than those of Theodore Roosevelt, President of the United States.[7]

Woodside's reference to Roosevelt holding the highest political position in America was due to him having been sworn into office following the tragic death of President William McKinley only weeks earlier. McKinley passed away on September 14 due to wounds he had suffered one week prior during an assassination attempt. Anarchist Leon Czolgosz shot President McKinley on September 6 during an appearance at the Exhibition in Buffalo, New York.[8] Roosevelt, the man whom Fred Clarke had joined for a hunting trip in New Mexico the previous winter, became the leader of the world's freest nation as a result of diabolical circumstances that unfortunately had occurred on two

3. *Barney Dreyfuss Battles Fellow National League Magnates*   49

other occasions during the nation's history. Days after President McKinley was shot, a man from Casper, Wyoming, who called himself Hans Wagner was tarred and feathered for sympathizing with Czolgosz. Newspapermen throughout Pittsburgh knew that if the Pirates' Wagner had been present during these proceedings, he would have agreed with this man's just punishment.[9]

When Woodside finished his speech during Pittsburgh's championship celebration at Exposition Park, Barney Dreyfuss offered a brief reply and thanked the railroad officials. Fred Clarke was dragged to the front where he made a short speech that was a hit with the cheering fans. Team secretary Harry Pulliam's modesty prevented him from speaking even though he was urged to do so by Pittsburgh's players. Pulliam kindly declined the offer, but did say that he would buy drinks for everyone that evening when the players continued their celebration.[10] Shortly after the season ended in Chicago on October 6, the Pirates embarked upon a spirited barnstorming trip. Fred Clarke's team returned to Pittsburgh on October 15 and was entertained by Dreyfuss during an extravagant dinner at the Hotel Schenley. Pulliam acted as the toastmaster just as he did at the dinner given by the railroad men weeks earlier.[11]

Besides showing deep generosity for his men with a grand banquet, it was rumored that Pittsburgh's owner also gave each player a huge bonus check for helping Pittsburgh win the National League pennant. While Pirates management would have preferred to remain anonymous in respect to this information, not wanting to gain any notoriety, the generous monetary offer became public when catcher Jack O'Connor bragged about it to his friends upon returning to St. Louis for the off-season. While O'Connor did not divulge the exact figure, one wild rumor suggested each player received a gift of $4,000. This did not seem feasible since even a successful club like Pittsburgh probably could not afford to give away that much money in bonuses. It was believed that $2,000 was the more likely figure.[12]

Besides this sum, Pittsburgh's players also were permitted to split the $3,000 that was collected during the field-day benefit activities at Exposition Park on October 4. Barney Dreyfuss' charges also received some monetary proceeds from the sale of souvenir pins and photographs. Of course, also counted in this tidy sum of cash was the final 15 days' pay for all of Pittsburgh's players.[13] While this fact tended to skew the bonus total slightly, that did not take anything away from Dreyfuss' munificent stance in rewarding his players for winning the 1901 National League pennant. While the will of Pittsburgh's collective team was the main reason why they pushed back the competition in 1901, individual efforts also defined the team's success. Fred Clarke's pitching staff turned in a stellar performance as Deacon Phillippe (22–12, 2.22 ERA), Jack Chesbro (21–10, 2.38 ERA), Jesse Tannehill (18–10, 2.18 ERA) and Sam Leever (14–5, 2.86 ERA) formed the National League's best foursome.

Southpaw hurler Eddie Doheny also did solid work for the Pirates as he went 6–2 and posted a 2.00 ERA after his release from New York. When the Pirates acquired Doheny in July, Fred Clarke predicted that the former Giants pitcher might benefit from a change of scenery.

> Eddie could not have pitched winning ball for New York, no matter how long he had been kept there, but a change may do him good. I don't say that he will come here and prove a wonder, but in the games he has pitched against me he has displayed enough ability to make me think that he is a pitcher, and a change of surroundings often means a great deal to a player. If you don't believe it, ask Lefty Davis. He tells me that he feels like a new man here, and yet he has no grievance against the Brooklyn club, and I doubt if he can tell himself why he did not make good with the Champions.[14]

Lefty Davis also performed brilliantly for Pittsburgh once he arrived in the Smoky City. The fleet-footed outfielder batted .313 in 87 games. Davis utilized his greatest asset of speed to its fullest effect as the former Brooklyn player scored 87 runs and stole 22 bases. Joining Davis in doing great stick work for the Pirates were Ginger Beaumont (.332), Fred Clarke (.324), Tommy Leach (.305), Claude Ritchey (.296) and Kitty Bransfield (.295). Honus Wagner topped all Pirates batters as he antagonized National League pitchers throughout the summer to the tune of a .353 average. While teammate Jesse Tannehill had the league's best earned run average at 2.18, Honus was tops in RBI (126) and stolen bases (49). For the second season in a row, the local star from Carnegie was Pittsburgh's offensive catalyst.

Wagner had made his major league debut with the Louisville Colonels after Clarke and Harry Pulliam secured his services from Paterson of the Atlantic League in July of 1897. Wagner immediately displayed supreme ability at the plate as he appeared in 62 games and batted .335. He followed up his National League initiation by hitting .299 in 1898 and .341 in 1899. When scouts first caught on to Wagner's exploits at Paterson in 1897, Pulliam made a strong push to bring the big fellow to Louisville. Fearful that Wagner might change his mind after Pulliam made his strongest sales pitch in person about the benefits of playing for the Colonels, Louisville's baseball executive hung around the prospect so he would not even leave to partake in dinner.[15]

Pulliam's confidence rose once the two men reached the train station. When they arrived at the depot, he offered to buy Wagner anything at an adjacent eatery from a plate of toast to terrapin for dinner. Wagner, however, nodded his head in disapproval to everything that Pulliam read from the establishment's menu. When Pulliam finished, Wagner blurted out "Get me some bananas." Pulliam immediately went out and purchased a bunch of the fruit which Wagner feasted on during the train ride to Louisville.[16] This prudent decision by Pulliam regarding Wagner in 1897 made it possible for thousands of Pittsburgh baseball fans to cheer for their hometown hero in 1901.

Barney Dreyfuss did not waste any time making decisions in respect to upgrading his Pittsburgh squad for the 1902 campaign. While the team was in Chicago finishing up their season, a report from Milwaukee stated that a rumor regarding shortstop Wid Conroy jumping from the local American League team to play for the Orphans in 1902 was inaccurate. It was learned on good authority that Conroy had already signed a contract to switch leagues and play for the Pirates.[17] Further tweaking of Pittsburgh's roster was put on hold for a few days as Dreyfuss battled throat trouble. His physician advised the magnate to spend a few weeks in North Carolina so he could avoid the heavy fog which hung over Pittsburgh during this season that was bothering him.[18] Before Dreyfuss became ill, he issued a statement explaining where the Pittsburgh franchise stood entering the off-season:

> Before Pittsburgh had won the 1901 pennant, I had made preparations to put a winner in the field next year. I had great satisfaction in having the champion club of the National League and the patrons of the game have shown splendid appreciation of my efforts to give them the best ball team in the world. The off season will not be one of worry for me nor will it be for my players. I know what is in store for me and they have freed themselves from care by signing for next season at satisfactory terms.[19]

Dreyfuss also announced that the story regarding Conroy was true. The former Milwaukee shortstop was joining the squad along with catcher Harry Smith, the man whom Connie Mack had stolen away from Dreyfuss one year earlier.[20] Former Pirates third baseman Jimmy Williams, who played against Conroy in the American League in 1901, could not believe Pittsburgh was able to pull off this coup. "But if that is true, president Dreyfuss has picked up the greatest shortstop in either league," said Williams. Williams also admitted he lost money by signing with Baltimore the previous spring and considered Dreyfuss the best man in either league to play for.[21] Such an admission seemed odd since he had deserted the man he considered to be the best magnate in major league baseball during the spring of 1901.

While Williams was paid a higher salary to play with Baltimore in 1901, he saw a loss of revenue due to bonuses, post-season receipts and money from Exposition Park's field day that would have been accrued had he remained with the Pirates.²² In respect to the Conroy signing that Williams was praising, Conroy's decision to join the Pirates did not prevent Ban Johnson and his cohorts from attempting to change the infielder's mind. In late October, Barney Dreyfuss received a letter from Conroy as he wintered in New Jersey. Conroy wrote that he had been approached by American League agents who made him very flattering offers to remain with Johnson's organization. Despite being tempted to join the American League team in St. Louis, Conroy rejected every overture.²³

Conroy told Dreyfuss that he intended to honor his contract with Pittsburgh. In the letter to Pittsburgh's owner, Conroy also stated that he was glad to be getting an opportunity to join the Pirates and become a member of a championship team.²⁴ At the end of October, Fred Clarke commented on the Conroy situation while he stopped off in Chicago to visit Orphans' president James Hart before leaving for a hunting trip. "Tell the American bunch that Barney has Conroy's contract in his safe," said Clarke. "If they are on the level they will leave the kid alone."²⁵

During a conversation with a baseball pundit from the *Chicago Record-Herald*, Clarke also denied the rumor that Dreyfuss planned on donating two players to the St. Louis Cardinals.²⁶ Manager Patsy Donovan saw star performers Bobby Wallace, Jesse Burkett, Emmet Heidrick, Dick Padden, Jack Harper and Willie Sudhoff desert his team after the 1901 campaign and jump to the rival American League squad in that city. Clarke put to bed any notion that Pittsburgh would weaken their squad to assist a National League competitor. "Nothing in it," said Clarke as he responded to this speculation. "We have not donated any players, and are not likely to. We have troubles of our own. We did well last season, but in this game everybody is for himself. Undoubtedly the Pittsburgh club would be willing to stretch a point in favor of a National League club, but baseball is business."²⁷

While many National League squads had been severely gutted as the war between both leagues heated up, Clarke and Dreyfuss were very lucky. The Pirates' only defection thus far had been Jimmy Williams. Efforts by the American League to reclaim Wid Conroy were a little different from standard contract jumping since agents of that league believed the shortstop rightfully belonged to their organization. While many baseball followers had been misled into believing Pittsburgh was not being targeted by the American League, the actions of men like press agent Frank Hough, Connie Mack and John McGraw proved this was not the case.

Baseball writer J. C. Morse was one of those people who still alleged that Ban Johnson was operating under a hands-off policy toward the Pittsburgh organization.²⁸ "No effect has been made to pillage the Pittsburgh Club, all talk to the contrary notwithstanding," said Morse. "This for the reason that it was decided to keep this club as strong as possible, thereby causing a disparity between it and the other National League clubs to be more marked. This policy will be pursued for another season. Pittsburgh will be stronger than ever in 1902."²⁹

At the National League meeting in New York prior to the 1901 campaign, Hough had assured Barney Dreyfuss the American League would not touch a single Pirates player. At the time, Dreyfuss realized this was a hollow proposition since he was aware that a league agent had traveled from Philadelphia to Carnegie for the purpose of offering Honus Wagner a large sum of money to sign a three-year contract.³⁰ Clarke Griffith, pitcher and manager of the Chicago White Sox, had traveled to Carnegie on a snowy night, acting as an ambassador on behalf of the American League. Griffith supposedly offered Wagner $20,000 to jump leagues, but the player rejected his proposal. Wagner had been more than happy to remain in his hometown and receive a salary bump from $2,400 to $2,700 to play for Dreyfuss in 1901. Some experts of the game rationalized that unsuccessful attempts to entice Wagner to join the American League were the reason that Johnson instituted his much-debated hands-off policy toward Pittsburgh's players that some perceived as being a false narrative.³¹

Posturing and arguing between the two leagues died down for a few weeks as pleasant stories about the Pittsburgh Pirates were reported once the offseason kicked into high gear. On Monday, November 4, 1901, Pirates center fielder Clarence "Ginger" Beaumont married Miss Norma Olive Vaughn at a ceremony in Honey Creek, Wisconsin.³² Letters from Beaumont and each one of his teammates trickled into the Pirates offices throughout the autumn, thanking Barney Dreyfuss for his kind gesture of giving each player a bonus for winning the National League pennant. Not much was going on at team headquarters as this gracious correspondence was being delivered by the postman. Dreyfuss was in Louisville to attend the unveiling of a Thomas Jefferson statue. Harry Pulliam was so busy dealing with football that he could not find time to see former President Grover Cleveland, a man he deeply admired, when he appeared at the Carnegie Library on Founders' Day.³³

Jesse Tannehill used rabbit hunting during the off-season as a means to relax and stay in shape. Following an invigorating trip with his brother, Lee, Tannehill covered a number of topics, from his hunting exploits to the American League, during a chat with Cincinnati writer Ren Mulford, Jr. "Hunting rabbits on the Kentucky side is good training for a player," declared Tannehill.

"I lost five pounds and that brother of mine, Lee, walked off eight—an average loss of two pounds a day. It takes good shooting to land your rabbit there, for if the cotton tail gets a six-yard jump on you he's gone. The mountain daisies are so thick he easily escapes."[34]

"The American League isn't any too chipper at this time," continued the outspoken player who was never afraid to make controversial statements. "I don't think it is as strong today as it was this time last year. There have been many family quarrels to alarm the players. To welcome some of the leaguers who deserted last year would be a heart punch."[35]

This serene, pristine landscape did not identify the baseball canvas for very long as verbosity and bombastic behavior on the part of its warriors quickly crept back into the consciousness of fans throughout Pittsburgh. While Tannehill's poignant, straightforward comments were only the opinion of a veteran player who freely spoke his mind, American League president Ban Johnson released a bombshell statement that seemed to be rooted in undeniable fact. Johnson claimed that two National League magnates had sabotaged efforts the previous summer to reach a peace accord between the warring factions.[36]

"Peace was not out of the question this year," was the stunning revelation made by Johnson. "It was during last June, that we met certain people whom we accepted as duly credited representatives from the National League. Negotiations for a cessation of hostilities had progressed until it looked as if a settlement had been reached.

"There would have been two leagues in the field next year under the terms of the compromise, but we would not have gone into St. Louis. While the peace plans were on I discovered a plot to steal away several of our clubs. Baltimore and Detroit were among them, and Manning (Washington Senators) was also in the deal. Negotiations ceased right there. I have reason to believe that John T. Brush's finger was in that pie, but it was Andrew Freedman who balked at the plans of the peace commissioners. He refused, as I have been given to understand, to listen to any such proposition. I have it on the best of authority that Freedman helped out two National League clubs in a financial way this year. That is one reason why he has such a hold in shaping the league's policy.

"I want to see the National League live and do well. There is room in this big country of ours for two major leagues."[37]

According to Johnson, Cincinnati owner John T. Brush and New York Giants baseball mogul Andrew Freedman were directly responsible for peace discussions falling apart. It was not known if Barney Dreyfuss was one of those men that Johnson classified as duly credited National League representatives who attempted to broker peace. Shortly after Johnson issued his statement to the press, Dreyfuss responded with comments of his own regarding the American League. He also criticized fellow National League owners for not showing enough foresight to sign players before they were tempted by extravagant offers from Johnson's rival organization.

> I am in favor of placing nothing to the way of the American League. I am content to let it rush on to its own doom. It cannot survive. It can't pay the salaries it has guaranteed on 25-cent ball. Last season the American had a good bit of sentiment in their favor, too, which assisted in bringing in the quarters. This year they will have no sentiment coming their way. They have taken National League players at almost double their payroll of last year. Let them go along. There can be but one ending. I will not give, sell or lend a player to a National League club. Why didn't these people do as I did—sign their men last summer, when they had a chance? It's too late to shout now.[38]

Ban Johnson fired the next volley in this battle of words between esteemed members of both the National and American Leagues. At the end of November, Johnson stated that Frank Hough did try to land some Pirates players for Connie Mack's Philadelphia Athletics. While the invasion of Pittsburgh had never been officially discussed by Johnson's organization, a man whose name certainly was familiar to local baseball fans hoped to place an American League franchise in Pittsburgh as competition for Dreyfuss.[39]

"Barney Dreyfuss was frightened by the visit of Frank Hough, who wanted to land a couple of his men for Connie Mack," said Johnson. "At that I think that Hans Wagner is the only Pirate who was ever approached. Colonel Kerr sent for Hough. The Colonel is ambitious to get back into the game, but I never figured Pittsburgh as a good place for two clubs. Both of them nearly starved to death in '90. Still Barney was scared, and Fred Ely lost his head, doubtless because he was a good friend of Colonel Kerr."[40]

Dreyfuss' only comment in response to the American League president was that Johnson tended to get silly at times.[41] While this war with the rival American League had been a major source of aggravation and infuriation for many National League team owners, a menace within the ranks posed a greater danger. Before Dreyfuss was scheduled to leave for the league meetings in New York on the evening of Saturday, December 7, with Harry Pulliam by his side, Pittsburgh's team owner declared that the upcoming meeting would be a mere formality. While the election of a new league president was expected to be one order of business for the owners in New York, Dreyfuss felt things would run so smoothly that these matters could be attended to through the mail. Even though Fred Clarke was not attending the meeting and remained at his home in Winfield, Kansas, Dreyfuss had extended his manager a written invitation to join him in New York.[42]

"Harry and I will be glad to have you go with us," wrote Dreyfuss, "but as you say you are willing to stand pat in the matter of players and as there are no deals on, there is no reason why you should come East before the holidays unless you desire to do so."[43]

The departure of Pittsburgh's baseball entourage for New York was delayed a day until Sunday night due to Dreyfuss being out of town from Wednesday evening until Saturday morning. Joining Dreyfuss and Pulliam on the 10 o'clock train leaving the Smoky City was Cincinnati owner John T. Brush, who had come to Pittsburgh a day earlier.[44] Brush's presence among the Pittsburgh contingent was very intriguing since the Cincinnati owner, along with New York Giants magnate Andrew Freedman, planned on making this meeting in New York anything but a formality. When Dreyfuss arrived in New York, he immediately declared that the National League's baseball moguls were a band of brothers facing the sporting future with confidence and unity of purpose.[45]

Besides being confident that the organization's eight owners were unified, Dreyfuss was also convinced that Albert G. Spalding, the man he supported for the National League presidency, would be elected to that post. While a unanimous vote supporting Spalding's election seemed out of the question, Dreyfuss believed a majority vote would not be a problem. Pittsburgh's owner reasoned that officials from the Boston, Chicago and Brooklyn clubs supported Spalding as well. He assumed the deciding vote would come from the Philadelphia camp since owner John I. Rogers was leaning toward approving Spalding for league president. Before the caucus began, Spalding told reporters that he preferred not to be elected through a unanimous vote.[46]

"I would rather give $10,000 than to be elected president of the league by a unanimous vote," said Spalding. "In fact, a vote of five to three would suit me best. Six to two would be all right, but a unanimous vote would put me in a neutral position, and if I take the place, I can see where vigorous measures would be necessary to straighten out the bad muddle a few men have allowed baseball to get into."[47]

As it turned out, Barney Dreyfuss' confidence regarding Spalding's election was misguided. John T. Brush and Andrew Freedman indicated from the start of these proceedings that they were willing to fight tooth and nail to prevent Spalding from assuming the presidency. Freedman shifted the balance of power from Dreyfuss and his allies to the faction headed by New York's owner and Brush by getting Boston magnate Arthur Soden to switch his allegiance. Since the Boston Beaneaters owned minority shares of stock in the New York club, Freedman threatened to transfer the lease of Manhattan Field to Ban Johnson of the American League. It was believed this threat enticed Soden to change his mind.[48] Freedman had purchased Manhattan Field so Johnson could not get his hands on this fine piece of property for a prospective American League team in New York. When the conclave in New York began, Freedman also demanded that his fellow National League owners help pay for the $15,000 rental on Manhattan Field.[49]

The first vote taken on December 12, 1901, to elect a National League president was a tie. Pittsburgh, Brooklyn, Philadelphia and Chicago supported Spalding, while St. Louis owner Frank de Haas Robison agreed with emissaries from New York, Boston and Cincinnati as they backed incumbent Nick Young.[50] Dreyfuss withdrew from the meeting around 3 o'clock in the afternoon and did not return until later that night. Pittsburgh's owner was visibly angry that the league's eight owners were deadlocked. Dreyfuss, never one to shy away from speaking his mind, indicated he had little use for the other magnates who were fighting so ferociously. Arising from this tension between Dreyfuss and the faction of owners led by Brush and Freedman was the rumor that Pittsburgh might seriously consider leaving the National League to join Ban Johnson's organization.[51]

Baseball fans throughout the city of Pittsburgh quickly realized why Dreyfuss was so agitated and a rumor regarding a move to the American League by the Pirates could be pursued. There was a good reason why Brush, Freedman, Soden and Robison were against Spalding's election, or any other person's for that matter, to the league presidency. An expose that appeared in *The Pittsburgh Press* reported that Brush had been working for more than a year on a scheme to organize an enormous trust for control of baseball. Brush planned to capitalize the National League at one million dollars and convert it into a corporation. Through this process, Brush, Freedman, Soden and Robison would take control of 57 percent of the company's stock. Brush also wanted to tie up the nation's largest cities and wage a bitter war against the American League, forcing that organization to surrender or crumble.[52]

Brush's syndicate trust plan fanned out beyond major league baseball. The American Association, which was started in the west by W. H. Watkins, one of Brush's able lieutenants, supported this policy. A year ago, Brush had insisted upon putting the American Association into motion to compete with the American League, but newspapers across the country got wise to the plan and his fellow National League owners killed the conspiratorial strategy. Had Brush been successful in carrying out this plan, his power would have increased to an astonishing degree. Despite Brush's illusions of grandeur at becoming the czar of a baseball empire, one well-known minor league executive believed his baseball trust plan would collapse.[53] "The Indianapolis man is counting upon the assistance of the recently formed National Association of Minor Leagues to make him the king of baseball," said the well-informed minor league official who preferred to remain anonymous, "but he will be disappointed."[54]

Confusion replaced contentious statements and bickering among National League magnates early in the morning on December 14. At 1:30 a.m. Albert Spalding was unanimously elected president, secretary and treasurer of the National League through the votes of Philadelphia, Pittsburgh, Chicago and Brooklyn on the 26th ballot. In making the selection unanimous, the four clubs that voted conducted the meeting following the precedent of Congress. Before the vote occurred, the faction that opposed Spalding left the meeting, leaving Nick Young as chairman instead of Boston's Arthur Soden, who had retired for the night. When Young left the session as well, Philadelphia owner Colonel John I. Rogers was named chairman pro tem of the meeting.[55]

A ballot was taken immediately to elect a president, and the four clubs that supported Spalding cast their vote in his favor. The names of Cincinnati, St. Louis, New York and Boston were called, but did not respond. Chairman Rogers considered these clubs present and not voting, and he declared that Spalding had been elected as the National League's new president. It was certain that this decision would not sit well with Brush and Freedman. During a contentious verbal skirmish the previous afternoon, Spalding had declared that Freedman must get out of the league for the good of baseball. Brush then offered a resolution that the meeting adjourn until January 7, even though a new president was not selected. This decree was voted down due to a 4–4 deadlock, and there was a two-hour adjournment.[56]

When the delegates returned at 8:15 p.m. on December 13, the count remained four votes for Spalding and four votes for Young following another round of voting. After A. G. Mills was nominated, another ballot was cast in which the choice between Spalding and Young remained deadlocked and Mills did not receive a single vote.[57] Had crafty maneuvers not been used by Dreyfuss and his allies, this logjam probably would have never been broken since the opposition seemed intent on remaining entrenched until the bitter end. The election of Spalding also killed the trust plan and John T. Brush's desire to become a baseball dictator.

Pittsburgh's owner issued an optimistic statement about baseball's future shortly after the proceedings in New York reached their conclusion. "It was either Spalding or a baseball trust," said Dreyfuss. "We preferred Spalding and hope that the successful fight which we made for him will receive the approval of the national game's many friends in Pittsburgh. There will be a National League next year. It will be stronger than ever before and Pittsburgh will be in it. In the future the business of baseball, like the game itself, will be clean and above board."[58]

John T. Brush and Andrew Freedman did not waste any time making their first move to circumvent Spalding's election as league president. On December 20, the owners who opposed Spalding filed an injunction to prevent him from assuming his duties as the National League's president. The case had been delayed a day so DeLancey Nicoll, counsel for the Freedman faction, could attend a funeral. Nicoll appeared before Judge Francis Scott of the New York State Supreme Court and presented injunction papers which read: "The Boston Baseball Association and others against the Brooklyn Baseball Club and others." While Soden and his Boston franchise were listed as the major plaintiff, there was no doubt that Freedman was orchestrating this legal action. Nicoll urged Judge Scott to issue an injunction that would compel Spalding to return the papers and records which he had procured from Nick Young.[59]

Judge Scott ruled in favor of Nicoll's clients and issued an injunction which prevented Spalding from performing his duties as league president. When Spalding's lawyer countered with a motion challenging the injunction, Judge Scott's ruling that future court proceedings involving both parties would be necessary indicated the case could be tied up in court for a year.[60] After this decision was handed down, Spalding sent a letter to the eight National League clubs which stated that he had been served with an injunction to take no further action as president-secretary-treasurer of the National League and American Association of Professional Baseball Clubs. Spalding also wrote that he took up the duties and responsibilities of the office immediately after being notified he had been elected as president. Prior to being ordered to refrain from acting within his official capacity, Spalding had made only a few preliminary arrangements regarding what was considered the proper conduct of his office.[61]

As long as this case remained tied up in court, the National League organization technically was in limbo. Without a president or ruling body, each team would be responsible for taking care of its own affairs. It should have come as no surprise that Andrew Freedman would treat his fellow magnates with such disdain since he also exhibited a contemptuous attitude toward his own manager and players. He bullied his players and was overbearing and abusive toward New York's manager. Freedman seldom attended league meetings and had the proceedings mailed to him. He forced his fellow magnates to chip in rent money for Manhattan Field even though revenue had been generated from football games played at the facility before the big New York colleges abandoned that site. Freedman retained the field to keep a potential American League team from competing against him in New York. Barney Dreyfuss was paying rent on Recreation Park in Pittsburgh for the same reason, but he never dreamed of asking his fellow owners to pay their share of this monetary burden.[62]

Spalding believed Freedman, a man with Tammany Hall connections in New York, was vulnerable at this time despite the fact that he was flexing his ownership muscles. A new municipal administration was taking control of New York City's government after January 1, 1902. Seth Low was replacing Robert Anderson Van Wyck as mayor. With Van Wyck out of office, Freedman could no longer use the threat of putting a street through any baseball park that might open its gates in opposition to the Polo Grounds, since Low had been an anti–Tammany Hall candidate. Some people felt Spalding's declaration on this issue meant that he was planning to use the threat of carving up the Polo Grounds as leverage to bring Freedman in line. This scenario was not likely since Spalding planned on using ethical measures to advance his agenda and Mayor Low was not the type of man who would allow individuals to alter the city map to settle personal grudges.[63]

The alliance of Andrew Freedman and John T. Brush was an odd relationship since the two men had been deadly enemies in the past. Brush attempted on different occasions to get Freedman out of baseball. When he failed to do so, he knelt at the New York owner's feet, begging for forgiveness and requesting friendship. Brush claimed he did this for the good of baseball, but his efforts certainly had not reaped any results as Freedman's behavior continued to place the game at risk.[64] While Freedman's method of dealing with issues was to do so in a confrontational manner, Brush preferred to work on things behind the scenes and attempted to bring people around to his point of view through discussion and diplomacy. When Brush, who also owned stock in the New York club, had proposed his trust scheme during the summer to Freedman, Robison and Soden, the four men agreed to keep this dark secret quiet for months.[65]

Albert Spalding, James Hart, Barney Dreyfuss and officials of the Philadelphia and Brooklyn clubs had been unaware that Brush planned on turning the National League into a syndicated corporation that would usurp the power of every owner. Brush's big problem heading into the National League meetings in New York regarding his trust plan was that he had only four votes that would support his proposal. When it came time to search out a fifth owner who possibly would be amenable to Brush's new vision regarding the National League, he decided that Dreyfuss was the man most likely to help Cincinnati's owner realize his dream.[66]

Early in December, before the league meeting, Brush had come to Pittsburgh and remained sequestered for a few days before he got up enough courage to go see Dreyfuss. When the baseball trust schemer met with Pittsburgh's baseball magnate, he gave his best sales pitch, hoping to convince Dreyfuss to join his group of National League owners.[67] "Here is the plan upon which I have been working for months," said Brush after he finished laying out the particulars regarding his trust plan for Dreyfuss. "Will you accept it or not? I must have an answer tonight."[68]

Dreyfuss informed Brush in a very straightforward manner that he would not be in a hurry to make a decision. He left the meeting without making a commitment to support Brush's syndicate trust plan. On the advice of a powerful friend in Pittsburgh, Dreyfuss caught an early train the next day to Louisville, where his wealthy relatives lived. While he did not directly ask for money from these men who had offered financial assistance one year earlier during his battle with William Kerr and Phil Auten, they said help in respect to this latest issue was there if needed. This made Dreyfuss feel strong, knowing that if he were forced into an expensive fight, he would not have to surrender since additional monetary resources were available if his dried up.[69] This mysterious trip to Louisville was the reason why Dreyfuss had not been in Pittsburgh from Wednesday through Saturday prior to leaving for the league meetings in New York on December 8.

Buoyed by the support of his Louisville friends, Dreyfuss decided at the New York meeting to battle Brush and his supporters to kill the trust plan that he believed would destroy professional baseball after one season. The non-committal posture of Dreyfuss after his discussion with Brush in Pittsburgh convinced Cincinnati's owner that the Pirates mogul was not on board in support of his plan. Brush realized that securing a fifth vote to validate and enact his trust blueprint was highly unlikely.[70] For weeks, both sides continued to posture and bloviate while attempting to gain sympathy for their position regarding Spalding's election as National League president and the subsequent injunction challenging that premise. Rumors also cropped up at times which lacked validity. One story claimed that National League entries from Pittsburgh, Brooklyn, Philadelphia and Chicago were going to join the American

League (the Phillies and Orphans would combine with the Philadelphia Athletics and Chicago White Sox). Under this plan, these squads would join a 12-club circuit with league holdovers Baltimore, Boston, Cleveland, Detroit, Washington and St. Louis (having just shifted from Milwaukee), as well as new franchises in New York and Cincinnati.[71]

This rumor was quickly killed following a meeting between Albert Spalding, James Hart, Ban Johnson and Barney Dreyfuss in Chicago on January 18, 1902. Johnson stated that while there would be no amalgamation between these four clubs and the American League, the two parties would act harmoniously. The four men at this conference sent a letter to Pat Powers, president of the minor league organization, asking him to join committees from the four clubs and the American League to establish uniform baseball rules.[72] While these baseball pioneers worked feverishly trying to bring about positive changes to the game, John T. Brush was busy denying that he had ever proposed the infamous trust plan during the December National League meeting in New York. This statement was ridiculous on its merits since stenographic notes from the meeting proved otherwise. Albert Spalding and Brooklyn owner Charles H. Ebbets argued that the combine plan was discussed and could be corroborated by other magnates who attended the conference.[73]

Barney Dreyfuss was instrumental in killing the syndicate baseball plan put forth by fellow magnate John T. Brush. Needing a fifth vote so his plan could be adopted, Brush met with Dreyfuss in Pittsburgh, hoping to bring the Pirates owner into his camp. Dreyfuss, who refused to make a commitment, diligently fought the trust plan during the December National League meetings in New York (courtesy of the National Baseball Hall of Fame Library, Cooperstown, New York).

Many of Barney Dreyfuss' fellow National League magnates seemed comfortable giving out lines of newspaper print boasting of their courage on the firing line during this time of crisis. Instead of engaging in rhetoric that sometimes only inflamed the situation, Dreyfuss preferred to remain in the background rather than aspiring to seek notoriety. For this reason, he extended his holiday stay in Louisville for weeks

3. Barney Dreyfuss Battles Fellow National League Magnates 63

after the Christmas season so he could avoid interviewers looking for a quote that could further stoke the fires of controversy. Other than taking an occasional trip like the one to Chicago for a conference with Johnson, Hart and Spalding, Dreyfuss remained isolated. While he was going to great lengths to keep his name out of newspaper articles, there was no question that his resolve was strong in supporting Spalding as the National League president.[74]

Baseball politics had been on the front burner for so many weeks that Pirates fans were ecstatic when any information about players or the upcoming 1902 campaign was gleaned from local newspapers. Fred Clarke gave out some pearls of wisdom for the baseball pundits while he was in Chicago visiting James Hart and Ban Johnson on Christmas Day. In this newspaper interview, Clarke claimed he was fairly confident that Pittsburgh would repeat its performance from the 1901 campaign during the upcoming season. He also stated that he was delighted over the present composition of his squad.[75]

> The only thing that will bother us will be cutting down to the 16 rule. You see, with a rule of that kind you can carry five pitchers, three catchers, the regular in and outfielders, and one utility man. Well, we have the 16 we were carrying last fall and have added Merritt, Smith and Conroy. Take out Yeager and we still have 18 men, all of championship quality, for Smith and Conroy are as good as they grow. Now then how are you going to arrange it?[76]

News like this about Clarke's confidence in his team making another strong showing in 1902 helped whet the appetites of fanatical Pirates fans who could not wait for the season to begin. A month after Pittsburgh baseball patrons were treated to the wise annotations of Clarke, they were further entertained by a story about star shortstop Honus Wagner. Bookmaker Johnny Fay, who was a great admirer of Barney Dreyfuss, had a long chat with Pittsburgh's owner during a short trip he made to Cincinnati on January 20, 1902. Fay relayed the story to Cincinnati newspapers of what Dreyfuss told him regarding the circumstances surrounding Wagner's signing for the upcoming campaign during the summer of 1901.[77]

"Hans dropped into Dreyfuss' office one day with a letter from Charles Somers, that Cleveland chap who owns the Boston American League club," said Fay as he recounted the story Dreyfuss told him. "In that letter Somers offered Hans $9,000 for two years; would put money in the bank, and Hans could draw on it whether he played or not."

"'Say, look at dis,' said Hans to Barney.

"'Well Hans, what do you want to do?' was Barney's query, after reading the letter.

"'I want to play right here,' was Wagner's reply.

"'Well, here is a contract; fill it out, and I will be satisfied,' responded Dreyfuss.

"Hans took the contract and put in $3,000, just $1,500 less than Boston offered him. Barney did the same thing with all of his players, and in each instance he got them to play for less than he would have offered had it been left to him. Dreyfuss is the best man baseball ever had connected with it. He knows how to handle players, and that is why he won the pennant last year."[78]

Besides knowing his players, it also seemed that Dreyfuss was a very competent owner, well versed in using the proper methods to bring about a peaceful solution in his battle with the Freedman-Brush faction. At the end of January, *The Indianapolis Sentinel* reported that it was absolutely a fact that John T. Brush planned on getting out of baseball. The story claimed that Brush could not continue as an owner under the old methods regarding how baseball was financed. Andrew Freedman, Arthur Soden and Frank de Haas Robinson reportedly were going to follow Brush's lead and dissolve their association with the teams they owned. Some viewed this simple declaration on Brush's part to mean that if he could not have a baseball trust that made him the game's supreme ruler, he was going to take his ball and go home.[79] Others reasoned that he was merely posturing to strengthen his side's position.

This stalemate lingered for months as neither side was willing to budge from what they believed was the proper vision regarding the National League's future. When Barney Dreyfuss returned to Pittsburgh in early February, he talked with a local reporter about baseball's state of affairs. Dreyfuss seemed excited over the fact that every Pirates player was signed, the grounds at Exposition Park were in excellent condition, and arrangements had been made for the training trip to Hot Springs. He planned on remaining in Pittsburgh until the team left for spring training unless a league conference called him to the east. When the reporter asked Dreyfuss about a rumor that he favored a four-club National League that would include Pittsburgh, Brooklyn, Chicago and Philadelphia, Pittsburgh's owner carefully chose his words responding to the question.[80] "I simply said that if nothing else could be done I prefer going into a four-club league to joining an eight-club trust," responded Dreyfuss.[81]

When the writer pressed the issue and asked Dreyfuss if there was any danger that the National League might be reduced to a four-club circuit, Pittsburgh's owner replied that he would rather not answer that question.[82] Due to his pragmatic, level-headed character, Dreyfuss knew that the National League's long-term health was predicated upon each of the eight teams coexisting in a harmonious manner. Many people connected to baseball held Dreyfuss in utmost esteem, and Chicago Orphans president James Hart thought Pittsburgh's owner should be nominated as a compromise candidate for league president. Hart believed proposing an alternative candidate such as Dreyfuss was a prudent move in case the courts ruled against Spalding's election to that post. When pressed about this matter, Dreyfuss refused to discuss the subject.[83]

A major fissure that seemed capable of destroying the rock of solidarity that Dreyfuss and his allies had built their principled case upon regarding Spalding appeared in late February. A meeting was held at the Hotel Schenley in Pittsburgh on February 22, 1902, where officials of the Pittsburgh, Chicago, Brooklyn and Philadelphia franchises reaffirmed their support for Spalding. The meeting was called by Barney Dreyfuss at the request of Spalding to consider his resignation. The meeting, originally schedule for 10 o'clock in the morning, was delayed until noon since Brooklyn's Charles Ebbets' and Philadelphia's John Rogers' train was delayed by a storm in the mountains. Albert Spalding was given a vote of confidence. The four club officials also refused to accept his resignation and returned the paper to him.[84] While James Hart had joined in this vote of confidence for Spalding, a man who was part of the Chicago franchise's ownership group, he publicly threw support to Dreyfuss as a compromise candidate during an interview in Chicago on March 3.[85]

> I've been in the game too long to take anything seriously in baseball. The common sense solution of the league trouble is a return to the old league lines, with eight clubs and a clean, strong man for president. Our old constitution is good enough. The only difference between the factions is the question of procedure with a president or under new conditions with a board of regents.
> I'm in no position to prophesy what the outcome will be or when the end will come. Did you ever realize, that the fans tire of magnates as they do of players? Barney Dreyfuss is the only popular mogul in the National League.[86]

Spalding and his supporters were anxious to see how the New York State Supreme Court ruled on the demurrer that had been filed by Philadelphia's John Rogers in opposition to John T. Brush and Andrew Freedman's injunction. The case was supposed to be presented on March 3, but was postponed by mutual consent for three days.[87] A little over three weeks after the case was finally heard, Justice Truax ruled against the demurrer presented by the Spalding lawyers which had claimed that the court had no jurisdiction in these injunction proceedings. This ruling on March 29 gave Brush and Freedman a huge victory in preventing Spalding from becoming president of the National League.[88] Harry Pulliam claimed the only thing that Judge Charles

H. Truax had decided to this point was that the New York court had jurisdiction in this matter.[89] While Pulliam's positive stance was commendable, it certainly did not seem practical for a drawn-out fight to continue as the 1902 baseball season loomed on the horizon.

On April 2, owners from the eight National League franchises met in New York in an effort to bridge their differences and unravel the tangled mess they had created. Albert Spalding decided to act in the best interests of baseball by resigning as league president so a man could be elected who was suitable to both warring factions. Many were surprised when Chicago's James Hart officially presented Spalding's resignation letter. Arthur Soden immediately was mentioned as a possible replacement, but the Boston owner graciously declined the nomination. Hart then proposed Pittsburgh's Harry Pulliam. The Pirates' secretary-treasurer turned around and nominated Pittsburgh native William C. Temple. Andrew Freedman initially was reluctant to elect any man who was not present at the caucus. Freedman did not want to make a commitment to a man until a candidate had explained his policies in relation to running the National League.[90]

As it turned out, Barney Dreyfuss ended up being the hero who may have possibly saved the National League. Dreyfuss was able to convince all of his colleagues that Temple was a man of integrity who had a reputation for loyalty and fairness.[91] His colleagues concurred with this assessment and voted unanimously in favor of electing Temple as the new National League president. When Pulliam and Dreyfuss placed Temple's name into nomination for the position, they probably did so with the assurance that he would accept if elected. Everybody connected to baseball were shocked when Temple declined to serve as president of the National League. Before the meeting in New York commenced, Pittsburgh's contingent had received a letter from Temple which stated he would gladly accept the presidency under certain conditions.[92]

The only feasible explanation attached to this refusal was that some of Temple's friends had persuaded him to change his mind. Some people believed he was reluctant to accept the presidency since it would prevent him from living in Florida from shortly before the Christmas holiday until May 15 as he usually did each year.[93] When it was announced at the New York meeting on April 3 that Temple had declined to accept the league presidency, fear abounded that past hostilities could be renewed during the night session. These worries were put to rest as a compromise plan was agreed upon regarding how the National League would conduct its business in 1902. Since a single candidate could not be agreed upon, a three-man committee that included

3. *Barney Dreyfuss Battles Fellow National League Magnates* 67

John T. Brush, Arthur Soden and James Hart was formed to oversee league affairs until next fall.[94]

Weeks earlier, when it looked as if a resolution would never be reached to breach the big divide between National League owners, Barney Dreyfuss had claimed that it would be business as usual for the Pirates regardless of the outcome.[95] "Delay or no delay in the settlement of the internal strife, the Pittsburgh club is going to play ball," Dreyfuss had declared. "The players have been ordered to report on March 29, ready to leave for Hot Springs, and if I did not feel entirely satisfied that Pittsburgh would play ball this year the same as usual, I would not go to the expense of sending the men to Hot Springs to get into condition."[96]

Barney Dreyfuss' steady leadership had been instrumental in allowing the National League to remain as a sustainable baseball institution. Since a resolution had been reached that was satisfactory to all parties involved, backroom deals and courtroom maneuvers were now ancient history. Games played on a baseball diamond were the focus once again. The time had finally arrived for Pittsburgh to defend its title and take another step toward being touted as a baseball dynasty.

4

Pittsburgh Breaks Out of the Gate in Splendid Fashion

Peace was finally brokered between the National League's two warring factions at the Fifth Avenue Hotel in New York on April 3, 1902. While Barney Dreyfuss had seemed prepared to fight in order to insure that other owners adhered to his principles of honesty and integrity when a league meeting began two days earlier, compromise ended up ruling the day instead of hostility. On April 1, three different National League schedules had been presented during the session by Charles H. Ebbets, Nick Young and Frank de Haas Robison. Before the three-man committee idea was unanimously accepted by all eight National League teams, Dreyfuss had leveled a threat that indicated a switch to another league was a possibility. "You can say for me that the people of Pittsburgh will have baseball this year," said Dreyfuss. "If the National League is not ready to play ball with me I will play somewhere else."[1]

Dreyfuss was issuing a warning to his fellow National League magnates regarding a move to the American League, even though he did not single out that institution when making this bold statement. Although Dreyfuss might have been using this hollow threat of a move to the rival organization to gain some leverage for his side in the war with John T. Brush and Andrew Freedman, American League president Ban Johnson claimed Pittsburgh would be welcomed with open arms. Johnson asserted that if Pittsburgh joined his circuit, no increase in the number of teams in the American League would be necessary since another city could be eliminated to bring in the National League's marquis baseball team. Johnson had expressed his feelings regarding this whole matter in an open letter that appeared on March 21 in the *Commercial-Tribune*, a Cincinnati newspaper he had worked for many years earlier.[2]

4. Pittsburgh Breaks Out of the Gate in Splendid Fashion

"Though a change in the American League circuit is not likely to occur this year," wrote Johnson, "there is one city in the circuit of the entangled National League for which room would be made at a moment's notice by the Johnsonites, and that city is Pittsburgh."

"Colonel Dreyfuss can continue to sit upon his high horse, for he still holds the key to the situation. It is not betraying a secret to say that Dreyfuss has but to say the word and the gates to the American League will be opened to admit him. Furthermore, no one is more familiar with these facts than Colonel Dreyfuss himself. He knows just where he stands, and all the bluffs of members of the Freedman faction about closing up their grounds for the season do not have to worry the Pittsburgh magnate in the least. If the National League is not in condition to protect Pittsburgh and furnish that city good baseball Dreyfuss knows where he can get that article, and he won't have to knock more than once for admission.

"With the only first-class team in the National League, and one of the best baseball cities on the map, Dreyfuss has no occasion for worry, even though the affairs of the National League look none too bright. Late though it is to think of changing a circuit, the American League would do it should Dreyfuss apply for admission."[3]

Once harmony was achieved by the National League's eight owners, discussion regarding that circuit's only first-class team switching leagues ceased. The selection of a committee to oversee the league's operations in 1902 until the issue of selecting a president could be addressed after the season guaranteed that Barney Dreyfuss would remain loyal to the Senior Circuit. Cincinnati owner John T. Brush was selected to be the chairman of this committee, while Arthur Soden of Boston and James Hart from Chicago were his associates. Nick Young was also re-elected as the National League's secretary-treasurer.[4] Dreyfuss' uncanny ability to multitask and deal with more than one situation had served him well during this long, drawn-out struggle. While he was busy fighting Brush and Freedman's attempt to kill their baseball trust plan, Pittsburgh's owner had to deal with a homegrown problem regarding his star player.

In late January, the *Pittsburgh Gazette* reported that Honus Wagner was giving careful consideration to retiring from baseball. Wagner was a thrifty man who judiciously watched his finances and was not prone to making any extensive financial splurges. Following the 1901 campaign, Wagner engaged in his second favorite passion in life after baseball. He spent most of the winter gaining pleasure and staying in shape for the upcoming season by hunting. Even though Wagner loved going hunting with his friends, this mode of living did not assist in fattening his bank account and actually slightly reduced his savings. He decided that he should enter a business venture that would allow him to earn some money during the off-season. When an opportunity arose to become involved in the saloon business, Wagner felt this was a business prospect that was too good to pass on.[5]

Wagner had the necessary cash available to act upon a good offer from an established liquid emporium. The only thing that remained in respect to finalizing this deal was for Wagner to receive the consent of Barney Dreyfuss when he returned from a trip to Louisville. Wagner was not sure if Dreyfuss would approve if one of his players mixed beer with baseball. Wagner thought so much of this business proposition that he threatened to quit baseball for good if Dreyfuss did not grant permission for his star shortstop to engage in the saloon business. Wagner's honest nature would not permit him to participate in any activity that Dreyfuss disapproved of regarding his players. This threat on Wagner's part did not have much meat on the bones since he had signed a contract to play for the Pittsburgh Pirates in 1902.[6] The outcome of this meeting between Wagner and Dreyfuss remained a mystery as talk about saloons and retirement quickly dissipated.

Issues such as the one involving Honus Wagner were not always handled at the organization's highest level through Barney Dreyfuss. Pittsburgh's owner confidently delegated responsibility on some matters because he had highly capable lieutenants like Harry Pulliam and Fred Clarke. Pittsburgh's fearless leader had left his home in Winfield, Kansas, and come to the Smoky City in early January to help with Pirates baseball affairs while Dreyfuss was engaged in the National League's political machinations. One way that Clarke kept himself busy in Pittsburgh was to go trap shooting with Deacon Phillippe and Honus Wagner. The three players often made a trip to Carnegie so they could become more proficient at target shooting. While Clarke, Wagner and Phillippe were developing as skilled marksmen, pitcher Sam Leever remained the squad's elite shooter.[7] Shortly after Clarke arrived in Pittsburgh, he told local reporters a funny story regarding his team's barnstorming tour the previous autumn.

> I told the boys we ought to play in our regular positions because that was what the people in the small towns paid to see. It went along all right until Pulliam left us and I had to go on the gate for four innings. When I came back Wagner was pitching, Bransfield was catching, and not a man was in his regular stand. Wagner was shooting them over against the locals, and if he had hit anyone he would have killed him. I took him out of the box in a hurry, for the semi-professionals do not know how to dodge like experienced men.[8]

Besides going on trap shooting jaunts with Wagner and Phillippe, Fred Clarke decided to use ice skating to stay in shape for the upcoming baseball season. Clarke and Phillippe skated daily at Duquesne Gardens during his time wintering in Pittsburgh.[9] While skating was beneficial in strengthening leg muscles, a true competitor like Clarke quickly gravitated toward a game that combined power and grace on skates. Pittsburgh's manager fell in love with the game of hockey and intended to start a team. Deacon Phillippe cancelled his proposed trip to Virginia so he could practice for Clarke's hockey team. Clarke hoped to form an all–Pirates hockey team that would challenge the winner of the Western Pennsylvania Hockey League trophy. It was rumored that third baseman Tommy Leach would be a fine addition to Clarke's squad since the diminutive player was a great skater.[10]

Hopes of putting together a hockey squad comprised entirely of Pittsburgh Pirates baseball players were shattered when Honus Wagner did not report at noon as he promised for the team's initial practice at Duquesne Gardens.[11] It turned out that Wagner felt more comfortable participating in a sport where shoes were part of the uniform rather than skates. He decided basketball was more his speed. On February 4, Wagner debuted for his hometown team in a road contest between Carnegie and McDonald. With the idea of forming his own team now a pipedream, Clarke decided to play the point for a local squad comprised of area bankers.[12] Clarke debuted for the Bankers on February 6, 1902. The huge crowd that turned out for this event at Duquesne Gardens was impressed with Clarke's work on the point. They applauded his every move as the Bankers defeated Quaker City, 3–2.[13]

Clarke also showed his humorous, good-natured side when he grasped the puck, dropped his stick, and started moving on skates as if he were playing left field at Exposition Park.[14] Fred's hockey career seemed to be progressing beautifully until the Bankers played a team from Cleveland at Duquesne Gardens on February 20.[15] During the contest, Clarke was banished to the bench so he could think over the sin of tripping opponents.[16] It seemed that Clarke enjoyed using some of the same rough-and-tumble methods on a sheet of ice that he utilized effectively as one of the National League's top players. Baseball matters also took up some of Clarke's time while he was in Pittsburgh. At the end of January, he received a letter from pitcher Jack Chesbro which stated he would join the Pirates' colony of players in Pittsburgh shortly and remain there until it was time to leave for Hot Springs.[17]

Clarke also received written correspondence from star hurler Jesse Tannehill in early February. Tannehill informed Clarke that he would be leaving in seven days to train for four weeks at Mt. Clemens, Michigan, in the company of former Pirates shortstop Fred Ely. Tannehill also wanted to know when the Pirates intended to start for Hot Springs so he could be on hand at the time fixed by Clarke.[18] During an interview with *The Sporting News,* Tannehill heaped lavish praise upon his Pirates teammates' hitting ability which gave Pittsburgh's star southpaw pitcher excellent support when he was on the mound.

"We had some good hitters last year in Pittsburgh," said Tannehill. "Wagner is unquestionably a star with the bat, and yet I don't think he hits a ball any harder than Fred Clarke. There is a fellow who can sting 'em. Bransfield was another gentleman who could hit the sphere a mile, but for timely hitting none of them compare with little Claude Ritchey. There is the chap who won many a game for us. He would go to the bat maybe as many as seven times and not get a hit, but just as soon as the score was close, there were men on two bags and we needed a run or two, he was there with a bingle."[19]

One player from Clarke's squad whose intangibles overshadowed his hitting ability could have been playing in another city during the 1902 season if Barney Dreyfuss had not been prudent and signed all of his players the previous summer. Manager Jimmy McAleer of the American League's St. Louis Browns squad claimed Dreyfuss beat him by two days in attempting to sign Jack O'Connor. McAleer, who had played with O'Connor, was determined to bring "Rowdy Jack" into the fold when he agreed to assume St. Louis' managerial post for the 1902 campaign. Dreyfuss got O'Connor's signature on a Pittsburgh contract because he acted swiftly upon realizing that McAleer was pursuing the catcher. McAleer's failure to land O'Connor could be attributed to his foolish decision to put off communicating with O'Connor until the two men met in person.[20]

Fred Clarke left Pittsburgh on March 11 and returned to his home in Winfield, Kansas. He planned on going directly from his winter home to Hot Springs and would not be returning to the Smoky City until the Pirates played their opening regular season game at Exposition Park.[21] Shortly after Clarke reached Winfield, he wrote to Barney Dreyfuss that if any of the Pirates reported overweight for spring training, he should send them out to his farm since there was much plowing work to be done.[22] One day before Dreyfuss received this letter from Clarke, Pittsburgh's owner announced on March 19 that current groundskeeper John Murphy had been released.[23] James Coyle from Minneapolis, Minnesota, who was recommended to Dreyfuss by pitcher Deacon Phillippe, was hired to succeed Murphy as groundskeeper at Exposition Park.[24] Murphy was expected to remain in Pittsburgh and continue his profession as a landscape gardener.[25]

As the reporting date to leave for Hot Springs grew near, Dreyfuss started receiving correspondence from his players stating their intentions regarding spring training. Infielder Jimmy Burke wrote that he and Jack O'Connor planned on working out at Hot Springs for a few weeks before the Pirates' spring training party arrived in Arkansas.[26] Jesse Tannehill informed Pittsburgh's devoted baseball fans that even though he did not like Hot Springs' mineral baths, a strict workout regimen at Mt. Clemens would melt away the winter pounds.[27] When Clarence Beaumont had shown up in Milwaukee on Valentine's Day, the outfielder told a local newspaper that he did not plan on heading to Hot Springs early to train on his own. Beaumont claimed that he was in perfect condition and needed only to work every day in order to keep his weight down.[28]

When Fred Clarke was in Pittsburgh looking after Pirates affairs and playing hockey, he offered some insight regarding the dedication of his players to working hard and staying in shape.

> The Pittsburgh players are willing workers. When requested to turn out for practice they are always punctual and stay on the field as long as anyone will pitch to them. In the spring we practice from 2 to 3 every afternoon with another quarter of an hour warming up before the game. This arrangement, I believe, gives the men all the exercise they need at that season of the year. Too much practice is as harmful as not enough, as it is not easy to strike a happy medium. After June 1, I do not believe in having much hard work in the morning and do not ask the players to turn out.
> Of course, they are compelled to report every morning, but when the warm weather comes I think they need all their strength and cannot see where they would be benefitted by working under the hot sun for an hour or so, rushing out for lunch and hustling back to dress for the afternoon struggle. There are times even in mid-summer when a few extra turns are necessary. For instance, a club may fall off in batting while away on a long trip, and I believe then in having the boys out as soon as they get home for morning practice against the best pitching that can be furnished. In this way men who have been suffering from slumps often regain their courage for knowing that in the trials there is nothing at stake, they go after the ball with confidence and regain the natural swing which leaves a man after he has been in hard luck for a week or so.[29]

The opportunity for Clarke to implement his philosophy regarding keeping a baseball team in shape during a long campaign finally moved from a discussion based in theory to practical application on a diamond. On Saturday, March 29, 1902, pitcher Deacon Phillippe was left in charge of getaway day in Pittsburgh for the Pirates baseball squad. Due to the absences of Fred Clarke, Barney Dreyfuss and Harry Pulliam, Phillippe was responsible for making sure the Pirates contingent bound for Hot Springs was present at the Baltimore & Ohio Station no later than 7:00 p.m. to board a special flyer bound for the Arkansas resort. A train carrying the 1901 National League champions was expected to depart the station at 7:45 p.m.[30]

Phillippe, Jesse Tannehill, Eddie Doheny, Jack Chesbro, Ed Poole, George Merritt, Chief Zimmer, Harry Smith, Kitty Bransfield, Claude Ritchey, Honus Wagner, Tommy Leach, Wid Conroy, Clarence Beaumont and Lefty Davis were expected to be on board the Pirates Express as it pulled out of Pittsburgh. Fred Clarke was going directly to Hot Springs from Winfield, and Sam Leever planned on departing from Pensacola, Florida, to join his teammates at the spring training site. Jimmy Burke and Jack O'Connor had already been at Hot Springs for weeks getting in some extra training work. A staff correspondent from *The Pittsburgh Press* also traveled with the pennant winners to give a detailed account of spring training's important events. Pittsburgh's spring training caravan was expected to reach Hot Springs on the morning of March 31.[31]

Hopes of arriving at the Arkansas resort on time were contingent upon nothing going wrong during the trip. After a long delay between Pittsburgh and Youngstown, Ohio on Saturday, the Pirates entourage did not reach St. Louis in time to make their connection. Instead of leaving St. Louis on a train heading for Hot Springs Sunday afternoon, the Pirates did not make their getaway until Monday morning at 2 o'clock. Some of Pittsburgh's more superstitious performers blamed this bad luck on the fact that only 13 players reported for duty in Pittsburgh on Saturday night instead of 15. Tommy Leach and Harry Smith were the two Pirates who had delayed their departure to Hot Springs. Teammate Chief Zimmer believed Leach was holding off making the trip so he could play for his indoor baseball team that was competing for the championship of Cleveland on April 3.[32]

While Zimmer made a valid point, the main reason why Leach did not accompany his teammates to Hot Springs was that his little son Nelson had not been in the best of health for weeks. Due to Leach being worried over his son's condition, a slight delay in reporting to spring training made sense since the Pirates' third baseman certainly would have difficulty concentrating on baseball.[33]

Second baseman Claude Ritchey also seemed to be worried over the ten pounds he lost during the off-season. Ritchey's major goal during spring training was to add that amount of weight before the practice session ended. He also went to great lengths to contradict a story that he had spent the whole winter in Pittsburgh.[34] While making this statement, Ritchey also touched upon a possible reason for his weight loss. "I was in Pittsburgh for eight minutes once this winter," said Ritchey. "My brother was ill in Hartford City, Ind., and I went there to take him home to Emlenton. On the way out I had to wait five minutes for a train, and on the return trip I made connections inside of

4. Pittsburgh Breaks Out of the Gate in Splendid Fashion 75

three minutes. I did not have time to call on Barney Dreyfuss, and he was unaware of my presence at the old stamping ground."[35]

The train carrying the Pittsburgh Pirates squad finally reached Hot Springs late in the afternoon on March 31.[36] When Pittsburgh's players finally hit the field for practice at Whittington Park on April 1, Wid Conroy and Honus Wagner made immediate impressions on Fred Clarke. He was pleasantly surprised with Conroy's work, while Wagner seemed to be in mid-season form as he proved to be the same solid ground coverer at shortstop as in 1901 after Clarke switched him to that position. Infielder Jimmy Burke dislocated his finger on a sharp grounder off the bat of Eddie Doheny. Burke was not expected to miss any time after Chief Zimmer snapped the bone back into place. Since Ritchey was well below playing weight, he and roommate Honus Wagner were permitted to go to and from Whittington Park in a street car on the first day of practice. The remainder of Clarke's squad made the trip from their hotel and back on foot to help eliminate stubborn winter fat.[37]

Moaning and groaning were the common sounds associated with Pittsburgh's players as they crawled out of their beds and limped to the street car heading for Whittington Park on April 2. The second day of spring training always seemed to be a sharp contrast from the first day's drills as players who looked nimble and lithe 24 hours ago now resembled men with cadaverous muscles. Compounding the issue for outfielder Clarence Beaumont was the fact that he was permitted to eat only two meals a day until his weight dropped down to 170 pounds.[38] Fred Clarke was not surprised that many of his players were afflicted with sore muscles after only one day of spring training.

> It was ever thus. I don't care how much road or gymnasium work a man does in advance, he is going to suffer after the first day on the diamond. Baseball brings into play every muscle of the body, and the ones that have not been worked since last fall naturally complain when aroused suddenly. The beauty about training at Hot Springs is that the baths take the soreness out quickly. We will regain our speed in a day or two.
> No one but a ball player, though, knows anything about the second day. It is a combination of a toothache and rheumatism, with the difference that it hits all parts of the body at the same time.[39]

While Pittsburgh's training schedule at Hot Springs could not be categorized as brutal, their sessions at Whittington Park, which was nestled between two ridges of the Ozark Mountains, certainly were productive. Each Pittsburgh player was expected to be out of bed by 8:00 a.m. every morning. Breakfast was a half-hour later and practice began at 9:30 a.m. The players returned to the hotel at 11 o'clock and had lunch at 1:00 p.m. Afternoon practice at the ballpark started at 2 o'clock and lasted until 3:30 p.m. Fred Clarke's troops hit the mineral baths at 4 o'clock and ate dinner at 7:00 p.m. Every member of the Pirates squad was expected to be in bed each night before the 11:00 p.m. curfew.[40]

Tommy Leach planned on joining his teammates in Hot Springs on April 5. Since Leach had spent a portion of the off-season playing indoor baseball, Fred Clarke seemed confident that his third baseman was in fine shape and would be ready for the Pirates' first exhibition game.[41] Sam Leever took the field for Pittsburgh's practice session on the morning of April 5 after he arrived on a late train from Florida the prior evening.[42] With Leever now in camp and Leach on his way to Hot Springs, this left catcher Harry Smith as the only player who was not on hand for spring training. When Smith did not arrive in Pittsburgh to leave with the Pirates party on March 29, many speculated that he had jumped to the American League. A few days after spring training started, Clarke refuted the rumor that Smith had been kidnapped by American League agents, stating that Smith was missing because he had appendicitis.[43]

After a short delay, Tommy Leach finally arrived at Hot Springs on April 7 with secretary Harry Pulliam and catcher Harry Smith. The whole squad was now in camp as Fred Clarke's team prepared to leave the practice field and begin a rousing series of exhibition games.[44] Clarke did not hesitate placing Leach in his starting lineup for a game against the Southern Association's Little Rock Travelers that afternoon at Whittington Park even though he had just arrived in camp. Pittsburgh easily handled the Travelers as Eddie Doheny, Jesse Tannehill and Ed Poole got in some mound work during a decisive 9–4 victory. Lefty Davis and Wid Conroy each rapped out three hits. Leach showed he was in great shape as he joined Clarke, Honus Wagner and Claude Ritchey in banging out two hits apiece.[45] One of Leach's safeties was a home run.[46]

One day after Pittsburgh's victory over Little Rock, Leach was injured during morning practice when a roller to third base took a funny bounce and struck him squarely in the eye. He had extreme difficulty seeing out of his eye which was swollen and black.[47] Such mishaps were a part of the process each spring for players as they toughened up both their bodies and minds for the long season ahead. Each baseball player had his own routine for getting into shape and preparing for another important campaign on the diamond. Fred Clarke used a unique method to insure that his bats would be of optimum use throughout the year. A few months before spring training began, Clarke had soaked 30 baseball bats in pickle juice so his war clubs would produce outstanding results at the plate.[48]

Pittsburgh made it two victories in a row over Little Rock as Clarke's

4. Pittsburgh Breaks Out of the Gate in Splendid Fashion

troops defeated the Travelers, 6–3, on April 8. The score was 3–3 through the sixth inning before Clarke and Sam Leever, who was expected to be handed the Opening Day pitching assignment against St. Louis on April 17, jumped to the forefront and led Pittsburgh to victory. Lefty Davis and Kitty Bransfield were the Pirates' hitting stars as each player rapped out two hits.[49] In respect to Pittsburgh's potential lineup for Opening Day, Clarke announced that he had decided to install Wid Conroy at short and planned on permanently keeping Honus Wagner in center field.

This meant that Clarence Beaumont would remain on the bench as a substitute player. It was speculated the possible flaw found in his game was that he lacked ginger.[50] This characterization seemed a bit odd since Beaumont's teammates had nicknamed him "Gin-

During spring training at Hot Springs, Arkansas, in 1902, outfielder Clarence "Ginger" Beaumont was relegated to substitute duty even though he batted .332 in 1901. Beaumont was temporarily demoted by Fred Clarke to send a message that showing up for spring training 15 pounds overweight would not be tolerated (courtesy of the National Baseball Hall of Fame Library, Cooperstown, New York).

ger" because he displayed pep and dash while playing. It was true that Beaumont did not look lively on the diamond at all times. When batting on some occasions, he dragged himself to the plate resembling a man booked for an early trip in the first carriage of a funeral procession. A moment later when he connected against a pitch, he would sprint to first base in record time. Beaumont consistently made plays on baseballs in the outfield that slower men would never reach.[51] Although such scrutiny over Beaumont's play was understandable, there was an underlying reason why he was not starting in center field. Manager Fred Clarke wanted to send a message to Beaumont that showing up for spring training 15 pounds overweight was totally unacceptable.

As it turned out, Beaumont's time on the bench was short-lived. During Pittsburgh's third consecutive exhibition game against the Travelers at Whittington Park on April 9, Lefty Davis suffered an injury as the Pirates demolished Little Rock, 18–6. Whittington Park's rocky infield was responsible for the severe accident that sent Davis to the sidelines. He slammed out a long drive to center field that seemed destined to be a three-bagger. As Davis motored around the bases attempting to leg out a triple, he tripped at second base. He fell and hit the rocky infield, bruising his leg and wrenching his body. He was expected to be out of commission for several days. The climate, accommodations and mineral baths in Hot Springs were all that could be desired helping athletes get into shape, but the infield at Whittington Park was dangerous. Each year, promises about laying down a good layer of soil over the rocks had been broken by the ballpark's owners.[52]

Beaumont actually started this game in center field as Honus Wagner was shifted to left so Fred Clarke could have the day off. With Davis now sidelined due to his injury, Beaumont's regular employment in Pittsburgh's starting lineup was guaranteed for the time being. During an intra-squad game between the Regulars and Yanigans on April 10, he recorded two hits, walked once, scored two runs and made three putouts.[53] Pittsburgh broke camp at Hot Springs after this practice game in order to play road contests against Little Rock and the St. Joseph Saints of the Western League. Hurlers Jack Chesbro, Sam Leever and Jesse Tannehill were brilliant on the mound as Fred Clarke's team shut out Little Rock, 4–0, on April 11. A crowd of 1,500 showed up to watch the defending National League champions.[54]

The game between Little Rock and Pittsburgh on April 12 was billed as a gala event that was second in importance only to the opening of the Southern Association season. Over 4,000 people were expected to witness this contest. Harry Pulliam had invited Arkansas Governor Jeff Davis and students from the Maddox Seminary who were expected to occupy a section in the grandstand. Unfortunately, poor weather ruined the festive day as the game had to be cancelled due to rain. The silver lining in this dark cloud from Pittsburgh's perspective was that the team would not have to rush after the game to catch their train to St. Joseph, Missouri. Instead of being forced to hustle from the ballpark to the team hotel and then rushing off to the railroad station perhaps without eating dinner, Pittsburgh's players had plenty of time to pack, eat a meal and board the train bound for St. Joe's. Before the Pirates departed, Clarke gave an assessment of where his team stood at this point in spring training.[55]

> The team has been so fortunate since it left home that I do not like to complain about losing this day. But it seems strange that we always strike rain here. Last year we had fine weather at Hot Springs and came here only to encounter a cloud burst. Little Rock has a fine team and I would have enjoyed another game with it,

especially before a large crowd. The Southern League will see a high grade of baseball this year if the other clubs are anything like as fast as the Little Rock team. Finn has several boys who will bear watching this year. They are nearly ripe.

I need not say that I am pleased with the condition of the Pittsburgh team. All that I ask for now is half decent weather until the season opens. If we get that, look out for us.[56]

The Pirates had a long train ride ahead of them. They left the station in Little Rock at 6:10 p.m. and were not expected to arrive at St. Joseph until around noon on Sunday, April 13. The train did make a morning stop in Kansas City so the players could eat breakfast. As Pittsburgh prepared to play the final games of their 1902 exhibition season, manager Fred Clarke received some good news regarding one of his players. Lefty Davis was recovering nicely from his injury and was expected to be ready for the season opener in St. Louis. During his absence, Ginger Beaumont's play improved each day to the point that a return to the form he exhibited in 1901 seemed realistic. As he reduced his weight, the star center fielder's speed and endurance increased.[57]

Pittsburgh easily handled the Saints once the games commenced against St. Joseph's squad. On April 13, Deacon Phillippe and Jesse Tannehill combined to toss a one-hitter as the Pirates defeated St. Joseph, 4–0. Wid Conroy was a demon in the field for Pittsburgh and chipped in with three hits at the plate. Honus Wagner also banged out three safeties while Ginger Beaumont recorded two hits.[58] Pittsburgh had a tougher time in the game against the Saints on April 14 as Fred Clarke's boys secured a tight, 4–3 victory. Jack Chesbro and Sam Leever were dominant on the hill as they kept St. Joseph off balance all afternoon. Clarke was Pittsburgh's batting star as he smacked three hits, while catcher Jack O'Connor gave his captain ample support by rapping out two safeties.[59] Tommy Leach delivered the game's big blow when he homered in the fourth inning, a long drive to the deepest part of left field. Clarke, who was on the coaching line, tried to hold Leach up at third base, but the little fellow wanted the home run and got it when he beat the throw to home plate.[60]

Claude Ritchey was unable to take his spot at second base late in this game because he was not feeling well. Wid Conroy took his place.[61] Honus Wagner manned the shortstop position for the first time in a game since spring training began. Clarke was confident that Conroy could be plugged into the second base position if Ritchey suffered an injury during the regular season. If Wagner played shortstop, Ginger Beaumont would be able to man his regular position in center field.[62] No matter where Wagner played on a baseball diamond, most people connected to the National League in some way believed he was the game's top player. Those with allegiances to the American League vehemently disagreed. St. Louis Browns manager Jimmy McAleer believed Philadelphia Athletics second baseman Nap Lajoie was superior to Wagner.

"I suppose the National League public, almost to a man, considers 'Hans' Wagner the greatest player in the game at the present time," said McAleer. "The Teuton is certainly a rare performer, but Lajoie is his superior. I don't think baseball has ever offered a player who could tie the Frenchman. He is almost in a class by himself when it comes to hitting and fielding, and he has rare speed in getting down to first and making the circuit of the bases. He played sensational ball all summer long in 1901. Great as Lajoie was when he was a Quaker, his all-around work, to my way of thinking, showed huge improvement last year over what he had ever showed before."[63]

On the morning of April 14, before Pittsburgh defeated St. Joseph that afternoon, Fred Clarke cancelled practice so the team could visit the house where Jesse James lived and was eventually killed. The house was located on a little hill on the north side of town. Admission to this historic site was 15 cents. The room where James met his fate was in the same condition as on the day he was shot. While this visit proved very entertaining for Clarke's squad, some of his players got an opportunity to act the role of marksmen during the Missouri State Championship Shoot on April 15. Clarke, Honus Wagner, Deacon Phillippe, Ginger Beaumont and Sam Leever competed against some of the state's top experts at shooting clay pigeons.[64] Leever put on a great performance at the shoot that even impressed authorities of this sport. After he struggled during the first round of shooting, he broke 14 out of 15 clay birds in both the second and third rounds. Leever was applauded and congratulated for his proficient shooting by well-known trap experts such as Fred Gilbert, J. R. Elliott, C. W. Budd and Jack Fanning.[65]

Pittsburgh closed out its exhibition season in fine fashion as they pounded the Saints, 17–2, on April 15. Honus Wagner and Kitty Bransfield led the Corsairs' relentless attack with four hits apiece. Lefty Davis also banged out three hits, while Fred Clarke, Claude Ritchey and Tommy Leach each bagged two safeties.[66] The Pirates closed out their short exhibition season with a perfect 7–0 record as Fred Clarke's squad outscored their opponents, 62–18. A potential eighth spring practice game against the Western League's Des Moines Midgets on April 16 was called off when owners of that club would not agree to Harry Pulliam's requested terms. Pittsburgh left St. Joseph that evening following their final exhibition matchup and traveled to St. Louis for the opening game of the regular season on April 17.[67]

Since the game against Des Moines was postponed, the Pirates were able to rest for a day once they arrived in St. Louis on April 16.[68] One of the first duties that manager Fred Clarke attended to when the Pirates reached St. Louis was to hand out uniforms to each of his players for the first road game of the season. When Clarke proudly handed Tommy Leach his jersey and pants, the little third baseman immediately started making speeches about the fact that his uniform was excessively large for the second consecutive year. In 1901, Leach had to put tacks in his trousers and wore garters on his arms to keep his sleeves from falling down over his hands. He had been pacified somewhat by the promise that he would receive clothes that fit in 1902.[69] Leach seemed to believe that the man who made Pittsburgh's uniforms was responsible, but one had to wonder if someone else connected to the Pirates was having a good laugh at his expense. "I guess that uniform man can't read figures," roared Leach. "Wonder if these fellows think I'm the Sultan of Turkey? I've got trousers five feet wide and they make me feel like a clown. Somebody will tell me soon that they will shrink in the washing."[70]

Fred Clarke certainly could not be ruled out if someone was playing a practical joke on Leach. Clarke, a notorious prankster, engaged in harmless mischief-making at times to keep his players loose. Although Clarke was just one of the boys on a baseball diamond, his position as captain and team manager anointed him as team spokesman with the press. While the Pirates relaxed the day before the opener on April 17, Clarke had a discussion with baseball writer Harold Lanigan of the *St. Louis Star* about his team's prospects for the upcoming 1902 campaign.

"We have had a splendid season of practice since we went to Hot Springs," said Clarke, "and the boys were never feeling better at this time of the year than they are at present."

"While our practice season was not a long one, beginning as it did on April 1, good use has been made of every day. We have missed but one since the commencement of the season and made up for that by playing on a Sunday, when we were not scheduled for a contest. The weather at Hot Springs was fine. The team is in perfect physical position, not a man being on the injured list at present, and of course we are going after every game we can get here.

"How many will we take? Well, you had better ask me something easier than that. I do not know how the Cardinals stack up and of course would not hazard a guess unless I did.

"Will we win that championship? That is another of those easy ones. I guess you want to get me into trouble, young fellow, by putting me on record now and then calling me in the fall. I will say this, however, we never had a better team and never started out with better prospects."[71]

Lanigan's article that contained Fred Clarke's quotes also talked about how the Cardinals players planned to approach opening against the defending National League champions. The St. Louis squad was excited to be starting the 1902 campaign against Pittsburgh. One anonymous player reasoned that a few victories over the Pirates would give his team a lasting psychological edge. "You see, if we can just beat this Pittsburgh bunch," said the Cardinal, "we will have half of the other teams scared to death and can sail along on our reputation for a while. If we get beat, the others will say that Pittsburgh is in championship form and we will not have to work any harder than we would if we faced some weak team first and won the series."[72]

The time for talking, practicing and training finally ended as the Pittsburgh Pirates opened their 1902 campaign against the St. Louis Cardinals at League Park on Thursday, April 17. Clarke selected Deacon Phillippe to pitch the opener, while St. Louis manager Patsy Donovan countered with Stan Yerkes. Both men were brilliant as the game remained scoreless through the first five innings. Pittsburgh finally got on the board in the sixth frame as they scored the only run of the ballgame. Tommy Leach reached base after Claude Ritchey was retired by lacing a sharp single to center field. Leach advanced to third base when Cardinals second baseman John Farrell booted Jack O'Connor's hot grounder. Phillippe stepped to the plate with two runners on base. He smacked a ground ball to Farrell that looked to be an inning-ending double play.[73] When Farrell tried to tag O'Connor as he ran toward the keystone sack, he became confused when O'Connor stopped and started heading back to first base. Farrell threw the ball to first baseman Doc Hazelton and retired Phillippe. O'Connor had ample time to reach second base before Hazelton could make a return throw to Farrell. While this was going on, Leach scampered home with the game's winning run.[74]

Phillippe was spectacular for Pittsburgh as he tossed a complete game and scattered seven hits. Leach supplied all of Pittsburgh's fireworks at the plate as he went 3-for-4 and blasted a double and a triple. Fred Clarke's lineup for the opener resembled one that he used on numerous occasions during the final months of the 1901 campaign. Lefty Davis was in right field after having returned from an injury to play in the club's final two exhibition games, Honus Wagner held down the shortstop position, and Ginger Beaumont was the starting center fielder.

Pittsburgh's string of shutout innings continued on Friday, April 18. Unfortunately, Fred Clarke and his teammates did not get a chance to see if starting pitcher Sam Leever could match Deacon Phillippe's shutout performance. Umpire Joe Cantillon called the contest, in which neither side scored

4. *Pittsburgh Breaks Out of the Gate in Splendid Fashion* 83

after three innings. Time was called briefly in the second inning during a small rain shower. When a dust storm struck the field as the third inning ended, Cantillon decided to call the game on account of darkness. Ten minutes later, the sun was shining once again, but by that time the Pirates were in their coach somewhere downtown heading for the team hotel.[75]

St. Louis' strong showing against the defending league champions became a distant memory once the two squads resumed playing baseball on April 19. Despite making four errors in the field, Pittsburgh defeated the Cardinals, 10–4, during a Saturday matinee that was witnessed by 12,000 fans. One reason Fred Clarke's brigade pulled out an easy victory was that St. Louis committed even more egregious fielding gaffes than their opponent. The Cardinals committed 11 errors as first baseman Doc Hazelton was the only player from Patsy Donovan's squad who did not make a fielding blunder. Jack Chesbro was solid for the Pirates even though his team was also lackluster at times in the field. Chesbro tossed a complete game and was charged with only one earned run.[76] Lefty Davis, Kitty Bransfield, Claude Ritchey and Jack O'Connor banged out two hits apiece and combined to score five runs.

The Pirates made it a clean sweep during the opening series as they pasted St. Louis, 10–2, in the finale on Sunday, April 20. It was Jesse Tannehill's turn to pitch, and the stellar debut of baseball's best southpaw put a smile on Fred Clarke's face. He exhibited his graceful, careless style of delivery and perfect control throughout the game. The contest was witnessed by an overflow crowd of 16,000 rooters who packed the stands and stood on League Park's field. After Pittsburgh opened up the scoring by plating two runs on three errors and Tommy Leach's triple in the second stanza, they put the game out of reach one inning later by placing a five-spot on the scoreboard.[77]

Ginger Beaumont opened up the third frame with a line drive single over the shortstop. Honus Wagner reached on an error after second baseman John Farrell fumbled his bunt. Pittsburgh loaded the bases when Kitty Bransfield reached first on a beautiful bunt to shortstop Otto Krueger. Beaumont tallied the inning's first run after third baseman Fred Hartman could not handle Claude Ritchey's sizzling grounder. Wagner was thrown out at home plate when Tommy Leach grounded to Krueger. Chief Zimmer stepped to the plate and drove home Bransfield and Ritchey with a sharp single over third base. After Jesse Tannehill drew a walk, Lefty Davis recorded the second out on a pop-up to first baseman Doc Hazelton. Clarke quickly made the score 8–0 as he drilled a single that brought Leach and Zimmer home, but was thrown out at second base trying to stretch his hit into a double.[78]

Tannehill went the route for Pittsburgh, allowing two runs and scattering five hits. Lefty Davis, Ginger Beaumont, Claude Ritchey and Tommy Leach rapped out two hits apiece for Pittsburgh. Ritchey and Leach both crossed home plate three times each as Leach also smacked a triple and scooted around the bases when George Barclay booted his short hit to left field. After the final game, the *St. Louis Star* pondered whether Pittsburgh was capable of winning all 140 games on its schedule.[79] Harold Lanigan gave a tongue-in-cheek assessment of the National League race after only three games. "Pittsburgh is so darned good that the race in the National League may be good and interesting after all," claimed Lanigan. "It should be Fred Clarke's valiant crew first and the rest of the field nowhere. That should aid in insuring a close race between the other aggregations."[80]

One of New York's newspapers was not quite ready to concede the National League pennant to Pittsburgh as Lanigan suggested. The *New York Press* believed one of the other seven squads possibly could shock the baseball world and beat out Pittsburgh for the 1902 National League pennant.

> On paper the Pirates look to be the best aggregation of the lot, but any of the other seven clubs is likely to spring a surprise on the confident champions, who recently have been boasting of their ability to walk away with the coveted bunting in an easier manner than they did last year. Pittsburgh has the advantage of having practically the same team that has played together for two years, and hence the Pirates probably will assume command at the outset. It will require several weeks for their opponents to get in their stride; but when they accomplish this purpose Captain Clarke and his men will find that they have a battle royal on hand, and that it will be a difficult proposition to shake off the teams which will be tugging at their coattails.[81]

The *New York Press* was right on point in that Pittsburgh had a huge advantage in one area over their National League competitors. The majority of Fred Clarke's squad had been playing together for two years while other National League clubs were trying out new players to replace those that had jumped to the American League. When Barney Dreyfuss returned to Pittsburgh after the series in St. Louis, he received some good news about one of those traitors who had jumped to Ban Johnson's league. The Pennsylvania Supreme Court in Philadelphia ruled in favor of the National League with respect to the Nap Lajoie case. The court declared that Lajoie's contract with the Philadelphia Phillies had been valid for the 1901 campaign. This meant he had illegally jumped to Connie Mack's Philadelphia Athletics franchise that season when his .426 average led the American League.[82] Johnson's response to this edict was to transfer Lajoie to the Cleveland Broncos franchise after the court rendered its decision. Had Lajoie remained in Pennsylvania, he would have been arrested for defying a court order.

4. Pittsburgh Breaks Out of the Gate in Splendid Fashion

After playing great baseball in St. Louis, the Pirates returned to Pittsburgh to play their home opener against Cincinnati on Tuesday, April 22. Pomp and circumstance was the day's theme as devoted baseball fans throughout the Smoky City celebrated the birth of a new baseball campaign while also recognizing the achievements of Fred Clarke's team in 1901. A huge parade was scheduled to kick off the afternoon's festivities.

Speech-making by local dignitaries was not part of the program since only a few people present at Exposition Park would be able to hear the orators. Harry Pulliam, who was overseeing the special celebration, also wanted Pittsburgh's players to be the main focus of this great event.[83]

The Pittsburgh Pirates arrived at the Monongahela House where the Reds were staying, and joined Cincinnati's players in the hotel rotunda at 1 p.m. on April 22. Players from both squads walked outside to waiting carriages that would form the long parade procession. Hours before the appointed time when the parade was scheduled to begin, young boys had grabbed prime spots of real estate along the route, hoping to catch a glimpse of their favorite Pirates player. The 50-piece Grand Army band led this pageant that ushered in another baseball season. Fans along the parade route had a grand time as the procession weaved through Water Street, Wood Street, Liberty Avenue, Seventh Avenue, Smithfield Street, Third Avenue, Grant Street, Fifth Avenue and Market Street in downtown Pittsburgh. The parade then passed over the Sixth Street Bridge into Allegheny and proceeded down Federal Street and Robinson Street before it reached Exposition Park.[84]

By the time these carriages carrying players from Pittsburgh and Cincinnati arrived at Exposition Park, the Pirates' home ballpark was jammed with passionate baseball fans. Club management allowed about 1,000 spectators to stand in front of the grandstand and right field bleachers although no ropes were stretched as was the case in the ballpark's designated standing room area. At 3:15 p.m. Fred Clarke and his players finally appeared and marched across the field behind the Grand Army band. This was followed by a procession involving both the Cincinnati and Pittsburgh teams to the center field flag pole, where the 1901 National League pennant flag was unfurled and raised at 3:30 p.m. As the flag whipped in the wind after being raised on this beautiful day, both squads marched back to home plate, where Tommy Leach was presented with a big leather chair by some admirers. Leach received this gift as a reward for a home run that he hit during the final game of the St. Louis series.[85]

Captain James Thornton of the Allegheny police force was the afternoon's hero during the pre-game celebration. When the band was in danger of losing its path to the pennant pole, Captain Thornton took control of the situation and prevented any snag in the proceedings. He also handled the record-breaking crowd perfectly.[86] Once the action started on Exposition Park's baseball diamond, numerous Pirates players followed Thornton's lead, providing great leadership as champions of their profession. Cincinnati and Pittsburgh engaged in a tight affair as 15,000 fans cheered on the Pirates. Sam Leever pitched splendidly as the Pirates defeated Cincinnati, 4–3. Leever showed great control throughout the complete game and was under duress only in the fourth inning when Cincinnati scored two runs.[87]

Lefty Davis, Fred Clarke, Honus Wagner, Kitty Bransfield and Tommy Leach were Pittsburgh's batting heroes as each player recorded two hits. Davis, Wagner, Bransfield and Leach scored one run apiece. Pittsburgh captured the game in the eighth inning after they had rallied from a three-run deficit to tie the score, 3–3. Tommy Leach led off the frame with a single. Chief Zimmer was instructed to bunt. Pittsburgh's veteran catcher laid down a slow tapper to first baseman Jake Beckley. Leach broke for second base like a flash as Zimmer was retired at first. Instead of stopping at second base as the Reds' players figured he would, he continued to run until he reached third. Leach scored the game's winning run as he crossed home plate in plenty of time after Leever smacked a fly ball to Dummy Hoy in center field.[88]

Pittsburgh raised its record to 5–0 as it slaughtered Cincinnati, 11–3 on Wednesday, April 23. Poor fielding was prevalent on both sides as the beautiful, sunny weather that had graced the opening game was replaced by high winds whose fury kicked up blinding dust that made visibility difficult at times. As *The Pittsburgh Press* said, "As the sun shines upon saint and sinner so does the dust blow over, on and around, champion and chump alike."[89] The two teams combined to commit nine errors during the game. Deacon Phillippe was the whole show on this windy afternoon as his pitching, hitting, and base-running set a pace that was too fast for his teammates as well as Cincinnati's players.[90] Phillippe tossed a complete game, struck out six Reds, went 2-for-3 at the plate, smacked a triple and scored two runs.

Losing had become a foreign idea to the Pirates as they were now undefeated through the exhibition season and the regular season's first two series against St. Louis and Cincinnati. The upstart Chicago Cubs (their new nickname penned by a Chicago reporter) quickly reintroduced Pittsburgh to the concept of being beaten when they came to town for a three-game series at Exposition Park. Chicago handed Pittsburgh its first loss of the season on April 24 as the Cubs prevailed, 5–3. Jack Chesbro's lack of speed during the first inning hurt Pittsburgh as Chicago put the game away early by scoring four runs. Errors were plentiful once again due to Exposition Park's grounds

4. Pittsburgh Breaks Out of the Gate in Splendid Fashion 87

being in poor shape. Spring flooding had wreaked havoc on the ballpark which prevented the field from getting a thorough rolling before the season started. Bunk Congalton recorded four hits against Chesbro and Charlie Dexter hit the first home run of the season at Exposition Park. Dexter tore around the bases after blasting an eighth-inning drive that almost hit the pennant pole in center field.[91]

Chicago made it two victories in a row over the defending champions when they defeated Pittsburgh, 4–2, on Friday, April 25, and moved into first place. Pittsburgh's Jesse Tannehill and Chicago's Mal Eason were locked up in a pitcher's duel as the score stood 1–1 heading into the eighth inning. Chicago sealed the game in that frame due a mistake by right fielder Lefty Davis. With three Cubs on base, Congalton knocked a high fly to right that looked playable. Unfortunately, Davis forgot to take the wind into account. Instead of catching the baseball, he was surprised to see the ball sail over his head and hit the scoreboard. Tomfoolery quickly ensued as Pittsburgh's fielders threw the baseball all over the diamond trying to retire Chicago's runners. Two Cubs crossed home plate during the confusion and a third player scored moments later when catcher Johnny Kling smacked a fly ball to Ginger Beaumont in center field.[92]

Baseball writer J. Ed Grillo looked like a prophet after Pittsburgh suffered their second defeat of the young season. Grillo had cautioned everyone before the series against Chicago started that Pittsburgh was going to lose games at unforeseen times. "It must not be supposed," said Grillo, "that the Pittsburgh team will go through the season without suffering a defeat. The Pirates will be thrown down many a time, that is a certainty, and those defeats are apt to come when they are least expected."[93]

Two consecutive losses certainly were not going to crush the resolve of a seasoned team like the Pittsburgh Pirates. Their confident demeanor, which bordered on cockiness at times, remained although they had been outplayed by a team that finished in sixth place the previous season. Even though the Pirates were currently in second place, they had busted out of the gate in splendid fashion during the season's first week. The Pirates' train was just starting to gather some steam. It would be only a matter of time before this powerful locomotive operated at full capacity, destroying everything in its path.

5

Executive Discipline Fails to Derail the Pirates Train

Pittsburgh had experienced only minor resistance from its baseball opponents until a hungry Chicago Cubs squad strolled into the Smoky City, determined to knock the defending National League champions down a peg or two. While many Pirates rooters believed their beloved team was capable of capturing the pennant, most knew that an undefeated season was impossible. After manager Frank Selee's Cubs defeated Pittsburgh in the series' first game on April 24, the *Chicago Journal* professed joy over the fact that Pirates players and fans finally had been put in their place.[1]

> Frank Selee's youngsters did valorous deeds down at Pittsburgh Thursday, skinning the Pirates in a close, hard game, getting up to the top of the National, and giving Clarke's fellows their first tanning of the campaign. So puffed up had the Pittsburgh fans grown that they almost believed it impossible to beat the champions, and would have accepted odds that the Pirates would not lose two games in every 25. If the youngsters can get two out of three at Pittsburgh the boys will have done splendidly, and will come back to the West Side sure of good support from the fickle populace, which ever loves a winner.[2]

Chicago's victory on April 25 guaranteed they would claim at least two out of three games in this series as was suggested. Hopes of pulling off a clean sweep were ruined when Pittsburgh rebounded in resounding fashion in front of 7,000 delighted fans with a 7–0 victory over the Cubs on Saturday, April 26. Sam Leever was brilliant as he tossed a complete game and allowed only three hits. Lefty Davis was Pittsburgh's batting star as he went 3-for-4 and scored two runs. Fred Clarke and Ginger Beaumont chipped in with two hits apiece. Chicago pitcher Bob "Dusty" Rhoads was roughed up early as he yielded two runs in the first frame and four in the second before finally settling down. When the second stanza ended, Rhoads was so upset that when he reached the bench, he threw his glove to the ground with excessive force. It was appropriate that a player nicknamed Dusty pitched on this particular day. Howling winds were a problem throughout the afternoon.[3]

During practice, a section of the right field fence had blown down, but a rebuilt grandstand withstood the strain admirably. The contest was completed in one hour and 35 minutes even though umpire Joe Cantillon repeatedly called time when clouds of dust blinded him and the players. Games at Exposition Park previously had been postponed due to unique circumstances such as fog and flooding in the outfield. None were ever cancelled on account of dust, and manager Fred Clarke was not ambitious to establish a new record at Exposition Park in that respect.[4] Pittsburgh's victory allowed Clarke's squad to move back into a first-place tie with Chicago. Four Pirates were hitting above the magical .300 mark during the campaign's first week and a half of action. Tommy Leach (.379), Lefty Davis (.361), Ginger Beaumont (.343) and Honus Wagner (.333) were members of this heralded club.

Beaumont's inclusion in this group probably would have been dismissed as unlikely during spring training. Many within the Pittsburgh press corps alleged that Fred Clarke had purposely floated the story regarding Wid Conroy playing shortstop in 1902 with Honus Wagner moving to center field. These baseball writers believed that Clarke did this to frighten Beaumont into dropping 15 pounds of excess weight during spring training.[5] Following their sixth victory in eight games, the Pirates made a short trip to Chicago for one day to play a game at West Side Grounds on Sunday, April 27. Pittsburgh and Chicago's squads left Saturday night on the same train bound for the Windy City. Each team had a Pullman, while umpire Joe Cantillon occupied a berth in a third car.[6]

A huge crowd witnessed a fine pitching duel between Deacon Phillippe and the Cubs' Jimmy St. Vrain. Both hurlers kept the opposition off balance all afternoon as they pitched shutout ball through seven innings. The Pirates finally got on the scoreboard in the eighth inning as they plated two runs and sealed the game. Phillippe led off and was plunked by a St. Vrain offering. A mistake by shortstop Joe Tinker helped put a second Pirate on base. Tinker was unable to record an out at any base when he rushed trying to complete a double play after Lefty Davis laid down a bunt. Pittsburgh filled the bases when St. Vrain hit Fred Clarke with a pitch. Ginger Beaumont slashed a sharp single to right field that drove home Phillippe and Davis with the game's only two runs.[7] Phillippe was brilliant on the mound as he tossed a three-hit shutout.

Part of this large crowd at West Side Grounds engaged in behavior that was prevalent when Pittsburgh had visited Chicago in 1901. Fans in the left field bleachers resumed their verbal conflict with Fred Clarke as they roasted and castigated him in a manner that was standard protocol one year earlier.[8] Pittsburgh left Chicago immediately after the game on a train bound for the Smoky City. The Pirates had a scheduled day off before a series with Patsy Donovan's St. Louis Cardinals started on Tuesday, April 29. Clarke did not plan on wasting an idle day as he held a Monday practice session for his team at Exposition Park.[9]

While Pittsburgh's players participated in the workout, *The Pittsburgh Press* reported on an interesting story regarding a historic trip that could become a reality if Pittsburgh won the National League pennant in 1902. Barney Dreyfuss was carefully deliberating the idea of sending his team on a trip around the world to play baseball if they won the championship. The plan, which originated with Harry Pulliam, was considered a joke when it was first discussed during Pittsburgh's last eastern trip in 1901. That attitude was quickly erased when Dreyfuss began treating Pulliam's scheme seriously. Pittsburgh's owner believed the venture was feasible, and his players were willing to put their support behind the idea if Dreyfuss devised a working plan that proved favorable.[10]

Discussions regarding playing games in exotic countries across the globe were something that was many months away from becoming a reality. At present, Fred Clarke was more concerned over Pittsburgh's upcoming series with St. Louis. The first game against the Cardinals at Exposition Park was postponed due to rain.[11] Even though players from both teams spent an idle day away from the ballpark, this did not mean that baseball news surrounding the Cardinals was not splashed across the sports pages of Smoky City publications. Former Cardinals outfielder Emmet Heidrick had recently criticized St. Louis owner Frank Robison for allowing so many players to jump to the rival American League for the 1902 campaign. Heidrick, who was now a member of the St. Louis Browns, claimed Robison failed to heed Barney Dreyfuss' warning that American League agents had been hot on the trail of Cardinals players during the summer of 1901.[12]

"By the way," said Heidrick, "had Mr. Robison acted upon Mr. Dreyfuss' advice and taken the trouble to walk down from the Waldorf Astoria to the Broadway Central, while we were in New York last August, he would likely have had us with him yet.

"Mr. Dreyfuss told him to act promptly if he wanted to hold on to us, as the American League was hot after us. I, myself, told Donovan about the American's offer the day I received it. The bunch of us thought Mr. Robison would make a call and swing us into line for 1902, but he never turned up, so not taking any chances on being left out in the cold, we signed with Mr. McAleer when he called upon us, after we had returned to St. Louis."[13]

Whether it was due to their success over St. Louis during the season's opening series or the perception that Donovan's team was an easy pushover, the Pirates exhibited a "this-is-too-easy" attitude and played loosely at the game's start when both teams finally hooked up on Wednesday, April 30. Pittsburgh did prevail over St. Louis, 7–4, although there were some anxious moments for Pirates fans throughout the afternoon. Lefty Davis saved the game for Fred Clarke's boys in the ninth inning when his great catch snuffed out a possible Cardinals comeback. With two men on and two out, Patsy Donovan strolled to the plate. Noticing that Pittsburgh's outfield was shading him toward left field, the left-handed swinging Donovan decided to circumvent this strategy by pulling the ball to right field. Donovan took a vicious cut at one of Jack Chesbro's offerings and sent a vicious line drive to right field.[14] Donovan's blistering drive looked as if it was heading to the fence. The baseball never made it to that destination as speedy right fielder Davis covered a vast amount of territory until he was under the ball and clutched it for the game's final out. It seemed that Davis had strong motivation for using his blazing speed to outrun a baseball that appeared destined to be an inside-the-park homer. He was hungry and did not welcome the prospect of an extra-inning game that would prevent him from going home to eat dinner.[15] Besides his stellar defense, Davis also had a solid day at the plate as he went 2-for-5 and scored one run. First baseman Kitty Bransfield was Pittsburgh's top offensive performer as he was a perfect 3-for-3 on the day.

Davis' desire to make it home for dinner was understandable since Allegheny and Pittsburgh's downtown area did become a bit congested during the late afternoon hours. Days earlier, Fred Clarke had some difficulty getting home. One of his Southern friends had recently given him a beautiful colored glass cane that was six feet long and rather frail. Clarke's status as Pittsburgh's star left fielder did not matter on this particular day as he navigated the area, looking to catch a trolley for home. These trolleys at 6 p.m. were filled with a mass of people who usually did not show much respect for people with canes. While Clarke did not suffer any injuries when he was knocked down on a few occasions, he did sigh more than once en route to his house.[16]

Suspense was tossed out the window when Pittsburgh and St. Louis battled once again on Thursday, May 1. Southpaw Jesse Tannehill was the beneficiary of a ruthless batting attack from his teammates as Pittsburgh crushed Donovan's squad, 18–6. Fred Clarke's boys put this game out of reach when they scored nine runs in the second inning. During that exciting inning, Kitty Bransfield and Claude Ritchey each scored twice, while Ritchey and catcher Harry Smith banged out two hits apiece during the frenzied second frame.[17] Every Pirates player recorded at least one hit during this offensive outburst. Ginger Beaumont took top batting honors on the afternoon as he went 3-for-4 at the plate, drilled a double and scored four runs. Ritchey and Smith rapped out three safeties apiece, while Clarke, Honus Wagner and Tommy Leach each smacked two hits.

Prior to Pittsburgh's game against St. Louis on Friday, May 2, Ginger Beaumont pulled up lame during practice. This gave Clarke a chance to use Wid Conroy at shortstop and move Honus Wagner to the outfield. Conroy put his cap on the side of his head, rolled up his sleeves and went to work with confidence and assurance that inspired Pittsburgh's spectators at Exposition Park. Wagner also got an opportunity to show off his cannon arm in this game when he gunned down George Barclay at third base. In the first inning, Wagner knocked in Pittsburgh's first run when he blasted a triple to right-center field that drove home Lefty Davis. With the score tied 1–1 heading into the fourth frame, the Pirates realized they would have to resort to scientific methods to score against Cardinals pitcher Bob Wicker, who seemed to be on top of his game.[18]

Kitty Bransfield led off by beating out a beautiful bunt to third baseman Fred Hartman. Claude Ritchey stepped to the plate and utilized the right side of the diamond as he legged out a bunt to first baseman Roy Brashear. After Tommy Leach was retired on a fly ball to Barclay in left field, Jack O'Connor drove Bransfield home with a single to right that also moved Ritchey to third base. O'Connor stole second base, and two more runs were plated when Lefty Davis whipped a two-out base hit to left field, giving Pittsburgh a 4–1 lead.[19] No more runs were scored by either team as Sam Leever raised his record to 3–0 on the season. Leever tossed a complete game and scattered eight hits.

One Pittsburgh baseball writer showed his cynical side regarding the report that Beaumont was scratched from the starting lineup due to a charley horse. Pittsburgh's correspondent for *The Sporting News* alleged the story about an injury was a ruse. He believed that Clarke wanted to see how the combination of Conroy at shortstop and Wagner in center field actually worked.[20] This conspiracy theory lost some of its validity due to Beaumont not being in Pittsburgh's lineup during their final game of this series against St. Louis on Saturday, May 3. Pittsburgh made it six victories in a row as they defeated the Cardinals, 9–5. The game was closer than the score indicated as St. Louis battled gallantly before Fred Clarke's boys put the contest out of reach with three runs in the seventh inning. Lefty Davis, Fred Clarke, Wid Conroy, Honus Wagner and Tommy Leach banged out two hits apiece for the Pirates. Catcher Jack O'Connor was Pittsburgh's offensive catalyst as he went 4-for-4 and drove home five of his team's nine runs.[21]

Deacon Phillippe raised his record to 4–0 as he tossed a complete game. Prior to the contest, St. Louis manager Patsy Donovan boosted the confidence of his troops by convincing his players they could hammer Phillippe's curves since the Cardinals had more success against him than any other team in 1901. When it was leaked to Pittsburgh's players that Donovan was predicting a victory for his team, the information infuriated them and caused their tempers to flair. This contentious atmosphere was great for baseball fans at Exposition Park as they were given an opportunity to watch two baseball teams passionately battle throughout the afternoon. When Pittsburgh finally clinched the game during the seventh inning, Clarke turned toward St. Louis' bench from his position coaching at third base to scold Donovan's team for their cocky attitude.[22] "Now, will you go back and sit down?" Clarke asked in a sarcastic tone.[23]

Clarke did not wait for an answer as he turned his attention to the game once again.[24] Clarke and his players were a confident bunch that believed they were baseball's supreme team, and quite possibly the greatest aggregation in the game's history. When another squad verbally challenged their superiority, the Pirates believed a swift response upholding the organization's honor was necessary. Some perceived this attitude as overinflated self-worth with puffed chests on the part of Pittsburgh's team. A baseball writer from Baltimore reasoned this type of attitude would serve Pittsburgh well if they decided to tour the world playing baseball after the season as had been suggested. "Out in Pittsburgh they are talking of sending their prize team around the world," he wrote. "As a matter of fact, the team had only to turn around to accomplish the feat, for their chests already reach half way across."[25]

Numbers certainly supported the confident swagger which Clarke and his players exhibited during the baseball season's first few weeks. When National League action concluded on Saturday, May 3, the Pirates found themselves in first place with an 11–2 record. The New York Giants were Pittsburgh's closest challenger, 2½ games behind with a mark of 9–5. Cincinnati was the next team assigned the daunting task of trying to break Pittsburgh's winning streak. Fred Clarke's squad left the friendly confines of Exposition Park to play three games against the Reds at the Palace of the Fans. Pittsburgh extended its winning streak to seven in front of more than 10,000 fans when they demolished Cincinnati, 11–2, on Sunday, May 4. While the Reds recorded more hits than Pittsburgh, the Pirates were able to manufacture clutch safeties. The difference in fielding was also glaring as Cincinnati's defensive work was suspect.[26]

Wretched fielding by Cincinnati basically gave Pittsburgh the game in the first inning. Lefty Davis reached when second baseman Erve Beck could not handle his hot line drive. Fred Clarke made it to first base after Jake Beckley fumbled his sacrifice bunt. Wid Conroy moved Davis and Clarke up a base with a beautiful sacrifice bunt before Honus Wagner drove home both players with a single. Kitty Bransfield followed by beating out a grounder to shortstop Tommy Corcoran. Wagner was forced at third base when Claude Ritchey smacked a ground ball to Harry Steinfeldt, who stepped on third and made the peg to first baseman Beckley. Unfortunately, he threw the ball over Beckley's head, which allowed Bransfield to score and Ritchey to move over to third base. Pittsburgh increased the lead to 4–0 when Tommy Leach's single to left brought home Ritchey.[27]

Those four runs were all Jesse Tannehill needed as he tossed a complete game and raised his record to 3–1 on the season. Tannehill also claimed the day's batting honors for Pittsburgh along with Honus Wagner. One of his two safeties was a three-run, line drive inside-the-park home run in the fourth inning.[28] Even though Pittsburgh's National League dominance had been irrefutable to date, the *New York Press* was not ready to concede the pennant to Fred Clarke's swashbucklers. The newspaper claimed Pittsburgh had moved to the front of the pack with a rush as expected, but that before the curtain fell on the 1902 season, Clarke's aggregation would have to reckon with one or two clubs which had not been counted upon to be in the running.[29]

Cincinnati certainly did not look to be one of those aforementioned clubs that was going to surprise Pittsburgh during the 1902 campaign. The Pirates made it two wins in a row over Cincinnati with a 6–2 victory on Monday, May 5, against manager Bid McPhee's squad. Reds hurler Bob Ewing had a rough day as he allowed 11 hits and exhibited gracious generosity by walking six Pirates. Sam Leever was crafty all afternoon as Cincinnati did minimal damage since most of their hits were scattered and not one Red reached first base with a free pass. Jack O'Connor had another fine day at the plate as he rapped out three singles. Honus Wagner scored three of Pittsburgh's six runs, stole a base, had another assist from the outfield and caught two fly balls playing for injured center fielder Clarence Beaumont. Wid Conroy once again fielded his position at shortstop in fine style.[30]

Pittsburgh extended its winning streak to nine games with another 6–2 victory over Cincinnati on May 6. Jack Chesbro and Bill Phillips were locked up in a tight pitcher's duel until Pittsburgh busted the game wide open by scoring five runs in the ninth inning. Chesbro aided his own cause by leading off the frame with a double to left field. Lefty Davis drew a base on balls before Fred Clarke moved both runners up one base with a sacrifice bunt. Pittsburgh loaded the bases when Wid Conroy worked out a walk. Honus Wagner smacked one of Phillips' offerings on the nose, but shortstop Tommy Corcoran handled the hot smash and nailed "Happy Jack" at the plate for the inning's second out. Kitty Bransfield cleared the bases with a triple to center field. Claude Ritchey then astonished Cincinnati's baseball faithful when he smacked a two-run homer to right field that produced Pittsburgh's final tallies.[31]

Infielder Jimmy Burke did a fine job at third base after he replaced starter Tommy Leach early in the game. Leach was ordered from the grounds for disputing a decision by umpire Bob Emslie.[32] Prior to Leach's transgression, Fred Clarke's team had not done much kicking against umpiring decisions they deemed as incorrect.

While Pittsburgh's players did not seem to be antagonizing umpires, the team was so loose that nobody took it personally when a player was chastised by his teammates for screwing up. Cincinnati baseball writer Charley Zuber chronicled a few times when roasting between Pirates teammates had occurred during the recently completed series.

"In the Sunday game, after Fred Clarke and Hans Wagner allowed Heismann's fly to drop safely between them, Clarke came in for an unmerciful roasting when he walked to the bench, as Wagner had called for the ball, and was therefore entitled to it without any interference. In Monday's game a similar play came between Ritchey and Wagner, and the little second baseman was given an awful verbal walloping by his players. In the same game Bransfield gave Sam Leever a stiff call for throwing Beck out at first on a fast grounder, when he easily could have retired Crawford at second on the play.

"'There is no bad feeling among the players,' claimed one of the Pirates players, "but every man is anxious to have the others keep awake all the time, and the only way that this can be accomplished is to impress them with their mistakes. And we do it in a way that they do not soon forget any break they may make.'"[33]

Such behavior shocked Cincinnati's fans, who were used to players from their team overlooking each other's faults and the manager acting as a peacemaker when trouble did occur on the field. This system sometimes could be an abject failure if things festered below the surface and eventually ruined team harmony both on and off the field. Fred Clarke and his players were charting their own course as they fought to secure another National League pennant. Pittsburgh's players were always willing to dispute unfavorable events on the diamond involving opponents or umpires. Clarke and his men never hesitated coaching each other or openly criticizing bad plays committed by fellow teammates.[34]

Pittsburgh returned home for a four-game series at Exposition Park against the Brooklyn Superbas after the short road trip to Cincinnati. Fred Clarke made an alteration to his pitching rotation for the first contest on May 7 against Brooklyn. Rather than pitching Phillippe, Tannehill, Leever and Chesbro in turn without interruption, Clarke decided to give left-handed hurler Eddie Doheny his first start of the season. Pittsburgh's manager was rewarded for showing faith in Doheny's pitching ability as the southpaw gave a creditable showing for the Pirates. He held Brooklyn in check until the eighth inning when the Superbas tied the score, 3–3, on RBI singles by Tom McCreery and Tim Flood. Doheny's teammates got the lead back and clinched the ballgame during their turn at bat in the eighth. Lefty Davis singled and promptly stole second base. Fred Clarke smoked a line drive over third baseman Charlie Irwin's head that brought Davis home and secured Pittsburgh's 4–3 victory.[35]

One day later, Pittsburgh lost a game for the first time in May as Brooklyn ended the Pirates' ten-game winning streak. Frank Kitson was brilliant for the Superbas as he held Fred Clarke's troops in check and walked away with a 4–1 win. Brooklyn left fielder Jimmy Sheckard's finger was in the victory pie all afternoon as he made great catches of drives off the bats of Fred Clarke, Wid Conroy and Honus Wagner. The crowd at Exposition Park was so impressed with Sheckard's defensive work that they gave him a round of cheers even though he played for the visiting team. Pittsburgh ruined Kitson's bid for a shutout in the eighth inning when Tommy Leach walked, stole second base and scored on a single that Lefty Davis drove past Charlie Irwin.[36]

While revenge certainly was on the minds of Pittsburgh's players on May 9, getting back on the winning track would not be so easy with one of their star players unable to play. Fred Clarke sat out this contest so a badly bruised finger on his right hand could heal. Clarke moved Honus Wagner to his spot in left field and reinstalled Ginger Beaumont in center field. These moves were not expected to unhinge Pittsburgh's juggernaut attack one bit since they had the best bench in the National League. Wagner was a star wherever he played and could do anything but pitch or catch. Wid Conroy could play at third base, second base, shortstop or in the outfield, while Jimmy Burke was clever at third and short. Pitcher Ed Poole also was a good infielder, and Jesse Tannehill always performed admirably in the outfield when called upon to serve in a pinch.[37]

Outfield duty was not on the agenda for Tannehill during this Friday afternoon game. He was called upon to pitch against Brooklyn's Bill Donovan. Pittsburgh's players were in a foul mood from the game's outset due to Brooklyn putting on too many airs after its victory the previous day. The Superbas seemed determined to make it two victories in a row as they smacked five hits and worked out a walk against Tannehill during the first three innings. Clutch hitting was lacking as the game's first run was not scored until the third frame when Willie Keeler crossed home plate on Tom McCreery's single. Some of the gamblers occupying Exposition Park cheered heartily when Keeler scored. This round of applause for the opposing team aroused Pittsburgh's players, who did not appreciate the laudatory praise for Brooklyn. The Pirates struck quickly and put the game out of reach before Brooklyn realized what hit it.[38]

After Donovan struck out Harry Smith to start the bottom of the third inning, Jesse Tannehill singled to center field. Lefty Davis followed with a single to right. Tannehill gambled and reached third base ahead of the throw by right fielder Willie Keeler, while Davis sneaked into second. Ginger Beaumont tied the game when he drove Tannehill home with a single. It looked as if Donovan might work his way out of this jam when Davis was thrown out at the plate on a grounder by Wid Conroy. That expectation was shattered when Honus Wagner drove home Beaumont and Conroy with a double to the right-center field fence.[39] While these three runs were enough to secure a Pirates victory, the assault against Donovan continued until the final bell sounded. When the dust settled, Pittsburgh extracted revenge in a big way with a 12–1 triumph over Brooklyn.

As the hour grew late at Exposition Park, Tannehill had started to work quickly since dinnertime was nearing.[40] Besides raising his record to 4–1 and tossing a complete game, he also went 3-for-4 at the plate and scored two runs. Lefty Davis, Honus Wagner and Tommy Leach offered commendable support as each player banged out two hits and they combined to score four runs. The Pirates did not give the Superbas a chance to catch their breath during the finale of this four-game series on Saturday, May 10. Pittsburgh rewarded the 4,700 faithful fans who showed up at Exposition Park despite shivering, cold weather with an 8–4 victory over the Superbas. While the temperature may have been cold in the stands, the atmosphere was hot and fiery on the baseball diamond. Umpire Hank O'Day was forced to file more complaints after this particular contest than he did in many a week during the 1901 season.[41]

Brooklyn's players were particularly galled over O'Day missing an obvious third strike against Honus Wagner in the fourth inning. On the next pitch, Wagner rapped an infield single to third baseman Charlie Irwin, who inexplicably tried to make a play at first and threw the baseball into Exposition Park's bleachers. Wagner moved over to third on Irwin's errant toss. Bransfield stepped to the plate and slammed a sharp grounder to pitcher Jim Hughes, who made an acrobatic stop and fired home, hoping to retire Wagner. The play was close, but Brooklyn's players became further agitated when O'Day called Wagner safe. After Pittsburgh scored two more runs in the inning, kicking on the part of Brooklyn's players against O'Day intensified. Tiring of the constant verbal attack, O'Day restored order and banished Willie Keeler from the game.[42]

Lefty Davis went 3-for-5 and scored one run. Honus Wagner, Claude Ritchey and Jack O'Connor chipped in with two hits apiece. Jack Chesbro raised his record to 4–1 as he tossed a complete game. Another week of playing solid baseball helped widen Pittsburgh's lead over their National League rivals. Through May 10, the Pirates sported a sterling 17–3 record. This gave Fred Clarke's team a five-game lead over New York, whose record stood at 10–6. Late Saturday night after Pittsburgh defeated Brooklyn, the Pirates boarded a train for Cincinnati to play a single contest on Sunday afternoon. Eddie Doheny and Ed Poole were the only pitchers that Clarke took with him on this short trip. No changes were expected in Pittsburgh's lineup since Clarke planned on remaining on the sidelines until the Pirates returned home to play Boston.[43]

As it turned out, Poole wasted his time making the trip to Cincinnati. Doheny was masterful as he tossed a six-hit shutout, while his teammates smacked 16 hits and routed Cincinnati, 10–0, on May 11. Since coming to Pittsburgh from New York, Doheny's work had improved due to his steady habits. While never a boozer when he played for the Giants, he had succumbed to some irregular night life habits at times that hindered his performance on the field. Doheny's eyes were opened when he came to Pittsburgh. "I like your plan of doing business here," he had told Fred Clarke upon his arrival, and without any more discussion, settled down to the business of following that script.[44]

Following this dominant performance by Pittsburgh over the Reds, Cincinnati writer Ren Mulford, Jr., heaped lavish praise upon Fred Clarke's team. Mulford firmly believed the Pirates were determined to rewrite baseball history before the 1902 baseball campaign concluded. "Those Pittsburgh chaps actually nursed the dream of equaling the never-to-be beaten record of the Reds of '69 (who posted a perfect 57–0 record that year), and when they were here last week they were still doing more mourning over the brace of games they lost to Chicago than crowing over their great string of victories. Pittsburgh is out to win the pennant of 1902 with the greatest percentage ever attained by a team of champions. That's Fred Clarke's ambition, and no one can challenge the declaration that it is one most laudable and calculated to keep the fires of enthusiasm burning at the head waters of the Ohio."[45]

Cincinnati owner John T. Brush probably did not care much about Fred Clarke and his team's ambition to be christened as the greatest team in baseball history. Hope and excitement at the outset of Cincinnati's game against Pittsburgh before a large crowd at the Palace of the Fans had turned to embarrassment and disappointment once the Pirates got rolling.[46] Shortly after this carnage on a baseball diamond reached its merciful conclusion, the report that Brush planned on reinstating a 1901 rule where each National League team reduced its roster to 16 players by May 15 gained new life. Initial announcements on this subject usually had been made by friends of Mr. Brush. Pirates management believed this rule was a ploy to get players from Barney Dreyfuss' stable that may be released so Pittsburgh could reach the limit. Brush had been trying to acquire a pitcher from Pittsburgh for weeks, but Fred Clarke refused to release any of his men.[47]

Using surrogates to advance his agenda became ancient history for Brush on the evening of May 11. As Harry Pulliam waited at the railroad station in Cincinnati on Sunday night so he could return to Pittsburgh, the National League executive committee chairman told the Pirates team secretary that he intended to enforce the 16 player limit rule. When Pulliam returned to the Smoky City, the number of angry members from Pittsburgh's management team increased to three when Pulliam reported to Barney Dreyfuss and Fred Clarke. Upon hearing the news regarding Brush's plan, Dreyfuss stated unequivocally that he would not obey the edict. "If Brush insists upon that rule the league will not get one of the three men let out by Pittsburgh," said president Dreyfuss in a threatening tone.[48]

This threat by Dreyfuss indicated that Pittsburgh's owner had some plan for protecting his surplus players in which their best interests would be taken into account. Dreyfuss claimed he observed the rule in 1901, even though the New York Giants carried extra men. Pittsburgh's owner vowed not to be foolish again. Fred Clarke declared that Andrew Freedman's team would also ignore the limit in 1902. Both men did not plan on observing the rule if New York cheated once again. Clarke, believing that Brush was determined to break up the Pirates' happy family, defiantly claimed the team's composition would not change for some time to come.⁴⁹ "The team will do its best to make the magnates sorry for their break," declared Clarke in an irritated tone. "The magnates of the National League are not in touch with the players or the public and their legislative acts show it."⁵⁰

This illegitimate proposal being propagated by John T. Brush had certainly put Clarke in a cantankerous mood as Pittsburgh prepared to open a four-game series against the Boston Beaneaters at Exposition Park on Monday, May 12. While he was not prepared to make any bold predictions or boast openly about the greatness of his Pirates squad, recent events galvanized him to be more determined than ever to do heavy damage in the National League before other teams hit their stride.

Clarke showed some contempt for his rivals when a fan congratulated Pittsburgh's manager before the first game against Boston for his team's performance in Cincinnati.⁵¹ "I see the Cincinnati writers predicted that you will have the pennant clinched by July 4," claimed the Pirates rooter. "I only wish we could box it up by June 4," snapped Clarke.⁵²

Boston gave Pittsburgh everything they could handle as Fred Clarke attempted to slip another victory in his back pocket. Sam Leever had to retire after one inning when his pitching arm could not stand the strain. When Jesse Tannehill came on in relief to start the second frame, it snapped a streak of 21 consecutive complete games for Pirates pitchers. Tannehill pitched marvelously as Pittsburgh pulled out a 4–2 victory. Boston pitcher Vic Willis was tough on everyone in the Pirates lineup other than Clarence Beaumont and Clarke, who was back in the lineup. Beaumont smacked a single and two doubles, and reached on a walk. Clarke made three hits for eight bases, and scored two of Pittsburgh's four runs. He also smacked the first Pirates home run of 1902 at Exposition Park when he blasted a drive to the center field corner of the bleachers in the fifth inning. Tommy Leach took quite a risk waving Clarke home from the third base coaching box. Pittsburgh's captain barely legged out his inside-the-park homer as the throw to home plate was a split second too late.⁵³

After not having to use a reliever all season until the first game of this series against Boston, Fred Clarke was forced to go to the bullpen once again when play resumed between these two teams on May 14 after rain postponed the previous day's contest.⁵⁴ Boston sent starter Jack Chesbro to the woods when they scored six runs in the first inning. After his wildness yielded four walks, he abandoned speed and curves and decided a strategy of aiming the ball to catcher Jack O'Connor waist high and over the pan was more practical. This course of action proved disastrous as the Beaneaters started lacing base-

5. Executive Discipline Fails to Derail the Pirates Train 101

balls all over Exposition Park. Rather than conclude that Chesbro was having a bad day, O'Connor blamed umpire Hank O'Day for his pitcher's failure to hit the target once in a dozen attempts. O'Connor kicked so long that he started to believe he was telling the truth. Fred Clarke did not agree with his catcher's assessment. He reasoned the Pirates were just having an off day and held his tongue in respect to O'Day's umpiring.[55] Ed Poole pitched the final eight innings as Boston defeated Pittsburgh, 10–5.

Southpaw Eddie Doheny got the Pirates back on track on Thursday, May 15. Doheny was brilliant as he tossed a complete game, allowed one run and scattered four hits as Pittsburgh defeated Boston, 5–1. His solid pitching and the methodical manner with which Pittsburgh dismantled the Beaneaters ended up being minor stories during the final game of this combative series. Boston first baseman Fred Tenney and Fred Clarke had been mortal enemies for many years. A running feud between these two players started blazing once again in the seventh inning when a dose of accelerant rekindled the flames. After Boston shortstop Herman Long had just completed a fast double play, Clarke beat out a slow roller to Long and collided with Tenney, who had spread his body out all over first base reaching for Long's wide throw.[56]

Not happy with being barreled over by Clarke, Tenney gave Pittsburgh's manager a verbal barrage of epithets.[57] When Clarke came in from left field to take his place in the first base coaching box after Boston finished batting in the eighth inning, the controversy was renewed.[58] During this heated discussion, Tenney suddenly reached out and tried to yank Clarke's nose. Clarke responded by kicking Boston's first baseman in the shins.[59] Tenney retaliated with a swift kick to Clarke's shins before he threw off his mitt and landed a punch against Clarke's jaw.[60] Both players began swinging at each other with clenched fists, but none of the blows struck either man in the face. Over a dozen players from the two squads ran to the scene, and Pirates catcher Jack O'Connor used a boxing referee's wedge technique to separate the combatants. Tenney fought with his teammates to let the bout continue since he wanted to inflict as much bodily harm on Clarke as possible.[61]

When order was finally restored on the field, umpire Hank O'Day banned Clarke and Tenney from the grounds. After the game, O'Day reported the incident to the National League's executive committee.[62] When asked to give his opinion of the play in question, Clarke readily admitted that he ran close to the first base bag in order to make Tenney drop the baseball. On the morning of Friday, May 16, Clarke received a short, terse message from league executive committee chairman John T. Brush. "You are off until the case is heard," read Brush's decree.[63] Clarke and Tenney had both been suspended by Brush.

Pirates fans were angry when Clarke received a suspension from Brush for his confrontation with Tenney. They believed Tenney was in the wrong for instigating the incident. This was the first time Pittsburgh's manager had lost his temper during the 1902 campaign. He was only acting in self-defense since Tenney struck him first. All through this series, Boston's players blocked throws, bumped players and pulled other tricks at the direction of manager Al Buckenberger. The champion Pirates took their licks without a whimper and dished out rough play in equal measure. Tenney was the only player from his team who squealed over Pittsburgh's counter-tactics. Ironically, Tenney acted as though he was ashamed for his role in this incident after it played out.[64] One thing that Tenney's and Clarke's prompt suspensions demonstrated was that the executive committee seemed to be serious about preserving order on the diamond in 1902.[65]

Fred Clarke was not missed one bit as Pittsburgh easily handled the Philadelphia Phillies on May 16. Hurler Jack Chesbro redeemed himself after a rough outing in his previous start two days earlier. He secured a 6–1 victory as he tossed a complete game, allowed two walks and scattered seven hits. The trio of Ginger Beaumont, Honus Wagner and Kitty Bransfield gave Phillies pitcher Doc White headaches all afternoon. Beaumont had two singles and a walk. Wagner blasted two three-baggers and reached base a third time on an error by left fielder George Browne. Bransfield rapped out three timely singles that drove home five of Pittsburgh's six runs.[66] Even though Clarke was suspended, he remained on the Pirates bench all afternoon. When Clarke once or twice forgot himself and coached his team, Philadelphia's players rebuked him when they heard the Pirates skipper's voice.[67]

A powerful hitting barrage was Pittsburgh's recipe for victory on Saturday, May 17, as the Pirates defeated their cross-state rival, 9–3. Ginger Beaumont, Honus Wagner, Kitty Bransfield and Jesse Tannehill did the heavy lifting for Pittsburgh with timely hitting that excited the crowd of 6,000. Beaumont drilled two doubles, and Bransfield blasted two splendid three-baggers and just missed smacking a third, while Wagner and Tannehill each banged out a double and a single. Seven Philadelphia errors also aided the Pirates' cause. Tannehill's earnest effort on the mound brought cheers from Pittsburgh's fans throughout the afternoon.[68] He tossed a complete game, struck out five Phillies, and raised his record to 6–1.

Pittsburgh's record now stood at 22–4 on the season. New York was still second with a mark of 14–8 that left them six games behind. Six regulars in

National League executive committee chairman John T. Brush suspended Fred Clarke after he became embroiled in a fight with the Boston Beaneaters' Fred Tenney on May 15, 1902. Unhappy over Clarke colliding with him at first base in the seventh inning, Tenney initiated the fight one inning later. Pirates fans were incensed that Brush would suspend Clarke for defending himself against Tenney's attack (courtesy of the National Baseball Hall of Fame Library, Cooperstown, New York).

the Pirates lineup were now batting above .300. Ginger Beaumont (.411), Honus Wagner (.359), Jack O'Connor (.348), Tommy Leach (.319), Fred Clarke (.315) and Lefty Davis (.303) were all doing lethal damage with the stick. Pittsburgh made another short road trip by train to play a Sunday matinee against the Chicago Cubs on May 18. After spending one day in the Windy City, the Pirates would return to Exposition Park to conclude their series with Philadelphia.[69] While the American League's Chicago White Sox were entertaining 2,000 people at South Side Park, the Pirates and Cubs packed in 15,000 fans at West Side Grounds.[70] Those rooting for Chicago went home disappointed as Pittsburgh's offensive onslaught continued during an 11–3 victory.

Deacon Phillippe made his first start in ten days after being laid up with a cold that had moved to his pitching arm. Phillippe went the route for Pittsburgh as he allowed three runs, eight hits and struck out six Cubs. Wid Conroy and Kitty Bransfield rapped out three hits apiece, while Claude Ritchey, Ginger Beaumont and Tommy Leach each recorded two safeties. This quintet also scored eight of Pittsburgh's 11 runs. Pittsburgh basically clinched the game with four first-inning runs. Given a second chance after catcher Frank Chance muffed a foul popup, Lefty Davis opened the game with a single. Davis moved over to third base when Conroy singled past shortstop Joe Tinker, and crossed home plate after Conroy was forced at second on Beaumont's ground ball. Cubs pitcher Jock Menefee recorded the inning's second out when he fanned Honus Wagner as Beaumont stole second base.[71]

Menefee's hope of getting out of this inning without more damage was thwarted by Kitty Bransfield's RBI single. Claude Ritchey kept the hitting parade moving when he slashed a single to center field that moved Bransfield to third. Pittsburgh added their final two runs of the inning and made it 4–0 after Chance threw the ball into center field as Ritchey attempted to steal second base, allowing both Ritchey and Bransfield to score.[72]

When the Pirates returned home to resume their series against Philadelphia after the short jaunt to Chicago, Pittsburgh was absolutely buzzing over some great news involving the city's Fourth of July Celebration. It seemed that President Theodore Roosevelt had agreed to give the keynote address during Pittsburgh's holiday observance after a committee of city officials visited him in Washington on Saturday.[73]

"Gentlemen, I am going to accept your invitation, and I do so with pleasure," replied President Roosevelt as he graciously agreed to this request. "I am delighted that this opportunity has been given to visit that great manufacturing center and to meet its really great people. I do not know what I can say any more than to assure you of the pleasant anticipations I already have of the visit that is before me."⁷⁴

Besides the keynote speech from President Roosevelt, Pittsburgh's Fourth of July Celebration was expected to include a Declaration of Independence reading, patriotic addresses, daylight and night fireworks, balloon ascensions, flying airships and all of the holiday trimmings.⁷⁵ Over at Exposition Park on that day, the Pirates were scheduled to play a morning-afternoon doubleheader against the Brooklyn Superbas. While being part of Pittsburgh's big Fourth of July Celebration thrilled the Pirates, there were still many games to be played before this glorious event occurred. When the series against Philadelphia resumed on May 19, Pittsburgh's players quickly realized that a tough battle was part of this afternoon's itinerary. Pittsburgh's Eddie Doheny and the Phillies' Bill Magee were sensational on the mound. Magee throttled the Pirates and held them to five hits, while Doheny kept his opponents from utilizing their nine hits.

The game was tied 1–1 heading into the ninth inning. Philadelphia was retired quietly as Doheny made quick work of them. When Wid Conroy led off Pittsburgh's home half, Jack O'Connor gave his teammate simple instructions. "Finish it up here, Wid, I am hungry," yelled O'Connor. Conroy obliged his veteran teammate by ripping a drive to right-center field that eluded Philadelphia's Roy Thomas. Conroy was panting on third base with a triple by the time Thomas' throw reached the infield. Ginger Beaumont was so eager to end the game that he swung at the first pitch and fouled out to first baseman Klondike Douglass. Honus Wagner promptly sent everyone home to eat a hot dinner when he drove in Conroy with a seeing-eye single between third baseman Bill Hallman and shortstop Rudy Hulswitt that gave Pittsburgh a 2–1 victory.⁷⁶

Pittsburgh pulled off the four-game sweep over Philadelphia as 2,200 spectators watched both teams battle for a second consecutive day with the Pirates once again securing victory in the ninth inning. Sam Leever allowed Philadelphia to score four runs through six innings before he was lifted for Jack Chesbro. Even though he was still suspended, Fred Clarke made a managerial decision and pulled Leever after he had to run the bases following his triple to right field in the bottom of the sixth inning. Trailing Philadelphia, 5–4, heading into the eighth frame, O'Connor singled, moved to second on Chesbro's sacrifice bunt, and scored the tying run when pitcher Doc White made a wild throw to first on Lefty Davis' infield hit. The Pirates claimed a 6–5 victory in the ninth inning on successive singles by Kitty Bransfield, Jimmy Burke and Tommy Leach. Burke did a fine job subbing for injured second baseman Claude Ritchey as he went 3-for-5 at the plate.[77]

The level of competition quickly rose for Fred Clarke's troops as the New York Giants rolled into town to begin a four-game series at Exposition Park. While New York had slipped into third place behind Chicago and now trailed Pittsburgh by 8½ games, this series was viewed as a huge barometer for the Giants, who believed they could compete on equal footing with the National League's top team. Both squads showed up in a fighting mood for the first game in front of 2,500 fans on Wednesday, May 21. Many of the rooters were actually Giants sympathizers since Pittsburgh native George "Heinie" Smith played for New York. The usual addition of a delegation of New York businessmen made this combination so powerful that supporters for baseball's greatest team on earth had to exercise their vocal chords strenuously to make a respectable showing.[78]

Those fans rooting for New York had their moment in the sun as the Giants defeated Pittsburgh, 4–3. Giants hurlers Dummy Taylor and Christy Mathewson were extremely stingy on the mound as they held the Pirates to four hits. Mathewson relieved Taylor in the seventh inning after he was tossed from the game for doing a pantomime to show his displeasure over a close umpiring decision that allowed Pittsburgh's Jesse Tannehill to draw a walk. Tannehill eventually came around to score the tying run that made it 3–3. New York secured victory in the top of the eighth inning. After Joe Bean was retired, Mathewson reached when Tannehill hit him with a pitch. George Van Haltren was retired on a fly ball to Honus Wagner in left field. Wagner's return throw to first base was so fast that it reached Kitty Bransfield before Mathewson made it back to the bag. Unfortunately, umpire Bob Emslie did not see the play. This blunder cost Pittsburgh the game as Jack Doyle smacked a double to right-center field that drove Mathewson home with the winning run.[79]

Undeterred by their first loss after six consecutive wins, the Pirates were more resolved after this minor setback. As on other occasions after a defeat during the season's early stages, the Pirates displayed their contempt for any team that had the audacity to show them up. The Pirates immediately put New York back in its place with a solid 6–0 victory on Thursday, May 22. Deacon Phillippe was near perfect for Pittsburgh as he tossed a complete game and allowed only two hits. A vast majority of those in attendance at Exposition Park believed both singles should have been ruled as errors. Fred Clarke, who also kept a tally on the Pirates bench, was positive that both plays should have been recorded as misplays. Those Pirates who made the miscues were the first to back Clarke's premise that proper interpretation by the official scorer would have resulted in Phillippe pitching a no-hitter.[80]

Solid hitting support made this game a breeze for Phillippe. Jack O'Connor was a perfect 3-for-3 at the plate and scored two runs, while Ginger Beaumont, Kitty Bransfield, and Phillippe rapped out two hits apiece. Besides suffering a convincing defeat at the hands of the league leaders, New York also lost a crucial player to an ugly injury. Center fielder George Van Haltren broke his leg when he slid awkwardly into second base.[81] Pitching proved to be the main story line once again on May 23. Eddie Doheny and New York's Frank "Tully" Sparks locked up in a monumental pitchers' duel as both men were determined to match Phillippe's record from the previous afternoon. Sparks allowed five hits for a total of eight bases, and gave up two walks. Doheny allowed seven hits for a total of eight bases, while he issued two free passes.[82]

Each team scratched out one run before Pittsburgh pulled out the ballgame in dramatic fashion in the ninth inning. Ginger Beaumont knocked a long fly to right-center field that eluded Giants outfielder Jim Jones. By the time Jones retrieved the sphere and threw it back into the infield, Beaumont was perched on third base with a triple. He remained at third as Honus Wagner was retired on a ground ball to Sparks. Time was called, and a conference was held in the center of the diamond by Jack Doyle, Frank Bowerman, Heinie Smith and Sparks to discuss strategy regarding Kitty Bransfield. They finally agreed to issue an intentional pass to Bransfield and take their chances facing Jimmy Burke. While this seemed to be the proper move on New York's part, it failed to work. Burke cleverly bunted toward first base. Beaumont, who knew what was coming, bolted for home plate once bat met baseball. Doyle made a one-handed stab of Burke's bunt, but could not make a successful throw to the plate as Beaumont scored the winning run that gave Pittsburgh a 2–1 victory.[83]

Attracting attention was not an easy task for the champions these days unless they did something out of the ordinary. Winning ballgames was not always sufficient to draw more than a few words of praise for Barney Dreyfuss' great team. While attendance figures were higher than in previous years and the players' work was appreciated by Pirates fans, the loyal rooters had lived upon a luxurious diet for so long this season that they did not become enthusiastic unless manager Fred Clarke served a new dish. During the series finale against New York on Saturday, May 24, Jack Chesbro supplied a new menu item for hungry baseball patrons. Strikeouts a la Chesbro was the delicacy served for 6,500 cheering fans at Exposition Park.[84] He surpassed the pitching performances of Doheny and Phillippe as he tossed a complete game, gave up one run on two hits, and struck out 11 Giants as Pittsburgh defeated New York, 6–1.

Jack Chesbro's 11-strikeout performance was tops in the National League so far this season.[85] After falling in a hard-fought contest against New York in the first game of this series, the Pirates had regrouped and quickly showed manager Horace Fogel's squad why they were baseball's greatest team. Even the absence of Fred Clarke from the lineup due to some suspect league jurisprudence did not disrupt the Pirates' momentum. No National League team had shown that it was capable of catching the 1902 Pittsburgh Pirates as they maintained their assault on baseball history. Water was wet, the sky was blue, grass was green, and the Pirates continued to win baseball games without much resistance from their opponents.

6

Honus Wagner and Jack O'Connor Heading to St. Louis?

There was no mystery at all surrounding the favorite to claim a National League pennant in 1902. After the Pittsburgh Pirates defeated New York on May 24, their record stood at 28–5. This exceptional mark gave them an eight-game lead over the Chicago Cubs, whose 17–10 record ordinarily would have been good enough to lead the league as Decoration Day approached. The 1902 campaign certainly was anything but ordinary as Pittsburgh seemed determined to have the race wrapped up before Independence Day. Pittsburgh's pitching staff was far superior to its National League competitors. The hitting prowess of Ginger Beaumont (.380), Jack O'Connor (.361), Honus Wagner (.333), Tommy Leach (.319), Kitty Bransfield (.317) and Fred Clarke (.315) was unparalleled and exposed other National League batting attacks as being pretenders.

There were many reasons for the Pirates' sensational start. Familiarity with having played together for almost two seasons was their main advantage over teams auditioning new players in 1902 due to American League defections. The unusual 1902 schedule also benefitted Pittsburgh greatly during the campaign's first month and a half.[1] The Pirates had played 24 games at home and nine on the road thus far. Of all the National League teams, Pittsburgh definitely was the squad that least needed such a favorable schedule.[2]

Having speed to burn on the base paths was another reason why Pittsburgh was dominating the competition in 1902. When Jesse Tannehill and Harry Smith were in Fred Clarke's starting lineup, there was not a poor base runner among the nine starters. On many occasions, Pittsburgh's opponents were forced into making glaring mistakes due to the daring base running of

Clarke's troops. Rival infielders always had to worry about what strategic maneuver Ginger Beaumont might use after speedy outfielder Lefty Davis reached first base. Beaumont was one of the best bunters in the business. He usually could assess the defense, find its weakness, and make one of his famous bunt hits either to the left or right side of the diamond.[3]

While the New York Giants were in town to play Pittsburgh, team captain Jack Doyle critiqued the Pirates in a very favorable manner. A former member of the famous Baltimore Orioles in the 1890s, Doyle could not be blamed for ranking that aggregation first when he compared the two teams. He was willing to admit the Orioles were weak in a few places, while he could not find any such issues with the 1902 Pittsburgh Pirates. Baltimore manager Ned Hanlon never had an infield that was as well balanced as Pittsburgh's, and Barney Dreyfuss was able to produce four outfielders who could field, bat, throw and run the bases. Doyle believed both squads had solid attributes which made them stand out in this discussion regarding these two great baseball aggregations.[4]

> For tricksters I think the Baltimore team was never equaled. Their motto was "Anything to win," and they could think up more smooth dodges than any other team I ever saw. They also originated some good plays, many of which are in use now. In this respect I think they surpassed the present champions. There are some good inside men here now, but the team is playing straight baseball rather than the tricky brand, and in this style of playing, Pittsburgh is as clever as any team that ever won the pennant.
>
> There is a strong man for every position on the field, and then one or two left to sit on the bench and wait until needed. Another unusual feature is that none of the players have any serious defects. There is not a glass arm in the lot and not one slow runner to block team plays after the leaders of the batting order are out of the way. Then the pitching staff is a wonderful one. A manager who has two first-class twirlers considers himself fortunate, but Clarke has a half dozen at his command.[5]

The cleverest team at playing "straight baseball" in the National League as Doyle claimed found itself on the sidelines for a few days. Pittsburgh had two days off before the Cincinnati Reds were to begin a series at Exposition Park on Tuesday, May 27. Fred Clarke and his boys rested an extra day when the first Reds contest was postponed due to rain.[6] While the Pirates relaxed, Brooklyn manager Ned Hanlon stated that his team was ready to challenge Pittsburgh's baseball supremacy. The Superbas' record currently stood at 12–19. Unlike Pittsburgh's favorable early schedule, most of Brooklyn's games had been played on the road. Hanlon believed some home cooking would quickly cure what ailed his team.[7]

I think you will find a big difference in us when we have been home a week. We have played but four or five games at home this year and have not had a chance to practice much. When we get home it will be practice every morning. Then we will have a chance to work a few tricks and get the pitchers to working right. I am confident that we will be right on top of Pittsburgh from now on.[8]

This attitude on Hanlon's part certainly was commendable, although it did not seem to be rooted in reality. Even a long layoff and brutally cold weather could not alter Pittsburgh's ascendancy above their National League brethren. Showing no rust after a three-day break, the Pirates used another ninth-inning comeback to secure a victory on May 28 in front of 800 people who braved the 42-degree temperature to sit at Exposition Park.[9] Jesse Tannehill, a pitcher Jack Doyle said reminded him of Clark Griffith, raised his record to 7–2 as Pittsburgh defeated Cincinnati, 4–3.[10] Tannehill should have tossed a shutout, but shoddy fielding by the Pirates allowed Cincinnati to score three runs and take a 3–2 lead in the sixth inning. Pittsburgh struck back quickly as they scored the tying run in the seventh frame. Lefty Davis and Fred Clarke, who was playing in his first game since being suspended two weeks earlier, drew consecutive walks. Davis came around to score when Reds third baseman Harry Steinfeldt made a bad throw after fielding Ginger Beaumont's bunt.[11]

Pittsburgh sent the small throng of fans home happy with a dramatic finish in the ninth inning. Jesse Tannehill opened the frame with a line drive over second baseman George Magoon's head that went for a thrilling triple when the baseball rolled between two Cincinnati outfielders. After Lefty Davis was retired, Reds pitcher Henry Thielman hit Fred Clarke with a pitch. Clarence Beaumont promptly ended the game by legging out an infield single that brought Tannehill home with the winning run.[12] Due to the cancellation of Tuesday's contest, Pittsburgh and Cincinnati played a one-game series. When Pirates management made the decision to postpone that game, team president Barney Dreyfuss declared that rescheduling the game for June 30 was in Cincinnati's best interest.[13] "Postponement won't hurt the Reds," was Dreyfuss' honest admission, "for they will likely be playing better ball later on."[14]

Following another day off on May 29, Pittsburgh hosted the Chicago Cubs at Exposition Park for a morning-afternoon Memorial Day doubleheader on May 30. The morning encounter was slow, but packed so much excitement that nearly all of the 7,000 people in attendance remained for the finish. Pittsburgh was cruising along, leading the Cubs, 7–1, before Chicago put five tallies on the scoreboard in the seventh inning. This outburst forced starting pitcher Eddie Doheny to the bench as Fred Clarke summoned Jack Chesbro from

Pittsburgh's bullpen. Chesbro stopped Chicago's batting spree as Pittsburgh prevailed, 8–6. His solid relief stint allowed Doheny to keep his record clean for 1902.[15] Ginger Beaumont, Tommy Leach and Harry Smith smacked two hits apiece for the Pirates.

During the afternoon contest in front of 12,000 patrons, Cubs pitcher Jock Menefee did something no other hurler had accomplished during the 1902 campaign. He was the first pitcher to keep Pittsburgh off the scoreboard as Chicago gained a holiday split with a 4–0 victory. The Cubs were given a rousing cheer when the 27th Pirates putout was completed, and Fred Clarke's team exited the field without a run to show for nearly two hours of hard work. The sixth inning proved Pittsburgh's undoing as miscues and too much kicking against umpiring decisions temporarily threw Pittsburgh off their game and allowed Chicago to score four runs. Pittsburgh's players lost their temper with umpire Tom Brown when he called the Cubs' Charlie Dexter safe at first base on a ground ball to shortstop Honus Wagner. The Pirates stormed around the field until they were so angry that Clarke and his players did not know whether they were at Exposition Park playing baseball or in Hot Springs engaging in a game of ping pong.[16]

Although an official game was not completed on Saturday, May 31, this combative attitude was displayed by both sides in a contest at Exposition Park that only lasted three innings.[17] The afternoon had been so bright and sunny as game time approached that Harry Pulliam and his staff did not give out rain checks. Fans that gave no thought to rain as they left for the ballpark were shocked when the skies darkened and clouds started rolling in when the game got underway.[18] Since a storm was fast approaching from the east, umpire Charley Power tried to hurry the game along, but Jack Chesbro's wildness interfered with his plans and caused the contest to drag.[19] Fred Clarke and his players had also been ordered to move things along in a speedy manner by Pittsburgh's front office due to the rain check issue, but they forgot that directive when Chicago grabbed a 2–0 lead in the first inning.[20]

That is where the score stood at the conclusion of the third inning when Power called time on account of darkness. A half-hour later, the game was postponed. Harry Pulliam immediately manned every gate at Exposition Park with club employees. The spectators formed an orderly line and each fan received a rain check which was good for any future game. Everything ran smoothly with no confusion and little delay.[21] Even though this game did not count in the standings, two incidents left manager Fred Clarke hot under the collar. In the top of the first inning, Chesbro's wildness allowed Chicago's Dusty Miller and Davy Jones to reach first base with free passes. Bunk Congalton laced a two-bagger between Clarke and Ginger Beaumont that brought Miller home with the game's first run. Jones also made a dash for the plate, but Beaumont's throw, which was relayed by Claude Ritchey to catcher Jack O'Connor, beat the Cubs' base runner.[22]

Jones was coming at full speed when O'Connor turned to tag him out. He collided with Pittsburgh's catcher, knocked him down and jarred the ball loose. O'Connor hit the ground and fell flat on his face.[23] Besides barreling over O'Connor, Jones knocked out the veteran catcher by delivering a sneaky elbow to his jaw. O'Connor was out cold for five minutes before he finally regained his faculties.[24] While O'Connor lay motionless on the field, half of Pittsburgh's players argued with umpire Charley Power for calling Jones safe, while the other half sprinkled O'Connor with ice water in an effort to revive him. O'Connor finally regained consciousness and was helped off the field. Chief Zimmer took his spot behind the plate as he sat in the dugout looking the part of the "before taking" man in a patent medicine ad.[25]

Umpire Power came under fire again in the third inning shortly before this game was called. It was so dark that the baseball could not be seen from Exposition Park's grandstand. Jack Chesbro struck out to lead off the inning. Lefty Davis reached when third baseman Charlie Dexter misjudged a ground ball that he had trouble grabbing while grasping in the darkness. Chicago pitcher Jack Taylor induced Fred Clarke to hit a foul pop-up to catcher Frank Chance. With Ginger Beaumont standing in the box, Taylor whirled toward first and picked off Davis, who had strayed too far from the bag. Clarke started arguing with Power, claiming that Taylor had committed a balk. The squabble became so heated that Power ordered Clarke from the field. Wid Conroy trotted out to left field to take Clarke's place moments before the game was delayed.[26]

Clarke attacked Power with such vitriol during this dispute that Exposition Park's rooters loyal to the Pirates cheered vigorously when Pittsburgh's manager was banished from the game.[27] Clarke and his players claimed their problem with Power stemmed from him incorrectly calling Davy Jones safe in the first inning. O'Connor certainly did tag Jones and only dropped the baseball after he was knocked unconscious. While Power may have made a mistake calling Jones safe, this did not give Clarke license to insult him over Taylor's alleged balk. Clarke had made great strides in controlling his temper since arriving in Pittsburgh, but incidents like this one proved there was room for improvement. Of course, a double standard did exist at times regarding repeat disciplinary offenders like Clarke. If a Pittsburgh player had run over an opposing catcher as Jones did, there would have been an uproar over their rough playing style.[28]

Jack O'Connor had shown great restraint turning the other cheek even though he was the victim of a dirty play. Instead of whining or wanting to fight Jones after he regained consciousness, he went straight to Pittsburgh's bench. Many Pirates fans wondered if Fred Tenney would have been so forgiving if he had been elbowed in the jaw. They concluded Tenney would have made a terrible scene and caused a suspension or two.[29] Further potential fireworks on June 1 were averted because of Mother Nature. The game at West Side Grounds was postponed due to rain.[30] After spending the bulk of the 1902 season at Exposition Park, Pittsburgh was slated to begin its longest road trip of the season thus far. The Pirates had only one scheduled home series in June sandwiched between their eastern excursion and a late-month trip through Chicago and Cincinnati.

Fred Clarke decided to leave pitcher Sam Leever and infielder Jimmy Burke in Pittsburgh during the eastern trip. Leever was sidelined with a weak arm and Burke was not needed since Wid Conroy could handle general utility responsibilities. It was a pity that Burke, who did fine work subbing for Claude Ritchey when he was laid up, could not be worked into the lineup more often.[31] The Pirates went east by train on the evening of June 2 dressed in their finest clothes, which were accentuated beautifully by Kaufmann's famous Panama hats, gifts from the owners in appreciation for their solid work thus far during the 1902 campaign.[32]

One day before the Pirates embarked from the Smoky City for Philadelphia, Harry Pulliam traveled to New York to attend a league meeting that was called by John T. Brush on behalf of Phillies owner Colonel John I. Rogers. Rogers had a grievance against New York magnate Andrew Freedman which he desired to air before all eight club owners. When Philadelphia had played New York at the Polo Grounds earlier that spring, Freedman withheld the Phillies' share of gate receipts for payment of rent on Manhattan Field. New allegations asserted that Freedman was now receiving free rent on the park and had netted a tidy $400 profit due to his methods of extorting money from fellow National League owners.[33]

When this special session ended on the night of June 3, Brush released a short statement which indicated that no problems existed among the league moguls.[34] "All differences which have influenced club members of the National League in the past have been amicably and satisfactorily adjusted," said Brush, "and the National League stands today a harmonious organization and a unit in the management and conduct of its essential affairs."[35]

Baseball fans hoped that Brush's statement indicated that Freedman had agreed to meet his obligations and pay his share of the expense for reducing the National League circuit to eight teams three years earlier. If this was true and Freedman had consented to be fair with his Manhattan Field lease, then harmony certainly was possible. If the Giants owner continued to circumvent honest debts, there was no hope peace would exist in the National League.[36]

While the details of this special session were being dissected by baseball writers who covered teams from the Senior Circuit, sporting editor Ren Mulford, Jr., of the *Cincinnati Enquirer* reported that St. Louis Browns outfielder and catcher Bill Maloney had been signed by Barney Dreyfuss. Mulford claimed Maloney would join the Pirates during spring training prior to the 1903 campaign.[37]

Action on the baseball diamond finally resumed for Fred Clarke and his players as they opposed Philadelphia on Tuesday, June 3. Clarke was forced to alter his lineup since Ginger Beaumont was unable to play because of stomach trouble. Honus Wagner took Beaumont's place in center field while Wid Conroy played shortstop. Deacon Phillippe allowed four runs and did not give up a single walk. Unfortunately, southpaw Doc White was even better for the Phillies as he held the Pirates to four hits. One of Pittsburgh's safeties was a seventh-inning home run by Wagner. Pittsburgh's star smacked a drive down National League Park's left field foul line. The ball landed fair and rolled up the embankment of a bicycle track. By the time left fielder George Browne recovered the baseball, Wagner had already crossed home plate. Philadelphia handed Pittsburgh its first road loss of the season by claiming a ten-inning, 4–3 victory. The Phillies secured victory in the tenth inning when Browne's single drove home Pete Childs from third base.[38]

Discussion about Pittsburgh's first defeat away from Exposition Park was secondary to a big announcement Barney Dreyfuss made on June 4. Dreyfuss issued a challenge to play any baseball team in the world for $5,000 a side, even if his club failed to win the National League pennant.[39]

"I am willing to back my team to the extent of $5,000 for a series of five games with the team which wins the American League pennant," said Dreyfuss. "I am willing that the opposing team may take on any player in the American League, to strengthen up with. I think the Pittsburgh team is the best ball team in the country, and, though I do not care to be personally interested in a post season series, I am willing to put up the money for my men and let the winner of the series also take the entire gate receipts. I think this is a fair proposition and it should bring about a series of games after October 15."[40]

Challenging the American League to a post-season series was a bold gambit on Barney Dreyfuss' part since many of his fellow National League owners despised Ban Johnson's rival league. Some of Dreyfuss' contemporaries were not interested in offering olive branches to a league that was waging a war against their interests. Dreyfuss viewed everything through a different prism. He realized his Pirates were quite possibly the greatest team in baseball history and was anxious to put both Pittsburgh's superiority and National League supremacy on display for baseball enthusiasts across America. Manager Connie Mack of the American League's Philadelphia Athletics immediately stated that he was willing to accept this challenge.[41]

> Barney is one of the nicest fellows in the business, and one of the very few magnates connected with the National League that possesses the slightest remnant of the true spirit of sportsmanship. He has a splendid team. It is really a shame that it is not a member of the major league. On the level, I think it would have a fighting chance to break into the first division in the American League. But when he talks about betting $5,000 that it could beat the winner of the American League pennant, he talks a good deal like a crow performs its ablutions—at random.
>
> The fact that he has everything beaten away off in the National League has affected his vision. He is looking through the inverted end of the glass. The American League race is too close for anyone to predict with any degree of accuracy which of the leaders will capture the coveted bunting—in fact, there is not a club in the league that is out of the running. We're going to be 'thar or tharabouts' at the finish, but whether we win the flag or not, there is nothing that would give me more genuine pleasure than playing a series of games with Pittsburgh as Mr. Dreyfuss suggests.[42]

Pittsburgh rebounded with a solid win over the other Philadelphia team on June 4 after suffering its first road defeat of the campaign one day earlier. Jesse Tannehill improved his record to 8–2 as the Pirates used some late-inning heroics to defeat Philadelphia, 7–4. The Phillies were scrappy from the outset and battled Fred Clarke's troops through seven innings before the Pirates grabbed control of the game. The score was tied 4–4 when Pittsburgh came to bat in the eighth frame. A base on balls to Lefty Davis, Fred Clarke's double and Ginger Beaumont's fly ball to center fielder Roy Thomas gave Pittsburgh a one-run lead. Pittsburgh padded the margin with two more markers in the ninth inning on singles by Kitty Bransfield, Tommy Leach, Harry Smith and Tannehill.[43]

The champion Pirates toyed with Philadelphia once again during this series' final game on Thursday, June 5, like a cat does a mouse, only to crush it in the end. Heading into the bottom of the eighth inning, Jack Chesbro had held Philadelphia without a run or hit while Pittsburgh successfully placed four tallies on the scoreboard. Philadelphia's Rudy Hulswitt ruined Chesbro's bid for a no-hitter in the eighth when he legged out a hard grounder to shortstop Honus Wagner. This hit seemed to unnerve Chesbro as the flood gates opened and Philadelphia scored four runs to tie the ballgame.[44]

6. Honus Wagner and Jack O'Connor Heading to St. Louis?

Fred Clarke and his players considered this rally on the Phillies' part as nothing more than a slight inconvenience. Wagner led off the ninth frame by working out a walk against Chick Fraser and scored on Kitty Bransfield's double. Fraser made his second mistake of the inning when he fielded Claude Ritchey's grounder and made a wild throw to first base. Bransfield easily scored and Ritchey moved over to third base. Fraser made yet another horrible blunder with Tommy Leach at the plate when he uncorked a wild pitch that allowed Ritchey to score. Leach followed by rapping a single then moved to second on Jack O'Connor's out. Chesbro reached first base after catcher Red Dooin failed to handle the third strike. Pittsburgh loaded the bases when Lefty Davis beat out an infield hit, and Leach and Chesbro scored the final runs of the inning when Fred Clarke laced a single to center field.[45]

Chesbro retired Philadelphia in order to secure Pittsburgh's 9–4 victory. Clarke was the Pirates' star at the plate as he smacked four hits and drove home three runs.[46] Chesbro raised his record to 8–2 as he allowed four runs and four hits. Pittsburgh packed their bags and left the City of Brotherly Love by train bound for New York to open a series against the Giants. Nothing was settled during the first contest on June 6 as the game was called on account of darkness after 11 innings with the score tied, 4–4. While New York was far superior to Pittsburgh both offensively and defensively in this game, Fred Clarke's boys made big plays in the clutch that prevented the Giants from claiming a victory. On one occasion when New York loaded the bases with one out, Eddie Doheny fanned the next two batters and ended that threat.[47]

Claude "Little All Right" Ritchey saved the game for Pittsburgh in the ninth inning. With Joe Bean at second base and Heinie Smith on first, Jack Doyle knocked what seemed to be a Texas League single behind the initial sack. The ball was a little fly, too far out for Kitty Bransfield and too far in for Lefty Davis. Both of New York's base runners immediately tore gravel around the sacks. Ritchey made a mad dash from his position at second base, dove for the baseball and caught it before it reached the ground. He touched first and recorded the second out, then threw to Wagner at second before Bean could get back to complete a triple play. Ritchey was cheered enthusiastically by the crowd of 5,600 people at the Polo Grounds. The accolades lasted for so long that he had to doff his cap several times to thank these rooters who appreciated his heady play.[48]

Threatening weather on the morning of Saturday, June 7, did not dampen the spirits of 10,000 fans who paid admission to watch Pittsburgh and New York compete in the second game of this series. New York fans were disappointed as Pittsburgh claimed a 6–0 victory. Deacon Phillippe was brilliant as he tossed a shutout, allowed only four hits, and did not permit any Giants player to reach third base. Besides doing yeoman's work on the hill, Phillippe also smacked a solo homer in the ninth inning into the Polo Grounds' right field seats. Pittsburgh secured the game with two runs in the first frame. Lefty Davis opened the inning with a triple and scored on Fred Clarke's single. Ginger Beaumont blasted a double that moved Clarke to third. Not wanting to have anything to do with Honus Wagner, Roy Evans issued an intentional walk to Pittsburgh's star shortstop. Kitty Bransfield's fly ball to center field brought Clarke home with Pittsburgh's second run.[49]

Claude Ritchey saved the game against the New York Giants at the Polo Grounds on June 6, 1902, that was declared a 4–4 tie. In the ninth inning, Ritchey started a fast triple play when he somehow caught Jack Doyle's short fly to right field. After diving to make the catch, Ritchey touched first base to retire New York's Heinie Smith and threw to Honus Wagner at second base to complete the triple play before Joe Bean reached the bag (courtesy of the National Baseball Hall of Fame Library, Cooperstown, New York).

Throughout the game, whenever Pittsburgh's players came up to bat, a contingent of Pirates rooters saluted their team by singing the following refrain from a popular song: "I've got my eyes on you-oo-oo-oo-oo." As the game progressed, thousands of fans loyal to New York joined in belting out this song in support of Fred Clarke's Pirates squad.[50] As another week of the current baseball season concluded, Pittsburgh's record stood at 33–7, good enough to lead second-place Chicago by 9½ games. The Pirates continued to have six regular players hitting above the .300 barometer which separated accomplished batters and ordinary hitters. Ginger Beaumont (.366), Kitty Bransfield (.328), Honus Wagner (.321), Fred Clarke (.320), Tommy Leach (.318) and Jack O'Connor (.308) gave Pittsburgh a hitting aggregation that was tough to beat.

Despite a prediction regarding umpires from a player

on a visiting team that played at Exposition Park before Pittsburgh embarked on the eastern road trip, Fred Clarke's team had not been at odds with arbiters during this tour. The unidentified player had felt that Pittsburgh would get the harpoon from umpires in the east since the defending champions were quickly cutting away interest in the league race. He believed something must be done to stir up life in games when Pittsburgh's shear dominance took root.[51] Action between Pittsburgh and New York at the Polo Grounds was put on hold for one day so Fred Clarke's troops could play an exhibition game against the Eastern League's Newark Sailors. The Pirates won the poorly played exhibition contest, 8–5, as Ed Poole was given an opportunity to pitch for Pittsburgh. Every regular from Pittsburgh's squad played in the contest except for Fred Clarke.[52]

While Clarke's decision not to participate in a meaningless exhibition was not big news, his conduct during the three-inning game against Chicago on May 31 was still being dissected by baseball scribes. There had been the best of feelings between reporters and members of the Pirates organization before this incident ruined that rosy relationship. After that game, many writers had written scathing commentaries about the day's events at Exposition Park. Clarke received a severe lacing in print. He took this roast so bitterly for a day or two that he would not even talk to old friends in the press. One rumor stated that Clarke had hired an attorney and was considering filing libel suits. A young apprentice subbing for Cincinnati writer Charley Zuber defended those who criticized Clarke for his behavior during that game.[53] "No team," said the ghost writer using Zuber's byline, "be it champion or tail ender, had a right to act as the Pirates did and not feel the slash."[54]

Pittsburgh finished the three-game series against the New York Giants on Monday, June 9. New York won, 5–3, and handed the defending champions their second loss on this road trip. Jesse Tannehill and Tully Sparks each allowed ten hits, while Pittsburgh's star southpaw did not issue a base on balls.[55] Through the season's first two months, Tannehill's control had been impeccable, as he had allowed only six walks.[56] Lefty Davis was sidelined and was replaced by Wid Conroy.[57] Fred Clarke moved himself to the leadoff spot, while Tannehill batted eighth and Conroy assumed the ninth spot in Pittsburgh's lineup. Conroy performed admirably as he went 2-for-4 and scored one run.

Besides being gracious in allowing their hosts to capture two games in this series, Pittsburgh also helped the Giants out with a minor crisis. Since New York was short on catchers throughout the three-game series, Jack O'Connor and Harry Smith helped out by warming up their pitchers.[58] Following their games against New York, the Pirates did not have to travel far, with Brooklyn next up on the docket. Two unexpected things happened to Pittsburgh during the first game of this series on Tuesday, June 10. They lost consecutive games for the first time since an April series against Chicago at Exposition Park, and Eddie Doheny suffered his first defeat of the season.[59] Brooklyn won a hard-fought game, 5–4, with the deciding run scoring during Brooklyn's three-run third inning when Tom McCreery scampered home on Doheny's wild pitch.[60]

The threat of horrible weather did not prevent 5,000 devoted baseball fans from attending this splendid contest at Washington Park. These rooters were rewarded for their faith throughout most of the afternoon until a rain shower drenched them during the game's final stages. Umpire Hank O'Day received his fair share of hoots and hollers from the boisterous crowd. Close plays were frequent during this game, and O'Day's work did not seem to please players in either Pittsburgh's or Brooklyn's dugout. Not wanting to feel left out, spectators who were on the edge of their seats all day roared displeasure over every doubtful ruling. These nervous fans even roasted O'Day when the Superbas benefitted from one of his decisions.[61]

Rainy weather persisted in New York, preventing the second game of this series from being played on June 11.[62] While there was no afternoon baseball action at Washington Park, a bombshell news story was released that evening regarding the Pittsburgh Pirates. A St. Louis newspaper claimed in its 6 o'clock evening edition that the local American League franchise was signing two of Pittsburgh's players. Telephone bells in newspaper offices across America jingled all night after the story broke as scribes attempted to confirm this rumor. Many guesses were made as to which players had been captured.[63]

The first snippet of information sent out of St. Louis at 8:00 p.m. further clouded the situation. Rumors heard on the street alleged that Jesse Tannehill, Ginger Beaumont, Lefty Davis, Eddie Doheny and every Pirate other than Fred Clarke, Jack O'Connor and Honus Wagner were named as having jumped to the St. Louis Browns. A second message stated that the Browns were claiming O'Connor and Wagner. Ban Johnson might as well have captured Harry Pulliam and Barney Dreyfuss, both of whom pronounced this story as ridiculous and false. A strong denial also came from O'Connor. Wagner simply commented that Dreyfuss could answer for him. The insinuation that O'Connor or Wagner possibly could be turncoats was preposterous since both players were obligated to play for Pittsburgh according to their contracts.[64]

A few days before this story rose to the surface, American League president Ban Johnson had stated that he intended to play a trump card that would shock the National League magnates. The reason for this stance on Johnson's part was Dreyfuss' alleged effort to persuade Bill Maloney to sign with Pittsburgh. St. Louis Browns team secretary Robert Hedges denied that O'Connor and Wagner had been signed, but smiled as he issued this statement.[65] Hedges also stated that while he was eager to find strong men for his squad, he would not stoop to the practice of signing men already under contract to another team.[66] This rumor asserting that O'Connor and Wagner were jumping leagues contradicted an article that appeared in the *Philadelphia North American* which claimed Ban Johnson's organization was tired of stealing players and that National League owners had grown weary of bribing their players to return.[67]

Even though the *Philadelphia North American* reasoned that both organizations eventually would sign an agreement to respect player contracts in the future, Barney Dreyfuss wanted to be certain he was covered no matter what the outcome.[68] Dreyfuss' brigade took care of business in a methodical fashion once play resumed at Washington Park on Thursday, June 12. Jack Chesbro supplied a coating of whitewash as Pittsburgh defeated Brooklyn, 5–0. Chesbro allowed five hits which were so nicely scattered that Brooklyn never mounted a serious threat. Honus Wagner had a great day as he figured in all of the run scoring and fielded his position brilliantly. The Pirates also stole seven bases off Superbas catcher Hughie Hearne.[69]

Not everything ran smoothly for Pittsburgh during this game. Fred Clarke felt compelled to argue with Hank O'Day in the seventh inning after Ginger Beaumont was picked off first base by hurler Doc Newton in a most ridiculous manner. As Brooklyn's pitcher threw to first base, Beaumont dropped on all fours about two feet from the bag and seemed to be stuck there like an insect on a piece of fly paper. Clarke's argument that Newton committed a balk had the desired effect as the crowd stopped jeering Beaumont and turned their attention toward roasting Pittsburgh's manager.[70] After gaining a split in this shortened two-game series, the Pirates traveled to Boston to complete the final leg of the eastern trip. The first game, scheduled for Friday, June 13, was postponed by a rainstorm which made Boston's South End Grounds field unsuitable for baseball.[71]

Barney Dreyfuss, who came home early to Pittsburgh while his team completed the road trip, offered a startling opinion that surprised many correspondents who covered the Pirates' exploits. Dreyfuss believed his champion team still had not yet played its best baseball in 1902 and was weeks away from hitting their stride. "The Pittsburgh team has not played its game but once this season, and that was on opening day at Exposition Park," Dreyfuss insisted.

"For two seasons the club has not shown its real speed until about the first of August, and I think history will repeat itself."⁷²

When a writer asked Dreyfuss if the remainder of the 1902 schedule, which was top-heavy with games away from home, would upset those calculations, he elaborated upon his initial statement.

> When the boys are aroused they play as well on the road as they do in this city. They have been trained to win without asking any favors from the umpires, and, being accustomed to playing before large crowds, they are not disconcerted by the rooting of unfriendly crowds. Nearly all of the National League clubs are playing a faster game now than in May, but Pittsburgh is capable of smoother work than it has done yet, and if the other clubs close the gap during the next two months I look for the champions to make a good finish. There is not the slightest danger of the Pirates being headed off in the race unless they become careless.⁷³

Carelessness was not Pittsburgh's problem when they played the Boston Beaneaters on Saturday, June 14. On a day when star Boston hurler Togie Pittinger was at the top of his game, Pittsburgh's players decided to leave their hitting proficiency at the team hotel. Deacon Phillippe's single in the third inning was the only hit Pittsburgh could muster against Pittinger as Boston claimed a 3–0 victory. Pittinger utilized lightning speed and a tantalizing rise pitch that forced hitters like Honus Wagner and Fred Clarke to send skyscraping fly balls to the outfield.⁷⁴ This contest concluded a rough week for the Pirates, who played four of their six scheduled games and lost three.⁷⁵

Despite having their toughest week of the 1902 campaign, Pittsburgh actually extended its National League lead. A winless week dropped the Chicago Cubs into third place. Brooklyn jumped up to the second spot and now trailed the Pirates by 10½ games. Pittsburgh's record stood at 34–10, while a recent spurt by the Superbas pushed their mark to 25–22. Following a day off on Sunday, the eastern trip closed for Pittsburgh on June 16. On Tuesday, the defending National League champions were slated to celebrate Bunker Hill Day by playing an exhibition game in Kitty Bransfield's hometown of Worcester, Massachusetts. On Wednesday, Fred Clarke's boys were scheduled to play in Wilmington, Delaware, before they finally returned home to face Patsy Donovan's St. Louis Cardinals on Thursday, June 19.⁷⁶

While Fred Clarke's team enjoyed a relaxing Sunday away from the diamond, two Pirates were mentioned in a *Denver Post* article about frugal baseball players. The article stated that Clarke was a smart businessman much in the same vein as 1890s star Billy Hamilton. Clarke saved his money and owned valuable farming property in Kansas. On the other hand, hurler Jesse Tannehill

6. *Honus Wagner and Jack O'Connor Heading to St. Louis?*

was similar to the great King Kelly, who used to let money burn a hole in his pocket. Tannehill was characterized as the most liberal spender among the Pirates.[77]

Pittsburgh was awarded a victory under the most unusual set of circumstances against Boston in the final game of the road trip on Monday, June 16. Although Jesse Tannehill was cruising along with a 4–0 lead in the fifth inning, the star southpaw failed to record his ninth victory of the season. With bad weather on the horizon, Boston's players slowed down the game while Pittsburgh batted in the fifth frame, hoping rain would wipe out the contest. Beaneaters shortstop and team captain Herman Long, who had been warned by umpire Joe Cantillon not to delay the game, allowed an easy grounder to go for a base hit. Boston pitcher Mal Eason was outrageously slow. When the rain shower finally came, 2,000 bleacherites scampered across the field to South End Grounds' grandstand. Cantillon, irritated that a regulation game was not completed due to the Beaneaters' stall tactics, wasted no time declaring the game forfeited to Pittsburgh by a score of 9–0.[78]

Boston's players vehemently protested Cantillon's hasty decision. Fans who either wanted their money back or a rain check for some future game failed to gain satisfaction since Cantillon awarded the game to Pittsburgh. Cantillon gave a short statement that evening explaining his decision, saying "I am boss of the field and will not allow any club to show me up as Boston attempted to do today."[79]

While Pittsburgh was awarded a victory due to this forfeit, Tannehill was not credited with a win according to National League rules since an official game was not completed. The Pirates left Boston and headed to Worcester to play an exhibition game in Kitty Bransfield's hometown on June 17. Pirates prospect George Merritt did fine work at the plate and banged out three hits for the Eastern League's Worcester Hustlers as they claimed an easy 8–2 victory over the defending National League champions. Jack Chesbro was horrible for Pittsburgh as he gave up seven runs and nine hits before being pulled in favor of Ed Poole.[80] Over 7,000 people were on hand one day later to watch Pittsburgh play in Wilmington. The Pirates took care of business without much resistance on June 18 as they defeated the Wilmington Sailors of the North Carolina League, 7–3.[81]

When the Pirates were in Worcester, baseball scribe J. Ed Grillo weighed in on the big rumor regarding Jack O'Connor and Honus Wagner jumping to the American League:

> That must have been a pipe dream when they sent out a story from St. Louis that Hans Wagner and Jack O'Connor had accepted the terms of the St. Louis Ameri-

can League Club and would jump the Pittsburgh team on the 20th of this month.

There is not much danger of any of Dreyfuss' players leaving him. Every man on the Pittsburgh team filled out his own contract last fall. He put in the figures he thought he was entitled to, and should therefore be well satisfied with his berth. Besides, Dreyfuss and his players understand each other very well.

No, it is not likely that Pittsburgh will lose any of its stars, but it is not unlikely that most of the National League magnates would be tickled to death if some of the champions' star players would jump before the present season is over, for the National League race, which has been a farce all season, would then be much more interesting.[82]

Besides being generous in respect to salary, Barney Dreyfuss also exhibited his charitable nature by giving his players bonuses and gifts. Prior to leaving Pittsburgh to begin their eastern invasion, Dreyfuss had given each player a beautiful Panama hat from Kaufmann's store. While such a gratuitous present was a nice gesture, not every player cut a statuesque figure while wearing these hats. *Chicago Daily American* writer Charley Dryden explained which Pirates would never be confused with a Roman god while sporting these chapeaus.

> B. Dreyfuss is responsible for the Panama epidemic. He paid $18 each for 18 hats and lavished them upon his young men at a total cost of $324. All the Pirates look very nice except Tommy Leach. Owing to the smallness of his stature and the immensity of his hat Tommy resembles a short-stemmed toadstool after a refreshing rain on a hot summer night. Hans Wagner is also a bird in his.[83]

Even those players who resembled distinguished socialites while accentuating their snappy attire with these hats could not compete with one member of Pittsburgh's traveling entourage. Harry Pulliam was baseball's Berry Wall (the New York socialite known for his stylish attire) and the game's snazziest dresser. His wardrobe was so extensive that his expenses for excessive baggage every year amounted to hundreds of dollars. Pulliam rarely used fewer than ten trunks on road trips, and when he came to the baseball meeting in New York the previous December, his luggage had included 12 trunks of clothing and numerous hat boxes. During these league conferences, Pulliam usually had a change of clothing for every hour in the day. When a young man meandered into the Fifth Avenue Hotel's café at the December meeting wearing a felt hat with a brim broader than anything ever seen on the plains, Pulliam went to his room and eventually reappeared with a gray felt hat with a brim that was three inches wider.[84]

While a debate regarding which member of the Pirates was the snappiest dresser might not yield a definitive consensus, most Smoky City fans were in agreement that Pittsburgh's play had been subpar during their recent road trip.

Fred Clarke's team posted a 5–4 record on a disappointing eastern trip that could only be categorized as mediocre given Pittsburgh's lofty standards. Consistency was a problem as numerous games were postponed due to poor weather. Having only played a little over four innings against major league competition in the past four days did not serve Pittsburgh well in the opening game of the series against St. Louis at Exposition Park on June 19. In the third inning, two miscues and four singles by Patsy Donovan's squad enabled St. Louis to score three runs. This was enough to get the job done even though the Pirates finally started playing their game and made the contest competitive. St. Louis prevailed in the end, 3–2, as Mike O'Neill outpitched Jesse Tannehill.[85]

Just as Fred Clarke had been the center of controversy during Pittsburgh's last game at Exposition Park on May 31, he once again instigated a hullabaloo as this contest concluded. When Clarke was retired for the final out of the game, St. Louis players claimed he ran too close to the first base bag and cut Roy Brashear's stocking with his spikes.[86] They held this opinion even though it was evident that Brashear's leg was not even cut and that his limp was for effect. Pirates fans believed Brashear had glanced down at his shoe in order to get the crowd's sympathy. This controversy escalated when Cardinals manager Patsy Donovan, while shaking hands with some friends after the game, insinuated that Clarke was at fault.[87]

When Barney Dreyfuss was informed of this charge by Donovan, he uncharacteristically lost his cool and threatened to fight Donovan if he showed up at his office to complain about Clarke's conduct. Dreyfuss had watched the play in question closely and believed that Brashear was only bluffing. He censured Donovan for his attitude and warned those friends loyal to Donovan that he would repeat these remarks if Patsy visited Pirates headquarters.[88] It was rumored that Donovan had made several stops throughout Pittsburgh that night saying Clarke had spiked Brashear on purpose. A mutual friend of Donovan and Dreyfuss claimed that Donovan told him that he did not think Clarke intentionally spiked his player.[89]

On Friday afternoon, Donovan was sauntering down Fifth Avenue on his way to Dreyfuss' office when he was accosted by a few friends. The fact that he never got a chance to visit Dreyfuss possibly prevented a new feud from starting. Ten minutes before Donovan was sidetracked by his friends, Dreyfuss' anger had exploded as he voiced his disapproval over some of Donovan's doings.[90] Being peeved over this incident was an understandable reaction on Dreyfuss' part since his team had not been receiving much love from the press in recent weeks. Boston writer and American League sympathizer Tim

Murnane was the latest pundit to make disparaging remarks about the Pirates. Murnane claimed that the Pittsburgh team was not really a strong one. He defended this claim by saying that if Fred Clarke, Claude Ritchey, Honus Wagner and two pitchers were removed from the roster, there would not be much left.[91]

No baseball game was played at Exposition Park on Friday, June 20, due to rain. Harry Pulliam made good use of the free time by balancing his rain check account and beginning preparations for handling big crowds at Exposition Park on the Fourth of July. Since the team was leaving for a short trip west after their game against St. Louis on June 21 and would stay away until July 1, these preliminary details had to be attended to by Pulliam two weeks in advance.[92] While Pirates management wanted to reschedule the postponed game for later in the season, Patsy Donovan and the Cardinals insisted on playing a Saturday afternoon doubleheader on June 21. Miffed over having to play two games on a travel day, Fred Clarke's squad extracted revenge by sweeping the doubleheader.[93] Pittsburgh claimed the first contest, 4–3, as Sam Leever pitched for the first time since May 20 and raised his record to 5–0.

Jack Chesbro tossed a complete game in the second contest and improved his record to 10–2 as Pittsburgh walloped St. Louis, 14–4. Fred Clarke used a new combination in both games as he benched Lefty Davis, moved Honus Wagner to right field, and installed Wid Conroy at shortstop. The new amalgamation played splendid baseball as Wagner performed in the outfield with his former dash and Conroy was brilliant in the field. Pittsburgh basically secured the first contest with three runs in the fourth inning. Claude Ritchey was plunked by St. Louis hurler Ed Murphy. After Tommy Leach drew a walk, Murphy was unable to catch Ritchey at third base when he fielded Conroy's bunt. Jack O'Connor's deep fly ball to George Barclay in left field drove Ritchey home. After Leever was retired, Clarke drilled a double to the right field fence near the foul line that eluded Patsy Donovan. Leach and Conroy scored to make it 4–0 as Clarke was thrown out at third trying to stretch his hit into a triple.[94]

St. Louis offered no resistance in the second contest as Pittsburgh clinched this game before the Cardinals knew what hit them. The Pirates took a 1–0 lead in the first inning when Fred Clarke led off by doubling to left field and scored on Ginger Beaumont's single. In the second frame, Pittsburgh sent eight runs across the plate before they stopped to recover their breath. In rapid-fire fashion, Wid Conroy singled to right field, Harry Smith moved him to second with a sacrifice bunt, Chesbro singled to center and Fred Clarke made the second out when he flied out to left fielder George Barclay. Beaumont's grounder to Roy Brashear should have been the final out, but St. Louis' first baseman fumbled the ball and allowed Conroy to score. Pittsburgh added seven more runs before the inning ended as Honus Wagner doubled, Kitty Bransfield singled, Claude Ritchey and Tommy Leach walked, Conroy hit a bases-clearing double and Smith singled.[95]

Beaumont gave a fine bunting exhibition in both games. Five of the six hits that he made were gentle taps that none of the Cardinals infielders could reach.[96] When all action was completed on this day, the Pirates' record stood at 37–11. Chicago and Brooklyn were both ten games behind Pittsburgh as the Cubs held down second place over the Superbas by five percentage points. Pittsburgh's list of .300 hitters was reduced to four during the week as Ginger Beaumont (.371), Honus Wagner (.317), Tommy Leach (.312) and Kitty Bransfield (.310) remained in this exclusive club. Pittsburgh's players packed their bags once again and boarded a train for Chicago to begin a four-game series in the Windy City on Sunday, June 22. Frank Selee and his young Cubs squad were hoping their early-season success against Pittsburgh would provide the positive impetus for them possibly to sweep this series and get back into the pennant race.

Deacon Phillippe did yeoman's work against the Chicago Cubs at West Side Grounds on June 22, 1902. Phillippe and the Cubs' Jack Taylor locked horns in a classic pitchers' duel that was not decided until the 19th inning when Chicago scored a run to secure a 3–2 victory. Both hurlers went the route for their respective teams (courtesy of the National Baseball Hall of Fame Library, Cooperstown, New York).

Chicago certainly took a step in the right direction when these two teams met at West Side Grounds on June 22 and played a historic game. Deacon Phillippe and the Pirates looked to be in total control until Chicago pushed a run across the plate in the ninth inning and tied the score, 2–2. From this point forward, Phillippe and Chicago's Jack Taylor were steady and brilliant as neither team could muster any semblance of an offensive attack. The score remained tied until the bottom of the 19th inning, when Chicago finally broke the logjam. Bunk Congalton led off by flying out to Ginger Beaumont in center field. Johnny Kling followed by hitting a single to left field and stole second base with shortstop Joe Tinker at the plate. Kling moved over to third when Tinker was retired on a groundout.[97]

Cubs team captain and second baseman Bobby Lowe, a native of New Castle, Pennsylvania, stepped to the plate. Lowe, whose single had tied the contest in the ninth inning, ended the game with a scorching base hit between third baseman Tommy Leach and shortstop Wid Conroy that gave Chicago a 3–2 victory. As Kling crossed home plate, the crowd of 13,000 people cheered their approval. The celebration was quick as tired players from both teams broke for their clubhouses and Chicago's fans went home.[98] Phillippe and Taylor probably would not have any trouble sleeping that night. Both hurlers did remarkable work by lasting all 19 innings.

This latest setback on the road left some to ponder whether the Pittsburgh Pirates were a trifle overrated. Their recent struggles away from Exposition Park seemed to validate the opinions of some baseball pundits that a favorable early season schedule, rather than superior talent, had been responsible for the Pirates' early success. While some gleefully awaited an opportunity to write the obituary regarding Pittsburgh's collapse, Fred Clarke and his players were determined to invalidate all of this talk about the team's anticipated downfall.

7

Jack Chesbro Becomes the National League's Top Pitcher

While many baseball writers believed, like Tim Murnane, that the Pittsburgh Pirates were an overrated club destined to collapse as the 1902 season progressed, one man stood in opposition to them. John Gruber, Pittsburgh's official scorer at Exposition Park and one of the most respected journalists in baseball, argued that the 1902 Pirates aggregation was one of the greatest ever organized. Gruber used the premise that Pittsburgh currently had a better winning percentage than any other club in baseball history ever did at this point of the season to justify his argument.[1]

Skeptics who believed Pittsburgh's heartbreaking 19-inning loss to Chicago would have devastating repercussions obviously could not grasp the determination and tenacity this great team exhibited. Pittsburgh rebounded in strong fashion against the Cubs on Monday, June 23, as Fred Clarke's boys claimed a sloppy game, 7–2. While brilliant fielding had been prevalent one day earlier, constant bungling plagued both squads, whose players seemed tired.[2] Pittsburgh committed three errors while Chicago's poor play in the field led to six miscues. Exhaustion did not prevent an ugly confrontation from occurring in the fourth inning. A verbal controversy escalated into a fist fight between Cubs shortstop Joe Tinker and the Pirates' Wid Conroy. Tinker was angry with Conroy for allegedly grabbing hold of him near the keystone sack and preventing him from advancing to that base during Sunday's game.[3]

When the pair met at that station in the fourth frame on Monday, a spirited scuffle ensued. Tinker landed the first blow when his right hand connected against Conroy's neck. It was an ugly swing that almost caused Pittsburgh's shortstop to lose his balance and fall to the ground. Conroy quickly recovered and retaliated with a straight arm jolt that caught Tinker under his left eye.

At this point, both combatants ignored boxing strategy and started punching wildly at each other until they were separated by umpire Hank O'Day and other players. Members of the Chicago and Pittsburgh squads attempted to restore Tinker and Conroy to good humor before both men were banished from the game by O'Day.[4]

Action from National League executive committee chairman John T. Brush was swift in respect to this unseemly behavior. Word came from Philadelphia on June 24 that Conroy and Tinker were both suspended ten days pending an investigation into the matter. It was unfortunate that Conroy received the same penalty as Tinker since he was only defending himself, but a baseball field was no place for a prize fight. Brush believed such suspensions would deter players from conducting themselves in an improper manner.[5] While Chicago president James Hart initially thought Tinker's loss would prove costly to his team, it was Pirates president Barney Dreyfuss who was angered over league jurisprudence once Brush investigated the incident.[6] Brush decided to reinstate Tinker after he had been banished for only a few games, while Conroy was suspended for 20 days.[7] This decision did not please Dreyfuss, who felt Brush's inequitable verdict was not fair to his team. "I will write a letter to Mr. Brush telling him how I think he compares with Solomon," said Dreyfuss after his anger cooled down a little.[8]

Pittsburgh's owner was certainly justified in making accusations that Brush was more severe doling out punishment to the Pirates than to other National League teams. In a recent game involving Brush's Cincinnati Reds, Heinie Peitz and Jake Beckley openly bragged about using foul language while disputing a decision by umpire Charley Power, but Brush did not suspend either player.[9] It was also indisputable that Chicago's roster was loaded with rowdy baseball players who had not even received a reprimand from Brush. The Chicago Cubs' Davy Jones had planted his fist into Jack O'Connor's neck and delivered a knockout blow in a game one month ago. Besides his recent encounter with Wid Conroy, Joe Tinker had also spiked Harry Smith during a play at the plate on Decoration Day that caused Pittsburgh's catcher to experience a few sleepless nights and forced him to the sidelines for a week.[10]

Some of Chicago's writers alleged that Conroy was a rowdy player who instigated Monday's fight at West Side Grounds even though facts did not substantiate this claim. In Pittsburgh, Conroy was perceived as a quiet, passive, gentlemanly player. There were some followers of the game who asserted that Conroy was not aggressive enough to suit Pirates management.[11] When Chicago and Pittsburgh played the third game of this series on Tuesday, June 24, catcher Johnny Kling was Tinker's inadequate substitute at shortstop for

7. Jack Chesbro Becomes the National League's Top Pitcher 131

the Cubs. Conroy's absence did not weaken Pittsburgh's unit one bit. Lefty Davis arrived from Pittsburgh on a flyer express train prior to game time and played right field, while Honus Wagner replaced Conroy at shortstop.[12] After Chicago grabbed a quick 3–1 lead through two innings, Fred Clarke's squad turned to more strategic maneuvers.

After having little luck against former college phenom Carl Lundgren during the first three frames, Pittsburgh utilized the bunt to take control of this game. Ginger Beaumont started the fourth inning with a little bunt to Lundgren. Unnerved by Beaumont's speed, Lundgren picked up the baseball cleanly and threw it into the grandstand, allowing the runner to reach third base. Honus Wagner beat out a bunt for a single which drove Beaumont home with Pittsburgh's second run. Kitty Bransfield followed by bunting toward first baseman Art Williams, whose throw to second was too late to force Wagner. Claude Ritchey moved both runners up 90 feet with a sacrifice bunt. Tommy Leach tied the baseball game by knocking in Wagner when Lundgren and catcher Mike Kahoe became entangled while trying to field his beautiful bunt. Harry Smith's infield out scored Bransfield and gave Pittsburgh a 4–3 lead.[13]

The Pirates added three more runs and claimed a 7–3 victory. Jesse Tannehill tossed a complete game and raised his record to 9–4. Claude Ritchey went 3-for-5 and scored a run, while Lefty Davis and Ginger Beaumont rapped out two hits apiece.

Rainy weather and wet grounds prevented Pittsburgh and Chicago from concluding their series on June 25. Rather than travel to Rockford, Illinois, for an exhibition game on Thursday, June 26, Fred Clarke agreed to remain in Chicago and play the fourth game of this series.[14] Clarke's decision proved to be a prudent one as Pittsburgh gave Chicago a demonstration of how the game of baseball should be played. Jack Chesbro was masterful on the mound and was backed by perfect fielding as Pittsburgh cruised to an easy, 8–1 victory.[15] Chesbro raised his record to 11–2 as he tossed a complete game, scattered four hits and struck out five Cubs.

Deuces were wild for the Pirates as Clarke's troops scored twice in the first, second, sixth and ninth innings. In the first frame, Lefty Davis' single, Ginger Beaumont's double, Chicago left fielder Jimmy Slagle's error and a fly ball allowed Pittsburgh to plate two runs. Another pair of markers were added in the second frame when Tommy Leach tripled, Chief Zimmer was hit by a pitch, Jack Chesbro moved Pittsburgh's catcher to second with a sacrifice bunt, and Davis smacked a double. In the sixth inning, Kitty Bransfield and Leach singled and scored on Zimmer's triple. Two more runs were added in the ninth frame when Clarke and Beaumont crossed home plate.[16]

Following a tough, 19-inning loss in the first game of this series against Chicago, Pittsburgh had responded like a true champion and won the next three stages at West Side Grounds. The Pirates received a well-deserved day off before they started a series against Cincinnati on Saturday, June 28. Harry Pulliam and Fred Clarke utilized this open date in the schedule by going to Louisville to visit some old friends. Upon their return to Cincinnati, both men denied the rumor that they had made this trip to scout some of George Tebeau's players from the American Association's Louisville Colonels.[17] No baseball game was played at the Palace of the Fans on Saturday afternoon as rain forced Reds management to postpone the contest at 3:00 p.m. Getting in the game scheduled for Sunday afternoon seemed unlikely due to a steady downpour that continued into the night.[18]

Since there were no diamond events surrounding the Pirates for baseball fans and writers to dissect during this two-day period, people resurrected the story regarding the rumored defections of Jack O'Connor and Honus Wagner that was reported a few weeks earlier. O'Connor's failure to return to the team as scheduled while recuperating from an injury gave rise to reports that Pittsburgh's veteran catcher had severed his ties with the Pirates organization. This premise was not true, as O'Connor's hand did not heal as soon as was anticipated. He remained in St. Louis a couple of extra days on account of poor railroad conditions due to the recent storm.[19]

Although the rumor surrounding O'Connor was false, this didn't mean members of Pittsburgh's team had not been contacted by emissaries from Ban Johnson's American League. Lefty Davis confessed that he was approached while the team was in Chicago.[20] "Just before we left Chicago for Cincinnati on Thursday I was approached by a representative of the Chicago American League Club and asked to make my price for playing under Comiskey next season," explained Davis. "I had no figure to give them, for I am well satisfied with Pittsburgh and know that President Dreyfuss will pay me all that I am worth."[21]

Davis was one of a few National League players who had come out with an honest statement claiming that the services of National League stars were currently being aggressively targeted by the rival organization. Prying players from Pittsburgh's roster seemed like a long shot for Johnson and his sneaky operatives since each member of the Pirates aggregation was perfectly satisfied and would not dream of abandoning an owner they liked and respected. Tommy Leach declared that there was not a man in the Pirates camp who would desert Barney Dreyfuss' ship, even if Johnson himself knelt before the players and sprinkled their paths with five dollar bills.[22]

7. Jack Chesbro Becomes the National League's Top Pitcher

Barney Dreyfuss' generosity was a big reason why it was highly unlikely that any of Pittsburgh's players would jump their contracts and join the American League. During their recent eastern trip, the Pirates had played three exhibition games. These contests netted over $1,900 for Dreyfuss and the Pittsburgh baseball organization. Half of this amount was divided among 18 players, with each man receiving $53. Even though only 15 players made this trip, the three men who were left behind in Pittsburgh shared in the amount equally with their teammates.[23]

While Dreyfuss did not seem to be concerned with tales about his players being targeted by American League agents, he was fuming over John T. Brush's decision regarding the Wid Conroy suspension. Brush issued his final statement concerning the Tinker-Conroy incident during Pittsburgh's trip to Cincinnati:

> Tinker is eligible to play again. He was reinstated yesterday, and I so wired Frank Selee at St. Louis, but I rather imagine he did not carry Tinker to the Mound City with him, or perhaps he wanted to give his new find, Glenn, a thorough try-out. Conroy's term of suspension was fixed at 20 days, and he can get into the game again on July 14. The statements of Conroy furnished the convicting proof that he was at fault. He was standing on second base when Tinker arrived, and, although there was no play at the bag, he interfered with the runner getting in. The rules of play specifically charge that a runner must avoid an infielder who is fielding the ball, but Conroy, according to the evidence, had no play before him.[24]

The Pirates extracted some revenge against Brush's team when Pittsburgh and Cincinnati finally played on Sunday, June 29. In between rain showers, the defending champions won the contest in convincing fashion by a score of 6–0. Sam Leever gave a masterful performance and certainly did not resemble a pitcher who had recently been afflicted with a sore arm.[25] Leever tossed a complete game, scattered five hits and raised his record to 6–0. Kitty Bransfield was Pittsburgh's top batter against Reds hurler Henry Thielman as he went 2-for-4 and smacked a double. Rain followed Pittsburgh and Cincinnati back to the Smoky City as both teams traveled by train to begin a series at Exposition Park on Monday, June 30. The first contest was postponed due to the rainy conditions.[26] Before the game was called off, Barney Dreyfuss offered an incentive to his players for each victory against the Cincinnati Reds. "A prize for each game you win from Cincinnati" was the offer made by president Dreyfuss in response to John T. Brush's decision regarding Wid Conroy.[27]

On July 1, the prospect of prizes and gifts being rewarded to Pittsburgh's players seemed remote. Reds hurler Bill Phillips held the Pirates down in good style and enjoyed a 3–2 lead as Pittsburgh came to bat in the ninth inning. As had been the case on many other occasions during the 1902 campaign when an opposing pitcher was stifling Pittsburgh's attack, Fred Clarke's players turned to their reliable strategy of "when in doubt, bunt." Stylish bunting by Ginger Beaumont, Honus Wagner and Kitty Bransfield shifted the game's momentum in Pittsburgh's favor. Beaumont led off and bunted so cleverly that he reached first base when third baseman Harry Steinfeldt made an errant toss. Wagner surprised Cincinnati by not swinging for the fences when he placed a beautiful bunt between Phillips and second baseman George Magoon for a base hit.[28] Kitty Bransfield kept the bunt parade going when he dropped the ball down toward third base. Many fans at Exposition Park felt he beat the play at first base. Even though it looked as if first baseman Jack Beckley's feet were off the bag when he received Steinfeldt's throw, Hank O'Day called Bransfield out. The crowd was still growling and complaining when Claude Ritchey came to bat and promptly drove the ball between first and second base for a single. Beaumont and Wagner both scored on Ritchey's clutch hit as Pittsburgh claimed the game, 4–3.[29] Ritchey and Davis were Pittsburgh's hitting stars on this afternoon as each man went 2-for-4 at the plate, with Davis' two safeties being rattling doubles. Deacon Phillippe tossed a complete game and struck out five in his first appearance since the 19-inning game against Chicago over a week earlier. Phillippe, who had been resting in Pittsburgh since Thursday after returning early to the Smoky City, seemed to benefit from having a week off to become rejuvenated after pitching in his historic game.[30]

It looked like an extra-inning contest was a strong possibility when southpaws Eddie Doheny and Noodles Hahn locked horns at Exposition Park on Wednesday, July 2. Even though Doheny allowed only two hits, Hahn's solid performance for Cincinnati kept the Pirates at bay as the score was tied 1–1 heading into the bottom of the eighth inning. At this point, the Pirates used their standard modus operandi of late-game heroics to claim another thrilling victory. Fred Clarke employed cerebral strategy to get things going for Pittsburgh by pretending that he was going to bunt. After this feint drew the infield in and made Hahn a little nervous, Clarke drilled a line drive over second base for a single.[31]

Cincinnati should have retired Clarke at second base when Ginger Beaumont followed with a ground ball to third baseman Harry Steinfeldt. Clarke ended up at third base after Steinfeldt made a wild throw to the keystone sack. This proved to be a costly mistake when Clarke scored on Honus Wagner's single to left field. Wagner moved up to second base as Beaumont was thrown out trying to move from first to third on his single and scored the game's final run on Kitty Bransfield's single.³² Pittsburgh claimed a 3–1 victory over Cincinnati that allowed Eddie Doheny to improve his record to 8–1. While Barney Dreyfuss was still fuming over Wid Conroy's suspension, he could take solace in the fact that his team had now beaten Cincinnati ten times in 1902 without suffering a single defeat.³³

Conroy's banishment was not the only issue Dreyfuss had with Reds owner and National League executive committee chairman John T. Brush. When rumors about a return to a 12-team league began to surface, Dreyfuss quickly denied that he was connected to this project in any way. Many people associated with baseball believed Brush was interested in returning to the old system that existed before the eight-club aggregation became a reality after the 1899 campaign. Harry Pulliam offered his opinion regarding the reasons behind Brush's deep admiration for the 12-club concept.³⁴

> Cincinnati never made much money in a small league. The old town draws a great deal of its patronage on Sunday and from a class that knows little about the game. These people come from Ohio, Indiana and Kentucky towns and keep well enough posted on baseball to be familiar with the star players and to know the standing of the clubs. In an eight-club league Cincinnati seldom stands high enough to allow its official excuse-makers a two weeks' vacation, but in the old 12-club league it could beat out several of the bad ones and keep away from the tail end of the procession.
> The Sunday excursionists would look up the Cincinnati papers, note that the Reds were not the worst in the league by a long shot, buy a $1.50 round trip ticket and sneak to the ballgame. The excitement of riding on a railroad furnished most of the sport and if the Reds were beaten they did not mind it much. Now Cincinnati is fighting for the cellar championship and the rural patrons of the club are ashamed to go to see them play.³⁵

The Cincinnati Reds happily moved on to their next baseball destination as Ned Hanlon's Brooklyn Superbas arrived in the Smoky City to begin a four-game series against Fred Clarke's Pittsburgh Pirates. Rain postponed the scheduled first game on July 3 between the National League's two top teams.³⁶ Pittsburgh currently held down the National League's top spot with a record of 43–12 while Brooklyn stood 11 games back at 36–27. Concerns that poor weather would ruin the Independence Day festivities at Exposition Park were allayed when the bright sun's rays burst from a cloudless sky at daybreak.³⁷ Even though President Theodore Roosevelt did not attend either game of the morning-afternoon doubleheader due to his commitment regarding other holiday festivities in Pittsburgh, Jesse Tannehill and Jack Chesbro performed in a manner befitting the country's Commander-In-Chief.

In the morning game, Tannehill held Brooklyn to two hits as Pittsburgh

Over 20,000 fans were on hand to witness a morning-afternoon doubleheader at Exposition Park against the Brooklyn Superbas on July 4, 1902. In the morning game, Jesse Tannehill tossed a two-hitter as Pittsburgh claimed a 3–0 victory. Jack Chesbro scattered five hits in the afternoon contest as the Pirates defeated Brooklyn, 4–0. During the second game, outfielders from both teams were forced to navigate water in the flooded outfield. While flooding was an occasional problem at Exposition Park, a smoky landscape was commonly prevalent due to the area's steel mills and factories (courtesy of the National Baseball Hall of Fame Library, Cooperstown, New York).

prevailed, 3–0, striking out seven Superbas as he raised his record to 10–4. Tommy Leach was Pittsburgh's hitting star as he went 2-for-3 and scorched a double. Jack Chesbro supplied a second coat of whitewash during the afternoon game as he scattered five hits while his teammates rapped out 13 safeties and secured a 4–0 victory. Chesbro continued his ascension as the National League's top pitcher and improved his record to 12–2. A remarkable feature of both games started before the morning contest concluded. Water from the nearby Allegheny River sneaked up through the sewers and began seeping into Exposition Park.[38] During the afternoon contest, water started to ooze under the outfield fences and quickly flooded different areas of the outfield.[39]

Throughout most of the afternoon, the outfielders were knee-deep in water. The professional manner with which these men performed despite such a handicap was a source of pleasure to the crowd at Exposition Park. Cozy

Dolan, Willie Keeler, Lefty Davis and Ginger Beaumont all made remarkable catches in the flooded outfield.[40] Beaumont was not bothered one bit when he was forced to find an island of dry land after the water in center field became waist-deep.[41] As John Gruber wrote, Beaumont took everything in stride and let the kid inside of him take over for the remainder of this game.

"Clarence Beaumont, in center for Pittsburgh, was also active," stated Gruber, "though not to such a degree as his rival. He had but two put-outs, and was obliged to break away through the water after only three hits. He considered the unusual conditions as a huge joke, and ran races with himself, holding his hands high and making the water boil prodigiously with his kicking feet. He had the last put-out of the game, a fly from Bill Dahlen's bat. After making the catch he held the ball aloft and then plunged into the water. The dive took him out of sight, and when he emerged, he blew hard and punched his fists into his eyes like a real swimmer."[42]

More than 20,000 rabid Pirates fans turned out to watch both games on the Fourth of July as Pittsburgh extended its winning streak to eight games.[43] Brooklyn hurler Bill Donovan's stellar performance ended that solid run on Saturday, July 5. Donovan scattered six hits and tossed a shutout as Brooklyn prevailed over Pittsburgh, 2–0. Although Honus Wagner did the most damage at the plate against Donovan by smacking a single and a double, the Pirates shortstop also committed three errors. Right fielder Lefty Davis' day could best be categorized as boring. He did not receive a chance in the field, while his best bid for a base hit was thwarted by Brooklyn's defense.[44]

This solid week in which Fred Clarke's team went 5–1 helped push their season mark up to 45–13. Brooklyn still held down second place with a record of 37–29 and trailed by 12 games. Official league averages showed that four Pirates were hitting over .300. Ginger Beaumont continued to be Pittsburgh's top batter with a .355 average while Kitty Bransfield (.309), Tommy Leach (.305) and Honus Wagner (.301) complemented the curly-haired outfielder at the plate quite nicely.[45]

The Pirates caught a railroad flyer to Chicago for a Sunday afternoon game against the Cubs.[46] It seemed fitting that Jack Taylor was opposing the Pirates in a game made possible by America's evolving railroad system which allowed quicker travel. Besides being a star pitcher for Chicago, Taylor was also a railroad brakeman. Those who witnessed this contest on July 6 at West Side Grounds probably went home convinced that if Taylor knew as much about the railroad business as he did about bending a baseball, he was destined to become a rail industry magnate in the near future. Taylor locked horns with Deacon Phillippe in a rematch of the 19-inning game from two weeks earlier.[47]

While Phillippe had his customary good control, the Cubs freely smacked the right-handed hurler's offerings all over the lot to the tune of 13 hits. This game was basically secured in the first inning by Chicago as Frank Selee's boys scored four runs against Phillippe.[48] That was all the support Taylor needed as he cruised to an easy 8–3 victory. Ginger Beaumont was the only Pirates player who did any heavy damage against Taylor as he went 2-for-5.

Following this short expedition to the Windy City, the Pirates hustled home by train to begin a three-game series against Philadelphia on Monday, July 7. It looked as if Pittsburgh was about to lose three consecutive games for the first time in 1902 as Phillies pitcher Herman "Ham" Iburg held them in check throughout the afternoon and carried a 3–2 lead into the eighth inning. Iburg had some fun at the Pirates' expense as his slow deliveries frustrated Pittsburgh's players.[49]

The slower Iburg pitched, the harder Pittsburgh's players swung. Honus Wagner lost his temper after taking a wicked cut and failing to connect with the ball, while Fred Clarke laughed as heartily as the crowd over one of his misses. Clarke and the boys ended up having the last laugh again after trailing going into the late innings. In the bottom of the eighth inning, the joke was on Iburg when Fred Clarke cracked a double and immediately signaled to set the bunting game into motion. Beautifully placed bunts by Ginger Beaumont and Kitty Bransfield, a base hit by Tommy Leach, and third baseman Bill Hallman's error plated three runs and gave Pittsburgh a 5–3 victory over Philadelphia.[50] Jesse Tannehill tossed a complete game and raised his record to 11–4.

No such mystery or drama on Pittsburgh's part was evident when these two teams met once again on July 8. Jack Chesbro was absolutely brilliant as he tossed his second consecutive shutout and beat the Phillies, 5–0. "Happy Jack" gave up six hits and did not allow a Quakers runner to reach first base after the fifth inning. Honus Wagner was busy all afternoon leaving his imprint on this game. He smacked a single, a double and a triple, and was robbed of a fourth hit when right fielder Shad Barry made a great catch on his sharp line drive. Wagner's fielding at shortstop was better than usual and even opened the eyes of warhorse Hughie Jennings, who was watching from Philadelphia's dugout.[51]

Pittsburgh clinched this game with three runs against Chick Fraser in the first frame. Lefty Davis started the inning by blooping a double into left field. Fred Clarke cracked a single past second baseman Cupid Childs that scored Davis. With Ginger Beaumont at the plate, Fraser uncorked a wild pitch that allowed Clarke to move to second base. Beaumont struck out attempting to sacrifice him over to third base. Honus Wagner brought Clarke home when he blasted a triple to left-center field. Kitty Bransfield drew a walk. Claude Ritchey smacked a ground ball to Jennings at first base. Jennings attempted to catch Wagner at home, but failed when Wagner made a spectacular slide over the plate as catcher Red Dooin received the ball.[52]

After this contest, Pirates management announced a change in start times for Saturday afternoon games at Exposition Park. Barney Dreyfuss and Harry Pulliam decided that all Saturday games throughout the remainder of July and August would start at 3 p.m. rather than 3:30. Always thinking of his paying customers, Dreyfuss made the change to accommodate those who wished to engage in evening recreation during the summer. An earlier start at Exposition Park gave patrons an opportunity to watch games without interfering with their arrangements for dinner and other evening leisure activities.[53]

The Pirates made it a clean, three-game sweep over their state rival as Fred Clarke's brigade crushed Philadelphia, 8–2, on Wednesday, July 9. Eddie Doheny was sharp while Philadelphia's Doc White, who usually pitched good ball against the champions, did not have his best stuff.[54] Doheny raised his record to 9–1 and went 2-for-4 at the plate, scored a run and pounded a double. Lefty Davis was Pittsburgh's offensive catalyst as he went 3-for-4 and crossed home plate on two occasions. Fred Clarke and Honus Wagner also supported the cause by recording two hits and scoring one run apiece.

As fans in the Smoky City prepared for their favorite team to open a three-game series against National League cellar dweller New York, most of the Pittsburgh newspaper articles preceding this initial battle centered on management issues regarding the Giants. John McGraw had jumped from the American League's Baltimore Orioles so he could pilot Andrew Freedman's team. McGraw was not present in the Smoky City when this series' first game was played, and he still had not arrived at the Monongahela House when some players were pressed at noon on July 11 to answer questions about his whereabouts. Most of the Giants professed their ignorance in respect to McGraw's plans, and New York baseball writer Sam Crane claimed there was nothing new to report about one of baseball's most fiery characters.[55] Team secretary Fred Knowles issued a short statement in an effort to appease all interested parties. "We are watching the papers here closely for news of the new manager," said Knowles, "and have no other source of information."[56]

One reason so many in the press were interested in McGraw's arrival was the report that New York's new manager had been talking to former teammates Joe Kelley, Wilbert Robinson and Cy Seymour. Some people speculated that McGraw might be talking to Kelley and Robinson about releasing some high-priced Baltimore men so they could play for the Giants. A telegram sent from

Baltimore stated that McGraw had left for Pittsburgh on the night of July 10.[57] It was unfortunate that McGraw was not on hand to watch his new team play that afternoon against Pittsburgh. One fan in attendance wondered if players named Smith, Wagner and Clarke (in respect to Giants right fielder Roy Clark) on both teams had possibly switched uniforms as New York defeated Pittsburgh, 3–1. Twenty-year-old Pittsburgh native George "Heinie" Smith, who had been managing New York for a month since Horace Fogel's dismissal, was the game's star at second base and the plate, where he went 2-for-4.[58]

Pittsburgh's fighting spirit was running rampant when the two teams met once again on Friday, July 11. The passionate attitude of Fred Clarke and his players aroused those who paid admission to express enthusiasm seldom witnessed at Exposition Park during the 1902 campaign. Pittsburgh did not seem concerned in the least when New York's Steve Brodie smacked a triple and scored on a fly ball in the first stanza. The Pirates responded with four runs in the home half of the fourth inning. Singles by Ginger Beaumont, Honus Wagner and Kitty Bransfield, a base on balls to Claude Ritchey, Jack O'Connor's bases-clearing triple and a passed ball by Giants catcher Frank Bowerman gave Pittsburgh the four tallies.[59] Deacon Phillippe made this early support stand up as he tossed a complete game and defeated New York, 6–3.

Pittsburgh's victory came at a terrible cost as speed-burner outfielder Lefty Davis was injured in the fifth inning and had to leave the game. Davis suffered a fractured leg when he caught his foot in the dirt near second base. He had led off the inning with a single and soon broke for second. Noticing that Bowerman's throw was going wide of the mark, he attempted to make a quick turn at the keystone sack. It was this sudden lurch that proved disastrous as his spikes got caught in the infield dirt. He dropped to the ground and rolled over in agony. Even though the pain was severe enough to make the Pirates' sprinter sick, Davis had the presence of mind to roll over on his stomach and touch second base with his outstretched hand before he became unconscious.[60]

At first, it was believed that Davis was suffering from a severe ankle sprain. This initial diagnosis proved to be false once he was carried to the clubhouse and Dr. Dickson discovered the bone was broken.[61] In a bit of an ironic twist, Davis broke his leg in the same manner that New York's George Van Haltren had almost two months earlier at Exposition Park on that exact spot at second base.[62] Jesse Tannehill relieved Davis in right field since manager Fred Clarke's ability to make strategic maneuvers with his lineup was limited because Wid Conroy was suspended.[63]

7. Jack Chesbro Becomes the National League's Top Pitcher

A few days after this game concluded, Tannehill placed the blame for Davis' injury at the feet of New York shortstop Charley Wagner, who had made his major league debut on July 1.

> We get roasted to a turn every time we are mixed up in an accident, but get no credit when we save an opposing player. It may not be generally known, but it is a fact that Lefty Davis broke his leg to save Charley Wagner from a spiking which would have been unintentional, had it been inflicted. Lefty intended to slide to second but saw that Wagner, who is a novice and does not know how to protect himself, was straddling the base and must surely feel the steel unless something was done to prevent the accident. Lefty immediately decided to stay on his feet and the lurch he made in trying to do this snapped the bone in his ankle. He will be in bed for three weeks, but young Wagner escaped uninjured. I would like to see Lefty get some credit for his generous act.[64]

Owner Barney Dreyfuss wasted no time wiring Wid Conroy, asking the infielder to rejoin the Pirates immediately to replace Lefty Davis. Dreyfuss planned on ignoring Brush's edict regarding the length of Conroy's suspension and threatened to play the infielder once he arrived in Pittsburgh. This ended up being a hollow threat on Dreyfuss' part since Conroy lived on a farm in New Jersey and did not get the message until Saturday morning. Knowing that he could not reach Pittsburgh in time for any game before Monday delayed Conroy's departure until Sunday night. Conroy finally arrived in the Smoky City on July 14, the date that he was eligible to resume playing after his 20 game suspension officially ended the previous day.[65]

Jimmy Burke manned the shortstop position for Pittsburgh during the series' final game against New York on Saturday, July 12. While the Pirates were without the services of Lefty Davis and Wid Conroy, manager John McGraw still had not reached the Smoky City to join his Giants squad. Unfortunately, all three of these men missed a great pitching performance during the finale of this series. Mr. Whitewash, better known as Jack Chesbro, recorded his third consecutive shutout as the Pirates defeated New York, 4–0. Ginger Beaumont and Fred Clarke accounted for five of Pittsburgh's eight hits. The pair also pulled off a beautiful double steal in the third inning when Clarke scampered home with Pittsburgh's first tally of the day.[66] Besides holding the Giants to five hits, Chesbro also recorded 11 strikeouts.

Pittsburgh's most recent triumph allowed Fred Clarke's club to reach the 50-victory plateau in only 66 games. The Pirates were 50–15 and had one game declared a tie when it was called on account of darkness. Of these 50 victories, Jack Chesbro had 14, ten in succession. During the past three games, Brooklyn, Philadelphia and New York were unable to score against a man who was now considered the National League's best pitcher. Chesbro had prevented his opponents from scoring a run in the past 35 innings. No team had pushed a runner across home plate against Chesbro since the Chicago Cubs scored in the first inning on June 26.[67]

Before the second-place Boston Beaneaters arrived in Pittsburgh to open a four-game series at Exposition Park, the Pirates traveled to Cincinnati to play a single contest against the Reds on Sunday, July 13. Jesse Tannehill and Noodles Hahn did fine mound work for their respective teams as Pittsburgh recorded four hits and Cincinnati rapped out eight safeties. The Pirates prevailed over their western rival with a 3–1 victory. Pittsburgh clinched this game by scoring two runs in the first inning. After Fred Clarke was retired by Hahn, Ginger Beaumont reached first on a bunt single. Tommy Leach drove him home with a double. Honus Wagner gave the Pirates a 2–0 lead when he cracked an RBI single that scored Leach. When Tannehill was put out of commission late in the game, Clarke summoned Sam Leever from the bullpen. Leever held the Reds at bay and preserved the win for Tannehill.[68]

Tannehill was forced from this game because of an accident. During a crucial stage of the game, the Reds' Jack Dobbs drilled a liner that was ticketed for the outfield and would have knocked in a run. Tannehill made a desperate attempt to stop the baseball by throwing up his left hand. The ball struck his left index finger, knocked the member out of joint, and caromed to second baseman Claude Ritchey, who threw to second. Shortstop Jimmy Burke fired to first baseman Kitty Bransfield to complete a double play that left the Reds swearing in their dugout. Tannehill went to the hospital with a badly dislocated index finger. Pittsburgh's star southpaw was not expected to pitch again until he felt no soreness in the battered finger.[69]

The Pirates hospital list had grown dramatically in the past few days. Lefty Davis, who had missed a few games because of a painful boil before his return to the lineup, was now sidelined indefinitely with a fractured leg. Honus Wagner was hobbling around, playing on a lame leg, while Claude Ritchey and Eddie Doheny were still plugging along despite being sick.[70] Illness certainly did not seem to hinder Doheny's ability to dominate Boston when the Pirates and Beaneaters played on Monday, July 14. The steady southpaw tossed a complete game and raised his record to 10–1 as Pittsburgh defeated Boston, 4–1. Honus Wagner starred at the plate for Pittsburgh as he went 3-for-4, scored a run, smacked a double and a triple, and drove home two runs. Manager Fred Clarke also chipped in with three hits.

Fans witnessed some of the best fielding of the season at Exposition Park as Tommy Leach, Claude Ritchey, Honus Wagner and Kitty Bransfield all made eye-popping plays that demoralized the visitors. Boston never quit in this game even though the Pirates scored all of their runs against Boston hurler Vic Willis in the first inning. Fred Clarke led off and reached base when his sharp ground ball caromed off Boston third baseman Ed Gremminger's shins. Ginger Beaumont followed his captain to the plate and reached base with a bunt single. Clarke moved to third base when Tommy Leach was retired on a long fly to center fielder Duff Cooley. Honus Wagner followed with a triple that scored two runs. Kitty Bransfield drew a walk before Claude Ritchey smacked a single to center field that scored Wagner and moved Bransfield to third base. He scored the Pirates' fourth run on Wid Conroy's long fly ball to Cooley.[71]

Fred Clarke's troops gained some extra satisfaction when they defeated the Beaneaters, 5–0, on Tuesday, July 15. Hurler Mal Eason, who had indulged in attacking personalities while working the coaching lines during Monday's game, was put in his place by Pittsburgh's proud baseball squad. Deacon Philippe was untouchable as he scattered four hits and did not allow a Boston runner to reach second base. Duff Cooley tried to stretch a single into a double, but he was gunned down at second base when Honus Wagner fired one of his famous clothesline throws from right field. Gene DeMontreville attempted to steal second base and was promptly gunned down by catcher Jack O'Connor.

Pittsburgh put this game out of reach in the sixth inning after Claude Ritchey scored in the first frame.[72] Fred Clarke opened the sixth inning with a single. Ginger Beaumont and Tommy Leach laid down safe bunts that loaded the bases. Clarke scored when Honus Wagner grounded into a force play at second base, and Beaumont came home on a fly ball to left fielder Ernie Courtney.

Wagner scored Pittsburgh's third run of the inning on Wid Conroy's single. Singles by Deacon Phillippe, Ginger Beaumont and Tommy Leach brought home Pittsburgh's final run in the seventh inning.[73] Due to their solid showing thus far in 1902, each one of Pittsburgh's players received a special bonus when the semi-monthly checks were handed out on July 15. Every man on the Pirates roster received a crisp, new extra bill of large denomination in addition to his check. Secretary Harry Pulliam went to the hospital to deliver Lefty Davis' check and bonus to him, while offering the best of wishes from Barney Dreyfuss.[74]

Every Pirates player also received a personal congratulation from the team president for playing great baseball. Dreyfuss assured them that he had the utmost confidence Pittsburgh would break all records for victories in 1902. He hoped they would cross the century mark, and Pittsburgh's players promised to accomplish that goal if possible. When asked by reporters to verify the bonus amount, Dreyfuss' grateful players only smiled and refused to discuss the matter.[75] Pittsburgh's performance against Boston on July 16 proved this bonus was richly deserved. The Pirates hammered Beaneaters hurlers Togie Pittinger and Ray "Dad" Hale en route to a convincing 9–1 victory. Pittsburgh smacked 15 hits as Ginger Beaumont and Kitty Bransfield led the batting barrage with three safeties apiece. Fred Clarke, Tommy Leach, Honus Wagner and Claude Ritchey each rapped out two hits.

Although Boston was crushed in this contest, they did succeed in doing something that no other National League club had accomplished in July. Star Pirates hurler Jack Chesbro finally was scored upon when Ernie Courtney crossed the plate in the seventh inning. Chesbro's shutout streak probably would have remained intact if the Pirates had exhibited a little faster fielding during the fateful seventh frame. Many fans and writers who followed the Pittsburgh Pirates' fortunes believed that Chesbro's record of pitching 41 innings without being scored upon would stand for a long time. Pirates official scorer John Gruber believed Chesbro had established a record that would never be broken in the National League.[76]

When Boston arrived in the Smoky City, manager Al Buckenberger hoped to gain a split in their four-game series against the defending National League champions. When Buckenberger's squad left Pittsburgh after the final game of this series, they limped away into the night's darkness without anything but gratitude for being alive. The boast by Boston's players that they were in second place to stay whetted the Pirates' appetite for beans, and Fred Clarke and his players never stopped until they cleaned the plate.[77] It was another feast for the Pirates as they defeated Boston, 8–2, on Thursday, July 17, and added a cherry to their delicious four-game sweep sundae.

Sam Leever raised his record to 7–2 as he tossed a complete game and held Boston to seven hits. Ginger Beaumont and Honus Wagner each went 3-for-4 and scored a run. After Boston scored a run in the first frame, Pittsburgh took control by countering with three tallies in the home half. Fred Clarke got the Pirates going by drawing a walk against outfielder turned pitcher Pat Carney. Ginger Beaumont and Tommy Leach followed with singles that loaded the bases. Carney refused to waver despite the early trouble and fanned Honus Wagner. Beaumont was also retired on this play when he got caught straying too far away from the second base bag. After Kitty Bransfield walked, Clarke trotted home when Carney plunked Claude Ritchey with a pitch. Wid Conroy gave Pittsburgh a 3–1 lead when Leach and Bransfield scored on his single to left field.[78]

The Buccaneers' decisive victory over Boston pushed their winning streak

7. Jack Chesbro Becomes the National League's Top Pitcher 145

to seven games. Chicago proved to be a thorn in Pittsburgh's side once again as the Cubs ended this streak during the first contest of a two-game series on Friday, July 18. Pirates nemesis Jack Taylor continued to throttle Fred Clarke's squad as he tossed a shutout and made several spectacular plays in the field. Eddie Doheny's unsteady pitching at the start allowed Chicago to score the game's only two runs. Bad luck also plagued Pittsburgh throughout the afternoon. Tommy Leach smacked two line drives that seemed destined to be hits but were caught. Ginger Beaumont was also called out twice at first base on bunts. In each instance, the National League's resident bunting expert lost his decision at the initial sack by a whisker.[79]

Jack Taylor had now beaten the Pirates three times in 1902. To put that in perspective, the National League's remaining hurlers had accomplished this feat only 13 times. Taylor had more victories against Pittsburgh than Boston, Philadelphia, Cincinnati and St. Louis. The Pirates did not allow Taylor's dominance to place them in an improper mindset heading into the second game of their series with Chicago on Saturday, July 19. Pittsburgh turned the tables on the Cubs as Jack Chesbro started a new shutout streak and raised his record to 16–2 by beating Chicago, 5–0. Chesbro was untouchable even though he was pitching with only two days' rest. The National League's top pitcher tossed a complete game and struck out six Cubs as he recorded his fourth shutout during July at Exposition Park. In his past 54 innings of work, he had only allowed two runs.[80]

Pittsburgh sealed this game away with four runs against Dusty Rhoads in the third inning. Wid Conroy, who had been on the outs with Chicago's players since the incident with Joe Tinker, started the inning with a single to left field. A beautiful hit-and-run play allowed Conroy to reach third base when Jack O'Connor rolled a grounder to the spot shortstop Mike Jacobs had vacated to cover the keystone sack. Jack Chesbro tried to knock the baseball out of Exposition Park and succeeded in driving a long fly to center fielder Jimmy Slagle near the pennant pole that brought Conroy home. O'Connor scored when Clarke followed with an RBI triple that sailed over the head of left fielder Dusty Miller and caromed to the bleachers. Clarke crossed home plate with Pittsburgh's third run when Ginger Beaumont smacked a single between short and third. Honus Wagner knocked a liner out of Jacobs' reach that landed for a double and allowed Beaumont to score Pittsburgh's fourth tally of the stanza.[81]

When all games were completed on Saturday, July 19, the Pirates held a comfortable lead in the National League. Pittsburgh's record stood at 56–16. Brooklyn was the nearest competitor, 16 games behind with a mark of 43–

35. Pittsburgh continued to have three players above the magical .300 mark as Ginger Beaumont (.365), Honus Wagner (.319) and Jack O'Connor (.303) led the Pirates' offensive attack. After spending a good portion of the 1902 campaign playing home games at Exposition Park, the Pirates embarked for the west on Saturday night to begin their longest road trip of the season. Following a Sunday doubleheader in Chicago, Pittsburgh was scheduled to reach St. Louis on Monday and play five games there, spread over an entire week. From the Mound City, Fred Clarke's troops would advance east to play the four teams on that end of the circuit before returning to Pittsburgh on August 16.[82]

Catcher Harry Smith and outfielder Lefty Davis were the only members of Clarke's squad who did not join the Pirates for this sojourn through five hostile baseball metropolises. Smith had injured his throwing arm a week before and needed seven more days of rest. He was not expected to be missed much since Jack O'Connor was throwing well and batting better than he had for several seasons.[83] Davis would be dearly missed on this trip since he was the life of the party. The Nashville lad constantly entertained the boys by singing, dancing or chattering. Davis had one song that he loved to hum day and night. "Melancholy Mose" was the title, and his teammates claimed they heard this song more often than the words "Play Ball." Davis currently was recuperating at Allegheny General Hospital. With his leg in a cast, he chafed over his treatment as this injury likely would prevent him from doing any training work for many weeks.[84]

Hopes of playing a doubleheader at West Side Grounds on July 20 were spoiled for two reasons. It started drizzling when the initial contest began, and a cloudburst eventually soaked both players and fans at the beginning of the second game. The first game was also not decided until the 12th inning, and only one round of the second match had been concluded when the threatened storm arrived. Pittsburgh should have claimed the first game in regulation, but became complacent after building a four-run lead. Chicago scored four runs in the ninth inning to tie the score, 6–6.

The Cubs looked as if they were going to secure this game in their half of the 11th inning, but a bizarre demonstration of base running helped Pittsburgh get out of a big jam.[85] Johnny Kling started the frame by reaching on Tommy Leach's error. Mike Jacobs followed with a single. Both runners moved up 90 feet when Germany Schaefer executed a perfect sacrifice bunt. Dusty Miller smacked a grounder to Leach, who threw to Chief Zimmer in time to cut down Kling at the plate. Kling reversed course and started back toward third base with Zimmer close on his heels. The Cubs catcher was too swift as he reached the keystone sack before Zimmer could tag him. At this point, Jacobs and Miller had strayed too far from their respective bases. Zimmer turned his attention toward retiring Jacobs. By this time, the entire Pirates squad was gathered on the infield, while most of Chicago's players were along the lines shouting instructions as Jacobs was chased back and forth. So many Pirates were involved in the play that they were in each other's way. Jacobs eventually secured second base without being touched, and Miller sneaked back to first base, which was left unguarded.[86]

The chase started once again when Kling inexplicably started for home just as Jacobs reached second base. This time, Zimmer finally tagged Kling, who slipped and fell down. Jacobs also tried for third base, but he was cut off and finally run down by Jimmy Burke, thereby retiring the side without a run being scored. During this comedy of errors, there were at one time 22 players on the baseball diamond. Every Pirates player handled the ball at least once. Even Claude Ritchey, who was not in the game at all, assisted in this peculiar double play by handling the ball once according to reliable eyewitnesses. Having barely avoided defeat, Pittsburgh took care of business in the top of the 12th inning. Ginger Beaumont led off and beat out a pretty bunt for a single. Tommy Leach was retired when he fouled out trying to sacrifice Beaumont to second base. This did not matter as Honus Wagner smacked a liner to the clubhouse in center field. If the house had not been there, Wagner could have run around the bases twice before the baseball stopped.[87]

Wagner's inside-the-park homer gave Pittsburgh an 8–6 lead, and Jesse Tannehill retired Chicago in order during their half of the 12th inning.[88] Making his first start since suffering an injury in Cincinnati a week earlier, Tannehill tossed a complete game and raised his record to 13–4. Thoughts of playing a makeup game for the second leg of Sunday's doubleheader on Monday, July 21, were destroyed by uncooperative weather once again in the Windy City. Delayed due to their decision to remain in Chicago, hoping to play the previously postponed game, the Pirates entourage traveled to St. Louis to begin a five-game series against the Cardinals.

The timing for this series against the Cardinals could not have been better for Pittsburgh baseball pundits who were searching for a good story. Newspapers throughout the Mound City still insisted that Honus Wagner planned on playing for the St. Louis Browns in 1903.[89] Smoky City baseball writers scoffed at this ridiculous rumor which had proven to be false when it originally surfaced a few weeks earlier. While Pittsburgh pundits, as well as devoted Pirates rooters for that matter, were confident Wagner would be playing with Pittsburgh in 1903, a new story suggested that Barney Dreyfuss' team might be competing in a different league next spring. *The St. Louis Star* printed a story that rekindled the possibility that Pittsburgh would be welcomed into the American League with open arms if Dreyfuss decided to leave the National League.[90]

> The American League's lone chance to triumph in its war with the parent body is to induce Barney Dreyfuss to place his Pirate band in Baltimore for the remainder of the present season and next spring move it on to Gotham. Friends of the Johnson organization are hopeful that Herr Dreyfuss will make the leap. His plant is easily the most important one in either league, and added to the American's circuit would make it fully 50 percent more formidable than it is at the present time.
>
> However, Mr. Dreyfuss made big money in the National League in 1901. He is also a big winner this year, so he will likely decide to let well enough alone and maintain his franchise in the present body.
>
> The National League can ill afford to lose the Pirates. In fact, were they to break camp and enter the Johnson organization the situation would be as good as sealed. As matters stand, Mr. Dreyfuss has the attraction to offer that can make or break either of the leagues.
>
> Mr. Johnson is known to be working overtime in trying to induce him to string with his body.
>
> If he is successful in annexing the Pittsburgher and his mighty band of players it will be a ten-strike, and not only save the American League from going under, but give the National League a solar plexus punch that it will have a hard time getting over.[91]

Similar rumors had been flying around in American League cities for the past few days. When this first report came by telephone from Cleveland, the message was shown to Barney Dreyfuss by a reporter. Dreyfuss evaded a potential interview by replying, "That's all news to me." Team secretary Harry Pulliam would not even comment about these reports. While Dreyfuss' noncommittal answer was neither a denial nor an admission, some wondered if the prospect of making a move to the American League contained any truth.[92] That question took on new meaning once the games commenced for Pittsburgh in St. Louis, as another decision by John T. Brush stoked the fires surrounding this rumored switch to Ban Johnson's American League.

8

Pirates Rooters Demand a Shift to the American League

Ban Johnson and other members of the American League hierarchy believed that Pittsburgh was ripe for the picking due to Barney Dreyfuss' dissatisfaction with recent events involving some of his fellow National League baseball magnates. Dreyfuss, whose puritanical approach in respect to honoring baseball's honesty and integrity was beyond reproach, was not pleased that some National League teams were confiscating players from the American League's financially troubled Baltimore Orioles franchise. Andrew Freedman's New York team was the major guilty party as manager John McGraw siphoned players from his former squad in an effort to rebuild the Giants. While many baseball writers reasoned that Dreyfuss' disgust over this matter could force him to consider a move to the rival American League seriously, the *Detroit Free Press* felt conditions would have to deteriorate significantly before Pittsburgh's owner pondered such a transfer.[1]

> Barney Dreyfuss' roast of the National Leaguers who were concerned in the Baltimore deal has aroused false hopes in the breasts of some of the American League enthusiasts.
> These look to see the Pittsburgh leader enter into negotiations for a shift of his team from the National to the American, something that will not transpire unless the National League situation becomes much worse than at present. Mr. Dreyfuss can make money in the National, even if other teams do not, and is so placed now, and will be so placed for a season or two anyway, that he can make the other clubs give him a better deal than he got while in Louisville. He has already spoken on the present situation and says that he will hold aloof from the Baltimore–New York affair and its promoters, and will also refrain from having conversation with Ban Johnson on any of the many baseball angles that are now of interest.[2]

While various baseball pundits debated the possibility of Pittsburgh shifting to the American League in 1903, Barney Dreyfuss' squad resumed their quest to capture a National League pennant in 1902. The Pirates opened a five-game series against St. Louis at League Park on Tuesday, July 22. Pittsburgh entered the game shorthanded as Fred Clarke was unavailable since he missed his train to the Mound City after traveling from Chicago to Des Moines on Sunday night. The Pirates were also without two other starters because Lefty Davis had not made this trip due to a fractured leg and Tommy Leach had an injury. Despite the absence of this great trio of baseball players, Pittsburgh crushed St. Louis, 9–3.[3] Deacon Phillippe was the beneficiary of this fine support as he tossed a complete game and raised his record to 11–6.

Jesse Tannehill, who worked in Clarke's place as Pittsburgh's left fielder, started the Pirates off in fine fashion by scoring two early runs due to Cardinals miscues. Tannehill led off the game and reached first base when St. Louis second baseman Roy Brashear fumbled his sharp grounder. After Ginger Beaumont was retired on a popup to catcher Jack Ryan, Claude Ritchey struck out and Tannehill stole second base, Honus Wagner drove him home with a single to left field. In the third frame, Tannehill reached first base when Cardinals third baseman Otto Krueger committed an error. He moved to second base when Beaumont was retired on a ground ball to Brashear before Ritchey knocked in the substitute outfielder with a double to left field that gave Pittsburgh a 2–0 lead. After St. Louis took a short-lived, 3–2 lead in the fifth inning, Pittsburgh claimed the contest with three runs in the sixth frame, three more in the seventh and a single tally in the eighth.[4] A trio of Pirates smacked nine of the team's 14 hits against Cardinals hurler Clarence Currie. Honus Wagner, Wid Conroy and Jimmy Burke each went 3-for-4 at the plate and scored five of Pittsburgh's nine runs.

Things did not go as well for Pittsburgh on July 23 as Fred Clarke rejoined his teammates in St. Louis. Sam Leever and Eddie Doheny were both ineffective as each man tossed four innings and gave up five runs during a 10–4 loss. The Cardinals' Homer Smoot, Patsy Donovan, Art Nichols and George Barclay certainly had their batting clothes on as the four players combined for 11 hits. Wagner was thrown out of the game by umpire Tom Brown for objecting to a terrible decision. Most fair-minded observers who analyzed baseball on a regular basis readily admitted that Brown was the only incompetent umpire currently working for the National League.[5]

While Patsy Donovan and his players basked in the glory of defeating the invincible Pittsburgh Pirates in convincing fashion, comments from emissaries of both the National and American leagues made their way into print. After traveling between Washington and Baltimore for several days, Ban Johnson journeyed to Boston for the first time during the 1902 campaign. Before he headed north, Johnson refused to outline his plans to expand the American League to a ten-club program when pressed by baseball writers, but he did profess that Barney Dreyfuss and his Pittsburgh Pirates franchise would be a welcome addition to his aggregation. Although Johnson had no knowledge of Dreyfuss' immediate plans, he hoped the Pittsburgh man eventually would consider joining the American League.[6]

> It would be an easy matter for Mr. Dreyfuss to rid himself honorably of the National entanglements before he joined the American. I feel sure the American League would be pleased to have Mr. Dreyfuss, but he must come to us with the same honorable record behind him as he now possesses.
> With Pittsburgh and New York in the American, a splendid 10-club circuit could be arranged. It could be easily manipulated, although the eight-club circuit is the ideal one. Of course there could be an eight-club circuit in which these two cities would be embraced, without working injury to this city.[7]

After being non-committal or offering no comment regarding a move to the American League, Pirates management finally addressed this rumor one day after Johnson made his remarks to a Washington reporter. The Pittsburgh Pirates planned on sticking to the old organization as long as the league conducted its affairs honestly and fairly. Harry Pulliam issued a clear statement indicating the Pirates planned on remaining loyal to the National League despite these overtures from Johnson to join the Junior Circuit.[8]

> You can state positively for the Pittsburgh management that it is done for all time with Ban Johnson and his colleagues. Under no circumstances will we form an alliance with the American League interests. The Pittsburgh club has been and will be loyal to the National organization. We cannot subscribe to the cut-throat policy, and for that reason, if no other, we would necessarily reject any overture from the American League. In fact, the proposition made is not now even being considered.[9]

This strong proclamation on Pulliam's part did not mean that Barney Dreyfuss was not vexed over the recent activities in which some of his fellow magnates were currently involved. Dreyfuss was disgusted with the behavior of John T. Brush and Andrew Freedman in relation to the theft of players from the Baltimore Orioles. He became further agitated when it was revealed that each National League club would receive a letter of assessment from league headquarters outlining what they owed to pay for these former Orioles. Dreyfuss intimated that he would refuse to pay for players purchased by another team if such correspondence was delivered to his desk.[10]

> I am given to understand that others have received notice of assessment for Baltimore, but I have gotten nothing as yet. Perhaps those who have run this affair do

not consider me in the $2,000 class and will pass me by. I am content that this should be the case. I have had nothing to do with the Baltimore affair, nor will I have now. Why should Pittsburgh pay for players sent to New York or Cincinnati? Let those who are benefitted pay the bills. I pay all my own bills, but do not care to pay those of other people.[11]

    This type of behavior on Freedman's and Brush's part seemed to indicate the two magnates were trying to implement part of their syndicate plan that was rejected by fellow owners earlier that year. Dreyfuss was exposed to further dubious leadership on Brush's part prior to Pittsburgh's game against St. Louis on Thursday, July 24. The National League executive committee chairman announced that Honus Wagner was suspended pending further investigation due to his confrontation with umpire Tom Brown one day earlier. The question of whether Wagner deserved to be benched or not by Brush seemed to be a secondary concern to many within baseball. People outside of Pittsburgh pondered the validity of keeping an incompetent umpire like Brown on the National League payroll. Fervent baseball fans in the Smoky City were surprised that Wagner was suspended for only showing displeasure over Brown's call and not being offensive at any time toward the arbiter.[12]

    Those fans that rooted passionately for baseball's greatest team should not have been surprised over Brush's action regarding the Wagner case. In the Conroy-Tinker situation a month earlier, Brush had ruled unfairly even though umpire Hank O'Day had stated in testimony that Tinker was the offender. Brush disregarded O'Day's assessment of those events and suspended Conroy for 20 days while giving Tinker a slap on the wrist.[13] Wagner's absence was deeply felt by the Pirates as St. Louis made it two triumphs in a row over Pittsburgh with a 5–4 victory.[14] Jack Chesbro saw his winning streak end at 12 games as the Cardinals proved Pittsburgh did not own the copyright on heroic, ninth-inning finishes. After Fred Hartman scored to tie the game, Jack O'Neill crossed home plate with the winning run when shortstop Wid Conroy threw home while he had Art Nichols caught in a rundown between second and third base. After O'Neill slid home under Jack O'Connor's tag with the winning run, Pittsburgh's catcher threw the baseball into League Park's grandstand in disgust.[15]

    Fred Clarke and his team were afforded the opportunity to think about these two recent losses against St. Louis during an off-day on Friday, July 25. Pittsburgh's recent troubles against the Cardinals certainly were given scant attention in newspapers across the country. The big story being regurgitated by the press surrounded Barney Dreyfuss' displeasure with how his players received detrimental treatment in respect to discipline and rumors about a

8. Pirates Rooters Demand a Shift to the American League

subsequent move to the American League. Contrary to initial reports, Dreyfuss did not go into a rage when he heard John T. Brush's decision regarding Honus Wagner's suspension. The only action Pittsburgh's owner took was to wire Fred Clarke, asking him if it would not be a prudent plan to secure a player for Wagner's place until the big fellow was permitted to play. Clarke responded that the best strategy would be to wait until the length of Wagner's suspension was announced.[16]

There were some cynical people that covered baseball who believed a strong movement was afoot on Brush's part to freeze Dreyfuss out of the National League. These skeptics thought a scheme had been developing by Brush since the season opened to make life difficult for Pittsburgh when it became apparent they would make a runaway race for the 1902 National League pennant. An unnamed National League representative claimed Dreyfuss was likely to regret his strictures placed upon the men who were responsible for engineering the Baltimore coup.[17] While Pirates officials emphatically denied they had any intention of moving to the American League, some loyal baseball fans from the Smoky City were prepared to demand that Pittsburgh shift to Ban Johnson's organization.[18]

The suspension of Honus Wagner by John T. Brush, without waiting to hear umpire Tom Brown's report regarding that incident, led many Pittsburgh fans to believe that the National League's executive committee chairman was conducting a personal vendetta against Barney Dreyfuss. In the past few days, 50 well-known Pirates baseball enthusiasts had expressed their desire that Pittsburgh should move to the American League in 1903. Dreyfuss was besieged with letters from concerned fans who sought some remedy to this problem.[19] This group of prominent loyal rooters who loved the Pittsburgh Pirates planned a meeting in order to voice their opposition to Brush's discriminatory practices regarding their beloved team.[20] *The Pittsburgh Press,* which was owned by partners of Dreyfuss in the baseball business, printed this consortium's mission statement in the newspaper's Sunday edition on July 27.[21]

> A public meeting of the loyal baseball rooters of Western Pennsylvania to protest against the outrages perpetrated by the Executive Committee of the National League, in the name of law and order, but in reality for spite, is a possibility.
>
> If the meeting be held, a resolution will be adopted requiring President Dreyfuss to enter the American League. Many prominent supporters of the game went on record last night as being in favor of the step.
>
> The actions of the board in the Conroy and Wagner case were sufficient to arouse the suspicion that certain league magnates have determined upon a course of action decidedly unfair to the champion team of the league and to the city that for years has been the most loyal in the country to the national game.[22]

As the merits of a potential American League shift continued to be debated in the Smoky City, Pittsburgh played the final two games of the series against St. Louis. The Pirates returned to the winners' circle on Saturday, July 26, as they defeated St. Louis at League Park, 5–1. Sam Leever was absolutely brilliant for Pittsburgh as he tossed a complete game and allowed only one hit, a single by outfielder George Barclay in the fourth inning. Barclay also scored the Cardinals' single run due to some lethargic backstop play by Jack O'Connor. Leever's curve ball constantly mesmerized Patsy Donovan and his players all afternoon. Digging the horsehide out of the turf in front of home plate also seemed to be too great a strain on O'Connor. On many occasions, he grabbed in vain attempting to catch Leever's low, sharp curves that were dancing everywhere. Barclay scored his run when O'Connor let a pitch get by him and then refused to chase the ball. His inaction spoiled Leever's shutout bid.[23]

Solid hitting by Donovan's team against Eddie Doheny enabled St. Louis to grab the rubber match of the series on July 27 in front of 12,000 fans.[24] The Cardinals claimed their third victory of this series by defeating Fred Clarke's Pirates, 7–6. Doheny was ineffective as he gave up seven runs before being pulled for a pinch-hitter in the eighth inning. Deacon Phillippe tossed one scoreless inning as Pittsburgh almost rallied late in the game after the Cardinals grabbed a 7–0 lead. As the Pirates left the field after Jesse Tannehill made the final out, they were assaulted by a group of rowdy, overzealous fans.[25] While the St. Louis newspapers kept this story out of their own columns, news about the attack was telegraphed to other cities. The *Cincinnati Enquirer* ran an article under a St. Louis dateline the next day.[26] The following article which appeared in *The Sporting News* gave a detailed account of this confrontation between players and fans.

> The Pirates were followed to their bus by a howling mob on Sunday, and had they not submitted in silence to taunts and insults they would have been mobbed. There was no occasion for the cowardly demonstration, and it is to be hoped that in the future the police will prevent a recurrence of the affair.
>
> While going to the bus Clarke was struck in the face twice and other attempts were made to land on him. The Champions, while huddled together in their conveyance, were shamefully treated. Burke, who is a St. Louis boy, grabbed a bat and started to make a fight, but his teammates pulled him back into his seat and held him there. The riot call brought a platoon of police in time to prevent the Pittsburgh players from being torn to pieces.
>
> One arrest was made and he was discharged in the police court, the evidence not being conclusive. The daily papers state that President Robison sent word to the police judge that he would pay the fines of all parties convicted of participation in the attack on the Pittsburgh players.[27]

8. Pirates Rooters Demand a Shift to the American League

This decision to help people who committed a crime by attacking a visiting team at his ballpark was a bit misguided on Robison's part. Such behavior toward Barney Dreyfuss and his team was unwarranted given the Pirates owner's assistance to Robison by sharing scouting tips regarding first-class minor league players. The fact that 2,000 sunset fans attacked Fred Clarke's champions with stones, bricks and clubs was not surprising given the contentious nature of this series between Pittsburgh and St. Louis.[28] The *St. Louis Star* had been guilty of stirring the emotions of these Cardinals fans when it accused Ginger Beaumont of trying to spike Art Nichols after Wednesday's game. Before Pittsburgh left St. Louis to travel east, *The Star* apologized for making this false accusation after Harry Pulliam criticized their insinuation that Beaumont was a dirty player.[29]

"Mr. Pulliam took exceptions to the writer for stating that Clarence Beaumont made an attempt to spike Arthur Nichols in the closing round of Wednesday's game," stated *The Star* in their written apology.

"'Beau is the last player in the business to deliberately injure a fellow professional,' declared Mr. Pulliam. 'I cannot believe it of him.'

"Beaumont must be given full credit for being a gentlemanly performer. He is one of the few members of that band whose deportment on the field can be termed perfect.

"However, Beaumont was guilty of making a pass with his feet at Nichols, Wednesday. It may have been accidental, and it is to be hoped that it was, as the former Brewer has always been a prime favorite here and bears a good reputation."[30]

Stories about spiking incidents and fans attacking players with bricks, rocks and clubs certainly did not paint the game of baseball in a good light. Such events indicated that baseball was played by unrefined men whose rowdy behavior incited fans to riot on occasion. This myth was quickly dispelled in respect to the players on Pittsburgh's squad through an article that appeared in the *Chicago American*. This story did not talk about the greatness of Barney Dreyfuss' charges on a baseball diamond, but rather discussed the business acumen each man possessed. It was estimated that the average wealth of the 18 players on Pittsburgh's roster was about $15,000. While this assessment may have been a bit on the conservative side, it was understood that all but two or three Pirates carried a rating at Dun and Bradstreet's and could draw checks for vast amounts.[31]

Manager Fred Clarke possessed 400 acres of the finest wheat land in Kansas and owned a coal mine in Des Moines, Iowa, from which he enjoyed a handsome income. Ginger Beaumont controlled the biggest meat market and packing industry in Rochester, Wisconsin. His market, which was the showcase of the town, contained slabs made out of Persian marble and a refrigerated plant that was enclosed in the best French plate glass. When Beaumont appeared distracted at times while batting or in the field, it may have been due to the fluctuations of the meat quotations or the conduct of the beef trust. Claude Ritchey, often referred to as the John D. Rockefeller of the diamond, owned five oil wells in Emlenton, Pennsylvania, that produced many barrels of black gold each day. The Oil King also was the largest individual stockholder and director of the First National Bank in that town.[32]

Chief Zimmer was the proprietor of a very successful cigar store and poolroom in Cleveland, Ohio. He also rented out a half-dozen dwellings in that area. Honus Wagner supposedly had $25,000 deposited at savings banks throughout Carnegie, Pennsylvania. Wagner, who did not believe in bonds, was satisfied earning three percent interest. On the other hand, Tommy Leach had many thousands invested in four percent government bonds. He also worked in a Cleveland machine shop that he owned during the winter. Jack O'Connor was an active politician, owned a grocery store in St. Louis, Missouri, and was boss of the area known as Kerry Patch. O'Connor could have been the director-general of the World's Fair in St. Louis, but he preferred to continue his baseball career with Pittsburgh.[33]

Deacon Phillippe was a sheep rancher in Ashton, South Dakota. Phillippe owned so much land that it took him three and a half days to cover his ponderosa's territory on a swift horse. He supposedly was also the heir to a big estate in France. Harry Smith was a contractor and bridge builder in Massillon, Ohio. Lefty Davis owned a shooting gallery in Minneapolis, Minnesota. Jack Chesbro owned a block of houses in North Adams, Massachusetts, and lived in an elegant mansion on Chesbro Avenue, which was named after him. Fellow Massachusetts resident Kitty Bransfield was a wealthy landlord who collected rent on two long rows of tenements in Worcester. Eddie Doheny ran a marble yard and epitaph studio in Northfield, Vermont.[34]

Wid Conroy owned a farm near Camden, New Jersey, while Jesse Tannehill operated a bar in Dayton, Kentucky. The city's mayor and council usually met in the backroom of his establishment, formulating policy for Dayton. Sam Leever, who at one time was a school teacher, currently held down the position of banker and broker in Goshen, Ohio. Ed Poole was a hunter and trapper who roamed the Pennsylvania wilds during the winter resembling Daniel Boone wearing his buckskin coat and coonskin cap. While Jimmy Burke had not made his mark in industry just yet, he was acquiring habits of frugality that would make him rich in the near future. Of course, Colonel Barney Drey-

8. Pirates Rooters Demand a Shift to the American League

fuss had made a fortune in his capacity as owner of the Pittsburgh Pirates.[35] No one could dispute the fact that Pittsburgh's players were also astute entrepreneurs besides being baseball's greatest team.

The Pirates received some good news prior to the first game of their eastern invasion against Brooklyn on Tuesday, July 29. Honus Wagner was reinstated to active status by John T. Brush. Pittsburgh's star received sweet vindication as it was revealed that umpire Tom Brown had lied in his report to the National League executive committee about Wagner's conduct during a game against St. Louis on July 23. Brush apologized to the maligned player as well as to the entire Pittsburgh club for this injustice inflicted upon the Pirates organization. A telegram received by *The Pittsburgh Press* from its correspondent covering the Pirates in Brooklyn explained why Brush rescinded Wagner's suspension.[36]

On July 29, 1902, National League executive committee chairman John T. Brush reinstated Honus Wagner after he had been unjustly suspended. Brush apologized to Wagner and the Pittsburgh Pirates organization for this injustice. Brush initially had suspended Wagner based on the false testimony of umpire Tom Brown regarding a confrontation between the two men during a game against St. Louis on July 23. Brown lied in his report to Brush that Wagner had thrown a bat at him (courtesy of the National Baseball Hall of Fame Library, Cooperstown, New York).

> Secretary Pulliam said that the Pittsburgh club has no grievance against Chairman Brush. Mr. Brush told the official of the Pittsburgh club that he had been misled by a false statement on the part of Umpire Brown in the game at St. Louis. Brown informed Brush that Wagner threw a bat at him but this was shown to be absolutely false and when Brush was made aware of the facts he immediately raised Wagner's suspension.[37]

Pittsburgh's squad was invigorated by Wagner's reinstatement and Tommy Leach's return from an injury. Wagner, Leach and Ginger Beaumont smacked

11 of Pittsburgh's 19 hits and combined to score six runs as the Pirates defeated Brooklyn, 14–1. The Superbas were lucky to escape without being shut out as they did not score until the eighth inning.[38] Deacon Phillippe tossed a complete game and scattered six hits while raising his record to 12–6. Six Pirates recorded multiple hits, and four players feasted against Superbas pitching by smacking six doubles. Ginger Beaumont and Claude Ritchey hit one two-bagger apiece, while Tommy Leach and Honus Wagner each blasted a duo of doubles.

Brooklyn wasted no time extracting some revenge from the Pirates on July 30. Superbas hurler Frank Kitson frustrated Pittsburgh all afternoon as Brooklyn claimed a 5–1 victory. Pittsburgh registered only six hits against Kitson. The fact that three of these safeties were contributed by Claude Ritchey gave an idea of how well Pittsburgh's hits were scattered. Jesse Tannehill worked for Pittsburgh and gave an admirable performance in every inning but the sixth. Two errors along with three singles and a hit batsman gave Brooklyn four runs and the game.[39] This loss dropped Tannehill's record to 13–5.

Pittsburgh bounced back on Thursday, July 31, as Jack Chesbro continued his domination over Ned Hanlon's team in 1902. He recorded his third shutout of the campaign over the Superbas as Pittsburgh defeated Brooklyn, 3–0.[40] Chesbro was locked in a tight pitcher's duel until the eighth inning with recently acquired hurler Roy Evans, who had been released by the Giants two weeks earlier. The Pirates scored the game's only three runs in the eighth inning. Wid Conroy led off and was hit by an Evans pitch. After Jack O'Connor was retired on a foul pop-up to third baseman Charlie Irwin, Chesbro smacked a single that moved Conroy to third base. Fred Clarke drove home Conroy and Chesbro with a screaming triple to left-center field. Pittsburgh's manager scored the third run on Ginger Beaumont's single.[41]

Nothing was settled during the final game of this series at Washington Park on Friday, August 1. The game was called on account of darkness by acting umpire Jesse Tannehill after ten innings with the score tied, 6–6.[42] Tannehill was selected by both teams to act as arbiter after umpire Charley Power tendered his resignation.[43] A bad throw by Pirates first baseman Kitty Bransfield prevented Pittsburgh from securing this game in regulation. Bransfield refused to be removed from Pittsburgh's lineup as he played despite a lame throwing arm that was wreaking havoc with his fielding record. He horribly botched a play in the sixth inning when his wild throw to home plate allowed Brooklyn to score three runs. The Pirates gallantly fought back with a three-run rally in the ninth inning that temporarily gave them a 6–5 lead. Brooklyn

8. Pirates Rooters Demand a Shift to the American League

tied the game in the home half when pinch-hitter Frank Kitson doubled and scored on Cozy Dolan's single.[44]

While the Pirates prepared for the next leg of their eastern invasion against the New York Giants, it was learned by accident that Barney Dreyfuss had shrewdly foiled a plot to raid players from Pittsburgh's roster.[45] John T. Brush, a man who easily could be mistaken for Dr. Jekyll and Mr. Hyde by Pirates baseball fans, once again was connected to a deceitful plan just days after he had apologized for arbitrarily suspending Honus Wagner. Dreyfuss was considered one of the best judges of players in the country. Brush and Andrew Freedman concocted a cunning scheme aimed at inducing Dreyfuss to tell them the names of players he had selected for the 1903 season. A circular letter was addressed to each club owner asking him to name the players claimed by that particular organization.[46]

Brooklyn immediately fell in line and named 40 players, including Joe Kelley, who had deserted the Superbas last spring and was playing with Baltimore. Some of the other National League magnates also informed Brush and Freedman of their plans for the 1903 season, but Barney Dreyfuss exhibited cool cautiousness. "I do not claim any players," responded Dreyfuss in respect to the letter he received from league headquarters. "If I need any I will go out and get them."[47]

Brush and Freedman were deeply disappointed over their failure to sneak a peek at Dreyfuss' famous dope book that contained information about baseball prospects throughout America. It was demonstrated that this request was not made in good faith when Brush claimed Kelley for his Cincinnati team, while Freedman grabbed Joe McGinnity for the New York Giants. This was done without permission from Ned Hanlon, since Brooklyn technically still owned the rights to these players. If Pittsburgh had claimed any players, Brush would have declared that Pittsburgh did not need any new material. Speaking as the head of the National League executive board, Brush would then have permitted himself and Freedman to go after players on Dreyfuss' list.[48]

Rumors regarding a Pittsburgh move to the American League resurfaced after this story about Brush once again abusing his position became public. The prevailing consensus among those who were tired of Brush's mischief indicated that leaving the National League would be in the best interests of Barney Dreyfuss and his team. The latest gossip stated that Ban Johnson planned on buying out the Pirates ownership group. After being bombarded with questions from many baseball scribes, an angry Harry Pulliam unequivocally stated that the Pittsburgh club had not been sold to Johnson. Pulliam added there was no chance of this purchase on Johnson's part happening in the future, while affirming that the Pirates would be a member of the National League in 1903.[49]

After spending a few days vacationing in Bedford Springs, Pennsylvania, Barney Dreyfuss responded to this rumor when some newspaper lads ambushed him upon his return to Pittsburgh. "I know nothing about it and I have made up my mind that the less I say the better these days of fake interviews," replied Dreyfuss. "As to the Wagner case the 'Sporting Life' has it right. I never gave out a talk roasting Mr. Brush, saying he was trying to ruin the game, etc. I didn't talk on the matter at all."[50]

John T. Brush's various attempts at derailing Pittsburgh's pennant train had failed as the Pirates continued humming along at a sweet pace heading into the season's final two months. Fred Clarke's team was constantly referred to as the greatest aggregation of players that baseball fans had seen in many years. Clarke was given much of the credit for developing a cooperative spirit among his players during the past few years that was reaping significant dividends in 1902. Although he played the game in splendid style and always delivered the goods when called upon, Pittsburgh's manager did let his temper get the best of him at times. Umpire Hank O'Day once told Brooklyn shortstop Bill Dahlen that his head was filled with mayonnaise dressing. Occasionally, Clarke's brain matter was served out of the same dish. Despite these infrequent lapses in judgment, Clarke's dedication to the game and his determination to implement a foundation of teamwork benefitted Barney Dreyfuss.[51]

Teamwork was evident on Pittsburgh's part during the first game of the series against New York on Saturday, August 2. Four lightning double plays by the Pirates cut a big figure as Pittsburgh defeated New York, 7–2. Eddie Doheny pitched a solid game against John McGraw's men and was accorded fine support in the field and at the plate. Fred Clarke had a field day with the stick as he went 4-for-5, smacked a double, scored three runs and drove home two teammates. Pittsburgh sealed the game away with three runs in the first inning. Clarke started the game by blasting a single past shortstop John McGraw. He moved to second base on Ginger Beaumont's nicely placed sacrifice bunt to first baseman Dan McGann. Clarke scampered home on Tommy Leach's single to left field. Leach ended up at third base after Jim Jones made a wild throw back to the infield and scored when third baseman Billy Lauder muffed Honus Wagner's grounder.[52] Lauder's miscue also allowed Wagner to reach second base. He scored Pittsburgh's third run when Kitty Bransfield smacked a sharp line drive single.[53] Beaumont, Leach, Bransfield and Harry Smith rapped out two hits apiece on the afternoon. Leach also drove home

8. Pirates Rooters Demand a Shift to the American League

three runs. Eddie Doheny tossed a complete game and scattered six hits as he improved his record to 11–3. Pittsburgh's record now stood at 62–20 as another week of baseball action concluded. The Pirates held a 17-game lead over the second-place Brooklyn Superbas, who posted a mark of 49–41. Ginger Beaumont continued to be one of the National League's best hitters with a .367 average. Honus Wagner (.317) and Fred Clarke (.302) joined Beaumont in Pittsburgh's .300 hitters' club.

The beautiful thing about Ginger Beaumont's deftness as a batter was the variety of ways he could reach first base. If opposing infielders played in looking for a bunt, he was likely to cut one through so fast that enemy players could not see the baseball. When they played back, he did something artistic in the "tapping line."[54]

Pittsburgh took a break from playing National League games so they could travel to Albany to meet the New York State League's Senators at Chadwick Park on Sunday, August 3. If the weather proved suitable, Jim Pastorius, from the South Side section of Pittsburgh, would do the pitching honors for the home squad at Fred Clarke's request.[55] Unfortunately, Pastorius' once in a lifetime opportunity was not realized. The game in Albany had to be postponed due to wet grounds.[56]

Fred Clarke stole the show when play resumed between Pittsburgh and the New York Giants at the Polo Grounds on August 4. The boss Pirate scored two runs, smacked four hits and stole a base. One of Clarke's safe drives was a double and another a triple, giving him seven total bases on the afternoon.[57] Pittsburgh hung on and secured a 9–7 victory as Deacon Phillippe claimed victory number 13 in 1902. The Pirates had some anxious moments in the ninth inning as John McGraw's troops battled back and almost erased a six-run deficit. Pittsburgh's players became complacent and played back in the infield, allowing the Giants to reach base with two bunt singles. Two little taps sandwiched between solid hits and a two-run error by Wid Conroy pared away four runs from Pittsburgh's lead. "Wake up and play the game," shouted Clarke, and before the echo of his command floated away the Pirates pulled themselves together and quickly ended the game.[58]

Many baseball writers wondered aloud if Fred Clarke planned on making a strong bid to become the National League's champion batsman. After getting four hits for the second consecutive game, Clarke was creeping up on the century mark with 94 safeties.[59] One day after Pittsburgh and New York combined to score 16 runs on 20 hits, pitching took center stage on Tuesday, August 5. The Giants' Christy Mathewson did a remarkable job handling Pittsburgh, but Jesse Tannehill was near perfect against John McGraw's team. Tannehill allowed only two hits and tossed a shutout as Pittsburgh claimed a 3–0 victory. Tannehill disposed of the first 19 New York batters before McGraw reached first base with a single.[60]

Solid fielding aided Tannehill's effort on five occasions. Jimmy Burke picked off a liner close to the ground at third. Fred Clarke caught a high drive near the left field bleachers, and Honus Wagner made one of those somersault catches for which he was famous. Wid Conroy and Kitty Bransfield also made fine plays. Tommy Leach was thrown out of the game in the seventh inning by umpire Bob Emslie. Leach, who was called out on a close play at first base, remonstrated so vociferously that Emslie sent him to the bench. When Leach tried to go on the field with Pittsburgh in the bottom of the seventh frame, a wordy confrontation ensued as the entire Pirates squad surrounded Emslie, who remained firm about his decision. Clarke called off the dogs only when Emslie threatened to forfeit the game to New York.[61]

Pittsburgh made it a clean four-game sweep over the New York Giants with a 2–0 victory at the Polo Grounds on Wednesday, August 6. Only half a game was played as it started raining in the top of the sixth inning.[62] Jack Chesbro gladly accepted this weather-shortened shutout as he raised his record to 18–3. One day after Pittsburgh's players showed their displeasure toward umpire Bob Emslie, John McGraw and his minions abused the arbiter ferociously. Jim Jones attacked Emslie and knocked off his mask after Emslie called a strike that New York's batter could not see. McGraw was rude on numerous occasions, but escaped banishment from Emslie. Pittsburgh scored both runs in the first inning when Ginger Beaumont crossed home plate on Kitty Bransfield's single and Tommy Leach came home when Jim Jones muffed Claude Ritchey's high fly ball to left field.[63]

On the same day that Pittsburgh put the finishing touches on a perfect record against the last-place New York Giants, American League president Ban Johnson issued a statement in Chicago regarding Barney Dreyfuss' franchise. Johnson joined the growing group of baseball executives who denied that Pittsburgh planned on switching from the National to the American League. Johnson adamantly repudiated the notion that Cleveland Broncos team president John F. Kilfoyl had brokered a deal to bring Pittsburgh into the American League fold.[64]

> We have not offered a franchise in the American League. Not only that, but Barney Dreyfuss has made no advance to us at all regarding his coming into the American League next season. We admire Mr. Dreyfuss as a sportsman and gentleman, and we realize that Pittsburgh is a great baseball town, but we have made no advances to Mr. Dreyfuss. I have no knowledge that Mr. Kilfoyl has done so,

8. Pirates Rooters Demand a Shift to the American League 163

either, and I am sure that he is not acting under the instructions of the league if he has done so, which I very much doubt."[65]

Mr. Dreyfuss' team moved to Philadelphia for a few days as Pittsburgh opened a four-game series against the Phillies on Thursday, August 7. The Pirates seemed to have the first game sewn up as Sam Leever carried a 2–0 lead into the last half of the ninth inning. Philadelphia pulled off a shocking comeback as they took liberties with Leever's offerings. The Phillies rallied with three runs to claim a 3–2 victory that allowed the astonished crowd to hurry home in time to eat supper. Catchers from both teams were banished from the game in the fifth inning by umpire Hank O'Day. Red Dooin was put off the field when Tommy Leach was batting, while mild-mannered Harry Smith exited the game after he complained about how O'Day was calling pitches with Philadelphia's Bill Duggleby at the plate.[66]

O'Day also threatened to banish the Phillies' Hughie Jennings and Pittsburgh's Kitty Bransfield for intervening on behalf of their respective teammates during the altercations involving each unfortunate catcher. When Jack O'Connor entered the game to replace Smith, Fred Clarke gave one important piece of advice to his player. "Now keep your mouth shut," Clarke yelled to O'Connor.[67]

Things did not get off to such a great start for Pittsburgh during the second game of this series on August 8. Deacon Phillippe started for the Pirates but did not last long as he retired after four innings with the score 4–1 in favor of Philadelphia. Jesse Tannehill came in and was magnificent as he did not allow the Quakers to tally again.[68] Tannehill went about his work in the usual blasé manner that some people incorrectly misinterpreted as a dispassionate attitude rather than a methodical approach that had produced successful results. According to the *New York Evening Telegram*, Tannehill tossed the ball in a nonchalant fashion and with about as much speed as it would take to get to Harlem from Seventy-Second Street and back in four hours.[69]

Tannehill was rewarded for his solid work when Pittsburgh rallied with five runs in the eighth inning and claimed a 6–4 victory. Wid Conroy led off with a double, and Harry Smith followed with a single. Tannehill drilled a single that scored Conroy. Fred Clarke rapped out Pittsburgh's third consecutive single that allowed Smith to scamper home with the Pirates' third run. Ginger Beaumont beat out a bunt to load the bases. Tommy Leach forced Tannehill at the plate on a ground ball to shortstop Rudy Hulswitt. The Pirates received a huge gift when Phillies catcher Red Dooin threw wildly to first base trying to convert the double play. Clarke and Beaumont scored on Dooin's errant toss. Honus Wagner's single drove Leach home with the Pirates' fifth and final run of the inning.[70]

Great pitching was at the forefront during a Saturday afternoon matinee at National League Park on August 9. Jack Chesbro and the Phillies' Doc White both gave epic performances as only one run was scored the entire game. Luckily for Chesbro, the Pirates secured the lone tally as the National League's top pitcher added another shutout to his resume. In the fifth stanza, Honus Wagner led off with a double. He moved over to third base when Kitty Bransfield blasted a single and scored the game's only run as Claude Ritchey grounded out to Hughie Jennings at first base. Jesse Tannehill, who played left field to give Fred Clarke a break, was thrown out of the game in the eighth inning for disputing an umpiring decision.[71] Chesbro tossed a complete game and scattered five hits as he raised his record to 19–3. Pittsburgh's record stood at 67–21 as they led second-place Brooklyn by 18½ games.

Before the final game of this series, Pittsburgh's players made their annual trip to Atlantic City on Sunday, August 10, to relax at the seashore before returning to action on Monday afternoon.[72] One teammate who was becoming a little stir crazy back in Pittsburgh planned on joining the squad during its stay in Atlantic City and beyond. Lefty Davis recently had the plaster cast taken off his broken ankle, with a rubber bandage being substituted. Davis hoped he could return to playing baseball sometime in September.[73] Davis had shown up at Pirates headquarters on Saturday and stated that he decided to take a trip to the seashore because he had become lonely while the team was out of town.[74]

"I think that I will go to Atlantic City for a week or more," said Davis to the newspaper boys who gathered at Pittsburgh baseball headquarters. "My ankle is slowly mending, and I can get around with a cane so I will not bring any injury to the wound by going away from home. I want to tell you that with the boys away from the city it's pretty hard sledding for a man who likes company like me to put in the time. With a team in sight there is ever something doing. Will I play this year? Well Alfy hopes to get out on the diamond for a swirl ere the snow falls. A man cannot tell, however, when he has an injury like mine."[75]

Rejuvenated by their peaceful day in Atlantic City, the Pirates jumped out to a 3–0 lead against Philadelphia on Monday, August 11. Unfortunately, rain started falling about ten minutes too early while Pittsburgh batted in the fifth inning. Since the contest was called before a regulation game could be completed, the Pirates were unable to add another win to their total.[76] As Pittsburgh prepared to play the final leg of their eastern invasion in Boston,

8. Pirates Rooters Demand a Shift to the American League 165

big news regarding John T. Brush and his Cincinnati franchise adorned newspaper sports pages across the country. Information that had been leaked out a few days before was confirmed regarding Brush selling the Reds and turning his franchise over to a new ownership group on August 16.[77] The syndicate that was purchasing the Cincinnati Reds from Brush was headed by businessman Garry Herrmann.[78]

Brush planned on continuing as the chairman of the National League executive committee even though he would no longer own the Cincinnati franchise. He also indicated that he might throw his hat into the ring when a new National League president was elected in the fall.[79] Even though it seemed that Brush and Barney Dreyfuss had been at odds on many occasions regarding different visions for running the National League, Pittsburgh's owner showed his gracious nature by helping out the Reds magnate despite their differences. Dreyfuss had released Ed Poole in July so Cincinnati could sign the free agent pitcher. When it was announced on August 12 that a rescheduled game between Pittsburgh and Cincinnati would be played on August 17, Poole requested to be assigned the task of throttling his former comrades. Poole, who did not relish being cast adrift by Dreyfuss, wanted an opportunity to extract vengeance from his former club.[80] "I did not expect to play any more ball this year," said Poole. "I was really disgusted with the game. Although I was on the bench, I'll bet I pitched more ball for Pittsburgh than any twirler on that team. I was the fellow on the firing line every morning, and I never worked harder in my life. When I was let out I was figuring on fishing the rest of the season, Cincinnati's bait caught me."[81]

Disgust and disappointment was the common theme for Fred Clarke's team in their first game against the Boston Beaneaters on Tuesday, August 12. The Pirates were absolutely horrible as they were shut out by Togie Pittinger, 11–0. Misplays by pitcher Eddie Doheny and shortstop Wid Conroy were costly.[82] Boston recorded only seven hits, but still scored 11 runs due in large part to three errors by Doheny and two by Conroy. Doheny was also ineffective on the mound, pitching for the first time in ten days. He had been on the sick list for more than a week. He was sent home to Pittsburgh for a few days of rest when the Pirates left New York and traveled to Philadelphia. Judging from the score of this game, Doheny still had not recovered from his ailment.[83]

Poor pitching ailed Jack Chesbro during the first game of an afternoon doubleheader against Boston on August 13 as he failed in the first attempt to win his 20th game. Chesbro received an awful jolt in the eighth inning when Boston hammered out seven hits that produced six runs.[84] This outburst gave the Beaneaters an 8–6 victory. Tommy Leach starred at the plate for Pittsburgh as he went 2-for-3, smacked a double, hit a home run and scored three runs. Honus Wagner and Claude Ritchey chipped in with two hits apiece. Deacon Phillippe settled things down during the second game as Pittsburgh won, 6–1. Phillippe tossed a complete game, gave up ten hits and improved his record to 14–6. Wid Conroy went 3-for-4 and blasted a triple, while Honus Wagner and Jesse Tannehill each recorded two hits.

Tannehill played left field in the second game because Wagner had to be shifted to first base. During the first contest, Kitty Bransfield injured his leg when he tripped over the bag while running to first base and tumbled to the ground. Bransfield, who immediately left the game, was expected to be sidelined for several days.[85] Fred Clarke also injured himself sliding into second base during the afternoon's proceedings.[86] As Pittsburgh gained a split in this doubleheader with Boston, a good news/bad news story surfaced out of New York. The good news for honorable baseball owners like Barney Dreyfuss was a bombshell report that Andrew Freedman was retiring from active management of the New York Giants franchise. On the negative side, it was announced that John T. Brush planned on increasing his stock holdings in the New York club and would become the organization's director.[87]

During his news conference, Brush stated that the New York club would spend any amount of money to guarantee the Big Apple had a winning team in the National League. Brush also took a swipe at the rival American League with a comment that indicated the war between both organizations was still raging. "I want to say that there will be no amalgamation of the National and American Leagues," stated Brush. "We have no peace measures to propose."[88]

The defending National League champions closed out their second eastern trip of the season one day after the big announcement in respect to John T. Brush succeeding Andrew Freedman as director of the New York baseball franchise. Despite having a crippled team, Pittsburgh defeated Boston, 6–1, on Thursday, August 14, and gained a split in this four-game series. A huge feature of the game was the batting prowess of Tommy Leach. The smallest player in the league set the 1902 total base record by smacking two home runs, a double and a single for 11 total bases. Leach also had a hand in many of Pittsburgh's six tallies as he scored three runs and recorded three RBI.[89] Jesse Tannehill raised his record to 16–5 as he tossed a complete game and scattered seven hits. Claude Ritchey joined Leach by striking four hits for the Pirates, while Tannehill chipped in with two. Barney Dreyfuss also sat in the dugout with his team due to Fred Clarke being out of commission.[90]

When Pittsburgh had embarked on this long road that began in Chicago on July 20, Fred Clarke's team held a 16-game lead over the second-place

8. *Pirates Rooters Demand a Shift to the American League*   167

Brooklyn Superbas. Almost one month later, after they posted a 13–7 record playing in five National League cities, the Pirates' lead had increased to 17½ games. Before returning home to the Smoky City, Pittsburgh's players enjoyed a second day at the seashore with friends in less than a week. The Pirates had a lovely time at Atlantic City as they relaxed and took a break on Friday before resuming action at Exposition Park the following afternoon. Pittsburgh also played an exhibition game against a local team. A crowd of 1,500 were delighted with the blowout against their home squad as the Pirates claimed an 18–1 victory.[91]

The Pirates suffered another injury to a crucial player that did not actually happen during the game against Atlantic City. After smacking five hits as Pittsburgh's starting right fielder, Jesse Tannehill was in high spirits as the team rode back to their hotel. When they reached their destination, Tannehill threw his right arm out of joint as he swung himself out of the bus. Barney Dreyfuss hailed a hansom cab and took his injured pitcher to the Atlantic City Hospital. The operation to restore his arm back to normal was a painful one that took more than an hour to be completed.[92] Once the bone was reset, Tannehill left the hospital. He told surgeons that he was frequently inconvenienced in this way and considered the whole matter to be inconsequential.[93] It was expected that he would not be able to take his turn on the rubber for several days.[94]

The conquering heroes returned home to Pittsburgh from this long road trip on Saturday, August 16, battered and exhausted. President Dreyfuss had charge of what was left of his baseball warriors. Although he was tired, Pittsburgh's owner wore a broad smile. He maintained a positive attitude despite the fact that Fred Clarke, Kitty Bransfield and Jesse Tannehill had been put out of commission due to various mishaps. His decision to take on the added expense of carrying Wid Conroy, Jimmy Burke and three catchers all season proved to be a prudent one during this emergency. Dreyfuss released a short statement regarding the status of first baseman Kitty Bransfield, who did not return to Pittsburgh with his teammates and went to Worcester for a period of recuperation.[95] "What was the use?" asked Dreyfuss. "He can't walk across the room now, and would be miserable in a boarding house. At home he will get the best of treatment, and may be able to play when we go East again. The team is a little mixed at present, but it was strong enough to win that closing game at Boston."[96]

Injuries to key performers had not been the only concern for Dreyfuss during the team's recent eastern swing. The final week of the trip frayed the nerves of Pittsburgh's little baseball magnate. Gumshoe bandits representing the American League camped on the trail of Pirates players day and night, hoping to persuade them to make a jump to the rival organization. Although Dreyfuss was not afraid of losing any of the highly prized members from his club, it was aggravating to know that thieves were afoot making bold promises in an effort to steal players from Pittsburgh's roster. Barney Dreyfuss returned to Pittsburgh without losing a man to American League operatives in this instance.[97] In spite of Dreyfuss' recent triumph over Ban Johnson's league, matters were destined to become more difficult for Pittsburgh's owner. The time had arrived for traitors to weave their web of betrayal by putting into motion a devious scheme that was designed to cripple the Pittsburgh Pirates.

9

Ban Johnson Lures Pirates Stars to the American League

While the Pittsburgh Pirates completed their road trip through the east, every member of the defending National League champions had been approached by American League agents at some point.[1] Fred Clarke stated that each man was offered more salary than he presently made playing for Pittsburgh. While Clarke did not specify how much money these American League agents had offered, figures quickly were leaked to members of the press. The *Boston Herald* reported that Jesse Tannehill had been offered $5,000 for 1903, while Jack Chesbro would be paid $5,500 to play for the American League. Honus Wagner could show no better than a stipend of $4,800 to switch leagues. Lefty Davis had been promised $3,000 for the 1903 season. A final surprising rumor stated that Clarke was concealing an offer of $20,000 for three years.[2] Chances of the American League landing the boss Pirate were pure fiction given Clarke's strong relationship with Barney Dreyfuss.

Clarke issued his statement regarding the American League's deception when he returned to Pittsburgh one day ahead of the Pirates squad. Dreyfuss corroborated his manager's assertion by giving out specific details regarding one man who was hot on the trail of Pittsburgh's players. Chicago White Sox owner Charles Comiskey had made numerous overtures toward two or three Pirates stars in an effort to bribe them to join the American League. Honus Wagner and Tommy Leach were the two players that Comiskey wanted most, and he made a magnificent offer hoping to obtain the best pair of infielders in the country.[3]

Rabid Pittsburgh fans gave no thought to these rumors about their favorite players as they poured into Exposition Park on Saturday, August 16, to watch a doubleheader between the Pirates and Phillies. The mood was festive throughout the day as Pittsburgh celebrated their return to the Smoky City by pulling off a twin bill sweep over Philadelphia. The Pirates were in top form despite being without the services of key performers Fred Clarke, Jesse Tannehill, Kitty Bransfield and Lefty Davis. Wagner subbed for Clarke in left field, Jimmy Burke played right field and Jack O'Connor worked at first base.[4] Pittsburgh claimed the afternoon's first game, 4–2, as Jack Chesbro secured his 20th victory of the 1902 campaign. Jack O'Connor went 3-for-4, while Ginger Beaumont, Claude Ritchey and Chief Zimmer chipped in with two hits apiece. Sam Leever was victorious in the second game, 6–2.

Unusual incidents were a part of this joyous afternoon as mirth and merriment defined the mood at Exposition Park throughout the doubleheader. During the break between games, a quartet marched across the field to the grandstand and gave a concert for the fans. After the first number concluded, a man stepped forward and introduced himself as the chairman of a relief committee representing striking miners of the anthracite district. When the chairman asked for financial aid, he was greeted with cheers and a shower of silver. Coins ranging from nickels to dollars were thrown onto the field from Exposition Park's box seat sections and grandstand. Some bills were tossed on the field as well. Players from both teams were pressed into service to gather up this generous donation made by Pittsburgh's rooters. A group of small boys left the stands and pitched in to help. One or two of these urchins loaded their pockets with some of this treasure before they were quickly chased off the diamond.[5]

Pittsburgh's fans were treated to an exciting play and a comical incident during the second game of this doubleheader. The thrilling moment occurred in the third inning after Tommy Leach drove Sam Leever home with a triple. Leach wasted no time taking advantage of Ham Iburg's slow delivery as he darted for home with Honus Wagner at the plate. Leach had the advantage since he was like a streak of lightning on the bases and catcher Klondike Douglass' view was obstructed by Wagner's huge body. The play at the plate was close, as was always the case during an attempt to steal home. Umpire Hank O'Day called Leach safe as he slid into the plate amid a cloud of dust and barely beat Douglass' tag.[6]

Wagner was also involved in the game's amusing moment that took place when a yellow dog sneaked under a fence, ran toward the pennant pole and then trotted over to left field. The crowd of 7,200 fans started a whistling chant that confused the dog. Finding it impossible to respond to all of the calls, the dog stood behind Jimmy Burke in right field until the Phillies were done batting that inning. When the frame ended, Wagner, who was acting

9. Ban Johnson Lures Pirates Stars to the American League   171

captain in Clarke's absence, decided that it was his duty to clear the field and started after the intruder. The cur did not stop to dispute Wagner's right to eject him as it took off at full speed toward the left field bleachers. Wagner followed until he was out of breath and threw his cap at the dog as a parting shot.[7]

Rowdy behavior was also prevalent as a fight occurred in the right field bleachers before the entire police force on the field restored order in that section of Exposition Park. Several arrests were made. During this skirmish, occupants of the left field stands became restless and walked across the grounds to get a better view of the fight. This tempted some boys who were watching the contest from the roof of a box car at the railroad yard beyond the left field

Fans were in a festive mood as the Pittsburgh Pirates swept a doubleheader against the Philadelphia Phillies at Exposition Park on August 16, 1902. An impromptu concert between games, a fight in the right field bleachers, and Honus Wagner doing his duty as acting team captain by chasing a dog from the diamond were some of the afternoon's side stories. In this photograph of Exposition Park, no young boys are sitting on the roofs of any box cars beyond the left field fence (courtesy of the National Baseball Hall of Fame Library, Cooperstown, New York).

wall to navigate Exposition Park's fence. The boys somehow scaled the fence and, holding on to the top with their arms, attempted to lower themselves down to the field. To get to the ground they had to drop 15 to 20 feet. Most of the lads plummeted like a load of bricks. No injuries were reported.[8] A good time was had by all as fervent fans from the blue-collar industrial city of Pittsburgh rooted on baseball's greatest team.

Honus Wagner had taken charge of the National League's top team while Fred Clarke was sidelined by a bad leg that was threatened with blood poisoning.[9] Wagner had filled the position as Pittsburgh's boss with dignity since taking over for Clarke. His Pirates teammates claimed that Wagner kicked less with umpires when he was the field general rather than only a private. They also declared that Wagner used excellent judgment directing strategy during a game. This statement was validated by Barney Dreyfuss. "I was surprised at the executive ability Hans displayed at Boston," said Dreyfuss. "I was sitting on the bench and know all that was going on there. Wagner ordered the plays and coached the boys intelligently."[10]

Pittsburgh's insurmountable lead now stood at 19 games over second-place Brooklyn as another week of baseball action concluded. The Pirates posted a mark of 71–23 while the Superbas' record stood at 55–45. After being home only one day to play their Saturday doubleheader against Philadelphia, Pittsburgh embarked on a short trip to Cincinnati to play a makeup game on Sunday, August 17. The fans in Porktown celebrated through the night after Cincinnati won its first game of the 1902 campaign against Pittsburgh, 2–1. The pitching of Deacon Phillippe and the Reds' Ed Poole was of the highest order as the former Pirates hurler extracted revenge against Pittsburgh just as he had predicted. When Ginger Beaumont was called out on strikes in the ninth inning to end the game, fans swarmed on the field and carried Poole to Cincinnati's clubhouse. This enthusiastic crowd was the largest of the season at the Palace of the Fans.[11]

The series against Philadelphia resumed at Exposition Park on Monday afternoon. Eddie Doheny raised his record to 12–4 as Pittsburgh fought back and defeated the Phillies, 7–4, on August 18. Tommy Leach put his defensive skills on display for all to see as the diminutive third baseman was the main act during the closing game of this series. Leach also delivered a clutch hit that swung the game in Pittsburgh's favor in the seventh inning. With two outs, Harry Smith occupied third base, while Ginger Beaumont stood at second. After Phillies first baseman and team captain Hughie Jennings let loose with one of his loud war cries in an effort to encourage pitcher Doc White, Leach promptly smacked the hurler's next offering to the gate at the entrance of the 25-cent stands in left field for a triple. Smith and Beaumont scored and gave Pittsburgh a 4–3 lead.[12]

Pittsburgh put the game away in the eighth inning when Jack O'Connor hit a three-run homer.[13] The Pirates now had a record of 4–1 since Honus Wagner assumed Fred Clarke's role as captain and manager of the club. While Clarke may not have been able to perform his duties on a baseball diamond, he still voiced his opinion regarding matters related to the Pirates squad. Pittsburgh's manager continued to be annoyed with Ban Johnson's agents from the rival American League. He seethed over their sordid methods aimed at convincing Pirates players to desert his champion squad. "I would like to follow in the footsteps of Kelley and McGraw and raid the American," declared Clarke. "I think I'll have to get Barney to send me out. There's no danger of me leaving Pittsburgh. Colonel Barney and I are partners for life and I would have to go into court and get a divorce to be freed from little Barney."[14]

While Clarke reiterated that his loyalty to Barney Dreyfuss was indissoluble, Pittsburgh's owner announced that he had been busy securing additional players for the 1903 campaign. Dreyfuss made these moves in the event some current Pirates were corrupted by the monetary promises being brandished about by unscrupulous emissaries of the American League. He signed pitcher George Merritt and outfielder Jimmy Sebring from the Worcester club to play for Pittsburgh in 1903. Merritt actually had some previous experience with the Pirates as he had won three games for Fred Clarke during the late stages of the 1901 season. Merritt and Sebring, regarded as two of the best minor league players in America, were expected to join Pittsburgh when the Eastern League season concluded.[15]

John McGraw's last-place New York Giants traveled to Pittsburgh to begin a series against the Buccaneers at Exposition Park on Tuesday, August 19. Fans in attendance rooted passionately for their Pirates due to the strong fighting spirit New York's players exhibited throughout this battle. The Giants hit the ball harder than the Pirates and fielded with equal aplomb. New York's Roscoe Miller carried a 4–3 lead into the ninth inning. Chief Zimmer led off the inning and was soaked by one of Miller's pitches. Honus Wagner sent Deacon Phillippe up to pinch-hit for Jack Chesbro. Even though Phillippe laid down a perfect bunt, catcher Frank Bowerman pounced on the ball and made an impeccable peg that forced Zimmer at second base.[16] Ginger Beaumont cracked a single to right field that advanced Phillippe to third base. Beaumont tagged up and moved to second base when Tommy Leach made the second out on a fly ball to left fielder George Browne. With the game on the line, Miller quickly gained the upper hand against Honus Wagner when Pittsburgh's star player made two vicious but futile attempts to connect against his offerings. Unfortunately for New York, Miller was unable to make a final clutch pitch as Wagner slapped a single between short and third that scored Phillippe and Beaumont to give Pittsburgh a 5–4 victory.[17] Leach was 2-for-3 at the plate and smacked a home run, while Chesbro improved his record to 21–4.

As the Pirates moved one step closer toward securing another National League pennant with this victory over New York, Chicago White Sox owner Charles Comiskey professed his desire to play Pittsburgh in a post-season series. Comiskey planned on accepting Barney Dreyfuss' earlier challenge regarding an October series between Pittsburgh and the American League champion. According to Comiskey, if the two parties reached an agreement to play a post-season series, one game would be played in both Pittsburgh and Chicago with a rubber match to be conducted on neutral grounds in New York or Philadelphia if necessary. While Dreyfuss had not yet informed Comiskey that he would play the series, he told Chicago Cubs magnate James A. Hart that he planned on accepting this challenge.[18] Of course, talk about such a series was irrelevant at this point since the White Sox currently were in fourth place, two games behind the league-leading Philadelphia Athletics.

Charles Comiskey's timing regarding his aspiration to play Pittsburgh in a post-season series was a bit suspect since he recently had courted Honus Wagner and Tommy Leach, hoping to sign both players for the 1903 season. While previous attempts by American League agents to entice Dreyfuss' players to desert the Pirates had always happened while Pittsburgh played on the road in 1902, no attack had been perpetrated on their home turf. This changed when the American League's top two executives made a secret trip to Pittsburgh, hoping to steal players from Dreyfuss for their organization. League president Ban Johnson and vice-president Charley Somers came to the Smoky City to make their best sales pitch during conferences with some of Pittsburgh's finest players.[19] Although no game was played between Pittsburgh and New York on August 20 due to rain, underhanded activity involving numerous Pirates players supplied a huge story for newspapers the following day.[20]

Johnson's treacherous scheme to steal players from Pittsburgh's squad may have done irreparable damage to the franchise if Barney Dreyfuss had not been tipped off about a traitor on his team. The *St. Louis Star* had informed Dreyfuss in June that catcher Jack O'Connor was a disloyal employee. While the initial accusation falsely stated that Honus Wagner was O'Connor's partner, further investigating on Dreyfuss' part proved the information regarding his catcher was accurate. Wagner had been tempted for two months by

9. Ban Johnson Lures Pirates Stars to the American League

American League agents with promises that he could have anything he wanted. All he had to do was name the salary figure and say how long he wanted his contract to run. These overtures aimed at convincing the National League's top player to abandon the Pirates were futile as Wagner was one of the first players to sign a Pirates contract that covered the 1903 and 1904 seasons.[21]

Due to receiving some solid information, Dreyfuss, Harry Pulliam and Fred Clarke were prepared to foil the plotters when they arrived in Pittsburgh on the evening of August 19. On August 20, Pulliam set up shop at the Hotel Lincoln, where Johnson and Somers were staying, while Clarke was stationed in Allegheny near Jesse Tannehill's apartment. When the first set of meetings began at the Hotel Lincoln as Jack O'Connor brought a group of teammates to Johnson's room, Pulliam telephoned Dreyfuss to alert him that the treacherous scheme was now under way. When Dreyfuss arrived at the hotel, Johnson and Somers barely escaped detection right before Pittsburgh's owner stormed into the room.[22]

Johnson and Somers believed they had avoided exposure as they traveled to the North Side and began working on the second phase of signing Pirates to American League contracts. They settled into Tannehill's Allegheny apartment and sent accomplice O'Connor out to bring in more players. Once again the two executives were foiled shortly after this conference got under way. Fred Clarke approached Tannehill's room, knocked on the door, and to the surprise of the plotters exhibited no inhibition whatsoever as he walked into the room and interrupted the meeting. Clarke and nine other players proved loyal during this attempt by Johnson to deliver a crushing blow to baseball's greatest team. It was initially reported that Tommy Leach was invited to attend this conference but had positively declined to do so.[23]

Barney Dreyfuss acted swiftly handing down punishment against the principle traitor when he suspended Jack O'Connor for violating Section 5 of his contract.[24] When Dreyfuss issued a statement to the press on August 21 that gave a detailed account of Johnson's and Somers' indecorous activities in the Smoky City, he also revealed that O'Connor had been released because of his traitorous intentions.[25]

> The causes leading up to this summary action on my part have been brewing for some time but the crisis was reached yesterday, when I was compelled to take this step in order that I might meet the issue in the attempt that is being made to wreck the Pittsburgh Club.
>
> Tuesday night Charles W. Somers, who is the vice president of the American League, came to Pittsburgh on a gum shoe mission. Accompanying him was one Ban B. Johnson, the president of that league, who came to aid his partner in his dirty work. O'Connor, I know, visited the Union Depot at the time of the arrival

of the Cleveland train, from which place this worthy pair came, which in itself was significant to what followed.

Somers and Johnson, evidently ashamed of their mission, made their way carefully to the Lincoln Hotel. Johnson waited behind a lamp post while Somers went in, and after seeing, as he thought, that his tracks were covered, registered as J. A. Benham, Saginaw, Mich. He did not register Johnson at all, such were his dark-lantern methods. Yesterday morning the plot began to unfold when O'Connor appeared on the scene with one of our unsigned players. After a protracted conference both players departed, and O'Connor returned a short time afterward with another of our players, whom he conducted to the hiding place of this precious pair. The scene was then transferred to a room in Allegheny, where another meeting was held with two more of our players, with O'Connor again present.

Upon his return from Allegheny Mr. Somers, alias Benham, arranged to leave on the 6 o'clock train for Cleveland. By this time, however, he became aware that his presence in Pittsburgh was known to the officials of the Pittsburgh Baseball Club, and he tried all he could to save his co-conspirator, Johnson, from public view. He first ordered a closed carriage for himself and Johnson to make their trip to the depot, but changed his mind at the last moment and drove away, leaving Johnson still under cover.

As both had to make the same train, Johnson, to cover his retreat, had the porters bring him down by the freight elevator, hidden among a lot of garbage cans. He then sneaked out by the back alley and trudged his way on foot to the Ft. Wayne Depot in Allegheny, where he waited under cover until the train came along which Somers, alias Benham, had boarded at the Union Station. I mention these details to show the dark lantern and sneak thief methods employed by this worthy pair.

I didn't believe they signed any of our players, and I hope the net results of their efforts will be shown in the future to be nothing. I have treated our men well and am willing to pay them as much as anybody can honestly promise to pay.

If, notwithstanding, any of our players at the expiration of their contracts choose to leave the Pittsburgh Club, well and good. But I will not stand for any treachery or disloyalty from anybody while in my employ. No player can be a stool pigeon for the American League and draw salary from the Pittsburgh Club at the same time.

I don't object to legitimate competition for the services of ball players, and had Johnson and Somers come here and acted in an honorable manner I would have been perfectly willing to have had them meet our unsigned players to talk business. But I do object to such people coming in between two days and in disguise and using one of our players to accomplish their ends.[26]

While Ban Johnson's and Charley Somers' sneaky maneuvers were not the methods usually associated with honorable brokers representing baseball, it was highly unlikely that Barney Dreyfuss would have granted permission for the American League emissaries to talk to his players about switching leagues while the season was still in progress. Although Jack O'Connor had

9. Ban Johnson Lures Pirates Stars to the American League

betrayed Dreyfuss' trust and was subsequently released, Pittsburgh was losing a veteran player who was a valuable backstop and an excellent coach. Nothing escaped O'Connor during a game, and Pittsburgh's pitching staff had improved greatly since he joined the Pirates in 1900. O'Connor's biggest faults as a player were that he could not hit southpaw twirlers and was reluctant to signal for curve balls.[27]

If O'Connor had acted honestly, no one in Pittsburgh would have blamed him for leaving the club if an American League owner had offered him a larger salary than he could expect to receive from the Pirates. Unfortunately, O'Connor acted as an emissary for the enemy while he drew salary from a generous owner like Barney Dreyfuss. Whether the American League bribed him or not to assist in their dirty work would never be revealed unless Johnson, Somers or O'Connor himself confessed to the deed. Some of O'Connor's friends in Pittsburgh suspected he was paid for his assistance. Pittsburgh was definitely better off removing a player from the team who could not be trusted.[28]

The crucial question that remained unanswered for baseball fans throughout Western Pennsylvania centered around which Pirates had held discussions with Johnson and Somers about jumping their contracts and joining the American League in 1903. That query was partially answered when Harry Pulliam announced that Deacon Phillippe, Sam Leever, Eddie Doheny, George Merritt, Kitty Bransfield, Claude Ritchey, Honus Wagner, Ginger Beaumont, Fred Clarke and Jimmy Sebring had signed contracts to play for Pittsburgh in 1903, while catchers Harry Smith and Chief Zimmer had accepted terms. The remaining players on Pittsburgh's roster were told they had until September 1 to re-sign for the following season.[29] Barney Dreyfuss paid tribute to Phillippe's sterling integrity shortly after the tall right-handed hurler inked his signature to a Pittsburgh contract for the 1903 season.[30] "If they were all like Phil," said Dreyfuss, "a baseball man's life would be one round of pleasure. You never have to watch that big fellow. He is a man."[31]

Initial reports that Tommy Leach had not attended any of the meetings organized by Ban Johnson and Charley Somers lacked validity since he seemed like a prime candidate to jump leagues. Leach held a blank contract in his possession for weeks with instructions to fill in any salary amount that he desired. While he had not yet returned the signed document, the star player did promise Barney Dreyfuss that he would sign with Pittsburgh for the 1903 campaign. Jesse Tannehill, Jack Chesbro, Wid Conroy, Jimmy Burke and Lefty Davis were the other Pirates who had not signed a contract for 1903. Tannehill claimed he would rather play in Pittsburgh than any other city, providing he was paid a good salary. Chesbro, who was always slow in signing, declared he would be a Pittsburgh Pirate in 1903. Burke wanted to remain in Pittsburgh, while Conroy and Davis supposedly had not been approached about jumping leagues on this occasion.[32]

The loyalty regarding some of these unsigned players certainly came into question when it was reported that six Pirates were promised a $1,000 bonus for jumping to the American League in 1903.[33] Another story claimed that two good pitchers on Pittsburgh's staff were prepared to jump leagues. One man was guaranteed to receive a two-year deal worth $16,000, while the other player was promised $15,000 for two years to join the American League. If this was true, Jack O'Connor's mission was a rousing success even though he had failed to land Honus Wagner, the man he was instructed to capture above all others.[34] O'Connor, who was disappointed when Wagner did not agree to jump with him months earlier, failed in this enterprise to deliver Wagner's signature on an American League contract as he had promised.[35]

When O'Connor originally agreed to jump leagues, it was understood that he would be playing for the Browns in his hometown of St. Louis. This plan was altered as the veteran catcher was now slated to join an American League entry in New York with other Pirates he had tempted to desert. Even though O'Connor had been handed his release and barred from Exposition Park, he remained in Pittsburgh.[36] He certainly was keeping a low profile as he made a concerted effort to stay off the city's main streets to avoid angry Pirates rooters.[37] A Pittsburgh politician who was a good friend of O'Connor's admitted that O'Connor was inspired by a money consideration to do this dirty work for Ban Johnson, but meant no harm. "Jack did wrong, but I think he did it without intending to do so," said O'Connor's friend.[38]

The treacherous action perpetrated by O'Connor, Johnson and Somers could have proved disastrous for Barney Dreyfuss if he had not received information about this secret meeting beforehand. Dreyfuss had employed detectives to keep an eye on O'Connor when he first received evidence that his catcher was plotting to destroy the Pirates.[39] In respect to being tipped off about the meeting aimed at stealing Pittsburgh's players, Harry Pulliam stated that information came from a man in Cleveland who had fleshed out Johnson's and Somers' intentions for their proposed trip to the Smoky City.

Correspondent A. R. Cratty, who covered the Pirates for *Sporting Life*, claimed deductive reasoning made it easy for Dreyfuss, Pulliam and Clarke to keep tabs on the American League agents' activities once they reached Pittsburgh.[40] Cratty deduced that the Hotel Lincoln was a likely destination to secure lodging by this pair since hostelry manager Frank Probst was a good friend of Somers and many baseball players. Somers' movements throughout the city were also easily chronicled since he was very recognizable even though the American League vice-president had shaved his mustache. Cratty also believed that careful planning had allowed Johnson to make his eventual escape through a freight elevator at the hotel in Allegheny. A few weeks earlier, a bride and groom who were being pursued by a group of friends had attempted to ditch their tormentors by hiding in that hotel. The situation was getting rather uncomfortable for the couple when a hotel employee whispered into the groom's ear, "I'll fix the freight elevator and you just step inside." The groom did so and made his escape utilizing the same method Johnson would use weeks later.[41]

While great detective work helped fill in some of the blanks for Pirates officials regarding the itinerary of the American League emissaries, there was no substitute for obtaining intelligence directly from one of the co-conspirators involved in this sordid affair. Dreyfuss had gotten an inkling about the conspiracy in Pittsburgh's camp while the team was in Atlantic City on August 15.[42] The original tale given out by the press regarding Jesse Tannehill injuring his shoulder getting off the team bus was a false yarn that Pirates officials released on purpose. Tannehill actually jerked his shoulder out of place engaging in a friendly wrestling match with teammate Jimmy Burke. Since Burke balked at going to the hospital to witness the operation that patched up Pittsburgh's injured pitcher, Dreyfuss was alone with Tannehill when he was treated by doctors.[43]

Under the influence of ether that was used for anesthesia, Tannehill started to mumble about a proposed raid by American League envoys aimed at fleecing players from Dreyfuss' roster. He revealed just enough of the plot to arouse the astonished baseball magnate's suspicions.[44] Tannehill implicated Jack Chesbro, Tommy Leach, Wid Conroy and ringleader Jack O'Connor in the scheme. For years after this incident, when a player was called into Dreyfuss' office, his teammates would call out, "Don't let Barney put you under ether!"[45] Dreyfuss at once had commenced an investigation that prepared the little owner for Ban Johnson's Pittsburgh invasion.[46] Shortly after pieces of information regarding Johnson's secret meetings in Pittsburgh became public, members of the conspirators' faction quickly started working the spin machine in an effort to help cover their tracks. In a dispatch sent out from Cleveland, Charles Somers admitted that he did make a trip to the Smoky City.

> Mr. Johnson and myself were in Pittsburgh, and while there we looked at several pieces of ground suitable for a baseball park, and found that the claims of the National League that we would not be able to find grounds were ill-founded.

There are plenty of good grounds there, so that will be the least of our difficulties. Yes, I am well pleased with the result of our visit, and am confident that if the American League places a team in Pittsburgh, it will win out over the National League, as it has in Boston, Philadelphia, Chicago and St. Louis. It will only be an illustration of history repeating itself.

The American baseball public has in two years placed its endorsement upon American League ball, and wherever we go we get the crowds. That we will fail in Pittsburgh is beyond my belief. The people there are sick of the Brush-Freedman regime and their methods, and will, I believe, welcome our league. As to O'Connor, whom I see has been suspended by Dreyfuss, I have been told that Dreyfuss said a month ago he knew that Jack had signed with St. Louis for next year.[47]

On August 21, 1902, Barney Dreyfuss announced that Jack O'Connor had been released due to acting as an agent for the American League. Dreyfuss accused O'Connor of acting as a liaison between a group of Pirates players and American League officials Ban Johnson and Charley Somers during a series of meetings on August 20. O'Connor professed his innocence, claiming that while he did meet the two men when they were visiting Pittsburgh, he did not influence any teammates to do so as well (courtesy of the National Baseball Hall of Fame Library, Cooperstown, New York).

Ban Johnson also wasted no time issuing statements aimed at defending his actions. During an interview in Cleveland, Johnson chastised Dreyfuss for claiming that he objected to the American League president's gumshoe methods in attempting to procure Pirates players for his league. Johnson replied that Dreyfuss certainly should not have expected several brass bands announcing their arrival at the train station. The remainder of Johnson's statement ran verbatim to the comments made by Somers.[48] While he was in Boston, Johnson further clarified the nature of his business during the recent trip to Pittsburgh:

We went to Pittsburgh to look over the ground so as to be prepared to intelligently discuss the situation when the American League holds its annual meeting in Chicago. We also talked with several of the members of the Pittsburgh team, and I can safely say that if we place a team in

Pittsburgh some of the men now drawing salaries from Mr. Dreyfuss will be members of that team. Those that we talked with like the American League, and, as they also like Pittsburgh, we will allow them to remain there, that is, of course, if we place a team in Pittsburgh.

I was amused at Mr. Dreyfuss' protest against our doing business with his men during the playing season. What did Mr. Dreyfuss do last year? He signed Burke during the playing season, as well as Conroy from Milwaukee. Dreyfuss later signed Harry Smith from the Athletics. Now Mr. Dreyfuss objects to the American League doing the same kind of business. The American League will ask no man to break a contract to go with them, considering it an open field now in going after unsigned ball players.[49]

The final culprit connected to this conspiracy of deceit aired his grievances regarding these events which reshaped the Pirates moving forward. Jack O'Connor denied any complicity in this affair as he took his turn at the pulpit of justification and persecution.

"Dreyfuss was wrong in his action," declared O'Connor, "and he will find it out. It looks now as if I was entirely to blame in this matter, but you will hear a different story in a few months from now. I met Johnson and Somers while they were in Pittsburgh, but there was no sneaking on my part to get them. Neither did I take any of the other players on the team to the American League officials. I told him some time ago I would sign where I could get the most money. He goes on what Clarke and Pulliam tell him, and the manager and secretary have had little use for me for some time."[50]

This off-field soap opera drama certainly broke the monotony of what had become a predictable season for some fans as it became apparent that it was only a matter of time before Pittsburgh clinched the National League pennant. While this cloak and dagger stuff certainly added a little spice, Barney Dreyfuss and Fred Clarke remained focused on matters that took place between the lines on a baseball diamond. Pittsburgh resumed the series against New York on Thursday, August 21, with a doubleheader. Sam Leever outpitched Christy Mathewson in the opener and allowed only three hits as Pittsburgh defeated New York, 2–0.[51] Leever raised his record to 10–4, while Tommy Leach and Honus Wagner each rapped out two hits and scored a run. Leach also smacked a triple and Wagner blasted a double.

Plucky Fred Clarke was back in left field although he was still hampered by an injury. This move was necessitated because Wagner had to replace Jack O'Connor at first base. The Pirates were lucky they were not given a coat of whitewash during the second game. They could not handle Joe McGinnity's delivery, and Deacon Phillippe's steady offerings were just to the liking of New York's hitters as they scored eight runs. Jimmy Burke also seemed to be out of place in right field even though he did not commit an error.[52] All of this negative karma was a recipe for disaster as New York won, 8–1. The Pirates' catching corps also became further thinned out when Harry Smith hurt himself in the first game. Due to Smith's injury and Jack O'Connor's discharge, Chief Zimmer was the only healthy catcher on Pittsburgh's roster.[53]

Smith's strained leg had to be placed in a plaster cast. He joined the list of walking wounded that included Lefty Davis (broken leg), Claude Ritchey (injured leg), Kitty Bransfield (knee injury), Jesse Tannehill (dislocated right arm), Honus Wagner (bruised legs) and Fred Clarke (injured leg). Wagner and Clarke remained in the game despite being handicapped by their injuries and continued to play on sheer nerve alone.[54] Clarke's battered squad was pressed into double duty action for the second day in a row as the Buccaneers opposed Ned Hanlon's Brooklyn Superbas in an afternoon doubleheader on Friday, August 22. Although the defending champions limped around Exposition Park for four hours, the Pirates still managed to pull out two victories.[55]

In the first game, Eddie Doheny held the Superbas to two runs and improved his record to 13–4 as Pittsburgh exploded for 14 markers against Frank Kitson. Tommy Leach was the heaviest contributor to the Pirates' blistering hitting attack. After being retired in the first inning, Leach smacked two singles, a triple and a home run.[56] Pittsburgh rapped out 17 hits as Wid Conroy went 3-for-4, while Ginger Beaumont, Honus Wagner, Claude Ritchey and Doheny contributed two hits apiece. Jack Chesbro just missed recording his fourth shutout against Brooklyn in 1902 during the second game as the Superbas pushed a single tally across the plate in the fifth inning.[57] Chesbro raised his record to 22–4 as Pittsburgh defeated Brooklyn, 7–1. Ginger Beaumont went 2-for-3 and scored two runs for the victorious Pirates.

Brooklyn gained some revenge during the third game of this series on August 23. The Superbas claimed a wild affair over Pittsburgh by a score of 9–8 as Sam Leever allowed 16 hits. Many of these safeties were hammered out to right field where youngster Bill Miller was making his major league debut. Miller, after being recommended by Tommy Leach, arrived in Pittsburgh on short notice to offer aid for Pittsburgh's depleted roster. Since Miller did not have an opportunity to visit a barber shop before reporting to Exposition Park, his flowing locks seemed out of place on the diamond. He was also as pale as a ghost because he had only recently recovered from an illness. The youngster also appeared nervous debuting in front of 5,000 critical admirers of the Pirates who compared him with Lefty Davis, Willie Keeler and Patsy Donovan.[58]

It was Miller's great misfortune to break into wonderful baseball company on the same day that Leever was committed to showing how poorly he could pitch. Miller did not endear himself to Pittsburgh's crowd from the start as he misjudged a fly ball by running in the wrong direction to catch the baseball. In fairness to Miller, his single in the sixth inning finally got Pittsburgh going as it put two runs on the board. Despite bad days by Leever and Miller, Pittsburgh still had a chance to tie the game in the ninth inning as Wid Conroy stood on second base when the contest concluded.[59] Miller went 1-for-5 at the plate, recorded two RBI and made no putouts in his debut with Pittsburgh that also ended up being the youngster's only appearance in a major league game.

As another week of baseball action ended, the second-place Brooklyn Superbas trailed Pittsburgh by 20 games. The Pirates were comfortably atop the National League with a record of 76–26, while Brooklyn stood at 59–49. Ginger Beaumont continued to be Pittsburgh's top batter with an average of .354. Honus Wagner (.311) and Tommy Leach (.305) rounded out Pittsburgh's .300 club. The Pirates added two more rookies to their roster before the team left Saturday night to play a doubleheader the following afternoon in Cincinnati. Pitcher Harvey Cushman and catcher Lee Fohl accompanied the Pirates entourage to Cincinnati. Cushman made the trip since Jesse Tannehill's arm had not been tested since his accident in Atlantic City and Deacon Phillippe usually struggled against the Reds. Fohl was signed to take disloyal catcher Jack O'Connor's place.[60]

O'Connor was still in Pittsburgh, intending to do more mischief as a paid American League agent. Many believed the removal of the restraint of club rules had emboldened the former Pirate to complete his assignment before he left the Smoky City.[61] Barney Dreyfuss received praise and accolades for his handling of the affair involving O'Connor, Ban Johnson and Charley Somers. Many newspapers from National League cities believed the national game needed more men who possessed Dreyfuss' honesty and integrity.[62] New York scribe John B. Foster was particularly vocal in commending Dreyfuss for striking a blow for clean baseball.[63]

"Something akin to a real sensation has taken place in Pittsburgh," said Foster, "where Barney Dreyfuss, owner of the team in that city, has suspended John O'Connor, one of his catchers, because the player was acting as a go-between for the American League. O'Connor is off the payroll for the remainder of the season, and probably permanently through with the Pittsburgh management.

"When Mr. Dreyfuss starts out to do a thing he does not do it by halves, and the punishment that has been visited upon O'Connor will cause more than one player to stop and think. It is presumed that O'Connor had already signed a contract with some American League club for 1903, probably with St. Louis, and not satisfied with that, he was aiding the American League to break up the Pittsburgh club and destroy its efficiency while under salary from the Pittsburgh management.

"Rather low-down business, and there are few who will believe that O'Connor was punished other than he deserved for his part in the business. It is said that Ban Johnson, president of the American League, and Charles Somers, vice president of the organization, had gone to Pittsburgh secretly to engage Pittsburgh players, and that, O'Connor was their stool pigeon in bringing the Pittsburgh men to them.

"Were there any motive other than purely mercenary, any good reason for O'Connor's conduct, there might be some excuse advanced for him, but there is not the slightest. No baseball club in the United States has been better treated than Pittsburgh. The players have been paid liberal salaries, have received half the profits of the exhibition games in which they participated and have been accorded the best accommodations in their travel across the country.

"Had O'Connor been desirous of signing with the American League, there was no reason why he should not have jumped, as other players have done, and let it go at that, but when he lent his services to injure his present employer and still continued to draw his salary, he engaged in contemptible business, and fair minded men will be glad that one baseball president in the present chaotic state of affairs has backbone enough to make it understood that he is running his team and proposes to continue to do so.

"The National League will not lose very much if O'Connor continues out of it for all time. His conversation on the field has never been free from profanity, and only recently, during the last visit of the Pittsburghs to the Polo Grounds, he offended by the language that he used."[64]

A small group of people scoffed at this notion that Dreyfuss was a paradigm of virtue. One wild rumor that painted Dreyfuss in a negative light was the story that he had used O'Connor one year earlier during mid-season to convince Jimmy Burke to play with Pittsburgh in 1902.[65] Somers and Johnson claimed they attempted the raid upon Pittsburgh's players because Dreyfuss had stolen Burke, Wid Conroy and Harry Smith away from the American League.[66] Both of these tales lacked validity. The deals Pittsburgh made regarding these three players were done in a very straightforward manner by Harry Pulliam. Pirates management did not try to do business with any of these men while they were still under contract to play for American League teams. In respect to O'Connor acting as an agent on Dreyfuss' behalf, Pittsburgh's owner signed Burke on the recommendation of his veteran catcher, who was Burke's neighbor in St. Louis. Burke did not sign with Pittsburgh until he was released by the Chicago White Sox on September 15, 1901.[67]

Barney Dreyfuss had grabbed Smith since he believed Smith was his property after purchasing the catcher from Connie Mack prior to the 1901 season. It was perceived that the signings of Burke and Conroy were done by Dreyfuss to get revenge against Mack for cheating him regarding the sale of Smith.[68] While this may have been an underlying motive at the time, Conroy's and Burke's acquisitions looked like shrewd moves as Pittsburgh prepared to play a doubleheader against Cincinnati on Sunday, August 24. Both men were now vital cogs in Pittsburgh's fluid baseball machinery due to a host of injuries that had crippled Fred Clarke's team.

An estimated 25,000 baseball fans witnessed their hometown Reds gain a split against baseball's best team. It was Deacon Phillippe against Cincinnati's Bill Phillips in the first game as Pittsburgh prevailed, 8–6. Owing to the overflow crowd standing on the field, many fly balls that would have been caught during a normal day on the diamond went as base hits.[69] Both teams combined to bang out 23 safeties in the first contest. Jesse Tannehill, who returned to action in left field as Fred Clarke shifted over to right, went 2-for-5 at the plate. Baserunners were plentiful during the second game of the afternoon's festivities as well as 25 hits were produced by Pittsburgh and Cincinnati. The Pirates were foiled in this game that was shortened to seven innings as Cincinnati claimed a 9–4 victory.

Rookie Harvey Cushman, who had recently pitched for a team in the Pittsburgh suburb of Millvale, was brutally roughed up by the Reds. Cincinnati catcher and antagonist extraordinaire Heinie Peitz started working on the young hurler from the coaching box in the third inning. Cushman became so rattled that he allowed nine Reds to cross home plate before he calmed down.[70] Club presidents from each team and the National League executive committee chairman sat together and watched both games. Barney Dreyfuss, Garry Herrmann and John T. Brush also dined at the St. Nicholas Hotel after the game. Brush offered his opinion regarding the recent conduct of American League agents operating in Pittsburgh. Brush claimed that Fred Ely was released by Pittsburgh in 1901 because Ban Johnson was plotting to use him as a stool pigeon much like Jack O'Connor.[71] Dreyfuss also offered his opinion regarding the current state of baseball.

> That was one of the grandest crowds I ever saw. I guess interest in the game is not dead. Now, I don't intend to be drawn into any controversy with Ban John-

son, but I do desire to say that he does not seem to be able to tell the truth. He has not told the truth in his defense of his actions at Pittsburgh. The American League took Harry Smith away from me after I had bought and paid for his release. He says he did not make any attempt to raid Pittsburgh until I signed Conroy. Why, Ban Johnson gumshoed into Pittsburgh last year."[72]

Pittsburgh was not the only National League franchise fighting to keep players on its roster from jumping to the American League. Brooklyn manager Ned Hanlon missed the game against Pittsburgh at Exposition Park on Monday, August 25, because he was on a scouting mission looking to replace players tempted to join the American League in 1903. Superbas hurler Frank Kitson was one of the most egregious offenders as it was rumored he had accepted a $4,000 offer to play for Detroit in 1903. After a poor performance three days earlier against the Pirates, Kitson was ineffective once again as Pittsburgh claimed an 8–6 victory. In the two games that he pitched against Fred Clarke's team, Kitson gave up 32 hits for a total of 45 bases. The Pirates scored five runs against him in the first inning on a walk, five singles, a double and three errors. Jesse Tannehill faltered a bit in the ninth inning as Brooklyn pushed four runs across the plate.[73]

Tannehill improved his record to 17–5 as the Pirates battered Kitson for 15 hits. Chief Zimmer was a perfect 4-for-4 at the plate. Ginger Beaumont went 3-for-5 and scored a run, while Fred Crolius played right field and rapped out three singles. Crolius' solid showing was crucial given Pittsburgh's shortage of outfielders. No further help would be available in September if rumors surrounding prospect Jimmy Sebring were true. A few weeks before, Sebring supposedly had accepted a $100 bonus from Frank Dwyer for promising to sign with Detroit before he inked his signature to a Pirates contract.[74]

Pittsburgh played its fourth doubleheader in six days as the Boston Beaneaters came to town and kicked off a three-game series with a twin bill at Exposition Park on Tuesday, August 26. Boston narrowly escaped being shut out in both contests as Pittsburgh's shear dominance was evident throughout the afternoon. In the first game, Jack Chesbro was so exceptional that Boston did not score a run until the ninth inning as Pittsburgh claimed an easy 8–1 victory.[75] Chief Zimmer and Claude Ritchey each had three hits, while Honus Wagner and Fred Crolius banged out two safeties apiece. Chesbro tossed a complete game and struck out six Boston batters as he improved his record to 23–4.

Eddie Doheny surpassed Chesbro's pitching performance during the second game as Pittsburgh defeated Boston, 3–0. Doheny gave his best pitching exhibition of the season as he allowed only two hits, one of which was a fluke.[76]

He also did heavy damage at the plate by smacking an inside-the-park home run. Fred Clarke was the game's hitting star as he went 3-for-4, blasted a triple and scored a run. Honus Wagner and Claude Ritchey chipped in with two hits apiece.

The following morning, before Pittsburgh played the final game of this short series against Boston, local newspapers printed a story which offered irrefutable evidence that some Pirates players were destined to receive a sizeable bonus at season's end. New York State Senator Thomas F. Grady, who was an admirer of baseball in general and the Pirates in particular, offered a purse of $1,000 in gold to the players who were tops in certain National League categories. The captain of the pennant-winning National League team would be awarded $250 under Grady's criteria. The player making the greatest number of sacrifice hits received $100, while the player on Pittsburgh's squad making the greatest number of timely hits was honored with a gift of $200. The Pirates pitcher with the best average at season's end also received $200, and Pittsburgh's top batter garnered $100. Grady also planned on giving $100 each to the best infielder and outfielder in the National League. Fred Clarke was practically assured of pulling down the $250 prize. It was quite probable that Pirates would secure $900 of the gold booty for their treasure chests, with sacrifice hits being the only uncertain category.[77]

Ginger Beaumont and Honus Wagner staked their claim to some of this prize money during the game against Boston on Wednesday, August 27. Each man went 3-for-5 at the plate as Pittsburgh secured a 7–2 victory. Beaumont rapped out three singles and scored a run, while Wagner smacked two doubles and recorded four RBI. Pittsburgh clinched the game with four runs in the fifth inning. Harry Smith got the parade going when he tripled to right field off Beaneaters hurler Mal Eason. Smith scored on Sam Leever's fly ball when right fielder Pat Carney made a wild throw attempting to cut him down at home plate. Fred Clarke singled to left field and quickly stole second base. He moved over to third on Ginger Beaumont's single to left field. Clarke scored on Tommy Leach's safe drive. Honus Wagner drove home Beaumont and Leach with a timely double.[78]

Clarke and Eason, along with Boston's Charlie Dexter, growled and snarled throughout this game. Dexter's presence in particular was not conducive to harmony. When both teams changed sides in the first inning, Clarke shook hands with his former teammate from Louisville. A few minutes later, this truce was forgotten as Clarke's and Dexter's acid tongues hurled insults at each other. On one occasion, when Dexter made a great defensive play at shortstop, Clarke did not miss a beat harassing his opponent after showing surprising dexterity in the field. "Did you catch that, Percy?" Clarke shouted from the bench.[79]

As Pittsburgh prepared to open a three-game series against the Chicago Cubs on August 28, *The Pittsburgh Press* reported that Chicago White Sox manager Clark Griffith had arrived in Pittsburgh the previous evening. It was reported that contract-jumper Deacon Jim McGuire, who had deserted Brooklyn for the American League in 1902, also made the trip to assist Griffith as he attempted to build on the framework established by Ban Johnson one week earlier. It was reported that Griffith came to Pittsburgh to see two pitchers, two infielders and a catcher. In light of this latest news, Pirates management stated that the names of those players who had been bribed by Johnson to join the American League and intended to jump ship would be released on Saturday. This article also claimed that Barney Dreyfuss planned on signing Pittsburgh native and St. Louis Browns shortstop Roderick "Bobby" Wallace for the 1903 campaign.[80]

If this whole business regarding some Pirates possibly deserting Barney Dreyfuss to join the American League was becoming a distraction, Fred Clarke's players certainly were not allowing it to affect their play. Pittsburgh slaughtered an old nemesis on Thursday, August 28, as they defeated Chicago, 11–3. The Pirates blitzed Cubs hurler Jack Taylor, who had held them in check throughout the 1902 season. One of the game's highlights was Wid Conroy's grand slam in the third inning that scored Tommy Leach, Honus Wagner and Claude Ritchey ahead of him. Conroy was able to sprint around the bases after his low drive to center field rolled behind the flag pole at Exposition Park. The score was 10–0 heading into the sixth inning when Deacon Phillippe went into cruise control and started taking some steam off his pitches.[81] Phillippe raised his record to 16–8, while Ginger Beaumont was Pittsburgh's offensive star as he went 4-for-5 and scored three runs.

Chicago evened the score on August 29 as rookie hurler Harvey Cushman dropped his second consecutive decision. The Pirates lost to Chicago, 9–3, even though they outhit their opponent, 7–6. Poor fielding was the culprit as Pittsburgh committed six errors with Wid Conroy committing two miscues and Tommy Leach one. In the first five innings, the Cubs scored six runs even though they knocked the ball out of the infield on only three occasions. Being a rookie, Cushman offered no complaint about his teammates' wretched fielding. Such atrocious support most likely would have drawn a vigorous protest from a shrewd veteran hurler like Jesse Tannehill who was never afraid to voice his opinion.[82]

Prior to the final game between Pittsburgh and Chicago at Exposition Park on Saturday, August 30, conferences were held between Pirates front

9. Ban Johnson Lures Pirates Stars to the American League

office officials and some players. While the results of these meetings were not announced, it was believed that some Pirates players had received advance money and planned on jumping to the American League. Newspapers reported that catcher Harry Smith, outfielder Lefty Davis and infielder Wid Conroy were possible turncoats no longer wanted by Pirates management.[83] When the Pirates hit the diamond against Chicago, it was evident that some tension was prevalent. Fred Clarke and Honus Wagner both lost their tempers on numerous occasions as they made life difficult for umpire Hank O'Day all afternoon.[84]

Nothing was resolved between Pittsburgh and Chicago through regulation as the Cubs tied the game 2–2 in the ninth inning. The Pirates finally settled affairs as the sun disappeared behind a cloud over Saw Mill Run when they came to bat in the bottom of the 12th frame. Jesse Tannehill led off the inning by drawing a walk off Carl Lundgren. Fred Clarke bunted the ball to first baseman Jock Menefee, who picked up the baseball, dropped it, repeated the performance and then kicked himself as Clarke slid safely into first base. Ginger Beaumont followed with a walk that loaded the bases. Tommy Leach rapped an infield single to shortstop Joe Tinker that drove Tannehill home with the winning run that gave Pittsburgh a 3–2 victory.[85] Tannehill tossed a complete game for Pittsburgh and improved his record to 18–5.

On the same day that Pittsburgh moved one step closer to clinching the National League pennant, Barney Dreyfuss announced he had changed his mind about playing a championship series with the pennant winner of the American League. Dreyfuss declared that he had had a change of heart due to recent attempts by that organization to coerce players to desert his squad. "I was willing to arrange a series of games with whoever won the championship of the American League," stated Dreyfuss, "but I have changed my mind now since Ban Johnson and Charlie Somers came here and tried to steal my players and did a lot of other underhanded things to me."[86]

Since winning the National League pennant was a mere formality and no post-season series against the American League champion would be occurring in October, two main goals still existed for Fred Clarke and his troops. Could the Pittsburgh Pirates reach the century mark in victories, and would they ultimately break the league record for most wins in a season (102)? While these two objectives were expected to be the key narrative surrounding the final weeks of Pittsburgh's glorious season, another subject likely would be meticulously scrutinized. The question still remained unanswered regarding which players planned on playing for the Pirates in 1903 and which were committed to deserting Barney Dreyfuss to play for Ban Johnson's American League aggregation.

10

Jack Chesbro and Jesse Tannehill Issue an Ultimatum to Dreyfuss

When Pittsburgh defeated the Chicago Cubs on Saturday, August 30, they entered a new arena of achievement that was befitting a team that quite possibly was the greatest in baseball history. Prior to this conquest, Chicago was the only National League team that still held out hope of claiming the season series against Pittsburgh. This prospect became unachievable when Chicago lost its 11th game to the Pirates and fell in line with Boston, Brooklyn, New York, Philadelphia, Cincinnati and St. Louis as teams that had been dominated by Fred Clarke's squad.[1] A peak at the standings offered further evidence that Pittsburgh was in a class of its own in relation to the National League's other seven franchises. The Pirates' record stood at 83–28, while second-place Brooklyn was 24 games behind at 60–53.

The Pirates left the Smoky City on Saturday night to begin their final eastern invasion of the 1902 season. They would be on the road for two weeks until they returned home to play a game against Cincinnati at Exposition Park on September 13. Before the train carrying Pittsburgh's baseball entourage pulled out of Union Station, Barney Dreyfuss was pressed by reporters to divulge details regarding several conferences he had held with players at his office that morning. While Dreyfuss refused to offer details of who was present for these discussions and what was said, he did give a short statement to the press prior to his team's departure.[2]

> I am not ready at this time to make a statement about the players we have signed for next season, or to say whether any of the men we want for next year have gone over to the American League and deserted the Pittsburgh club. I will say this, however, Pittsburgh will have a championship team next year, and the club

10. Chesbro and Tannehill Issue an Ultimatum to Dreyfuss

will be even stronger than it is this season. That is all I care to say about the matter at the present time.[3]

Dreyfuss offered no insight into whether he still considered September 1 the deadline for Pittsburgh's players to declare their intentions to remain with the Pirates or play in the American League in 1903. While Dreyfuss diligently continued to keep the matter a secret, Ban Johnson had attempted another covert operation in an effort to steal one of Pittsburgh's top players. Johnson made a trip on Saturday, August 30, to Worcester, Massachusetts, hoping to sign first baseman Kitty Bransfield to an American League contract. Johnson registered at a local hotel under the name of R. B. McRoy and sent for Bransfield, who was recuperating at his home from a knee injury. After speaking with Johnson, Bransfield signed a two-year contract to play for Pittsburgh that was presented in person by team secretary Harry Pulliam.[4]

This story was corroborated by a traveling salesman who made the trip back to New York by train in the company of the American League president following his unsuccessful attempt at landing Bransfield. In an odd set of circumstances, Johnson was on the same train to New York that had carried Pulliam from that city to Worcester.[5]

This news was minor in comparison to the shocking narrative that was put forward by Pittsburgh correspondent A. R. Cratty in his article in *Sporting Life* on September 1. Careful and vigilant investigating by Cratty revealed the identity of each Pirates player who was being courted by the American League and had been bribed to desert Barney Dreyfuss. Cratty believed Dreyfuss' problems had started about three weeks earlier while he was vacationing in

While at his home in Worcester, Massachusetts, recovering from a knee injury, first baseman Kitty Bransfield received a visit from American League president Ban Johnson on August 30, 1902. Johnson initiated another covert operation, hoping to steal Bransfield from the Pirates. Following his meeting with Johnson, Bransfield signed a two-year contract to play for Pittsburgh that was presented in person by team secretary Harry Pulliam, who also made a trip to Worcester (courtesy of the National Baseball Hall of Fame Library, Cooperstown, New York).

Bedford Springs. An American League baseball magnate had called on Pittsburgh's owner at the Pennsylvania resort to discuss a proposition where the Pirates would move from the National League to join Ban Johnson's organization. Dreyfuss listened to the owner but informed him that he was not interested in joining the American League. Fearing that Johnson would not be happy with this decision, Dreyfuss commenced signing Pirates players for the 1903 season in case American League representatives started tampering with his men.

While Dreyfuss was able to sign most of his players, there were some on the squad who believed the hot air being offered by Johnson's hirelings. Dreyfuss was particularly amazed at the actions of a few men whom he relied upon to give him at least courteous treatment.[6] Tommy Leach was linked to this group of conspirators even though initial reports had stated that he did not attend any meetings when Johnson and Charley Somers were in Pittsburgh on August 20. Leach's betrayal was surprising since he was a favorite of Dreyfuss' who had been groomed to take over as the team's third baseman by the Pirates owner and manager Fred Clarke in 1901. When the boy's future had looked suspect during that season because of a leg injury, Dreyfuss sent Leach to Bonesetter Reese for treatment in Youngstown, Ohio. The doctor's high fee did not deter Dreyfuss one bit since he adored Leach and wasn't concerned how much it cost to get his player back on a baseball diamond.[7] All of the bills for his therapy were paid by the Pirates organization, and Leach received full salary while he was sidelined.[8] Many people in Pittsburgh were astonished that a player could be such an ingrate after team management had done so many things to help advance his career.[9] "I had an idea that ball players were not so bad as they were painted," said one angry fan who was a banker on Smithfield Street, "but, if Leach leaves Barney Dreyfuss it's all off with me."[10]

Cratty also reported that pitchers Jack Chesbro and Jesse Tannehill knew weeks ago that they would not be back with the Pirates next year. During Tim Hurst's Friday night Irish fair in Pittsburgh on August 29, which Cratty had attended, the writer noticed that Dreyfuss took Chesbro aside and began talking to him. They did the gesticulation act for some time, and the discussion certainly appeared heated given the demonstrative body language of both men. It was rumored that Chesbro demanded a $17,000 contract over two or three years to remain in Pittsburgh. In respect to Tannehill, he banked on his ability being worth $1,000 more than any other pitcher playing major league baseball. Infielder Wid Conroy was the fourth person mentioned in Cratty's article. Conroy's defection was not seen as a major loss since he was considered by some Pirates fans to be the biggest disappointment that ever stepped on

10. Chesbro and Tannehill Issue an Ultimatum to Dreyfuss 193

Exposition Park's field. While Conroy was an excellent glove man, he was a poor ground coverer, consistently allowed balls to elude him near second base, and was a light hitter.[11]

It seemed that outfielder Lefty Davis had also fallen into disfavor with Pirates management. Club officials asserted that Davis' ankle injury was no longer sufficient for him to remain idle. It was rumored that Dreyfuss and his partners were angry with Davis over his reluctance to play. They treated him with great consideration but had not received equal respect in return. When Davis was roasted in the newspapers, he told his sob story to a reporter from Chicago. He declared the Pittsburgh club still had not given him an opportunity to sign for the 1903 season. Davis also informed the reporter he had turned down a fine offer from the American League months before because he was still under contract with Pittsburgh.[12] During a recent trip to the Pirates' team office, Davis had irritated Barney Dreyfuss when he tried to cover up his complicity in the American League affair with a line of nonsensical chatter.

"Some of these newspaper men are going to have a lot to answer for," declared Davis. "Their pipe dreams are ever that a lot of players are going to jump. I'll swan if I have heard of a single man who is going to leave."

"Well, if you haven't I have," retorted Dreyfuss angrily.[13]

There was also some good news surrounding the Pittsburgh Pirates that offset this negative discussion about players acting with traitorous contempt. Second baseman Claude Ritchey, a man who remained loyal to Dreyfuss, announced that he had secured a license to marry Miss Sophie Boyer from his hometown of Emlenton, Pennsylvania. Miss Boyer was the daughter of an oil refiner from that town.[14]

This combination of trustworthy and unfaithful players that made up Fred Clarke's squad prepared to begin the season's home stretch run with an exhibition game against the New York State League's Utica Pent-Ups on Sunday, August 31. Unfortunately for the 6,000 fans expected to be in attendance to watch the Pirates, the team failed to make a railroad connection in Buffalo and could not reach Utica in time to play the game. Gate receipts totaling $1,500 were returned to these disappointed rooters.[15]

The Pirates kicked off their final eastern invasion of the 1902 campaign with a Labor Day doubleheader at Brooklyn on September 1. Pittsburgh celebrated the holiday by sweeping both games from the Superbas. In the morning contest, Jack Chesbro pushed his record to 24–4 as Pittsburgh defeated Brooklyn, 4–3. The afternoon game was a crazy affair as Sam Leever and the Pirates prevailed over their nearest National League nemesis, 8–7. Chesbro was Pittsburgh's top hitter in the first contest as he went 2-for-3. Tommy Leach, Wid

Conroy and Jesse Tannehill rapped out two hits apiece for the Pirates during the afternoon game, while Jimmy Burke went 4-for-5 and smacked a double. Burke also had the honor of recording the game-winning hit in each contest.[16]

In the morning game, the score was 3–2 in Brooklyn's favor when Pittsburgh came to bat in the ninth inning. Tommy Leach started off the rally on the right foot with a single over second base. Honus Wagner repeated Leach's trick to put two Pirates on base. Both players moved up 90 feet when Jesse Tannehill laid down a beautiful sacrifice bunt. Burke gave Pittsburgh the lead for good when his single inside the right field foul line drove home Leach and Wagner. Burke and Wagner were at it once again during the afternoon game when they worked their magic and secured another ninth-inning victory. With the score tied, 7–7, Wagner smacked a single, stole second base and scored on Burke's single before the Superbas even knew what hit them.[17]

Besides scoring the winning run in both contests, Wagner was also involved in an amusing play in the first inning of the second game. Brooklyn's Willie Keeler reached first base after Burke fumbled his ground ball near second base. Keeler moved over to third base on Cozy Dolan's single to right field. Bill Dahlen smacked a ground ball to third baseman Tommy Leach. The bounder was easily handled, but Leach fired the baseball over first baseman Honus Wagner's head into the bleachers. Wagner vaulted the low fence and dove into a mass of humanity, searching for the ball. After Keeler, Dolan and Dahlen had scored, Wagner came out of the stands and threw a pop bottle to catcher Harry Smith. This was the only loose object he could find since the crowd had kept the ball away from him.[18]

While Pittsburgh's lead over second-place Brooklyn now stood at 26 games in the National League, a tight pennant race was developing in Ban Johnson's rival American League. The first-place Philadelphia Athletics were clinging to a half-game lead over the St. Louis Browns. The Boston Americans were one game back in third place, and the Chicago White Sox held down the fourth position, 2½ games behind the league leaders.

Any infinitesimal mystery or ambiguity involving the National League race withered on the vine when the inevitable occurred on September 2. The Pittsburgh Pirates clinched the National League pennant when they defeated Brooklyn during the first game of an afternoon doubleheader. In the process, Pittsburgh also established a record that still stands of capturing the pennant at the earliest date in the season.

Pittsburgh secured its second consecutive National League pennant in fine fashion as they defeated Brooklyn, 5–3. Deacon Phillippe raised his record to 17–8 as he tossed a complete game and scattered 11 hits. Wid Conroy went

3-for-3, scored two runs and smacked a double. Down 1–0 in the third inning, Pittsburgh put a single run on the board when Conroy drew a walk and eventually scored on Ginger Beaumont's fly ball to center field. After Brooklyn grabbed a 2–1 lead, Conroy went to work once again in the fifth inning when he singled to left field. Catcher Eddie Phelps, who was making his major league debut, moved him over to second with a sacrifice bunt. Conroy scored his second run of the day when Fred Clarke cracked a single.[19]

Clarke's brigade of swashbucklers took the lead for good with two runs in the sixth frame. Tommy Leach worked pitcher Jim Hughes for a walk and scored on Jesse Tannehill's double to center field. Conroy's base hit brought Tannehill home with Pittsburgh's fourth run. The Pirates added an insurance marker in the eighth when Wagner singled and was forced at second base by Tannehill. Burke and Conroy both hit safely, bringing Tannehill home with the Pirates' final run of the game.[20] Spirits were still high for Pittsburgh over their groundbreaking achievement even though Fred Clarke's boys dropped the second game, 3–0. Rookie hurler Harvey Cushman saw his record drop to 0–3 as Brooklyn's Doc Newton held the Pirates to three hits. Although this was Cushman's best outing since he joined Pittsburgh, a lack of control continued to plague the youngster. While about three-fourths of his deliveries crossed home plate, they were coming in a few inches too high.[21] "The only way I can account for it is that I am not accustomed to pitching from the raised pitcher's rubber," said Cushman as he discussed his control problems. "On the amateur fields, the diamond is level, but I find that in the National League the rubber is several inches higher than the home plate. In time I will become accustomed to this and may find it an advantage, as other pitchers have done, but at present it is a handicap."[22]

Now that Pittsburgh had clinched the National League pennant, youngsters like Cushman and Phelps were expected to get a long look from Fred Clarke. Two goals still remained for Barney Dreyfuss' championship squad before the 1902 season ended. Their first objective was to win 14 more games so they could reach 100 victories. Once this was accomplished, another three victories would break the National League record of 102 wins established by the Boston Beaneaters in 1892 and 1898. Boston was the next stop for Pittsburgh on this road trip as they opened a four-game series against the Beaneaters on Wednesday, September 3. First baseman Kitty Bransfield rejoined the team, hoping to be back in Clarke's starting lineup. Once Bransfield put on his uniform and started practicing, the big first baseman realized he could not stand the strain and watched the game from Pittsburgh's dugout.[23] Before Bransfield arrived in Boston, Harry Pulliam bragged over some recent correspondence between the two men. "Ban Johnson made a strenuous effort to secure Bransfield when the first baseman was ill at his home in Worcester," said Pulliam, "but I telegraphed Kitty, and the American League president got a very cold reception in Massachusetts."[24]

While Pittsburgh was still committed to winning baseball games even though the pennant had been clinched, blowing out an opponent in the first game of a series certainly dampened hope for success at the gate for the remaining contests. The Pirates crushed Boston, 12–5, on September 3 as southpaw twirler Eddie Doheny improved his record to 15–4. Boston's players could not touch Doheny's delivery and became even more discouraged when the Pirates teed off against Mal Eason. Pittsburgh cinched the game by scoring five runs in the first two innings and added five more tallies in the sixth inning, aided by Eason's wildness and errors by Gene DeMonteville and Billy Lush. The Pirates eventually grew weary and played loosely enough to allow Boston to score some runs. Jesse Tannehill, who had been playing hurt for days, retired before the game ended as second baseman Claude Ritchey gave it the old college try and replaced him in right field.[25]

Clarke and his troops experienced a surprising problem during a doubleheader against Boston on Thursday, September 4, as the Pirates failed to score a run over 18 innings of play. Boston won the first game, 1–0, as Togie Pittinger outpitched Jack Chesbro. Great fielding also aided the Beaneaters, who scored the game's only run in the second inning when Herman Long crossed home plate after Tommy Leach and Jimmy Burke both fumbled Billy Lush's ground ball. Shortly after the first game concluded, it began raining in torrents. The storm lasted for 15 minutes, and the field, which had been muddy already due to rain earlier in the day, was filled in with sawdust so the second contest could begin.[26] Pitchers Sam Leever and John Malarkey were brilliant as neither team was able to score a run through nine innings. At 5:25 p.m. Hank O'Day called the game due to darkness even though many fans in attendance who voiced their anger believed a few more innings easily could have been played.[27]

Pittsburgh suited up and played the fourth doubleheader of the week on Friday, September 5. The Pirates rediscovered their batting prowess in the first game against Boston, exploding for 13 hits and defeated the Beaneaters, 6–3. Deacon Phillippe improved to 18–8 as he tossed a complete game and scattered five hits. Ginger Beaumont went 3-for-5, smacked a double and scored a run, while Wid Conroy also banged out three safeties, drilled a triple and crossed home plate twice for the Pirates. Fred Clarke and Tommy Leach aided the cause with two hits apiece.

Things did not run very smoothly during the second game as Boston

10. Chesbro and Tannehill Issue an Ultimatum to Dreyfuss   197

crushed Pittsburgh, 12–1, in a game that was shortened to eight innings when Hank O'Day stopped the contest due to darkness. Harvey Cushman's performance on the mound was brutal in the first inning as he allowed five walks and four singles that led to six Beaneaters runs. Cushman was not much better in the second frame as four more runs crossed the plate on four bases on balls and two more hits. With a victory now looking improbable, the game had some vaudeville flavor injected into it as Honus Wagner took the mound in the third inning. Wagner supplied entertainment for Boston's fans and gave a solid pitching effort the remainder of the afternoon. The Beaneaters scored only two unearned runs on four hits during Wagner's 5 ⅓ innings of work, and he struck out five.[28]

The Pirates left Boston Friday night and traveled to New York to begin the third leg of their road trip against John McGraw's Giants. More than 8,000 fans sat in the Polo Grounds stands during the series' first game on Saturday, September 6, and watched New York give the poorest exhibition of ball they had played since McGraw took over the reins in July. Lousy pitching, catching that was a grade inferior than the pitching, muffed fly balls and a bundle of mental errors were the norm as Pittsburgh claimed an easy 9–3 victory. Eddie Doheny had the Giants at his mercy until the ninth inning when two singles and a double produced two runs for New York.[29] Doheny scattered seven hits, tossed a complete game and raised his record to 16–4. Honus Wagner went 3-for-5 and scored two runs, while Claude Ritchey and Jimmy Burke rapped out two hits apiece.

Following their lopsided victory over the Giants, Fred Clarke bade his players farewell before he departed on a train bound for Pittsburgh. Once Clarke reached the Smoky City, he made a second trip to Des Moines, Iowa, with his wife, Annette. The couple was making this journey to celebrate the golden wedding anniversary of Clarke's parents, William and Lucy. Honus Wagner was chosen to handle managerial duties during Clarke's absence. Wagner expected to have Kitty Bransfield back at first base for a Monday afternoon doubleheader against New York. Pirates management also planned on using Jimmy Sebring in right field if he reported to the Polo Grounds in time for the twin bill. Clarke issued explicit instructions for Wagner to keep Sebring busy and give the youngster plenty of practice until he returned from Des Moines in a week.[30]

Before Pittsburgh continued their series against New York on September 8, the team journeyed to Utica on Sunday so they could play the game that had been cancelled one week earlier due to railroad travel problems. Hurler Harvey Cushman was excellent against non–major league competition as he tossed a shutout against the Pent-Ups. Ginger Beaumont scored the game's only run in the first inning on his infield hit, a fielder's choice, a walk and a fly ball to center field. Harry Smith played left field for Pittsburgh as a replacement for Fred Clarke. Since the weather was threatening during the first part of the afternoon, only 1,000 fans witnessed this low-scoring Sunday affair.[31]

The Pirates were unable to recapture the winning formula that was utilized in Utica when they locked horns against New York in a doubleheader on Monday, September 8. New York claimed the first contest as Joe McGinnity bested Jack Chesbro, 3–1. The Giants made it an afternoon sweep when they pounded Sam Leever for 13 hits and secured a 7–4 victory. During the dual battles that lasted over three hours, the pitching duel between Chesbro and McGinnity was the only feature of the afternoon. Jimmy Sebring made his major league debut as he played right field for the Pirates in both contests. He gave a solid performance during his big league baptism, going 2-for-9 at the plate and playing flawlessly in the field. Following Sebring into the fold was pitcher Warren McLaughlin from the Connecticut State League's New London Whalers, who was expected to join the Pirates on September 9.[32]

As the Pirates played some of their worst baseball of the season against New York, new information regarding which players were posing a problem to continued harmony on the team was unearthed by A. R. Cratty. These new reports singled out Jesse Tannehill and Lefty Davis as members of the troublemakers' society that was causing problems for Fred Clarke and Barney Dreyfuss. It had been management's intention to play Tannehill in the outfield every day he was not pitching. Dreyfuss and Clarke did this so they could punish him and get as much work out of him as possible after he had been implicated with the other American League conspirators a few weeks earlier. A poor throw from the outfield at Brooklyn on September 2 was the reason this plan was abandoned. Jimmy Burke had taken Tannehill's place in right field until Sebring's arrival.[33]

Before Clarke left the team to attend his parents' wedding anniversary, he and Tannehill also had a verbal confrontation on Saturday prior to the game against New York. Clarke and Tannehill snapped at each other for a few minutes before each man calmed down. Supposedly, this was the third time they had engaged in a fight during the past three years. Clarke and Tannehill actually became involved in a physical conflict on one occasion during spring training at Hot Springs, Arkansas. Pat Egan, a correspondent for the *Pittsburgh Times* who was a friend and confidante to many of Pittsburgh's players, relayed a story surrounding the third clash these two men had engaged in during their first season together in 1900 after the Pittsburgh-Louisville merger. Tannehill walked away victorious after this particular scrap.[34]

"Barney understands that you are lazy," Clarke yelled before the fight started. "Get a hustle on you."

"That's all right," retorted Tannehill. "You go and play left field and I'll pitch the game."[35]

While the problems between Pirates management and their malcontent star pitcher had been festering for years, the tribulations regarding Lefty Davis had only recently boiled to the surface. Davis had fallen out of favor in Dreyfuss' eyes due to his lifestyle choices in recent months. Prior to the 1902 season, he chose Jesse Tannehill, a player who had never been known for his convivial habits, as his roommate. The two players took up quarters in Allegheny, and from that time forward, his play slipped horribly because of too much nighttime carousing before he broke his leg. Davis sealed his fate in Dreyfuss' eyes on the night that Ban Johnson and Charley Somers were in Pittsburgh. As Dreyfuss and Harry Pulliam went out for a late-night walk to discuss baseball matters, they came upon Davis, who was hanging out with a bad crowd on a city side street.[36]

Davis practiced at Exposition Park every day, hoping to return to Pittsburgh's starting lineup. Pirates management had soured on the outfielder so badly that he had to beg for practice balls on three occasions.[37] He still hobbled a bit when he ran at full speed, but was able to leap about the diamond in his old form. Hopes of getting a chance to return to his old position were slim for Davis since Jimmy Sebring was expected to get the bulk of playing time in right field for the remainder of the season.[38] Davis claimed the only reason he was unfaithful to Dreyfuss and had signed an American League contract was that Pirates management had not treated him right.[39] Dreyfuss informed his outfielder that he could look for a position with another club since Pittsburgh did not want him next year.[40] Dreyfuss also issued a brusque statement in response to one of Davis' friends in Pittsburgh who believed management was unfairly criticizing the player.[41]

> I don't suppose that I am the man accused of slinging the hammer, but let me say that Davis has no one but himself to blame for his present condition. He was paid well for his services and we treated him just as we do other players. Early in the season I learned that he was not taking the best care of himself. I gave him ample warning. He failed to take heed, and, of course, in the interest of discipline a move had to be made. Mr. Davis was laid off. Instead of then realizing that he was not giving us value received for money paid him, he went back to his old tricks. I cannot see any place where the man was not treated right. He is being paid his salary in full, though we have not had his services for some weeks

past. I have heard of clubs cutting men off the payroll whenever they were hurt, but I do not make moves of that kind. Mr. Davis was paid for playing ball and not having a good time.[42]

Although Jack O'Connor was no longer a Pirate, the veteran catcher claimed that he was constantly being shadowed by detectives since his suspension and release.[43] Continuing surveillance on O'Connor was a prudent move on Dreyfuss' part since O'Connor still seemed intent upon earning the $800 stipend that was promised by Ban Johnson. It was rumored that Johnson had made a second trip to Pittsburgh to look over suitable grounds for a ballpark if the American League decided to invade the Smoky City. O'Connor supposedly was Johnson's companion throughout the afternoon as both men sized up potential sites. It was reported that the best this duo could do was to find spots in Carnegie and Homestead, both of which were about a 45-minute ride from downtown Pittsburgh.[44] This story was corroborated when it was reported that Johnson and Charley Somers indeed had made a second trip to Pittsburgh.[45]

While Barney Dreyfuss admitted that Johnson had secured options on two plots of land while he visited Pittsburgh, he did not seem concerned that a local American League team might be offering stiff competition in 1903.

"I cannot prevent the American League from coming as near Pittsburgh as they can get," said Dreyfuss. "I have no mortgage there. The field is open and the American can enter if it sees fit, as I have heard they have already done. I am satisfied that the people of Pittsburgh and vicinity will patronize the club playing the best ball, and so we have no fear. I will not fight to keep the American out. I will hold the people, though, by giving them the best ball they have ever seen. If I cannot outdraw and beat the American League at its own game on the square in Pittsburgh I am willing to step down and out. We have given the people of Pittsburgh good ball, and they are with us. We will hold them, for our club next year will be better than is the team which has just won the championship for us the second time."[46]

While Dreyfuss was positive beyond the shadow of a doubt that Jack O'Connor was still trying to wreck his ball club, he did not believe the latest story perpetrated by New York Giants manager John McGraw. McGraw claimed that O'Connor was disloyal to Dreyfuss before when he had acted as a go-between helping to steal Jimmy Williams from the Pirates during a trip to Hot Springs in 1901. Dreyfuss scoffed at this notion, believing O'Connor had not turned until he was bribed by American League officials in the summer of 1902.[47] Dreyfuss also did not put much stock in McGraw's accusations

10. Chesbro and Tannehill Issue an Ultimatum to Dreyfuss   201

since his dealings after jumping to the Giants from the Baltimore Orioles could be characterized as shady.

Hopes of extracting revenge against McGraw's New York squad for the two defeats one day earlier were ruined when the final game of this series at the Polo Grounds was postponed due to rain. This deeply incensed Pittsburgh's players, who were anxious to get back on the baseball diamond and defend their reputation as baseball's top team. "We wanted to get even for the double defeat of Monday," said one of Pittsburgh's players. "And what we would have done to McGraw and his tribe would have been plenty. They would have received their worst thrashing of the season."[48]

Although no baseball game was played against New York, Barney Dreyfuss took care of an important business matter that morning before the contest was cancelled. He held an impromptu meeting at the team hotel with pitchers Jack Chesbro and Jesse Tannehill in an effort to find out what their salary demands were for remaining with Pittsburgh in 1903.[49] The salary mandate staggered Pittsburgh's team president when Chesbro and Tannehill issued their ultimatum regarding how much money it would take to keep them in the fold.[50]

"I want a two years' contract calling for $17,000," said Chesbro.

"I'll sign for the same figures," chimed in Tannehill.

Dreyfuss gave a long, low whistle before he offered a response. "Is that all?" he softly asked.

"Yes, that's all," said Chesbro, who acted as the spokesman for this pair, "and we'll get it or we'll jump to the American League."[51]

Dreyfuss had anticipated a large salary demand on the part of both men, but these figures were even more excessive than he had imagined. He informed the two pitchers that he would talk to them again in a hour.[52] Dreyfuss walked into the hotel bar and took some time as he attempted to regain his composure and contemplate these ridiculous demands. After much deliberation, he left the bar and rejoined his two star slab artists. "Boys," Dreyfuss said, "the Pittsburgh club is not owned by Andrew Carnegie, nor are we in business solely for your benefit. I'll give each of you $11,000 for two years, and if this isn't satisfactory, you may jump to the Johnson crowd if you see fit. Will you accept?"[53]

Dreyfuss also informed Chesbro and Tannehill that he could go no higher than this figure. He declared this was a "take it or leave it" offer that gave them a huge increase over their present salaries. The two players walked off and told Dreyfuss later in the day that they had decided not to accept his offer. Both men readily acknowledged that the contracts called for $1,000 more than Ban Johnson's organization had offered them. When asked to issue a response about the attitude of Chesbro and Tannehill regarding their ingratitude, Dreyfuss refused to get tangled up in a war of words over this setback. "I have made them their final offer," said Dreyfuss stoically. "That is all I have to say, but Pittsburgh, with or without them, will have a team next season that will be fighting for the pennant from flag-fall to finish."[54]

In spite of this latest obstacle regarding Pittsburgh's two top pitchers, many Smoky City fans believed that Chesbro and Tannehill would not carry out their threat to jump to the American League.[55] When the Pirates arrived in Philadelphia to complete the final portion of this eastern jaunt, they did so in a more crippled condition than they had been throughout the 1902 campaign. Second baseman Claude Ritchey was called home to Emlenton due to the death of his grandmother. Jimmy Burke was slated to replace Ritchey. Although his injured leg had improved, Kitty Bransfield was incapacitated with a new malady, a boil on his butt cheek that was lanced during the team's day off in New York. Bransfield still hoped to cover first base during the Philadelphia series despite this latest health problem.[56]

A small crowd witnessed the first game of this series between the Pirates and Phillies on Wednesday, September 10, as most of the baseball fanatics from the City of Brotherly Love opted to catch the Philadelphia Athletics play against Baltimore. Attendance had dropped significantly during this eastern trip since Pittsburgh clinched the National League pennant.[57] Pittsburgh secured its 90th victory of the season as they defeated the Phillies, 5–1. Kitty Bransfield celebrated his return to the starting lineup by smacking three singles. The Pirates sealed away this victory with two runs in the seventh inning. Ginger Beaumont drew a walk and promptly stole second base. Beaumont scored on Tommy Leach's single. Leach moved to second base on the throw to the plate and came around to score when Bransfield drilled a single.[58] Disgruntled hurler Jesse Tannehill pitched for the first time in 11 days and won his 19th game of the season.

Pittsburgh's dominance over Philadelphia continued on September 11 as the Pirates swept an afternoon doubleheader against their cross-state rival. Pittsburgh claimed the first game, 7–5, as Jack Chesbro raised his record to 25–6. The Pirates had a much easier time in the nightcap as pitcher Warren McLaughlin made his 1902 debut and cruised to an 8–2 victory. Jimmy Burke and Wid Conroy smacked two hits apiece in the first contest, while Ginger Beaumont, Eddie Phelps, Jimmy Sebring and Chief Zimmer each recorded two hits during the second game. Chesbro was a bit wild as his seven walks were nearly twice as many he had given up in any previous game in 1902. He initially did not want to give up the baseball when ordered to do so by Honus Wagner in the ninth inning after Sam Leever was called on to relieve, but eventually capitulated and allowed the change to be made.[59]

McLaughlin was brilliant in the second game as he held Philadelphia to two hits until the seventh inning.[60] The Pirates played with a patchwork lineup throughout most of this game. Kitty Bransfield became involved in a heated dispute with umpire Arlie Latham in the first inning after he was called out on strikes. When the rhubarb ended, Latham ordered Bransfield and Wid Conroy from the grounds. Wagner took Conroy's spot at shortstop, Sam Leever entered the game in left field, and Eddie Phelps replaced Bransfield at first base. Pittsburgh clinched this game against Chick Fraser with four runs in the third inning. Chief Zimmer legged out a hit to shortstop Henry Krug. McLaughlin struck out trying to advance Zimmer with a sacrifice bunt. Ginger Beaumont doubled to left field. Tommy Leach drove Zimmer and Beaumont home with a triple. After Wagner struck out, Phelps was hit by a pitch and promptly stole second base. Jimmy Sebring ripped a single to right field that drove home Leach and Phelps.[61]

Barney Dreyfuss was absolutely elated over Jimmy Sebring's play since he had joined the Pirates. "He hits like a pile driver, and is an apt scholar," said Dreyfuss after Pittsburgh swept Philadelphia.[62] The National League champions had no trouble making it four victories in a row over the Phillies on Friday, September 12. The relative ease with which the Pirates made a clean sweep gave the few Philadelphia spectators who attended these games the impression that if pressed, Pittsburgh could have inflicted more damage.[63] Sam Leever tossed a complete game and raised his record to 13–6 as Pittsburgh defeated Philadelphia, 5–2. Honus Wagner was Pittsburgh's batting star as he went 3-for-4, smacked a double, scored a run and drove home three teammates.

Pittsburgh clinched this contest with three runs in the first two innings. Ginger Beaumont led off the first and reached third base when Paddy Greene made a wild throw after he fielded his ground ball at the hot corner. After Tommy Leach was retired on a fly ball to center fielder Roy Thomas, Honus Wagner brought Beaumont home with a single to left field. Pitcher Bill Duggleby's wild pitch moved Wagner to second base before he scored on Kitty Bransfield's single. The Pirates added another tally in the second frame when Wid Conroy walked, moved to second on Eddie Phelps' sacrifice bunt and scampered home on Beaumont's clean single to center field.[64] The newly crowned National League champions returned to Pittsburgh on Saturday morning after being on the road for two weeks. During their final eastern invasion of the 1902 campaign, the Pirates had compiled a record of 10–5.

As baseball's greatest team became acclimated once again with their home surroundings, *The Pittsburgh Press* stated in its Saturday edition that Pittsburgh likely would not lose a single man to the American League who was on Fred Clarke's list of players he wanted back for 1903. The article also reported that one or two men who were not on that list wanted to get back with the club and had asked for a conference with team management. Their request was not expected to be granted until Clarke returned from Des Moines.[65] The question surrounding which players planned on deserting to the American League and who was remaining with Pittsburgh could not be easily answered. One story claimed that Jesse Tannehill and Lefty Davis would experience the same fate as Jack O'Connor.[66] Baseball scribe Pat Egan claimed that Tannehill would defect to the American League while Jack Chesbro, Harry Smith and Tommy Leach were expected to remain in Pittsburgh.[67] Another report out of St. Louis stated that Chesbro had signed along with O'Connor to play for the Browns in 1903.[68]

Not one National League ballplayer had stepped forward to offer a tribute or any kind words about O'Connor since he had been released by the Pirates.[69] As was usually the case, he took it upon himself to bloviate as he repudiated Dreyfuss' traitor charges once again and professed his innocence.

> While I was catching a game in Pittsburgh one afternoon, a telegram was delivered to me. It was from Charley Somers, and he told me that he would be in town that night and for me to meet him. I called, as it was no open secret that I, as well as other members of the team, were out scanning for the best pecuniary offers, though I don't think there was one in that lot who would have left Mr. Dreyfuss without giving him a chance to pay us the same money.
>
> I didn't sign with Somers, nor did I steal any men for him. I was the most surprised individual in the world when I was served with notice of suspension and then with notice of release. When Mr. Dreyfuss handed me my check I tossed it over to him and said, "Barney, I'll bet this that I have not signed with any American League club nor tried to steal any of your men." He didn't take the gamble.[70]

Another problem that had been festering for some time exploded following the game between Pittsburgh and Cincinnati on Saturday, September 13. The Reds defeated Pittsburgh, 6–4, due to some ragged play by Jesse Tannehill. His teammates believed he exhibited a lackadaisical attitude on the field throughout the afternoon. He also drew the wrath of acting manager Honus Wagner when he disobeyed orders in the ninth inning. With runners at first and second and nobody out, he was instructed to bunt and move the runners up a base. He received the order, but instead he swung at the ball and was retired on a popup to second baseman Heinie Peitz. This total disregard for orders proved disastrous when Ginger Beaumont's hot infield smash was converted into a game-ending double play.[71]

Had Tannehill bunted the runners over as instructed, Cincinnati's infielders would have been in on the grass with runners on second and third and one out. Under that scenario, Beaumont's sizzler would have reached the outfield for a hit and driven home at least one run. A stormy scene ensued in the clubhouse after the game when Wagner called out Tannehill for not obeying orders in the ninth inning.[72] The Reds' Jake Beckley and Sam Crawford had also taken extreme liberties against Tannehill's pitches and smacked three hits apiece. Being disgusted over Tannehill's performance amid rumors that he was a traitor, Pirates fans at Exposition Park had urged Wagner to send his starter to the woods so a more competent hurler could take the mound. In spite of the cold weather, this game attracted a large crowd since it was Pittsburgh's first game at home in two weeks.[73]

This massive throng of fans were severely enraged and roasted Tannehill over his perceived lack of effort throughout the afternoon. He had made no attempt to field batted balls and acted altogether the part of a person who allowed his room in Allegheny to be used as headquarters for men who were determined to sabotage Barney Dreyfuss' club.[74] Most of the baseball reporters in Pittsburgh scratched their heads, wondering what had spoiled Tannehill during the past few years. When Tannehill first joined the Pirates, he was an ambitious young man with a cheerful disposition. He did not become a high-priced player in terms of salary until Barney Dreyfuss took control of the team. In spite of this, his attitude changed during the past few years to the point that he categorized baseball writers along with umpires as being all bad.[75]

Since the 1899 season, some malady or disability had always seemed to crop up that kept Tannehill out of action when meaningful games were played in August and September. It was also rumored that he had recently complained while the team was at the Marlborough Hotel in New York because Barney Dreyfuss intended to keep him at work until October 15. Even though each Pirates player was paid through October 15 in his contract, Tannehill believed he should be permitted to start on a barnstorming trip on October 6.[76] The desire to collect extra money seemed to be at the heart of this matter as he wanted to be paid his salary and earn additional coin playing baseball for a team other than the Pittsburgh Pirates. A remark Tannehill once made to one of his younger teammates helped offer insight into this new-found selfish disposition.

"You will come near making a record," exclaimed the young player admiringly.

"Record be blamed," retorted Tannehill. "It's the money I'm after. I am too old to be looking for the records."[77]

After playing only one game on their home grounds at Exposition Park, the Pirates traveled to St. Louis to begin a two-game series at League Park on Sunday, September 14. Acting captain and manager Honus Wagner, who had played the past four games with a broken hand, was ordered to remain in Pittsburgh. Barney Dreyfuss had charge of the team until it reached the Mound City. Fred Clarke was expected to meet his teammates in St. Louis and play left field against the Cardinals.[78] The Pirates, whose record stood at 93–34, needed to secure seven more victories in their remaining 12 games to reach the heralded century mark for wins.

Operating on all cylinders, they dismantled St. Louis, 9–6, in a game that was shortened to eight innings. The final count was deceiving as Warren McLaughlin had to overcome some miserable fielding by Wid Conroy and Jimmy Burke to notch his second victory of the season. Travel issues and hunger seemed like plausible excuses for this wretched defensive performance. The team's arrival in St. Louis was delayed by three hours due to a train wreck, and the players had only enough time to eat a light lunch on their way to the ballpark.[79] Clarke's return to the lineup was a rousing success as he went 2-for-2, blasted a double and scored two runs. Jimmy Burke also smacked two hits and scored two runs, while Tommy Leach went 2-for-4, tripled and scored two runs.

Pittsburgh made it two victories in a row with a 6–1 win over the Cardinals on Monday, September 15. Sam Leever was untouchable as he tossed a complete game, scattered seven hits and raised his record to 14–6. Ginger Beaumont and Jimmy Sebring did most of the heavy hitting damage for Clarke's squad that seemed to toy with the Cardinals throughout the afternoon. Beaumont, who was ambitious to lead the National League in hitting, recorded four hits while Sebring was credited with three safeties. The Pirates scored three times in the first inning on Beaumont's double, Clarke's single, Tommy Leach's fly ball to center fielder Homer Smoot, Sebring's single, Clarke's and Sebring's double steal, and Jimmy Burke's single. Two more runs were added in the fifth frame when Beaumont beat out a bunt and was forced by Clarke. Leach brought Clarke home with a triple, and Sebring's single scored Leach. Pittsburgh added a final run in the sixth inning.[80]

Two new players on Pittsburgh's squad made a positive impression upon many people during the team's short trip to St. Louis. Jimmy Sebring and Eddie Phelps received lavish praise for their performance in the two games. Third baseman Bill Friel from the American League's St. Louis Browns gave Sebring a glowing assessment after he watched Monday's game. "That Sebring is scarcely of age yet," said Friel. "He lives near me, and I tried for two years to get him to turn professional. He wound up the 1901 campaign with Worcester. Sebring, mark my word, is going to have a successful career."[81]

Phelps, a man who was expected to replace St. Louis native Jack O'Connor as Pittsburgh's catcher in 1903, received his round of complimentary praise from baseball writer Harold Lanigan of the *St. Louis Star*. "Phelps, Pittsburgh's new catcher, is also a rare performer, apparently," remarked Lanigan. "He goes at his work as though he had been in the professional arena for many years, instead of being a 'dub.' Phelps is put up on good lines. His throwing whip is a corker, and Monday he raced to the edge of the grandstand for a splendid capture of a foul fly from Wicker's bat."[82]

The Pirates and Cardinals traveled to Pittsburgh and relaxed for a day before opening a three-game series at Exposition Park on September 17. While baseball was not played for one afternoon in the Smoky City, American League executives never seemed to take a day off as another story surfaced regarding their efforts to inflict serious damage against their rival organization. Barney Dreyfuss received word that the placing of a club in Pittsburgh by the American League was contingent upon Ban Johnson's success at invading New York. After having made no inroads for weeks in his efforts to secure grounds for a team in New York, Detroit Tigers owner Sam Angus went to the Big Apple hoping to acquire a piece of property where a ballpark could be built.[83]

Dreyfuss learned that the latest American League scheme involved taking control of South Field, an improved lot of land on Amsterdam Avenue that was owned by Columbia College. South Field was located near the 116th Street station on the Sixth and Ninth Avenue elevated roads, and could be reached by several trolley lines. Angus was sent to New York to broker this deal since the American League syndicate did not trust Johnson with such a delicate task. Political winds in New York certainly seemed to be blowing in the syndicate's favor since Mayor Seth Low formerly resided as Columbia College's president. They also believed Low would be receptive to this venture as a means to gain revenge against New York Giants owner and Tammany Hall man Andrew Freedman, who was on the other side of the city's political fence.[84]

The American League had a huge obstacle to overcome since this property was valued at $2 million. Johnson and his syndicate would have to raise half of that amount before they could even contemplate finalizing a deal. Even if the syndicate miraculously secured the funds, it was still possible that the college trustees would not approve the sale due to some of the American League's crooked business methods.[85] These college board members were not the only people who questioned some of Ban Johnson's policies. A group of conservative American League magnates did not endorse Johnson's tactics and felt he had advanced his own interests at the expense of their pocketbooks. On September 15 and 16, National League owners held a quiet meeting in New York. While the official news release stated that this conference was conducted so the eight club leaders could talk over league matters, it was rumored that most of the discussion centered upon reaching a peace agreement with the American League.[86]

It was reported in newspapers across the country that an unidentified representative of the American League also attended this meeting in New York and came to talk about brokering peace within major league baseball. One of the key points made by everyone connected to this summit was that the high salaries being demanded by players from both leagues made it imperative that peace be attained.[87] Discussions about peace being achieved in baseball disappeared in the Smoky City when the Pittsburgh Pirates returned to action against St. Louis on Wednesday, September 17. Pittsburgh secured win number 96 as they defeated the Cardinals, 12–3. Jack Chesbro tossed a complete game and raised his record to 26–6. Kitty Bransfield was Pittsburgh's top batter as the big first baseman went 3-for-5 and smacked two doubles. Jimmy Sebring, Fred Clarke, Tommy Leach, Honus Wagner and Wid Conroy chipped in with two hits apiece. Clarke scored four runs, while Sebring, Leach and Wagner each crossed home plate twice.

Two local lads who played for St. Louis received adulation and cheers throughout the afternoon. Pittsburgh native and Cardinals third baseman Red Calhoun accepted a gold watch and chain from admiring fans prior to the game. Patrons also cheered the exploits of hurler Alexander Pearson from Beaver County as he held the Pirates in check for three innings. Things turned bad for Pearson in the fifth inning when Fred Clarke changed tactics and started using a clever combination of bunting and the hit-and-run to net six runs during the next two innings. Honus Wagner twice sacrificed when there was a runner on second base and another on first, and in both instances Kitty Bransfield followed with a long hit that drove in two runs.[88]

It took the National League champions ten innings to defeat Patsy Donovan's team on Thursday, September 18, by a score of 7–6. Even though the Pirates rapped out 15 hits against the Cardinals' Jim Hackett, they did not secure the game during regulation play. If Jesse Tannehill had pitched as well as he batted, this game would have been an easy afternoon at the park for the southpaw. He pitched horribly, and St. Louis would have scored more runs if not for perfect defensive support by his teammates that allowed him to secure his 20th victory of the season. Fred Clarke pulled off the game's defensive gem in the tenth inning when he robbed Donovan of a base hit. Donovan led off the frame by knocking a low fly ball to left field. Playing it safe would have allowed Donovan to reach base, while making a desperate attempt to catch the fly ball and missing it probably would have given the player three bases. As usual, Clarke had the nerve to attempt the more difficult play. He made the catch, did a somersault and held the ball above the ground while he did his tumbling act.[89]

This great defensive play took all of the fight out of Donovan's troops. After Chief Zimmer was retired in Pittsburgh's half of the tenth inning, Tannehill walked. Jimmy Sebring followed with his third hit of the day, a blistering single over second base that almost decapitated Jim Hackett. Clarke hit a blast to right field that eluded Donovan, who retrieved the ball as quickly as possible, but the lame Tannehill limped across home plate with the winning run before his throw reached catcher Art Weaver.[90] These two teams observed a one-day hiatus on Friday, September 19, as the Pirates instead played an exhibition game in the Pittsburgh suburb of Homestead against a team comprised of men who worked in that area's steel mills.

Pittsburgh secured an easy 7–3 victory as Clarke showed mercy toward manager Howard Risher of the Homestead team, who was his friend. Sam Leever and Claude Ritchey took turns in center field after Honus Wagner retired from the game. Clarke also played a few innings at third base when he switched positions with Tommy Leach. Homestead scored three runs after this combination was formed in the eighth inning. Harvey Cushman had a great day on the slab as he struck out 13 of the steelworkers.[91]

The Pirates and St. Louis played for the last time in 1902 on Saturday, September 20. Pittsburgh secured its 98th victory of the campaign with a 7–4 victory over the Cardinals. Warren McLaughlin tossed a complete game and garnered his third win against no defeats. McLaughlin was backed by excellent fielding as Fred Clarke's squad entertained the fans with spectacular defensive plays all afternoon.

In the eighth inning, right fielder Jimmy Sebring made a spectacular catch as he raced to the fence and grabbed Homer Smoot's fly ball. Tommy Leach went to the corner of the St. Louis bench in the ninth frame and snagged a foul ball after the St. Louis players under shelter had harassed him for attempting the play. Catcher Chief Zimmer also caught a difficult foul ball and nailed four Cardinals runners who attempted to steal. Offensively, the Pirates clinched this victory in the eighth inning. Singles by Fred Clarke, Tommy Leach and Eddie Phelps, Honus Wagner's walk, Claude Ritchey's sacrifice and Wid Conroy's out at first base brought home three runs and gave Pittsburgh the game.[92]

Seven games remained on the schedule as the Pittsburgh Pirates' passionate pursuit of rewriting baseball history reached its final stages. By winning two consecutive National League pennants, Fred Clarke's squad definitely possessed the bona fides to be categorized as one of the game's elite franchises in recent years. The Chicago Cubs and Cincinnati Reds were the only obstacles that stood between them and baseball glory. If the Pirates could win five more games, their status would transform from the sport's eminent power in 1902 to the greatest aggregation in baseball history.

11

Pittsburgh Breaks Record as Tommy Leach Fight Intensifies

The Pittsburgh Pirates left the cozy confines of Exposition Park to play a Sunday doubleheader against the Chicago Cubs on September 21. Pittsburgh needed to sweep in order to reach the century mark in victories for the 1902 campaign. Sam Leever and Deacon Phillippe, who had not pitched since September 5, were slated to do the hurling duties against Chicago. Twenty-game winners Jack Chesbro and Jesse Tannehill were not available since they had pitched in the recent series against St. Louis. Leever and Phillippe certainly were no slouches as they had combined to win 32 games in 1902. The team's .300 club included Ginger Beaumont (.353), Honus Wagner (.316), Fred Clarke (.305) and Kitty Bransfield (.300).

An interesting story awaited the Pirates entourage when they arrived in the Windy City. It was reported that the American League franchises in Detroit and Baltimore would be shifted to Pittsburgh and New York respectively for the 1903 season. League vice-president Charley Somers was the man credited with making this statement. While it seemed to be a foregone conclusion that the Baltimore franchise would be moved, the chances of Detroit being transferred to Pittsburgh looked remote.[1] A second article which appeared in the *New York Sun* alleged that six of the best players who had helped Pittsburgh win the National League pennant were expected to play for the American League entry in New York. Former Pirate Jack O'Connor, along with current players Jesse Tannehill, Jack Chesbro, Harry Smith, Lefty Davis, Wid Conroy and Tommy Leach, allegedly had signed American League contracts several weeks earlier and received advance money from Ban Johnson's organization.[2]

This report also stated that these men were receiving lucrative salaries so they could abandon Barney Dreyfuss and desert to the rival league. No player was getting less than $3,500 on a two-year deal, while one pitcher would be paid $14,000 and another was going to receive $12,500. Since Chesbro had recently requested a salary of $17,000 covering two years to remain in Pittsburgh, it was inferred that he would be the player who received $14,000, or the magnificent salary of $7,000 a year.[3] Harry Pulliam dismissed this yarn, claiming he did not think Barney Dreyfuss would lose many players. Pulliam also asserted that Pittsburgh had not made as much money in 1902 as was popularly believed, due to the team's high salary list and runaway pennant race. He also responded with his opinion regarding Jack Chesbro's extravagant salary demands.[4] "If he can get $17,500 for two years they can have him as far as we are concerned," stated Pulliam.[5]

The Pittsburgh Pirates captured their 100th victory of the 1902 season during the second game of a doubleheader against the Chicago Cubs on September 21. Sam Leever, who had missed time earlier in the season due to an arm injury, secured the record victory. Leever scattered eight hits and raised his record to 15–6 as Pittsburgh defeated Chicago, 4–1, and reached the century mark in victories for the first time in team history (courtesy of the National Baseball Hall of Fame Library, Cooperstown, New York).

Focus and concentration continued to be the Pirates' theme in the face of these distractions as Fred Clarke's squad recorded victories number 99 and 100 against the Cubs on September 21. Deacon Phillippe tossed a complete game and raised his record to 19–8 as Pittsburgh claimed a 4–1 victory in the first game. The Pirates smacked 11 hits off Carl Lundgren as Fred Clarke, Honus Wagner, Jimmy Sebring and Wid Conroy recorded two safeties apiece. Pittsburgh also claimed the second game by the same 4–1 score as Sam Leever went the route and improved his record to 15–6. Ginger Beaumont was the Pirates' top hitter as he went 3-for-4, blasted a double

11. Pittsburgh Breaks Record as Tommy Leach Fight Intensifies 213

and scored two runs. Clarke smacked a single and a double, while Wagner stroked two doubles.

Some fireworks were supplied by Fred Clarke during the second contest when Hank O'Day made a mistake in a decision at second base that adversely affected the Pirates. Clarke complained to O'Day about his error in judgment and eventually lost his temper. O'Day threw Clarke out of the game and then banished him from the field altogether since he was slow exiting after the ejection. Ginger Beaumont had four hits on the afternoon during his return to the lineup after being sidelined for a few games.[6] Getting back into action was crucial for Beaumont since he was locked in a battle with Cincinnati's Cy Seymour for the National League batting championship. Beaumont currently held a three-point edge over Seymour, while fellow Reds Sam Crawford and Jake Beckley rounded out the league's top four batters.[7]

Pittsburgh needed to win three of their final five games to set a new National League record for most victories in a season. When the season was 154 games, the Boston Beaneaters turned the trick in 1892 and 1898. It could not be overlooked that Boston was involved in tight pennant races those two years (the split season format was used in 1892), which was not the case with Pittsburgh in 1902. There was a small minority of people who believed the Pirates had been lucky to hold together their fine team while National League rivals were hit hard by American League defections.[8] Pittsburgh's devoted baseball rooters mocked such suggestions. These fans reasoned that if the Pirates equaled Boston's record of 102 victories, their performance would be far more creditable since the team could possibly play only 139 games in 1902.[9]

Out of those five remaining games against Cincinnati, the Pirates were scheduled to play four contests at Exposition Park and one in Porktown.[10] Due to some strange scheduling, Pittsburgh and Cincinnati would have to wait almost a week before they opposed each other on Saturday, September 27. During this break in the schedule, Fred Clarke's troops sojourned along the east coast and Canada, playing exhibition games to stay sharp. The Pirates traveled to Buffalo on Monday, September 22, and defeated George Stallings' Bisons of the Eastern League, 5–1. The weather was absolutely beautiful as 8,000 people turned out to watch the champions. Jack Chesbro pitched for Pittsburgh and allowed only six hits.[11] Following the game in Buffalo, Pittsburgh journeyed to Toronto for a game against the Maple Leafs on September 23. After Toronto scored three runs in the first inning, Pittsburgh took control of this game with an offensive explosion and claimed a 7–3 victory behind Deacon Phillippe's masterful pitching.[12]

Fred Clarke had to retire from this game in the second inning when he received word that his sister who lived in Chicago was seriously ill. Jimmy Burke took Clarke's place as he started west on the first available train. If Kitty Bransfield was unable to return to the lineup so Honus Wagner could be shifted from first base to the outfield, the team would be horribly handicapped since Burke was not a natural outfielder.[13] When Pittsburgh played against Montreal on Wednesday, September 24, Wagner was at first base, Burke played left field and Bransfield sat in the dugout. The National League champions scored three runs in the first inning and never were in danger as Pittsburgh defeated the Eastern League's Montreal Royals, 8–3, in front of 4,000 enthusiastic fans. Warren McLaughlin remained undefeated in a Pirates uniform as he held Montreal to six hits.[14]

While the Pirates blazed a trail through Canada, more dominos started falling back home as Barney Dreyfuss officially jettisoned another traitor from his squad. On September 24, outfielder Lefty Davis was handed his release and told to remove his clothes from Exposition Park's locker room and move on. Davis would have received this bad news weeks ago when it was discovered he was giving aid and comfort to the American League if he had not been in Atlantic City listening to the sad sea waves while nursing his broken ankle. Dreyfuss did not have the heart to give the ungrateful player his release until he had entirely recovered from an injury he received while playing for Pittsburgh. Davis was free to go to the American League with no fear he would be sued under the two years' option clause, since the Pirates waived all claim to him.[15]

It had also been rumored that Jesse Tannehill would receive his notice of release shortly, but for some reason the southpaw hurler still remained on Pittsburgh's roster. Baseball experts reasoned that Dreyfuss intended to hold him until October 15 instead of allowing him to go on a barnstorming tour on October 5.[16] During recent weeks, Tannehill had not earned his paycheck and continued to deny some of the charges leveled against him. The fact that his room in Allegheny had been used as a meeting place for the conspirators was irrefutable. On that fateful August day, Fred Clarke immediately discovered the collaborators were holding a conference in Tannehill's room. When Clarke arrived, the players quickly changed the subject and talked about everything but the business that brought them there. Some players left before Clarke, while the remaining Pirates went with him. As Clarke left the room, he gave a farewell wave to Tannehill, who seemed to be alone at the time.[17]

This was not the case, however, since Ban Johnson was hiding in the freight elevator. Tannehill always told the joke to his Pittsburgh friends of how Clarke was fooled, but the Pirates manager knew full well what was going

11. Pittsburgh Breaks Record as Tommy Leach Fight Intensifies

on since team management had been tipped off to the American League syndicate's activities. In respect to Lefty Davis, his career possibly might continue to flourish if he fell into good hands as he had when the tutelage of Clarke and Deacon Phillippe helped him develop into a top-notch outfielder. Davis was a good-natured Southerner who sang and danced his way through life without wasting much time doing serious thinking. Since he was always likely to act upon the first suggestion offered by a friend or companion, falling in with a bad crowd once he reached his next baseball destination guaranteed an abbreviated big league career.[18]

In light of this recent development, Harry Pulliam certainly did not include Davis and Tannehill in the category of National League stars as he offered an opinion regarding some recent news surrounding the American League's invasion of Pittsburgh.

"I think the American League may break into New York," said Pulliam, "but that is not what is worrying me. It is another matter, which will come out soon. Peace is not in sight, and there will be no peace in my estimation. I know one thing. It has been publicly broadcast that Johnson has stolen our stars, but I know that such is not the case. There will be less contracts broken this year than there were last. Johnson's aim now is to get into Pittsburgh along with New York. But this he cannot do. He has many obstacles to overcome before he can drop Detroit and invade the Smoky City."[19]

While this debate continued to rage in the Smoky City over whether the American League was invading Pittsburgh, the Pirates played the final two games of their exhibition tour before returning home to oppose Cincinnati. On Thursday, September 25, Pittsburgh defeated the Worcester Hustlers, 3–2. While Kitty Bransfield was disappointed since he was unable to play in his hometown, former Hustler Jimmy Sebring was in the lineup and received a stirring reception from the patrons. After the game, Worcester hurler Fred "Cy" Falkenberg was signed by Pulliam for the 1903 season, and George Merritt reported to the Pirates before they left to play their final exhibition game in North Adams, Massachusetts, on September 26.[20] Rain prevented this contest from being played as fans lamented the missed opportunity to watch hometown hero Jack Chesbro pitch for Pittsburgh. The North Adams native, who had been in town for a few days, rejoined his team when they left that evening for Pittsburgh.[21]

On the same day the exhibition game in North Adams was cancelled, Barney Dreyfuss made a surprising announcement given recent events involving the American League's numerous attempts at stealing his players. Dreyfuss revealed that arrangements for a post-season series between his champion

Pirates and a team of American League players had been completed. Rube Waddell, Cy Young, Harry Davis, Bill Bradley and Monte Cross were just a few of the players who would comprise this team of American League All-Stars. Cleveland Broncos star second baseman Nap Lajoie was also on the squad, but would not participate in any of the games played in Pittsburgh since he risked being arrested if he set foot in Pennsylvania. That state's courts had ruled against Lajoie breaking his contract with the Philadelphia Phillies prior to the 1901 campaign so he could jump to the American League.[22]

This series, which followed the best-of-seven format, was scheduled to be played in Pittsburgh, Cleveland, Detroit and Chicago from October 7 through October 13. Dreyfuss exhibited supreme generosity by allowing Pittsburgh's players to receive his portion of the gate receipts from this post-season series.[23] One small glitch in this plan involved the single game scheduled in Chicago. Cubs owner James Hart believed the contest should be held at West Side Grounds rather than the Chicago White Sox's home ballpark. While Dreyfuss had not made his intentions known in public, it was believed that he would not allow players still under contract to commit an injustice against Hart and the Cubs franchise by patronizing the American League grounds.[24] The initial roster of Pirates players selected to oppose this All-Star team included Tommy Leach, while pitchers Jesse Tannehill and Jack Chesbro were suspiciously absent.[25]

In Dreyfuss' eyes, playing a series against the best players the rival league had to offer was an opportunity to show the baseball world that the 1902 Pittsburgh Pirates were the greatest team in the game's history. He also wanted to prove the National League was far superior to Ban Johnson's upstart organization. One positive result of the recent American League raids against Dreyfuss' players was that this action had galvanized the city and club of Pittsburgh into becoming strongly partisan for the National League.[26] The reason for Leach's inclusion on the post-season roster became clearer when Dreyfuss announced that Leach had signed a 1903 contract. Tannehill's exclusion came as no surprise since his days with the Pirates were numbered. To punish him for deserting the Pittsburgh team, Dreyfuss ordered him to report to Exposition Park every day until October 15.[27]

Forcing Tannehill to report for duty each day prevented the southpaw hurler from taking part in the barnstorming exhibition games that were scheduled around the team's final regular season contests against Cincinnati. Tannehill also would be divested from the monetary proceeds that were shared by players who performed in these games.[28] During the barnstorming swing through New York, Canada and Massachusetts, Tannehill, his brother Lee and

11. Pittsburgh Breaks Record as Tommy Leach Fight Intensifies

Lefty Davis hung around Tannehill's Allegheny flat. Tannehill made numerous efforts to receive permission from Dreyfuss to join a barnstorming excursion in Cincinnati, but Pittsburgh's owner rejected the request. Dreyfuss figured he should not grant favors to a man who had proved himself to be a traitor and an ingrate.[29] Dreyfuss believed Jesse and Lee Tannehill would play for Charles Comiskey's Chicago White Sox team in 1903 but still did not know what Jack Chesbro's intentions were and didn't seem to care.[30]

Chesbro took the mound against Cincinnati on Saturday, September 27, as Pittsburgh finally played a game against National League competition after a five-day hiatus. The Pirates assaulted hurler Rube Vickers and gained an easy 13–6 victory as Chesbro raised his record to 27–6. The fourth, fifth and sixth stanzas were Vickers' undoing as the Pirates erased a 4–0 deficit by scoring all of their runs on 14 hits that went for a total of 19 bases during those three innings. Left fielder George Merritt made three safe drives, Chesbro two, Jimmy Burke two, and Ginger Beaumont rubbed it in by making two in one inning. It was a good thing the Pirates inflicted heavy damage since Chesbro did not pitch his usually solid baseball.[31] The Pirates connected for 19 hits as every player had at least two safeties except for Jimmy Sebring, who was credited with a lone single.

Deacon Phillippe, Sam Leever, Eddie Phelps and Chief Zimmer were the two batteries that went to Cincinnati with seven other Pirates on Saturday night to play a single game against the Reds on September 28. If rain prevented that contest from being played, it was decided that the game would be rescheduled as part of a doubleheader in Pittsburgh on Thursday. Pittsburgh's roster was a bit depleted heading into the final week of the 1902 season. Tommy Leach was still at home in Cleveland recuperating from a sore arm. Kitty Bransfield had practiced with his teammates on Saturday, but was not expected back in the lineup until the final series against Cincinnati began at Exposition Park on Thursday afternoon.[32]

Due to this shortage of players, acting manager Honus Wagner was forced to use two pitchers and two catchers out of position so he could put nine men in the field against the Reds. Wagner was prepared to fill vacancies at third base and left field, but it was not until the Pirates arrived in Cincinnati that he discovered a hand injury which Claude Ritchey had suffered in Saturday's contest would prevent him from playing. Wagner shifted to second base and catcher Eddie Phelps was placed at first. Pittsburgh's battered squad could not overcome Reds hurler Noodles Hahn's stellar performance as Cincinnati defeated the incapacitated Buccaneers, 3–2. A crowd of 8,500 turned out for the game in spite of unfavorable weather.[33] On a bright note for Pittsburgh,

Wagner became the first National League player to score 100 runs when he smacked a homer.[34]

Although the home team won, many fans were upset with umpire Hank O'Day because he called the Reds' Mike Donlin out on a close play at first base in the seventh inning. When the game concluded, an angry mob surrounded O'Day, who had to be escorted to the dressing room by policemen. Some people who did not storm the field threw cushions at the umpire. After police finally cleared the field, irate rooters stood outside the ballpark and waited for O'Day. They perpetrated another attack against O'Day, who was saved by police once again and whisked to safety.[35] With their season away from Exposition Park now concluded, the Pittsburgh Pirates had posted a sterling record of 47–21 on the road in 1902.

Kitty Bransfield, Claude Ritchey, Fred Clarke, Tommy Leach and Eddie Doheny were all expected to be available for the Pirates' final series at home against Cincinnati that started on October 2.[36] During this little break before the season's final series, the Pirates' barnstorming tour continued with two games in the Pennsylvania towns of Charleroi and Rochester.[37] Pieces of interesting baseball news were chronicled during this interruption in Pittsburgh's National League schedule. Pirates management announced that hurler Kaiser Wilhelm of the Southern Association's Birmingham Barons had signed a contract to play for Pittsburgh in 1903.[38] It was also reported from New York that former Giants owner Andrew Freedman's retirement from baseball was now official as John T. Brush finalized the deal to purchase his club on September 29. Brush planned to gain total control of the franchise by making an offer to Boston Beaneaters magnate Arthur Soden to purchase the small block of stock he still owned in the New York team.[39]

Another story with indirect connection to the city of New York was released on September 30 under a Cincinnati dateline. Jack Chesbro had revised his salary demands in an effort to remain with Pittsburgh. It looked as if Chesbro probably would still have to shave a few dollars from this recent estimate of his worth or Pirates management would allow the pitcher to fly into the American League's arms. "We will pay liberally to retain him," explained Harry Pulliam, "but if he wants $7,500 he'll have to guess again."[40]

Pulliam also claimed that if every player lived up to the contract he had signed a year ago, Pittsburgh would not lose a single man to the American League. He substantiated this bold proclamation by explaining that Chesbro and Jesse Tannehill were under contract to play for the Pirates in 1903. Both players had signed a binding document in the summer of 1901 where, in exchange for an extra financial inducement, they agreed to give Pittsburgh a team option on their services for the 1903 campaign. Such a document was considered more binding than Nap Lajoie's Philadelphia Phillies contract that was declared legal by the Pennsylvania Supreme Court. Every Pirates player had signed the same type of contract and did so voluntarily, naming the amount of salary they wanted for the 1902 season.[41]

If Pittsburgh management released any of these men, as was the case with Jack O'Connor and Lefty Davis, they could keep the bonus drafts handed out by the American League and move on with a clear conscience. Those players who were not handed their releases and had given their word to management were legally bound to play for Pittsburgh until the 1903 season concluded.[42] While local baseball fans dissected this latest information, the Pirates played their final tune-up game before the season-concluding series with Cincinnati. On October 1, Pittsburgh and the Beaver Valley's Rochester squad played to a 3–3 standstill that was called on account of darkness after 11 innings. Harvey Cushman struck out 11 Rochester batters as Honus Wagner once again fielded a patchwork unit. Claude Ritchey was on his honeymoon, Fred Clarke remained out of town, and Wid Conroy, Tommy Leach and Kitty Bransfield were unfit for work.[43]

When the Pirates took the field against Cincinnati on October 2, Conroy and Bransfield remained on the sidelines, while Ritchey, Clarke and Leach manned their positions against the Reds. Pittsburgh's expectation of setting a new league mark for victories received a sobering jolt as Cincinnati claimed this contest, 6–4. Bill Phillips would have tossed a shutout if not for two errors by third baseman Harry Steinfeldt that figured in all four Pirates runs. Sam Leever struggled on the mound all afternoon serving up six runs and 15 hits. While Leever was a great pitcher, it seemed he had recently started working too methodically for his own good. Quickening the pace seemed like a good strategy for Leever moving forward.[44]

Cincinnati was without the services of star outfielder Cy Seymour and pitcher Henry Thielman, who had become involved in a fist fight during an exhibition game in Indianapolis on Tuesday afternoon. Seymour was unable to play due to injuring his hand during the scrap. When the Reds arrived in Pittsburgh on Thursday morning, Theilman was not with the squad. Team management speculated that he had left the train when it made a stop in Columbus, Ohio, during the night.[45] The Pirates certainly were not going to show Cincinnati any sympathy since they had been dealing with injuries and other issues for weeks. Playing a weakened squad was also beneficial for Pittsburgh since the margin for error was now nil in their quest to establish a new league record for victories.

Throughout the 1902 campaign, Fred Clarke's troops did their best work when the stakes were high and the team's supremacy was challenged. Realizing that the prospects of rain ruining Saturday's season finale were great, Pittsburgh's players made a conscientious effort to secure the game against Cincinnati on Friday, October 3. Pittsburgh claimed its 102nd victory of the season with a 5–1 triumph over the Reds, tying the National League record. Jack Chesbro walked into the winner's circle for the Pirates once again as he tossed a complete game and raised his record to 28–6. Chesbro's teammates bailed out the star hurler throughout the afternoon as he allowed 13 hits, gave up three walks and hit a Cincinnati batter.[46]

Honus Wagner did more than any other Pirate to beat the Reds. Kitty Bransfield returned to the lineup at first base, so Wagner shifted back to shortstop and put on a phenomenal fielding display. He handled everything that was hit his way and also traversed into the outfield on three occasions to snatch chances that should have gone for base hits. In the third inning, he threw Jake Beckley out from deep short, and a moment later turned the trick again when he fielded Sam Crawford's ground ball near the keystone sack and threw a perfect strike to first base. For good measure in the sixth frame, Wagner sprinted out to left field and speared Rube Vickers' fly ball. Fred Clarke, who nearly broke his neck trying to reach the baseball, pulled up laughing. Second baseman Claude Ritchey was also sensational in the field as his new bride beamed with pride while she watched her husband from the grandstand.[47]

The urgency Pittsburgh's players exhibited during this game was vital given their perceptive nature in accurately assessing the weather conditions for the season's final game at Exposition Park on Saturday, October 4. The baseball diamond was muddy due to weather so raw that many local colleges actually cancelled their football battles scheduled for that afternoon.[48] Despite the horrible conditions, Barney Dreyfuss was determined to play the game so his team could attempt to establish a new league mark for victories. When Cincinnati's Joe Kelley and Jake Beckley called at the local club's office around noon, they were told the game would be played if rain ceased long enough so the groundskeeper could get the field in shape. The pitcher's rubber and home plate were covered by a heavy canvas. The Cincinnati representatives were informed that it would take one hour to get the well-drained field in shape after the rainstorm passed.[49]

Kelley received word at 1:30 p.m. that the game would be played. Cincinnati's players were not happy over the prospect of playing a game on a cold, rainy day when they could instead be placing a few bets at the local racetrack. Following a meeting involving Cincinnati's players at the Monongahela House

11. Pittsburgh Breaks Record as Tommy Leach Fight Intensifies 221

where the team was staying, manager Kelley stated that his men were determined to defeat the Pirates and spoil their precious record. Unfortunately, some indecision entered into the equation when it came time to leave for the ballpark. Pirates management feared that the Reds intended to forfeit the contest, but a minute or so after 3 p.m. the bus containing Kelley's team arrived at Exposition Park. It took another 15 minutes before the Cincinnati squad could be induced to send a man to the plate.[50]

While the Pirates had taken their turn with batting and fielding practice, members of the Reds declined to go through with the formality. Some, including Kelley and Cy Seymour, used this time to sit in the dugout smoking cigarettes. After a tedious delay, Kelley was forced to name his battery. Fred Clarke protested when Cincinnati's skipper said that first baseman Jake Beckley would pitch, with young hurler Rube Vickers manning the backstop position for the Reds. "Be game and play it out," said Clarke, but Kelley only chuckled and refused to attempt an honest fight to win the game.[51]

Once this game started, the farcical quality it possessed did not sit well with the paying public. Barney Dreyfuss was so indignant with the attitude of Kelley and his players that he had employees go through the stands to tell patrons that their money would be refunded at the box office when the game concluded. Hank O'Day had his hands full right at the outset of this contest and was forced to restore order in the first inning. He used his power to reestablish stability when Kelley walked to the plate to take his turn at bat smoking a cigarette. Kelley initially refused to comply with O'Day's order to stop smoking, but when threatened with ejection from the contest, he complied. While the Pirates scored eight runs against Beckley before Kelley brought in Cy Seymour to relieve him in the fourth, the abysmal performance of Rube Vickers behind home plate took center stage. Through the first four innings, Vickers committed six passed balls.[52]

This game was never in question as Pittsburgh banged out 14 hits and claimed an 11–2 victory. Deacon Phillippe tossed a complete game and improved his record to 20–9 on the last day of the 1902 season. Kitty Bransfield went 3-for-5, while Ginger Beaumont, Fred Clarke, Jimmy Sebring, Chief Zimmer and Phillippe contributed two hits apiece. Despite this travesty executed by Joe Kelley and his Cincinnati players, Pittsburgh's accomplishment could not be diminished. They now held the record for most wins during a single season with 103. After the record-setting game ended, 600 spectators took Barney Dreyfuss at his word and lined up at the box office to receive money they had spent in anticipation of witnessing an actual baseball game. When Reds business manager Frank Bancroft asked for his share of the gate receipts, Dreyfuss pointed to an empty cash drawer. "We are not going to take money from our friends under false pretenses," said an agitated Dreyfuss to Bancroft.[53]

Some Smoky City baseball writers believed Kelley and a host of other Cincinnati players should be censured by the league for such contemptible conduct. While the National League executive committee could not punish these players since the season had officially concluded, it was hoped they would be publicly reprimanded for their behavior to prevent such unpleasant displays in the future.[54] As these scribes clamored for the game's integrity to be upheld by league executives, St. Louis writer Harold Lanigan offered some final thoughts about the 1902 National League campaign. He also shared his opinion on lost revenues as it was reported that Pittsburgh, New York, Chicago and St. Louis made money in 1902, while the Brooklyn, Cincinnati, Philadelphia and Boston franchises showed deficits.[55]

> No better proof of the honesty of baseball, nor the greatness of the National League magnates, who have suffered more than words can tell in late years, was ever evidenced than by the one-sided race that was run in the parent body. Pittsburgh, within six weeks after the campaign was started, had a lead of some 200 points. That meant the bunting in a walk.
>
> The Pirates were so good that they killed the race. Pittsburgh, by being in front, not being weakened, and trying all the time, cost the other seven National League clubs, say $250,000. That money would have been made, not lost as it was, had the race been anything more than a procession. St. Louis, and, perhaps, other cities, which have had two clubs, were just as willing to continue the National League article as they were the brand offered by the American League.
>
> Thus had the parent body had anything like the exciting race that was in vogue in the American League, it would have attracted just as many people as ever before. But the Pittsburgh team was kept intact; the Pirates had the rest of the field shut out before the quarter way mark was reached, and I figure it cost the National League a quarter of a million dollars. Surely, baseball is honest and certainly the National League club owners are game.[56]

Lanigan's premise regarding lost revenue due to Pittsburgh running away with the National League pennant certainly was valid. The Pirates finished the 1902 season with a record of 103–36, while their nearest competitor, the Brooklyn Superbas, were 27½ games behind with a mark of 75–63. What Lanigan failed to take into account when reaching his conclusion was Pittsburgh's monetary impact from games in which they had participated. The 1902 National League champions played in front of 602,613 people in games at home and abroad. That total was pushed up to 649,120 due to attendance of 46,507 at exhibition contests.[57]

Ardent baseball fans who had watched the 1902 Pirates play at Exposition

Park or road ballparks in other cities were fortunate to witness some of the best players from that era. Center fielder Clarence "Ginger" Beaumont, who excelled at placing bunts or smacking line drives to the outfield, was the National League's batting champion with a .357 average. Beaumont was supported quite nicely by Honus Wagner (.330), Fred Clarke (.316) and Kitty Bransfield (.305), who made up the remainder of Pittsburgh's .300 hitters brigade. Wagner also paced the National League in runs scored (105), doubles (30), RBI (91) and stolen bases (42). Tommy Leach took league honors for triples (22) and home runs (6). Beaumont (100) and Clarke (103) also joined Wagner in the century club for runs scored.

While phenomenal hitting was a key ingredient in Pittsburgh's tasty pennant recipe, solid pitching was the team's bread and butter during this momentous season. Jack Chesbro was the National League's top hurler as he went 28–6, buttressed by a 2.17 ERA. Chesbro also led the circuit with eight shutouts. Four other Pirates hurlers topped 15 victories as Deacon Phillippe (20–9, 2.05 ERA), Jesse Tannehill (20–6, 1.95 ERA), Eddie Doheny (16–4, 2.53 ERA) and Sam Leever (15–7, 2.39 ERA) rounded out one of the best pitching staffs in baseball history. Although this was the fourth time Tannehill had won 20 or more games in a Pirates uniform, his time in Pittsburgh came to an end. When the season ended, he was handed his unconditional release, paid in full through October 15, and told to remove his baggage from Exposition Park.[58]

By giving Tannehill his outright release, Pirates management was sending the message that they did not plan on resorting to legal proceedings to hold disloyal men to binding contracts. Due to his discharge, Tannehill was also not permitted to take part in the series against the American League All-Stars or the Pirates' annual field event competition. It was reported that Tannehill told a friend he had been the real agent of the American League while O'Connor had assisted in the devious plan as his helper. Since Tannehill's abrasive attitude did not always sit well with teammates, choosing him to spearhead the American League's gambit was an odd selection because he was not likely to carry much influence with fellow players. He was part of a clique of players that had attempted to drive Ginger Beaumont from the team when he debuted in 1899. Tannehill, Tom McCreery and Fred Ely were chums who ridiculed Beaumont and considered him to be the funniest thing to ever put on a baseball uniform.[59]

Following the announcement of Tannehill's release, Barney Dreyfuss also gave out the list of players who had signed to play for Pittsburgh in 1903. Deacon Phillippe, Sam Leever, Eddie Doheny, George Merritt, Kaiser Wilhelm, Warren McLaughlin, Cy Falkenberg, Chief Zimmer, Harry Smith, Eddie

Phelps, Kitty Bransfield, Claude Ritchey, Wid Conroy, Tommy Leach, Jimmy Burke, Fred Clarke, Ginger Beaumont, Jimmy Sebring and Honus Wagner had signed contracts and were now off-limits to American League emissaries.[60] Legal, binding documents such as these did not seem to inhibit Ban Johnson's underlings from still making overtures. Detroit Tigers owner Samuel Angus announced that he was dickering to secure the services of National League batting champion Ginger Beaumont.[61] When Beaumont received a telegram from Detroit pitcher Win Mercer urging him to desert Pittsburgh, the Pirates outfielder immediately hunted up Dreyfuss.[62]

"What do you intend to do about it?" asked Dreyfuss after Beaumont informed the owner that Detroit wanted him to jump leagues.

"I am going to stay in Pittsburgh," he replied without any hesitation.[63]

Such a bold attitude at this time by the American League was a bit perplexing considering that the series between their best players and the Pittsburgh Pirates started on Tuesday, October 7, at Exposition Park. Despite this latest attempt by Johnson's operatives to steal players from Barney Dreyfuss' squad, Pittsburgh's owner and his players had no intention of cancelling this series. The Boston Americans' Cy Young faced Sam Leever in the first contest as science trumped brute strength. The National League champions' inside game was too much for the muscle of their opponents. Pittsburgh's fundamentally sound play on defense helped give Fred Clarke's squad a 4–3 victory over the All-Americans. The Pirates clinched the contest in the third frame when they padded a 2–0 lead by putting up two more markers on Ginger Beaumont's triple, Fred Clarke's double, a passed ball and Honus Wagner's run-scoring ground out to first baseman Harry Davis.[64] A heavy rain shower settled in at Exposition Park after the third inning. To insure that an official game was completed, Pittsburgh discarded their mixed batting style and tried to hit the ball out of the lot. This approach and the dark skies worked wonders for Young, who had the Pirates at his mercy throughout the remainder of the game.[65]

Determined to show their superiority against competition from a league that had conspired to steal some of the team's best players, Pittsburgh took a 2–0 lead in this series against the All-Americans on Wednesday, October 8. Deacon Phillippe was brilliant as he tossed a three-hitter and claimed a 2–0 victory. Cleveland hurler Addie Joss matched Phillippe for four innings until the Pirates scored their first run.[66] Honus Wagner reached first base in the fifth frame on second baseman George "Scoops" Carey's error. Wagner moved to second base as Kitty Bransfield was retired and came home when Claude Ritchey lined a single that caromed off the shins of shortstop Monte Cross. Wagner also had a hand in Pittsburgh's second run in the eighth inning when

11. Pittsburgh Breaks Record as Tommy Leach Fight Intensifies

his double drove Fred Clarke home with an insurance marker.[67] Phillippe's performance was remarkable considering he originally was not slated to start this game. That honor was expected to fall upon Jack Chesbro, who was permitted to represent the Pirates in this series. When game time approached, Chesbro claimed he could not take the mound since he was sick. This excuse did not seem valid since he looked in the best of health before and after the game. It may be that Chesbro's fellow Pirates reasoned that the star pitcher shirked his responsibility because he was afraid of American League rules such as the no-foul-strike rule.[68]

The true story surrounding Jack Chesbro's last days as a member of the Pittsburgh Pirates came to light on October 9. It was reported that the champions had held a meeting prior to their game the previous afternoon where it was decided that Chesbro should be asked to pitch the game. He promised to do so, but when game time came, he failed to appear in uniform. On Thursday morning, his teammates held a second meeting and voted unanimously to count him out of a share of the monetary proceeds from this series.[69] Since Barney Dreyfuss allowed his players to have total control over this matchup against the All-Americans, they were permitted to divide the money to suit their own pleasure.[70]

Following weeks of uncertainty regarding where he would be playing in 1903, Jack Chesbro finally made a decision on October 9, 1902. Angry over being cut out of the monetary proceeds from a post-season series against a squad of American League All-Stars, Chesbro left Pittsburgh and finally decided to jump leagues and join the New York Highlanders. Pittsburgh's players unanimously voted to give Chesbro no share of the money since he had refused to pitch a game against the All-Americans on October 8. In this photograph, Chesbro is wearing the spangles of the American League's New York Highlanders (courtesy of the National Baseball Hall of Fame Library, Cooperstown, New York).

This action by his teammates was the last straw in Chesbro's eyes. During a recent negotiating conference, Dreyfuss had laughed at Chesbro in the team's crowded office at the Smith Building when the pitcher reiterated his desire to be paid $7,500 a year to remain in Pittsburgh. Chesbro perceived this outburst of mirth on Dreyfuss' part as an insinuation that he was not telling the truth regarding $7,500 being the amount Ban Johnson had offered to jump leagues. Chesbro became indignant and the discussion morphed into a heated argument before Harry Pulliam was called in to restore peace. While Pulliam was successful calming things down, Dreyfuss later wished Chesbro "good luck" and "good bye."[71]

On the evening of Thursday, October 9, Jack Chesbro left Pittsburgh and went west to play for Joe Cantillon's All-Nationals baseball team that was barnstorming across the country. After his teammates had cut him out of the monetary spoils from the series against the American League All-Stars, he appealed this decision before Pittsburgh's club directors. Dreyfuss told Chesbro that management had no right to interfere in this affair, but did inform him that they backed the players' action. Chesbro immediately announced that he was quitting the National League in general and the Pittsburgh Pirates in particular.[72] Dreyfuss was so infuriated with Chesbro's attitude that he declared Chesbro would never again play on any team owned or controlled by him.[73] On the same day that Chesbro declared his status as an ex–Pirate, Fred Clarke's troops played a previously postponed game in the Monongahela Valley town of Charleroi. Pittsburgh won the game, 8–2, while Charleroi captured a special trap shooting contest, 90–62.[74]

As the Pirates prepared to play the third leg of their series against the American League All-Stars, a report out of Cincinnati claimed that Jesse Tannehill might pull the disloyalty stunt once again by deserting the American League. Even though he confessed he had signed a contract to play for that league's New York entry in 1903, the pitcher felt he could be induced to play for the National League's Cincinnati Reds if the terms were satisfactory. Such a move likely would lead Pittsburgh management to become re-engaged in this battle for his rights with Cincinnati and the American League.[75] While Tannehill was busy proving how much of an ignorant despot he truly could be, his former teammates clinched their big series against the best players Ban Johnson's American League had to offer. Since it had been decided a week earlier that this series would last four games rather than seven as originally planned, the official 0–0 tie in Cleveland on Friday, October 10, guaranteed a Pittsburgh triumph.[76]

Pittsburgh's Sam Leever and the All-Americans' Bill Bernhard dazzled on the mound as each pitcher scattered four hits before the game was called on account of darkness after the 11th inning. Even the heralded debut of the Cleveland Broncos' Nap Lajoie could not swing the game in his team's favor.

11. Pittsburgh Breaks Record as Tommy Leach Fight Intensifies

Lajoie went 0-for-4 and failed in the clutch when a ninth-inning single would have won the game for the All-Americans. The best he could do was to hit a harmless ground ball to shortstop Honus Wagner.[77] Stellar twirling was the main theme once again during the final contest of this series on Saturday, October 11, in Cleveland as Deacon Phillippe and Cy Young locked up in a monumental pitchers' duel.

The All-Americans claimed a 1–0 victory as they scored the game's only run in the seventh inning. The All-Americans avoided being swept in this series when Lajoie reached first base when third baseman Tommy Leach booted his grass cutter, moved to third on Bobby Wallace's single and an error by right fielder Jimmy Sebring, and scored when Dick Harley smacked a base hit.[78] Although the American League gained a modicum of retribution by claiming this game, the Pittsburgh Pirates were undisputed champions of baseball by virtue of winning two out of the three completed games in this series.

While Barney Dreyfuss, Fred Clarke and Pittsburgh's players basked in the glory of being crowned baseball's greatest team, information was unearthed which indicated that everything was not rosy during the team's trip to Cleveland. American League vice president Charley Somers placed himself in a bad light by tampering with Pittsburgh's Tommy Leach and Harry Smith. Although Somers imagined he had been very secretive, Pirates management was aware of his movements at all times.[79]

Following this latest attempt by the American League to destroy the harmonious atmosphere on Pittsburgh's squad, Barney Dreyfuss issued a statement regarding how things currently stood regarding three players who had listened to the rival organization's sales pitch.

> I have known for many weeks that Leach, Smith, Conroy, Tannehill, Chesbro and O'Connor each accepted a draft of $1,000 from the American League. Some of these players were deceived by the syndicate agent and when they came to their senses decided that they could not afford to sell their reputation, so they returned the drafts uncashed. I saw the drafts given to Leach, Conroy and Smith. These were returned to Somers. Some of the drafts were on the Hanover Bank of New York and others upon a Cleveland bank. Somers knows that our players are all under contract. He should have known it when he came here in the summer, and he has no excuse for not knowing it now.[80]

Now that the grind of a long baseball season was finally over, the Pittsburgh Pirates embarked upon the final leg of their barnstorming trip that had also served as a victory tour for the champions. Baseball fans from the small Pennsylvania localities of Sharon and Manor received a rare opportunity to watch the greatest team in the sport's history perform on a diamond. Since Fred Clarke left the team immediately after the All-Americans series and returned to his farm in Winfield, Kansas, catcher Chief Zimmer was Pittsburgh's manager during these final contests.[81] The barnstorming tour was a rousing success from a financial standpoint as each player pocketed over $400 playing these fall exhibition games.[82]

As the loyal players from Barney Dreyfuss' squad finally had a chance to relax and reflect on their great baseball achievement, the final chapter of Jack Chesbro's and Jesse Tannehill's Pittsburgh careers was written. While the two pitchers toured across America with Joe Cantillon's All-Nationals team, Tannehill claimed that he and Barney Dreyfuss had never gotten along during their time together.[83] Baseball correspondents from Cincinnati were also holding Dreyfuss accountable for the failure of Reds management to land Tannehill for their team. Writers such as J. Ed Grillo believed Dreyfuss was interfering with a deal because he refused to waive claim to Tannehill. This account was false since Dreyfuss had offered only friendly advice to Cincinnati president Garry Herrmann and was not impeding a deal in any way. Dreyfuss had told Herrmann that it would be useless to open negotiations with a dishonorable man like Tannehill.[84]

This debate abruptly ended when Tannehill informed Herrmann that he had signed a contract to play with the American League's New York squad in 1903.[85] In spite of Pittsburgh's two star hurlers exhibiting vitriolic behavior for months, Fred Clarke traveled to Chicago so he could hold a conference with Jack Chesbro. Clarke claimed that he had hunted for Chesbro in a Chicago hotel and found him and Tannehill in a local saloon.[86] In a letter that appeared in a newspaper that was sympathetic to the American League's cause, Tannehill declared it was Clarke who was enjoying a cold, frothy beverage in this tavern. Tannehill also took a swipe at Dreyfuss when he alleged that the Pirates owner sat in the bleachers with field glasses and signaled signs by waving a newspaper during a game against the Philadelphia Phillies in 1901.[87]

Chesbro's claim that Clarke had promised to meet him at a Chicago hotel, but was afraid to face the tourist's party and did not keep the appointment, received a stiff rebuttal from Pittsburgh's manager.[88] "That is a lie," said Clarke. "I called three times at the hotel and each time was told that Chesbro was out. Then I went to a saloon kept by Joe Cantillon, the man who is managing the baseball excursion to the coast, and there I found the two Pittsburgh players. Tannehill and Chesbro failed to mention this fact."[89]

Chesbro was also irked over not receiving a check for the final installment of his 1902 salary. There was no malicious intent on the part of Dreyfuss in respect to Chesbro's delay in getting paid money that was rightfully his. The check was mailed to Chesbro in Kansas City, but for some reason it was forwarded to Topeka, Kansas. Postal authorities in Topeka returned the letter to Dreyfuss back in Pittsburgh. He re-mailed the check to Chesbro so it would reach Los Angeles while Cantillon's touring baseball team was in that city.[90] Chesbro also planned on suing the Pirates organization for $300 that was allegedly due him for his share of gate receipts from exhibition games played by Pittsburgh during their barnstorming tour. He claimed Clarke was unjustly withholding this money from him.[91] Chesbro's financial situation took another major hit when his $8,000 salary for playing in the American League for the 1903 campaign was decreased to $5,000 since he mistook $3,000 advance money handed him for a bonus.[92]

While it was certainly possible that Chesbro had misinterpreted the terms of his deal with Ban Johnson, the likely scenario that deceitful methods had been used by the league president to manipulate him and other Pirates seemed more feasible. The initial promise by Johnson to the conspirators that they would play for an American League team in Pittsburgh was an absolute lark. Under the guidelines of the Pennsylvania Supreme Court's ruling regarding Nap Lajoie's Philadelphia Phillies contract, any players who jumped their contracts to play for an American League team in Pittsburgh would have been arrested once they set foot on the home grounds.

Deception on the American League syndicate's part was one of the major reasons why Tommy Leach, Harry Smith and Wid Conroy had decided to remain with the Pirates.[93] Leach sent a letter to Pirates management that reiterated his intention to play for Pittsburgh in 1903. Harry Pulliam affirmed that Leach's letter corroborated the team secretary's previous contention that Pittsburgh would not lose these men claimed by Ban Johnson. "Don't pay any attention to anything you may read in the newspapers or to any gossip you may hear to the effect that I am going to the American League," wrote Leach. "I will be with you and no one else next season."[94]

Barney Dreyfuss echoed the sentiment of his star third baseman when he issued this statement during a late October trip to New York:

> I have 22 players under contract and my salary list will be $82,000. I don't expect to lose one of the men now under contract, except by mutual agreement. As to the National League players Ban Johnson claims to have under contract, I have no opinion to express except that in the language of the turf I know something and it will be found that Mr. Johnson is either deceiving himself or is being deceived by others.
>
> Harry Smith, Leach and Conroy will positively be found wearing the uniform of the Pittsburgh National League team next season. Ban Johnson is not worrying us nor is he causing the National League the anxiety he thinks he is. The old

organization will explode a bomb in the American League camp before long which will rock that body from stern to stern.[95]

Dreyfuss failed to elaborate on what the old organization had up its sleeve or why he was in New York. He also rejected a story out of Cincinnati which claimed he was planning on selling the Pittsburgh baseball franchise and buying a racing stable.[96] American League president Ban Johnson certainly did not intend on allowing Dreyfuss to have the final word regarding which players legally belonged to his organization and which did not. Unconcerned over Smith's and Conroy's reversals over joining the American League, Johnson focused all of his energy and outrage on Leach for claiming he planned on remaining with the Pirates. Johnson accused Leach of having been the go-between in the American League's dealings with Tannehill, Conroy, Smith, Chesbro and others.[97] Such an allegation defied logic since Leach was a young player without much major league service who did not fit the profile of a man who was leading a desertion movement. Pittsburgh's veterans certainly were not likely to be influenced by a player who was their junior.

Johnson's accusation did not make sense in the eyes of Smoky City baseball fans who believed Dreyfuss had made no mistake in identifying the true traitor. Jack O'Connor's political savvy made him the perfect foil for the American League's purposes just as veteran Fred "Bones" Ely had filled that role one year earlier. Johnson also claimed that Leach, Smith and Conroy had not returned the bonus money they received two months earlier, as was asserted by the three players. In respect to Leach, Barney Dreyfuss easily disputed Johnson's assertion since he could prove Leach sent a letter and the bank draft to Charley Somers in Cleveland. Dreyfuss had a post office receipt for when the correspondence was mailed in Pittsburgh and had received a receipt stipulating the letter was delivered to Somers. Dreyfuss also weighed in regarding the ridiculous yarn that Leach had been the ringleader of this conspiracy.[98]

> I have known for weeks, in fact, ever since Leach decided that he would not jump his contract, that the American League was going to try to make him unpopular with the Pittsburgh rooters, simply for revenge. He was the man that the trust wanted and now that it knows that he can't be bribed, it is trying to make trouble for him.
>
> Tannehill first circulated the story that Leach was the syndicate's agent. Leach came at the time of the charge and asked me to investigate it thoroughly because it was not true. I knew every move that had been made and that Leach was not guilty, so I sent him away happy by assuring him that an investigation was not necessary.
>
> Here are a few facts. On the day that Somers and Johnson sneaked into Pittsburgh, who was it that slipped up to the station to meet them—Leach or

O'Connor? Why it was O'Connor, the man who, according to Johnson, collected $800 from the American last season when he was employed to work for the Pittsburgh National League team. It was also O'Connor, who took Johnson and Somers to the Lincoln Hotel and then went to Allegheny, got Tommie Leach and guided him to the same place. Who was it, after learning that Harry Pulliam had discovered the whole plot, telephoned from a booth on the office floor of the hotel, to Johnson's room to call the meeting off for the time? O'Connor. It was also O'Connor, who waited until Johnson came downstairs and then took him in a cab to Jesse Tannehill's room in Allegheny.

Somers rode over in a Millvale car. It was also O'Connor who took the other players to Tannehill's room. We know other details about the conspiracy that convince us that we did not make any mistake in blaming O'Connor and Tannehill, but I have mentioned enough to prove that Johnson has trumped up the latest charge against Leach to punish Tommy for being too honest to jump his Pittsburgh contract.[99]

Besides making such specious allegations against Leach, Ban Johnson did not plan on letting the third baseman get away without a fight. According to Johnson, Leach would play baseball with the New York American League team or not at all in 1903.

When we came to sign the Pittsburgh players last August, I found that all business must be done through Leach. He was spokesman for the crowd. So I sent for Leach, and it was through him that all my negotiations were conducted. He got the other players together and brought them to me to sign contracts. Moreover, it was through Leach that we paid them their advance money, later. The contract which Leach signed with us is ironclad and calls for his salary whether he is able to play or not. There is no way to get around it, and he must play for us. That's all.[100]

Battle lines were drawn as each side seemed to be fervidly committed to using the Tommy Leach situation as an opportunity to make a final stand in this war between the two leagues that had been raging for years. Angered over the American League's recent success at stealing players from Pittsburgh, loyal Pirates patrons had become war-weary. Some people believed the time had arrived for men of conviction and courage to step forward and broker peace between the warring factions. Barney Dreyfuss realized that two leagues existing in harmony was the best solution to insure that baseball had a long, healthy life. Understanding that such an undertaking also served his self-interests regarding the continued prosperity of the Pittsburgh Pirates franchise, Dreyfuss put forth the man who could tackle these problems and usher in a new baseball era.

12

Pirates Win Third Consecutive Pennant Despite Loss of Stars

American League president Ban Johnson clearly believed he was justified in forcing star third baseman Tommy Leach to play for a team in his organization during the 1903 campaign. Johnson reasoned that he was backed by the law on this issue since Leach had accepted bonus money and signed a contract to play for a New York squad in the American League. From the opposing side of the aisle, Barney Dreyfuss maintained that Leach never agreed to such conditions and was not permitted to do so by law since he was already under contract to play for Pittsburgh in 1903. As this contract issue was heartily debated in the press, baseball writer and sports editor John B. Foster of the *New York Evening Telegraph* recalled comments Dreyfuss had made the previous spring. It seemed that Dreyfuss had anticipated such chicanery by the American League many months earlier when he talked about his players' contracts during a discussion with Foster in New York.

"They are not signed to one-year contracts either," said Dreyfuss. "Every man has signed with the Pittsburgh Club for two years, and the ten-day clause has been stricken out of all the contracts that I have made out for my men. I told them exactly what they might expect and that I would gladly meet the salaries that they would be offered for the next year by any rival club. They said they were perfectly satisfied and there was not a man who did not name his own terms before he was signed."[1]

While Dreyfuss was extremely confident that he would prevail in retaining Tommy Leach, another problem still existed in respect to the American League's desire to place a competing team in Pittsburgh. American League executives announced in early December that grounds would be broken for a new ballpark in Pittsburgh within 30 days.[2] The land in question was on the

12. Pirates Win Third Pennant Despite Loss of Stars

summit of Soho Hill, located on the western edge of the Oakland residential district. The plot, which contained eight acres, was certainly big enough to build a serviceable ballpark for the American League. This real estate was rather expensive, even though homes in that area were so close to the mills of Second Avenue and the South Side that they were constantly smothered with smoke and soot from industrial establishments like the Jones & Laughlin furnace which had grown so rapidly during the past five years. Owners of the property hoped to receive $300,000 for the land.[3]

Former Pittsburgh Pirates owner William Kerr was part of this consortium wishing to promote the idea that a Smoky City team could prosper in the American League. When word reached Barney Dreyfuss that businessmen affiliated with this venture were close to purchasing property to build a ballpark, he pulled a map of the city out of his desk and immediately found the location. This piece of property was about 800 feet farther away from the streetcar line than the beautiful Clarke plot which the American League syndicate coveted. Attempts to grab control of the Clarke property had been thwarted since the land likely would not be leased for amusement purposes with a hospital to be built at that location in the near future. Dreyfuss had exhibited great foresight purchasing and renting out vacant lots in Pittsburgh and Allegheny to prevent the rival organization from getting their hands on prime real estate.[4]

In spite of this latest setback, Dreyfuss remained unfazed over any potential competition from an American League franchise in Pittsburgh.

"I was given to understand yesterday," said Dreyfuss, "that S. F. Angus had practically agreed to let go of his Detroit holding for $36,000. Colonel W. W. Kerr and Phil Auten are believed to be the men who want to back the American Club in Pittsburgh. While I am not exactly willing to get out and escort the Americans into town, the gate is open, and I wouldn't lift a finger to stop them. I know if they do come in there'll be a funeral later on and we'll be the pallbearers.

"They couldn't break in at a more opportune moment for a fight. We have the money, the players and the sentiment of lovers of fair play. It is not a possible feat for Ban Johnson to shuffle up eight winners, and these clubs raided to strengthen Pittsburgh will be surely weakened. They've got one hard proposition in framing up a winner for New York, and the contract of putting two first division teams in the field will be a hard one to fill."[5]

When pressed to discuss the situation regarding an American League team competing in Pittsburgh during the 1903 season, Ban Johnson claimed the chance of making such a move was very small. Although Johnson did not rule out the possibility of invading the Smoky City at some future date, he refuted the report that a Pittsburgh syndicate had purchased the American League's Detroit franchise. Johnson also declared that a deal to secure grounds in Gotham had practically been finalized so an American League team could be placed in New York for the 1903 campiagn.[6]

"We are going into New York next season, without a doubt," said Johnson in a statement released from Chicago. "We are not ready to give out the location of our grounds there, because that would be of no advantage to us. We have never been in the habit of disclosing our locations in other cities, and it will not be wise for us to do so in this case. Whenever we have given out that we intended going to a town we have always made good the announcement, and we will do so this time. The American League has not laid out $20,000 for ground leases and advance salaries for nothing.

"There is no truth in the story that we are going into Pittsburgh instead of New York, as some of the papers have hinted. When the season opens next spring you will find us in New York. The list of players I have given out is correct, and every man who is on that list has signed an air-tight contract, with the ten-day clause cut out. If they can get out of that, baseball contracts are not much good."[7]

One of these players on the roster of the American League's New York team was former Pirates catcher Jack O'Connor. In Pittsburgh, his actions in the whole mess regarding Johnson and Charley Somers were viewed as being treasonous by those who supported Barney Dreyfuss and his baseball team. O'Connor did not agree with this character assessment as he believed a player had the right to shop his services to other teams, just as ownership was justified in dropping a player if a better man was found to fill that job. In November, O'Connor conducted a bizarre interview for an attentive baseball writer in his hometown of St. Louis.

During this long diatribe, O'Connor claimed he knew detectives had been tailing his activities three months earlier. He stated that he bribed one of the gumshoes by buying him drinks at a local tavern. In return, the investigator ditched his partner and pretended to keep an eye on O'Connor for Dreyfuss' benefit.[8] O'Connor also issued a mocking narrative of how his release was handled by Pittsburgh management.

> Pulliam planned to make the imposition of the sentence of suspension upon me theatrical and impressive. His purpose was to bring me to repentance and have the awful fate that threatened me serve as a warning to the others. Barney, Harry and Fred, president, secretary, manager, respectively, swooped down on me while I was in the reading room of the Pittsburgh Hotel, which I patronized. They

approached me with solemn countenances and, dear me, it did not occur to me that Pulliam had for once had a chance to make the most of a situation. Suppose each had worn a Salvation Army uniform, with Barney beating the big drum, Pulliam playing the banjo and Clarke doing a turn with the tambourine. I felt inclined to laugh as they solemnly approached to officially notify me that my doom was sealed, but I restrained myself and affected an air befitting the occasion.

"Jack," said Dreyfuss while Harry hawked and Clarke cougared, "here's a letter for you." "Thanks, Barney," I replied, as I put the letter, without breaking the envelope, in my pocket, treating it as an ordinary communication. Before the hand that conveyed the document to its resting place, had returned to my side, the three executioners said in chorus: "Read it now."

"Anything important?" I queried as I reached for the fatal missive. "Read it right now," voiced the officials in unison. I broke open the envelope, glanced over its contents and said unconcernedly, "That's all right." The silence that followed was embarrassing to us all. I wanted the other fellows to show their hand and quietly refolded the letter, placed it in the envelope and returned it to my pocket. Barney broke in with: "There's five days' pay due you." Pulliam and Clarke repeated the words: "Five days' pay." "When do I get it?" I queried. "Come to the office," said Barney. "To the office," intoned Pulliam and Clarke. "I'll go with you, but you can mail the check, if that is all the same to you," I observed. "To the office," thundered the trio and there we went.

"What's my offense, Barney?" I asked the little president. "T-r-a-i-t-o-r," the trio thundered. "Not I," said I. "I have looked over my own interests and not anybody else's. Guess that treachery or disloyalty is on in baseball," was my answer. "Now Jack, why did you not come to us?" Pulliam began, but I broke in with: "Say, I'm suspended and my only business here is to get the five days' pay you say is coming to me. Further than that there'll be nothing doing." The check was made out and I bowed myself out.[9]

While this tongue-in-cheek account obviously contained a touch of drama aimed at entertaining readers, O'Connor did offer some lucid material during his interview. He explained that Pulliam and Clarke had started giving him the cold treatment after some players on Pittsburgh's team asked the veteran catcher for advice regarding salary. Supposedly, one of these men was Honus Wagner, who requested O'Connor's assistance getting all the money he deserved for the 1903 season. When asked by O'Connor if he had been approached by American League agents, Wagner responded in the negative. Although O'Connor did not see where he could help, the catcher told Wagner he should be getting top-notch figures. He advised Wagner to make his salary request known to Pirates management. If Barney Dreyfuss was unwilling to meet those figures, O'Connor recommended that Wagner fall in line with people who were willing to pay what he was worth.[10]

Although Jack O'Connor's confession supplied good reading for many baseball fans, Pirates patrons believed this rant was an indictment that the veteran catcher was guilty of the charges leveled against him by Barney Dreyfuss. The fact that O'Connor believed he had the right to shop his services as a free agent was disingenuous since he technically was under contract to play for Pittsburgh in 1903.[11] Pirates supporters were never shocked when new information surrounding this traitorous group's deceitful nature became public. Jack Chesbro's name emerged in the local press when it was reported that he had been paid twice at the close of the 1902 campaign. American League president Ban Johnson claimed he had forwarded Chesbro two weeks' salary under the impression that the star hurler had been docked pay by Dreyfuss for violating his Pittsburgh contract. Chesbro obviously had no rightful claim to that money once he received his final paycheck from Dreyfuss.[12]

During his long, blistering epistle against Pirates management, Jack O'Connor seemed to single out Harry Pulliam for the largest doses of vitriol and contempt. There was definitely some bad blood between these two men. This particular development was a bit surprising since Pulliam had always gotten along splendidly with Pittsburgh's players since he joined the organization in 1900. Of course, being a loyal employee and devoted friend to Dreyfuss increased the likelihood that men who betrayed Pittsburgh's owner would turn against Pulliam. Whether the discussion was about disloyal players or a competing American League team coming to the Smoky City, Pulliam was the ideal ambassador who always articulated Dreyfuss' policies beautifully.

"There is again talk of putting an American League team in Pittsburgh," said Pulliam after he returned from a November business trip in the east. "While the Pittsburgh Club does not invite opposition, it is here to stay to the limit, whether there is opposition or not, and will give Pittsburgh first-class ball next season, or even better than for three years past. Barney Dreyfuss spent his money lavishly to give this city a championship team, and has succeeded. The team won the pennant twice in succession and could certainly win it again next year.

"If the American League breaks into Pittsburgh, which I am almost sure it will not, it will have to furnish A No. 1 ball to compete against us. The public will then have an opportunity to choose between straight, honest, home-made baseball or syndicate ball. If there is to be opposition, I hope local people will be connected with the other side. Businessmen of Pittsburgh are honest and reasonable. That cannot be said of the syndicate people who control the American League. They are too much addicted to gum shoes and garbage cans."[13]

The qualities of decency, dedication and unwavering allegiance which endeared Pulliam to Barney Dreyfuss could also be utilized on a higher level. In mid–November, it was rumored that Pulliam had been involved in initial discussions regarding a peace agreement between the National and American Leagues. While Dreyfuss laughed at the suggestion that Pulliam was working on the adoption of a peace plan, it seemed odd that Pulliam was present at a meeting in New York on November 13 which included American League officials. Various conferences between Pulliam, Ban Johnson, Detroit Tigers owner S.F. Angus, Cleveland Broncos president John F. Kilfoyl and Philadelphia Athletics president Ben Shibe were held at the Waldorf-Astoria Hotel.[14]

Further evidence that something was afoot regarding efforts to bring this acrimonious war between the two leagues to an end became public on November 30. *The Pittsburgh Press* reported that Harry Pulliam had suggested forming a committee from both major leagues to examine and report on the validity of contested contracts of players held by magnates from both leagues. Pulliam also recommended that owners agree not to interfere with men thus held, hoping to stop contract-jumping and double-dealing in contractual relations that were currently occurring between players and management.[15] Many people believed that some of the things Pulliam was endorsing regarding a peace agreement with the American League would be considered during the upcoming National League meeting in New York.

Early information pointed to the re-affirmation of the executive board at the National League's annual meeting on December 9.[16] One baseball publication based out of Philadelphia claimed in an editorial that W. C. Temple would be the next president of the National League. This assertion that Temple had consented to accept the office one year after he rejected such an offer due to health issues was news to Barney Dreyfuss and his partners. Contrary to the report of this weekly Philadelphia periodical, Temple seemed to have no knowledge of any such agreement.[17] Temple probably could be elected by a unanimous vote if he were to become a candidate, but it did not seem likely that he would consent to serve since he was a busy man. Regardless of Temple's intentions, Barney Dreyfuss and a group of owners were advocates of the selection of a president to lead the organization in its fight against the American League syndicate.[18]

On December 3, Temple announced that he would not accept the presidency of the National League if nominated and elected.[19] Dreyfuss responded that while he preferred that a strong candidate be put forward for the league presidency, continuing the executive committee overseen by John T. Brush for another year would be acceptable since they did fine work in 1902.[20] When delegates arrived in New York on December 8 for league conferences at the

Hotel Victoria, Chicago Cubs president James A. Hart maintained that if Temple was unwilling to accept the office as president, he knew of no other man that could be put forward as a candidate. Dreyfuss and Pulliam arrived in New York at breakfast time and declared that the coming session would be free from bickering.[21]

The first order of business was a meeting with American League representatives Ban Johnson and Charley Somers on the morning of December 9. The two league executives presented their compromise peace proposition and were rejected in resounding fashion, according to New York Giants owner John T. Brush.

"So far as I am concerned the American League is dead," said Brush. "We will have nothing to do with it. Yes, Johnson and his people are here with their ideas. We have refused to accept them. They declare they have New York and Pittsburgh. They have not. I admit they can get into Pittsburgh, but know that they dare not go. They have brought some person whom they call Robison from Pittsburgh as a character witness to show that they can get into Pittsburgh."[22]

Giants manager John McGraw backed Brush's comments when he asserted that there was no chance of a compromise between the National and American Leagues. McGraw interpreted the National League schedule for 1903 proposed by schedule committee chairman Barney Dreyfuss to mean war to the death.[23] This vindictive attitude by New York management seemed counterproductive when it became known, as the league meeting progressed, that negotiations had been going on for some time to broker a peace accord between the two warring factions.

American League representatives had made the first overture toward an agreement two months before. One of the current sticking points centered around whether there would be two eight-club leagues that harmoniously coexisted or a 12-team aggregation as had been proposed by National League owners.[24]

Nothing earth-shattering occurred during the second and third days of these sessions as standard league business was the only news to report. On Tuesday, December 9, the Pittsburgh Pirates were officially awarded their second National League pennant, and a check for $100 was rewarded to owner Barney Dreyfuss when this resolution passed.[25] Another nugget of gossip that was cultivated after the closed door meetings ended on Tuesday centered around John Montgomery Ward being considered for the National League presidency. Currently, Ward oversaw a prominent law practice in New York. Ward was also one of the most popular men in baseball and was thoroughly familiar with the game due to his time as a player and manager.[26]

Things started getting interesting during the third day of meetings when it was reported that Harry Pulliam's name had been tossed into the ring for the office of league president. This news came one day after the announcement that Pulliam had been re-elected to his post as secretary-treasurer during the Pittsburgh club's annual election of officers in Jersey City. Dreyfuss was also retained as team president, while Oliver S. Hershman replaced W. Kelsey Schoepf as vice-president.[27]

Pulliam's re-election to his post within the Pirates organization became moot on the final day of National League meetings in New York on December 12. By unanimous vote, the league's eight baseball magnates selected Pulliam to be the next president to lead their organization. Dreyfuss and his colleagues were so impressed with Pulliam's credentials that he was also named to the offices of secretary and treasurer and given authority to appoint his own assistant.[28] Two owners gave succinct reasons for why they elected Pulliam.

"I am for Pulliam," said Cincinnati Reds owner Garry Herrmann, "because he likes everybody and everybody likes him."

"We had to weaken Pittsburgh so we took its most valuable man," stated president James A. Hart of the Chicago Cubs.[29]

Barney Dreyfuss actually cried when he realized that he had lost his friend and faithful partner, Harry Pulliam.[30] Dreyfuss also stated that while he was sorry to lose Pulliam, he was very supportive of this action because the National League needed him.[31] A star at advertising and brilliant doing executive work, Pulliam had been consulted on any important move Dreyfuss had made during their time together in Pittsburgh.[32] A mutual friend of the Pirates executives believed finding a replacement for Pulliam would be a difficult task.

> Barney certainly will miss the sec. I will even say that the playing part of the club will not be benefitted by the man's departure, for he helped to smooth over breaches that arose in the team. I know that during the year that the team won the flag for the first time Pulliam went to down-hearted boys in Philly and gave them a good, strong talk. They had been dubious of the outcome of the race, as the umpires seemed to be throwing it into them. Pulliam's courage won the day. The boys stood to the breach like winners, and got there.[33]

Pulliam's policy for running the National League was a simple one based on honesty and integrity. He vowed that he would be fair and firm in his dealings with all parties.[34] In order to prove that his words did not have a hollow ring, Pulliam took immediate action to insure that he could never be accused of exhibiting partiality toward Barney Dreyfuss.

"I will sell out my stock in the Pittsburgh Club; this is not obligatory, but I will do it anyway," said Pulliam. "I want to start foot free. It will hurt me to cut away from Barney Dreyfuss, who has been with me so long, but I feel that the president of an organization such as the National League should not have financial interest in any club. I will resign as secretary of the Pittsburgh Club before January 1, when I assume control of National League affairs."[35]

Barney Dreyfuss quickly killed the rumor that Frank McQuiston would replace Pulliam when he declared that a new team secretary would not be appointed until February.[36] Dreyfuss was also forced to refute a story that claimed the Pirates planned on moving from Exposition Park to a magnificent field that would be built on the Aaron French Estate at Penn and Linden Avenues in Point Breeze. This local gossip maintained that a large amusement center that included merry-go-rounds, switch-backs and hockey and skating rinks would be built next to a new ballpark.[37] An organization known as the Pittsburgh Amusement Company had $500,000 capital and $250,000 in bonds to purchase this land. They were considering this project since the Pittsburgh and Western Railroad on numerous occasions had threatened to condemn the property where Exposition Park was located so they could convert it into a freight yard. The fact that the Pirates had a six-year lease at Exposition Park did not prevent this story from gathering steam.[38] "We cannot be evicted as long as we pay rent until our present lease expires," was Dreyfuss' only comment regarding a potential move to a ballpark in Point Breeze.[39]

While it seemed unlikely that the Pittsburgh Pirates would be moving to new ballpark in the near future, it was looking far more certain that no American League team was destined to occupy a baseball diamond in Pittsburgh for the 1903 campaign. After being promised by American League representatives in New York that something might be done for them, a conglomerate of Pittsburgh businessmen hoping to place a team in the Smoky City were mystified when no action was taken in support of their cause.[40] Ban Johnson readily admitted that the proposition was not even considered during a meeting on December 22.[41] Johnson had also stated to a National League representative during the recent conclave in New York that the American League had no rightful claim to Tommy Leach. Johnson confessed that all his blustery talk about Leach's case was an arrogant bluff since he knew baseball law prevented the American League from securing Leach's services.[42]

Ban Johnson's recent positions regarding American League policy and Harry Pulliam's election as National League president gave strong indication that peace between the two organizations was inevitable. Johnson readily admitted that brokering a peace agreement between the two leagues was a certainty. Committees from both sides of the aisle were scheduled to meet in Cincinnati on January 5, 1903.⁴³ Barney Dreyfuss refused to discuss the peace proposition or engage in any lengthy discussion relevant to the matter. "Out of courtesy to the conference committee I would rather not be quoted," said Dreyfuss.⁴⁴

When the time came for this conference to begin in Cincinnati, American League delegates met at the Grand Hotel and National League representatives hunkered down in the St. Nicholas Hotel.⁴⁵ On the night of January 8, 1903, Harry Pulliam received a telegram from Dreyfuss urging the National League president to join him in Cincinnati. Dreyfuss, who had left Louisville at 4 o'clock in the afternoon, wired Pulliam the minute his train arrived in Cincinnati, asking him to be present at this important conference. Pulliam specifically had not made the trip for this vital meeting since no one had extended an invitation to him until he was summoned by Dreyfuss.⁴⁶

On January 9, the two league committees went into joint session at the St. Nicholas Hotel. The National League committee consisted of Harry Pulliam, Garry Herrmann, Frank de Haas Robison and James A.

American League president Ban Johnson claimed that Tommy Leach would play for his organization in 1903 or not at all. Besides giving Leach advance money to join the American League, Johnson asserted that Leach had been the actual ringleader of the conspiracy regarding Pirates players jumping leagues the previous summer. Barney Dreyfuss argued that Leach had not agreed to jump leagues and was not permitted to do so since he had signed a contract to play for Pittsburgh in 1903. In December, Johnson finally admitted he had no lawful claim to Leach's services (courtesy of the National Baseball Hall of Fame Library, Cooperstown, New York).

Hart. The two committees remained in conference with the exception of a brief lunch until late at night. When they adjourned for the day, the territorial question had been settled. After Ban Johnson once again rejected the formation of a single, 12-team league, representatives got down to determining the eight cities in which the American League would place teams for the 1903 season. A resolution to this matter was reached when Johnson's organization was permitted to enter New York, since those plans had already gotten under way. As a compromise, the American League agreed to stay out of Pittsburgh if a satisfactory agreement regarding the player issue could be reached.[47]

The joint committee held a meeting on Saturday, January 10, to tackle the question of disputed players and which side owned their rights. Throughout this long process, the National League wing was kept busy with long distance phone calls to out-of-town magnates. When a deal was finally hammered out, the American League was awarded nine disputed players while the National League received seven. In respect to the Pittsburgh Pirates, infielder Wid Conroy was given to the American League, while third baseman Tommy Leach and catcher Harry Smith remained with Barney Dreyfuss. It was also agreed that all money received by rewarded players should be returned to the teams that lost them. A great triumph was finally achieved by these heralded negotiators as it appeared a peace resolution had been reached to bring this major league war to an end.[48]

Resistance to the agreement ratified by these committees representing each league was immediate as John T. Brush of the New York Giants, Ned Hanlon of the Brooklyn Superbas and John I. Rogers of the Philadelphia Phillies admitted they would not abide by this treaty. These three men believed the report was incomplete since the American League was not punished for their actions over the past two years.[49] Brooklyn president Charles Ebbets was also not pleased that Willie Keeler and Bill Donovan had been awarded to the American League. Ebbets planned on fighting for these two players he believed had been stolen from him by the American League syndicate.[50] Brush was angry over the fact that a competing American League team was permitted to move into New York while Barney Dreyfuss somehow escaped the same fate in Pittsburgh.[51]

On January 16, Brush filed for a court injunction to prevent the National League from ratifying the peace agreement that was brokered in Cincinnati. In court documents, Brush requested the injunction against Harry Pulliam within his capacity as league president. Pulliam, who was shocked when papers were served on him at the Hotel Walton in Philadelphia, immediately left for Cincinnati.[52] Another session aimed at ironing out these differences among National League owners was scheduled for that city on January 19 and 20. A resolution was passed at this meeting which slightly appeased Brush. The National League Committee stipulated that the American League claim to New York territory was limited to the Borough of Manhattan. The hearing regarding Brush's injunction was also postponed during this conference.[53]

On the morning of January 21, a majority report was read at the conference before Brush was permitted to articulate his feelings through submission of the opposition minority account at 5:00 p.m. Given the chance to air his opinion and put various grievances on the record, Brush lifted the injunction request against the National League which immediately vacated a restraining order against having a vote on the peace plan. After hours of intense discussions, the agreement was brought to the floor for a vote at 10:00 p.m. When roll call was taken, Brooklyn and Boston voted for adoption of this agreement, along with Pittsburgh, Chicago, Cincinnati, Philadelphia and St. Louis. Seeing the hopelessness of any further dissent, Brush and the New York Giants delegation fell into line. Brush's reversal made this adoption to bring about peace with the American League a unanimous vote that ended one of the most stubborn fights in baseball history.[54]

Harry Pulliam's steady stewardship had been critical in getting this deal done when it looked at times as if the peace process would unravel. With this time-consuming, difficult task now behind him, Pulliam officially tendered his resignation as secretary of the Pittsburgh Athletic Company on January 25.[55] William Henry Locke, sports editor for *The Pittsburgh Press,* eventually was selected as Pulliam's replacement during a February meeting of the club in Jersey City. Now that peace had been achieved between the two leagues, contract jumping and secret, covert meetings were a thing of the past. Barney Dreyfuss issued his final statement regarding anything connected to American League efforts to steal his players when he refuted a claim that Pittsburgh had no right to outfielder Jimmy Sebring's services.[56]

"As early as last June, I bought the release of Sebring and gave Pat Hurley $1,500 for that document," said Dreyfuss. "The youngster had signed a two years' contract with Worcester, and I simply assumed that contract. Hurley did not tell the fielder about the deal at the time. Later on he had a row with Frank Leonard (Worcester's manager), and while anxious to break away, Frank Dwyer came along. Telling him that he had purchased his release from Hurley, Dwyer succeeded in getting Sebring to sign a Detroit contract. When the falsity of Dwyer's claim was proved and he learned of Hurley's transfer of his contract to me, Sebring repudiated the Detroit contract, which had been obtained under false pretenses. I sent Mr. Angus the true story of the transaction and he has never since laid any claim to the player."[57]

Jimmy Sebring's continued development was viewed as critical by many Pirates fans for Pittsburgh to be a legitimate candidate to capture a third consecutive National League pennant in 1903. Sebring had done fine work for Pittsburgh during the final month of the 1902 campaign as he batted .325 in

19 games. Sebring and catcher Eddie Phelps were expected to make a seamless transition as replacements for deserters Lefty Davis and Jack O'Connor. A group of pitchers that included Bucky Veil, Irvin "Kaiser" Wilhelm and Fred "Cy" Falkenberg seemed capable of replacing Jack Chesbro and Jesse Tannehill. Cincinnati baseball writer J. Ed Grillo believed Pittsburgh would not be hampered on the baseball diamond by any of their player defections to the American League.

> Notwithstanding the fact that the Pittsburgh team has lost four players from its last year aggregation, it cannot be figured that the champions have been weakened in any way. Chesbro and Tannehill were unquestionably great pitchers last season, and won a large majority of their games for Pittsburgh.
> One would naturally suppose that the loss of two such stars would weaken a team considerably, but the owners of the club do not seem to think so. Manager Clarke still has a great pitching staff, and the youngsters that Barney Dreyfuss has purchased for the team are expected to develop into finds of the first water. The Pirates will not miss O'Connor and Lefty Davis. Sebring, the young man who played right field for the team the latter part of the season, proved to be Davis' superior in every respect, and he has really added additional strength to the outfield.[58]

Fred Clarke also seemed confident that his stable of young hurlers would do fine work in 1903. Before the opening game on April 16 in Cincinnati, Clarke critiqued the potential of his current pitching staff.

> While we have lost two cracks in Jesse Tannehill and Jack Chesbro, they came from the lots, and I believe I have some youngsters who are every bit as good as they were. I don't think any manager in the league can beat me on the count of promising youngsters. Fred Falkenberg has lots of pluck and the brains to make his stand good. Fred Veil is from Bucknell College, and he is the best little big man I ever saw. When he was in college he was considered a better pitcher than Christy Mathewson. Irvin Wilhelm looks to be a jewel. Without stretching the truth, I can say that I never saw a right-handed pitcher who was so hard for a left-handed batsman to touch. Old Bill Kennedy is in good shape to help out. Ed Doheny is still with us. Then there is George Merritt, recalled from Worcester. Sam Leever makes No. 8, and that winds up the pitching list.[59]

Writers and readers who were astute enough to realize that Clarke did not mention pitcher Deacon Phillippe need not have worried. Since he was pitching in the opening game against the Reds that afternoon, Pittsburgh's manager assumed everybody knew Phillippe was part of the pitching staff. Clarke and Grillo both seemed to be accurate in their evaluation of the Pirates squad as Pittsburgh swept the season-opening four-game series against Cincinnati before returning home to face the St. Louis Cardinals at Exposition Park on April 21. Grillo's assessment regarding Jimmy Sebring was also prophetic as the young outfielder became an instant fan favorite in the Smoky City. The fans fell in love with Sebring when he smacked two home runs during an 8–4 victory over St. Louis on April 23. In the second inning, he raced around the bases after he blasted a drive to deep center field that rolled to the flag pole. He duplicated this feat in the fifth frame when his speed allowed him to score after a high drive struck the center field fence.[60]

While Grillo's acumen regarding Sebring was dead on, the baseball writer and Clarke both missed the mark when it came to the potential of Pittsburgh's young pitchers. Replacing Jack Chesbro's and Jesse Tannehill's 48 victories during the 1902 campaign was a tall order for a group of unproven twirlers. Cy Falkenberg, Kaiser Wilhelm and Bucky Veil fell well short of that mark as the three men combined to win 11 games. Former Brooklyn Superbas hurler Bill Kennedy pushed that total to 20 victories as he went 9–6 during the 1903 campaign. Due to substandard work from the bottom of Pittsburgh's rotation, staff aces Deacon Phillippe, Sam Leever and Eddie Doheny were heavily counted upon to keep the Pirates in the hunt for a third consecutive National League pennant.

Rookie outfielder Jimmy Sebring became an immediate fan favorite at Exposition Park due to his work during a game against the St. Louis Cardinals on April 23, 1903. Sebring exhibited ultimate speed and hustle when he legged out inside-the-park home runs in the second and fifth innings as Pittsburgh defeated St. Louis, 8–4. Sebring's work in right field during the final month of the 1902 campaign had allowed Pirates rooters to quickly forget his predecessor, contract jumper Alfonzo "Lefty" Davis (courtesy of the National Baseball Hall of Fame Library, Cooperstown, New York).

Things certainly were tougher for Pittsburgh during the 1903 campaign. Besides losing 40 percent of their record-breaking pitching staff from 1902, Fred Clarke's troops faced stiffer competition in 1903. John McGraw's New York Giants were much improved after a last-place finish in 1902. Frank Selee's young Chicago Cubs squad was also hungrier in 1903 following a fifth-place finish the previous year. When May ended, the Pirates found themselves in third place with a 25–16 record. They trailed first-place Chicago by four games, while the second-place Giants were 2½ games in front of Pittsburgh. At this point of the season one year before, Pittsburgh's record stood at 30–6.

Pittsburgh did not get off to a very good start in June as Eddie Doheny was slaughtered by the New York Giants, 10–2, at Exposition Park. This defeat at the hands of John McGraw's team ended a modest four-game winning streak. As it turned out, this loss proved only a minor inconvenience for Fred Clarke's troops as they proceeded to reel off 15 consecutive victories. During this dominant run that propelled Pittsburgh to the top of the National League standings, the Pirates' pitching staff recorded six straight shutouts. Deacon Phillippe defeated New York, 7–0, on June 2, while Sam Leever turned the trick against McGraw's team one day later as Pittsburgh claimed a 5–0 victory. Boston was Pittsburgh's next victim when rookie hurler Kaiser Wilhelm made it three shutouts in a row as the Pirates defeated the Beaneaters, 5–0, on June 4.

The Pirates established a new record with their fourth consecutive shutout on June 5 when Eddie Doheny defeated Boston, 9–0.[61] One day after Pittsburgh broke the previous mark of three consecutive shutouts, they pushed that record up another game as Deacon Phillippe defeated Boston, 4–0. Although umpire Hank O'Day called the game in the bottom of the sixth inning due to rain, passionate Pirates rooters did not believe this achievement was cheapened by not playing a complete game.[62] Philadelphia was Pittsburgh's final victim during this shutout surge as Sam Leever defeated the Phillies, 2–0, on June 8. When the Phillies finally broke loose and scored a run against Kaiser Wilhelm in the fourth inning on June 9, it snapped a stretch of 56 shutout innings.[63] What made this achievement even more remarkable was that it occurred when Jack Chesbro, who had been christened "Mr. Whitewash" for his shutout exploits in 1902, was no longer a member of the team.

Fred Clarke's team grabbed control of the National League race by going 34–12 in June and July. On August 1, the Pirates stood on top of the standings with a record of 59–28 that put them 7½ games in front of the second-place Chicago Cubs. As the Pirates continued to barrel their way toward a third National League pennant, Clarke lost another crucial member of his record-breaking pitching staff from 1902. Eddie Doheny exhibited bizarre and irrational behavior as the 1903 season moved into the summer. During a contest against the New York Giants at the Polo Grounds on May 18, a riot almost broke out due to Doheny's conduct. With a teammate on first base, Doheny stepped to the plate and hit a harmless popup to the infield. In accordance with baseball rules at the time, umpire Bob Emslie called him out while the ball was still in the air.[64]

Doheny ran toward first base, carrying the bat with him. Halfway down the line, he tossed his bat aside and almost hit Giants catcher Frank Bowerman, who was dancing under the ball. The crowd, not realizing that Doheny had already been declared out, believed he was attempting to interfere with Bowerman. Angry rooters heckled and roasted the southpaw hurler over his action. Doheny lost his temper and foolishly bowed to the spectators in mock courtesy. Fuel was added to the fire later in the game when Fred Clarke was called out for interfering with Bowerman. When the contest concluded, a mob of about 1,000 people descended on the Pirates and started throwing rocks. Police arrived and escorted Pittsburgh's players to the clubhouse before anyone was injured.[65]

While this reaction on Doheny's part could be categorized as losing his cool during the heat of battle, there was no denying that he began to exhibit delusional behavior in July. For two weeks, he believed detectives were shadowing him. He could not be swayed in his thinking even after Pittsburgh team secretary William Henry Locke tried to convince him this was not the case. Although he was not being followed by anyone, he told the detective yarn to more than one friend. A deeply religious man, Doheny seemed to be fretting over his performance as a player more than past years. Intimate friends of the pitcher claimed this problem regarding mental worry became more glaring during the summer heat.[66] On July 28, while the Pirates were in Cincinnati, team management announced that Doheny had deserted the team while laboring under a mental hallucination and returned to his home in Andover, Massachusetts.[67] Fred Clarke claimed there was no chance that Doheny would return to the Pirates ever again.[68]

This assertion by the Pirates leader was believed to be subject to adjustment since Clarke was angry when he made his initial statement.[69] Clarke softened his stance once he received information that Doheny returned home because he was ill rather than deserting over being unhappy with his teammates. In early August, Clarke received letters from Doheny's wife and Dr. Edward C. Conroy which stated that Doheny was improving rapidly and would report to the team without delay.[70] Doheny rejoined the Pirates on August 15 during a series in Boston. He appeared glad to get back as he exchanged affable greetings with his teammates, donned his uniform and accompanied them to the ballpark.[71] Things seemed to be going well for Doheny following his return until the Chicago Cubs blitzed him for a 13–8 victory during the first game of a Labor Day doubleheader on September 7 at Exposition Park. He deserted the Pirates a second time and never returned.

Fellow hurler Bill Kennedy relayed an interesting story about Doheny shortly after he had returned to his Andover home in late July. Kennedy suggested that Doheny was suffering mentally before Pittsburgh left home for a western trip in July. Weeks earlier, Doheny scared Kennedy, who roomed near him at the Monongahela House in Pittsburgh. Kennedy was awakened in the middle of the night by a pounding on the door. He rose from his bed, opened the door and saw Doheny standing in the hall in his night robe. Doheny disclosed the perplexing information that he had been given an electric shock through the wall. "I'll wager," said Doheny, "that they're trying to work a panel game on me."[72]

While Doheny's room did not have a secret panel of sliding walls where a thief could enter Eddie's room while he slept and rob him as the reference to a panel game indicated, Kennedy joined the anxious hurler in his room to investigate. Together they searched for wires that may have shocked the scared southpaw pitcher, but found nothing. While Kennedy initially did not mention this incident to anyone, it weighed on his mind for weeks. Following Doheny's first departure from the Pirates, Kennedy unburdened himself of this midnight experience that made his hair stand on end.[73] Losing Doheny for the remainder of the 1903 campaign was a severe blow since Fred Clarke's pitching staff was now reduced to two reliable hurlers. Doheny's desertion was also critical because Barney Dreyfuss' dream of playing a post-season series against the American League champion was about to become a reality.

When it became apparent that the Pittsburgh Pirates and the Boston Americans would win their respective pennants, magnates of both franchises agreed to meet in a post-season series to determine which aggregation was the superior team. Dreyfuss and Boston owner Henry J. Killilea hammered out an agreement that called for the two squads to play a best of nine series that would begin in Boston on October 1. This championship battle was referred to as the World Series since the slate of games ultimately would decide which league had the greatest baseball team on Earth.[74] The Pirates took care of their end of the bargain when they clinched a third consecutive National League pennant with a doubleheader sweep over the Boston Beaneaters at Exposition Park on September 18.[75]

When the 1903 campaign concluded, Pittsburgh had outdistanced the second-place New York Giants by 6½ games with a record of 91–49. In the American League, Boston's margin was much wider as they posted a mark of

12. Pirates Win Third Pennant Despite Loss of Stars

91–47 and finished 14½ games in front of the second-place Philadelphia Athletics. Despite entering the World Series severely handicapped by injuries and a thin pitching staff, the Pirates looked as if they would cruise to an easy victory in this post-season series as they quickly grabbed a 3–1 lead against Boston. Deacon Phillippe was brilliant on the mound for manager Fred Clarke as he claimed victories in Games One, Three and Four. While Phillippe's performance was commendable, the inability of any other Pirates hurler to complement the staff ace spelled Pittsburgh's doom. While it had been reported that Sam Leever caught a cold in his pitching arm during the closing weeks of the season by pitching on a raw, windy day, it was believed a trap shooting mishap had also contributed to his injury.[76]

Unfortunately for Barney Dreyfuss, Fred Clarke and his players, Pittsburgh never won another game as Boston secured four consecutive contests and claimed the 1903 World Series five games to three. Players underperforming due to injuries and having to rely on one dependable hurler like Phillippe were too much to overcome. Some Pirates fans believed the outcome of the World Series would have been different if Leever was not handicapped by an injury. Numerous Pirates insisted Eddie Doheny's desertion also badly weakened the team. This news was surprising since some players quietly acknowledged they had grown nervous as the season progressed when Doheny was on the mound. His availability basically became a moot point on a fateful July day in Cincinnati when he initially bolted for home while playing billiards with Ginger Beaumont after he yelled that one of the supposed detectives shadowing him was in the pool hall.[77]

Doheny's teammates had hoped he would be well enough to participate in the World Series. When doctors made it clear that he would not be able to contribute, the team did what they believed was a touching gesture to lift the spirits of their teammate by returning his uniform to him.[78] This action had the opposite effect as Doheny interpreted it to mean that his baseball career was over. He was heartbroken when he received the uniform.[79] Doheny, who followed the World Series between Pittsburgh and Boston, became extremely agitated when he learned that the Pirates had lost Game Seven, 7–3, on Saturday, October 10.[80] Mrs. Doheny sent for Dr. Edward C. Conroy to attend to her husband at their home on 112 Main Street. When Conroy arrived, Doheny angrily informed the doctor that his services were no longer required.[81]

On Sunday, Conroy instructed nurse and faith healer Oberlin Howarth to care for Doheny. When Howarth arrived at the home, he initially succeeded in calming down Doheny and convinced him to go to bed. When Howarth turned his head, Doheny reached under the bed and grabbed the leg of a cast-iron foot rest he had hidden. In a fit of crazy, homicidal rage, Doheny struck Howarth in the back of the head with the foot-rest leg and knocked him to the floor. Doheny continued striking Howarth even though he was unconscious.[82] Contrary to reports that police officers had to overpower her husband after they were held at bay for some time, a tragedy was averted by the quick thinking of Doheny's wife.

"Ed blamed the doctor for keeping him out of the Pittsburgh-Boston series," said Mrs. Doheny as she explained the events surrounding Doheny's outburst after he was taken into custody by police, "and after a mad outbreak over the loss of Saturday's game he chased the doctor when he called. After that he seemed to cool down, and I went to another part of the house. I soon heard scuffling and other rounds of fighting in my husband's room, and catching my baby, I ran there. As I threw open the door I saw my husband standing over Mr. Howarth, who had evidently been knocked down by Mr. Doheny, who was standing over him with something in his hands, and, I suppose, was about to hit him again.

"Baby screamed and I cried, 'Eddie! Eddie! Don't do that.' He turned and looked my way with eyes which did not seem right, then he dropped whatever he had in his hand, and when I asked him to go back to bed he did so quietly. Then I ran and called the neighbors to help Mr. Howarth. The story that the officers had to come in and overpower my husband is not true. When they came to take him away to the asylum he went with them, harmless as a child."[83]

Howarth was expected to survive this heinous attack brought about by the instability of Doheny's mental condition. Doheny was taken to the police station and examined by doctors. A judge immediately issued an order to have Doheny committed to the Danvers Insane Hospital, where he would receive treatment. After Game Eight of the World Series was postponed on Monday, October 12, and rescheduled for the next day, Fred Clarke traveled to Andover and had a comforting talk with Mrs. Doheny.[84] Clarke also visited Eddie at the state mental hospital in Danvers. This meeting was a depressing time for Clarke, who struggled to keep his equanimity as he quietly talked to his former star pitcher, who looked fragile and emaciated.[85] Barney Dreyfuss expressed deep sorrow when he issued a statement regarding the tragic events surrounding Doheny's mental breakdown.

> I feel very much for Mrs. Doheny. She is a lovely lady, and they have as pretty a boy as I ever saw. Doheny was very fond of his wife and his child. I had no idea that his case would terminate this way. We lose a great pitcher in him. I was in

hopes he would come around all right for next season. Doheny I considered as good a left-hander as there is in the country when he was in condition.[86]

Eddie Doheny never played baseball again as he remained institutionalized until his death on December 29, 1916. The loss of yet another star hurler from the great 1902 pitching staff was too much for the Pirates to overcome in 1904 as their three-year reign on top of the National League came to an end when John McGraw's New York Giants claimed the pennant. After participating in the first modern World Series in 1903, it took Pittsburgh six more years before they had another opportunity to meet the American League champion in a post-season series. In 1909, Pittsburgh claimed its first World Championship over the Detroit Tigers, four games to three in the World Series. Five men from the 1902 Pirates who experienced the disappointment of losing against Boston in the World Series in 1903 were still on Pittsburgh's roster in 1909. Honus Wagner, Fred Clarke, Tommy Leach, Deacon Phillippe and Sam Leever were the remaining holdovers from baseball's greatest team that finally won a World Championship in 1909.

Following that World Series victory, these five men who were members of all four Pirates squads that claimed National League pennants between 1901 and 1909 never played for a first-place team again. Sam Leever played his last big league game in 1910 before he spent one season in the minor leagues. Deacon Phillippe retired from major league baseball after the 1911 campaign. Both players were still members of the Pittsburgh Pirates when their big league careers ended. Tommy Leach's time in Pittsburgh came to an end when he was traded to the Chicago Cubs on May 30, 1912. Fred Clarke retired as a full-time player following the 1911 season and remained as Pittsburgh's manager until he called it quits in 1915. Honus Wagner's illustrious career came to an end when he retired following the 1917 season with a lifetime batting average of .328 and 3,420 career hits.

Other members of that record-breaking 1902 team were not so fortunate in remaining with Pittsburgh as many years as these grizzled veterans. Following a horrible season in 1904, first baseman Kitty Bransfield was traded to the Philadelphia Phillies on December 20. Ginger Beaumont and Claude Ritchey were shipped to the Boston Doves on December 11, 1906, as part of a package to acquire Latrobe native Ed Abbaticchio. Infielder Jimmy Burke joined the St. Louis Cardinals in 1903. Catcher Harry Smith was sold to the Boston Doves on June 14, 1908. Fellow backstop Chief Zimmer was claimed off waivers by the Philadelphia Phillies in January of 1903 so he could act as a player-manager for that team.

Three of the four men who had been disloyal to Barney Dreyfuss and jumped to the American League's New York Highlanders quickly wore out their welcome before the 1903 campaign concluded. In June, it was reported that manager Clark Griffith was anxious to get rid of Lefty Davis and other players who had proved to be traitors to the National League.[87] On September 26, 1903, Jack O'Connor was dropped from the club payroll because Griffith believed his catcher would have broken up the team if he had stayed with New York much longer.[88] O'Connor was traded by the Highlanders to the St. Louis Browns on October 6, 1903. Davis played for New York only one year as he hit an anemic .237 in 1903. Southpaw Jesse Tannehill also spent one season in the Big Apple before he was traded to the Boston Americans for pitcher Tom Hughes on December 20, 1903. Following a mediocre season with New York, Tannehill topped the 20-victory mark for Boston in 1904 and 1905.

Jack Chesbro's ascension as one of the game's top pitchers continued during his time in New York. In 1904, Chesbro put the team on his back and almost singlehandedly secured an American League pennant for the Highlanders as he posted a record of 41–12, supported by a 1.82 ERA. The strain of hurling 454 ⅔ innings in 1904 may have been too much for Chesbro as he topped 20 wins only one more time over the next four seasons with New York. Wid Conroy, who was awarded to the American League through the peace agreement that was ratified by both leagues in January of 1903, remained as Chesbro's teammate with the Highlanders through the 1908 season.

The 1902 Pittsburgh Pirates' place in history could be perceived as fleeting since they held the record for most victories in a season for only two years. In 1904, the New York Giants secured 106 victories during the first year the National League schedule was expanded to 154 games. While the 1904 Giants were unable to eclipse the 1902 Pirates' winning percentage of .741, that mark was obliterated in 1906 when the Chicago Cubs finished the season at a .763 clip with a record of 116–36. The fact that Pittsburgh's record did not stand over a long period of time certainly did not mean their achievement lacked legitimacy.

Although there was evidence that the Pirates' path to glory in 1902 was made easier due to Barney Dreyfuss' team not losing many players to American League raids up to that point, this did not diminish the fact that they were the first true powerhouse team of the 20th century. Fred Clarke's five-man pitching staff put on one of the best single-season performances in the game's history. Players such as Clarke, Honus Wagner, Tommy Leach and Ginger Beaumont were also some of the top players from that era of baseball. Looking beyond numbers, the 1902 team achieved greatness because they expected to

12. Pirates Win Third Pennant Despite Loss of Stars 253

win every game and took it personally when they lost. The belief of the Buccaneers players that they were far superior to any other team in the National League was certainly justified. Considered during that record breaking season to be the greatest squad ever, the 1902 Pittsburgh Pirates rightfully earned their place as one of the top teams in baseball's long, rich history.

Appendix A: 1902 Pittsburgh Pirates Roster

Pitchers

John Dwight Chesbro ("Happy Jack"—"Algernon"—"Algy") b. on June 5, 1874, in North Adams, Massachusetts—5 feet 9—180 lbs

Harvey Barnes Cushman—b. on July 5, 1877, in Rockland, Maine

Edward Richard Doheny ("Ed"—"Eddie"—"Irish") b. on November 24, 1873, in Northfield, Vermont—5 feet 10 ½—165 lbs

Samuel Leever ("Sam"—"The Goshen Schoolmaster"—"The Pedagogue"—"Professor") b. on December 23, 1871, in Goshen, Ohio—5 feet 10 ½—175 lbs

Warren A. McLaughlin—b. on January 22, 1876, in New York, New York—170 lbs

Charles Louis Phillippe ("Deacon"—The Great Phillippi"—"Phil") b. on May 23, 1872, in Rural Retreat, Virginia—6 feet ½—180 lbs

Edward Isaih Poole ("Ed") b. on September 7, 1874, in Canton, Ohio—5 feet 10–175 lbs

Jesse Niles Tannehill ("Tanny"—"Powder") b. on July 14, 1874, in Dayton, Kentucky—5 feet 8–150 lbs

Catchers

Leo Alexander Fohl ("Lee")—b. on November 28, 1876, in Lowell, Ohio—5 feet 10–175 lbs

Michael Joseph Hopkins ("Mike"—"Skinner") b. on November 1, 1872, in Glasgow, Scotland—5 feet 8–160 lbs

John Joseph O'Connor ("Jack"—"Peach Pie") b. on June 2, 1866, in St. Louis, Missouri—5 feet 10–170 lbs

Edward Jaykill Phelps ("Ed"—"Eddie"—"Yaller"—"Smilie") b. on March 3, 1879, in Albany, New York—5 feet 11–185 lbs

Harry Thomas Smith ("Smithy"—"Schmidty") b. on October 31, 1874, in Yorkshire, England—5 feet 8 ½–165 lbs

Charles Louis Zimmer ("Chief") b. on November 23, 1860, in Marietta, Ohio—6 feet–190 lbs

Infielders

William Edward Bransfield ("Kitty"—"Branny") b. on January 7, 1875, in Worcester, Massachusetts—5 feet 11–207 lbs

James Timothy Burke ("Jimmy"—"Sunset Jimmy") b. on October 12, 1874, in St. Louis, Missouri—5 feet 7—160 lbs

William Edward Conroy ("Wid"—"Widow") b. on April 5, 1877, in Philadelphia, Pennsylvania—5 feet 9—158 lbs

Thomas William Leach ("Tommy"—"Wee Tommy"—"The Wee") b. on November 4, 1877, in French Creek, New York—5 feet 6 ½—150 lbs

Claude Cassius Ritchey ("Little All Right"—"Old Reliable"—"Little Ritch") b. on October 5, 1873, in Emlenton, Pennsylvania—5 feet 6 ½—167 lbs

John Peter Wagner ("Hans"—"Honus"—"The Flying Dutchman"—"The Carnegie Dutchman") b. on February 24, 1874, in Mansfield, Pennsylvania—5 feet 11—200 lbs

Outfielders

Clarence Howeth Beaumont ("Ginger"—"Beau"—"Clarry"—"Red") b. on July 23, 1876, in Rochester, Wisconsin—5 feet 8—190 lbs

Fred Clifford Clarke ("Cap"—"The Boss") b. on October 3, 1872, in Winterset, Iowa—5 feet 10 ½—165 lbs

Frederick Joseph Crolius ("Fred") b. on December 16, 1876, in Jersey City, New Jersey

Alfonzo DeFord Davis ("Lefty") b. on February 4, 1875, in Nashville, Tennessee—5 feet 10—170 lbs

George Washington Merritt ("The Worthy") b. on April 14, 1880, in Paterson, New Jersey—6 feet—160 lbs

William Alexander Miller ("Bill") b. on May 23, 1879, in Bad Schwalbach, Germany—6 feet 2—170 lbs

James Dennison Sebring ("Jimmy"—"Jeems") b. on March 25, 1882, in Liberty, Pennsylvania—6 feet—180 lbs

Appendix B: 1902 Pittsburgh Pirates Statistics

Batting Statistics—Team Batting Average .286

	G	AB	R	H	2B	3B	HR	RBI	BB	SO	SB	AVG	SLG
Mike Hopkins	1	2	0	2	1	0	0	0	0	0	0	1.000	1.500
Warren McLaughlin	3	11	1	4	1	0	0	3	0	3	1	.364	.455
Ginger Beaumont	130	541	100	193	21	6	0	67	39	40	33	.357	.418
George Merritt	2	9	2	3	1	0	0	2	0	2	0	.333	.444
Honus Wagner	136	534	105	176	30	16	3	91	43	51	42	.330	.463
Jimmy Sebring	19	80	15	26	4	4	0	15	5	7	2	.325	.475
Fred Clarke	113	459	103	145	27	14	2	53	51	38	29	.316	.449
Kitty Bransfield	102	413	49	126	21	8	0	69	17	29	23	.305	.395
Jimmy Burke	60	203	24	60	12	2	0	26	17	13	9	.296	.374
Jack O'Connor	49	170	13	50	1	2	1	28	3	11	2	.294	.341
Jesse Tannehill	44	148	27	43	6	1	1	17	12	12	3	.291	.365
Lefty Davis	59	232	52	65	7	3	0	20	35	12	19	.280	.336
Tommy Leach	135	514	97	143	14	22	6	85	45	45	25	.278	.426
Claude Ritchey	115	405	54	112	13	1	2	55	53	15	10	.277	.328
Chief Zimmer	42	142	13	38	4	2	0	17	11	14	4	.268	.324
Fred Crolius	9	38	4	10	2	1	0	7	0	6	0	.263	.368
Ed Poole	1	4	0	1	0	0	0	0	0	2	0	.250	.250
Wid Conroy	99	365	55	89	10	6	1	47	24	41	10	.244	.312
Deacon Phillippe	32	113	16	25	2	2	1	12	2	18	0	.221	.301
Ed Phelps	18	61	5	13	1	0	0	6	4	4	2	.213	.230
Bill Miller	1	5	0	1	0	0	0	2	0	2	0	.200	.200
Harvey Cushman	4	10	0	2	0	0	0	1	0	5	0	.200	.200
Harry Smith	50	185	14	35	4	1	0	12	4	24	4	.189	.222
Jack Chesbro	35	112	11	20	3	1	0	8	3	28	1	.179	.223
Sam Leever	29	90	6	16	3	2	0	8	3	10	1	.178	.256
Ed Doheny	22	77	8	12	1	1	1	8	1	7	2	.156	.234
Lee Fohl	1	3	0	0	0	0	0	1	0	1	0	.000	.000
Total	1311	4926	774	1410	189	95	18	660	372	440	222	.286	.374

Pitching Statistics—Team ERA 2.30

	W	L	ERA	G	GS	CG	SHO	IP	H	R	ER	HR	BB	SO
Honus Wagner	0	0	0.00	1	0	0	0	5.1	4	2	0	0	2	5
Ed Poole	0	0	1.13	1	0	0	0	8.0	7	4	1	0	3	2
Jesse Tannehill	20	6	1.95	26	24	23	2	231.0	203	78	50	0	25	100
Deacon Phillippe	20	9	2.05	31	30	29	5	272.0	265	90	62	1	26	122
Jack Chesbro	28	6	2.17	35	33	31	8	286.1	242	81	69	1	62	136
Sam Leever	15	7	2.39	28	26	23	4	222.0	203	73	59	2	31	86
Ed Doheny	16	4	2.53	22	21	19	2	188.1	161	68	53	0	61	88
Warren McLaughlin	3	0	2.77	3	3	3	0	26.0	27	13	8	0	9	13
Harvey Cushman	0	4	7.36	4	4	3	0	25.2	30	31	21	0	31	12
Total	102	36	2.30	151	141	131	21	1264.2	1142	440	323	4	250	564

Chapter Notes

Chapter 1

1. Frederick G. Lieb, *The Pittsburgh Pirates* (1948, reprint Carbondale: Southern University Press, 2003), 42–43.
2. *Ibid.*, 43.
3. "Dreyfuss Has It: Pittsburgh's Club Will Be His Property in a Few Days," *Sporting Life,* November 4, 1899, 4.
4. Circle, "Pittsburgh Points: A Loophole Spoils the Sale," *Sporting Life,* November 11, 1899, 3.
5. *Ibid.*
6. "Dreyfuss Has Three Offers: He Is Dealing With Pittsburg, Chicago and New York," *The Pittsburg Press,* December 7, 1899, 5.
7. *Ibid.*
8. "Union Station Smallpox Scare: Train Held Up Until Suspected Cases Were Examined," *The Pittsburg Press,* December 9, 1899, 1.
9. "Collapse of a Packing House: D. E. Francis, The Pork Packer, Caught in the Ruins," *The Pittsburg Press,* December 9, 1899, 4.
10. "Gossip About The Big Deal: Dreyfuss Admits That It Was Practically Closed Monday," *The Pittsburg Press,* December 9, 1899, 5.
11. *Ibid.*
12. Pirate, "Gigantic Deal: Star Colonels Sold to Pittsburg Club," *The Sporting News,* December 16, 1899, 3.
13. "Gossip About the Big Deal: Dreyfuss Admits That It Was Practically Closed Monday," 5.
14. "Gigantic Deal: Star Colonels Sold to Pittsburg Club," 3.
15. "Gossip About the Big Deal: Dreyfuss Admits That It Was Practically Closed Monday," 5.
16. "Gigantic Deal: Star Colonels Sold to Pittsburg Club," 3.
17. "Gossip About the Big Deal: Dreyfuss Admits That It Was Practically Closed Monday," 5.
18. "Late News: Dreyfuss Elected President—Will Control Pittsburg Club," *The Sporting News,* December 16, 1899, 1.
19. Circle, "Pittsburg Points: The Coming of the New President Awaited," *Sporting Life,* January 6, 1900, 8.
20. Al. E. Gheny, "Happy Pittsburg: Nothing To Worry the Smoky City Fans," *The Sporting News,* February 3, 1900, 3.
21. "Base Ball Caught On the Fly," *The Sporting News,* January 27, 1900, 5.
22. *Ibid.*
23. "Dreyfuss Has Three Offers: He Is Dealing With Pittsburg, Chicago and New York," 5.
24. Al. E. Gheny, "Coming to a Head: Circuit Complications Will Soon Be Settled," *The Sporting News,* March 10, 1900, 2.
25. Al. E. Gheny, "No Doubt About It: Association Is Dead Sure To Be a 'Go,'" *The Sporting News,* February 10, 1900, 3.
26. *Ibid.*
27. Gheny, "Coming To a Head: Circuit Complications Will Soon Be Settled," 2.
28. "League's Fast Outfielders: New York Is the Only Club That Cannot Boast of Speedy Trio," *The Pittsburg Press,* March 18, 1900, 14.
29. "The Day at Thomasville: The Pirates Were Tired After Four Hours of Hard Work," *The Pittsburg Press,* March 18, 1900, 14.
30. Al. E. Gheny, "Barney Explains: Did Not Go East to Consult With Freedman," *The Sporting News,* March 24, 1900, 2.
31. "Base Ball Caught on the Fly," *The Sporting News,* March 31, 1900, 5.
32. *Ibid.*
33. "Base Ball Caught on the Fly," *The Sporting News,* April 7, 1900, 5.
34. "Tips By the Managers," *The Sporting News,* March 24, 1900, 2.
35. Al. E. Gheny, "Headless Horde: Pirates a Bunch of Brainless Players," *The Sporting News,* April 14, 1900, 5.
36. *Ibid.*
37. *Ibid.*
38. Al. E. Gheny, "Hint To Dreyfus: Let Fred Clarke Manage the Pittsburg Team," *The Sporting News,* April 28, 1900, 3.
39. Al. E. Gheny, "Very Louisville: Pittsburg

Public's Opinion of the 1900 Pirates," *The Sporting News,* May 5, 1900, 5.
40. "Why Dick Cooley's Batting Average Was So Small," *The Pittsburg Press,* March 30, 1903, 10.
41. *Ibid.*
42. Al. E. Gheny, "Rumors of Deals: Rube Waddell May Figure in a Trade," *The Sporting News,* May 19, 1900, 3.
43. *Ibid.*
44. "Baseball: Rain Interfered at the Island," *The Mail And Empire,* July 25, 1900, 8.
45. "Waddell Has Been Loaned to Milwaukee," *The Sporting News,* July 28, 1900, 1.
46. "Good Fielding; Bad Batting: Pirates Take a Decided Brace in One Branch of the Game," *The Pittsburg Press,* May 23, 1900, 5.
47. "Rain Spoiled Another Game: All-Day Storm at St. Louis Prevented the Cardinals and Pirates From Meeting," *The Pittsburg Press,* June 24, 1900, 14.
48. *Ibid.*
49. "O'Connor Deal Is Not Closed: Col Dreyfuss Waiting for Word From President Robison," *The Pittsburg Press,* May 22, 1900, 5.
50. "Reds May Move To Washington: Poor Attendance at Cincinnati Said To Have Angered Brush," *The Pittsburg Press,* June 8, 1900, 5.
51. *Ibid.*
52. "The Pirates Need a Leader: Not Playing for Dick Cooley As They Did Fred Clarke," *The Pittsburg Press,* June 18, 1900, 5.
53. "Hurst Dislikes the Pirates: Sir Timothy Cannot Forget the Protest Filed by Dreyfuss," *The Pittsburg Press,* June 19, 1900, 5.
54. "Rain Spoiled Another Game: All-Day Storm at St. Louis Prevented the Cardinals and Pirates From Meeting," 14.
55. Circle, "Pittsburg Points: A Poor Western Trip by the Pirates," *Sporting Life,* June 30, 1900, 3.
56. *Ibid.*
57. "Accidents Hurt More Than Loss of the Game: Williams and Ritchey Crippled in Yesterday's Farce," *The Pittsburg Press,* July 14, 1900, 5.
58. Al. E. Gheny, "In Second Place: Pirates Have Forged Ahead of the Phillies," *The Sporting News,* August 18, 1900, 4.
59. *Ibid.*
60. Al. E. Gheny, "Wager Big Money: Pittsburg Sports Gamble on the Ball Games," *The Sporting News,* August 25, 1900, 4.
61. *Ibid.*
62. Al. E. Gheny, "Bright Prospects: Pirates Should Soon Pass the Brooklyn Bunch," *The Sporting News,* September 29, 1900, 3.
63. Circle, "Pittsburg Points: Splendid Start on the Eastern Trip," *Sporting Life,* September 8, 1900, 5.
64. Al. E. Gheny, "Base Ball Crazy: Pittsburg Wild Over Pirates' Pennant Prospects," *The Sporting News,* September 15, 1900, 1.

65. Gheny, "Bright Prospects: Pirates Should Soon Pass the Brooklyn Bunch," 3.
66. *Ibid.*
67. "Late News: Dreyfuss Will Punish Loafers," *The Sporting News,* October 13, 1900, 1.
68. *Ibid.*
69. Al. E. Gheny, "Patrons Pleased: Second Place Satisfies the Smoky City," *The Sporting News,* October 20, 1900, 3.
70. "Base Ball Caught on the Fly," *The Sporting News,* October 20, 1900, 5.
71. "H. C. Pulliam Will Manage the World's Championship Series: Players Decided Last Night To Put Him in Charge of Pittsburg-Brooklyn Games," *The Pittsburg Press,* October 14, 1900, 14.
72. "Pirates Were Outclassed by the Champions," *The Pittsburg Press,* October 16, 1900, 5.
73. "Pirates Gave the Champions Another Game," *The Pittsburg Press,* October 17, 1900, 5.
74. "Phillippe Was Too Clever for Pitcher Howell," *The Pittsburg Press,* October 18, 1900, 5.
75. "The Punch Bowl Goes To Pitcher Joe M'Ginnity," *The Pittsburg Press,* October 19, 1900, 5.
76. *Ibid.*
77. Francis C. Richter, "Brooklyn on Top: Wins the Cup From Pittsburg in Easy Fashion," *Sporting Life,* October 27, 1900, 7.
78. "Tips by the Managers," *The Sporting News,* October 27, 1900, 2.
79. A. R. Cratty, "Angry Owners: Col. Dreyfus' Bed in Pittsburg Evidently Not One of Roses—What the Gossips Say About Pittsburg Club Affairs," *Sporting Life,* December 29, 1900, 7.
80. "Gossip of the Players," *The Sporting News,* December 29, 1900, 2.
81. *Ibid.*
82. Al. E. Gheny, "Utter Nonsense: Story That Writers Will Be Barred in 1901," *The Sporting News,* November 3, 1900, 2.
83. Gheny, "Patrons Pleased: Second Place Satisfies the Smoky City," 3.
84. Al. E. Gheny, "To Keep Williams: Dreyfus Will Not Trade Him for Doyle," *The Sporting News,* November 24, 1900, 3.
85. Al. E. Gheny, "Pulliam Denies: Will Not Be With Chicago Club in 1900," *The Sporting News,* December 1, 1900, 2.
86. "Gossip of the Meeting," *The Pittsburg Press,* December 14, 1900, 5.
87. Francis C. Richter, "Dreyfus Dumped: Pittsburg's Club Can't Let Well Enough Alone," *Sporting Life,* December 29, 1900, 7.

Chapter 2

1. Al. E. Gheny, "Pulliam Denies: Will Not Be with Chicago Club in 1900," *The Sporting News,* December 1, 1900, 2.

2. A. R. Cratty, "Angry Owners: Col. Dreyfus' Bed in Pittsburg Evidently Not One of Roses—What the Gossips Are Saying About Pittsburg Club Affairs," *Sporting Life,* December 29, 1900, 7.
3. *Ibid.*
4. "Col. Dreyfuss Says Pulliam Will Be Missed," *The Pittsburg Press,* December 17, 1900, 5.
5. *Ibid.*
6. "Gossip of the Meeting," *The Pittsburg Press,* December 14, 1900, 5.
7. "Jennings May Be the Pirates' Next Manager," *The Pittsburg Press,* December 21, 1900, 5.
8. "Base Ball Caught on the Fly," *The Sporting News,* December 29, 1900, 5.
9. Francis C. Richter, "Dreyfus Dumped: Pittsburg's Club Can't Let Well Enough Alone," *Sporting Life,* December 29, 1900, 7.
10. Al. E. Gheny, "To Keep Williams: Dreyfus Will Not Trade Him for Doyle," *The Sporting News,* November 24, 1900, 3.
11. "Up Against It: Barney Dreyfus in a Bad Position in Pittsburg After Making a Phenomenal Success," *Sporting Life,* December 22, 1900, 11.
12. A. R. Cratty, "Pittsburg Points: Owners Pleased Over League Meeting Results," *Sporting Life,* December 22, 1900, 9.
13. *Ibid.*
14. "Baseball Gossip," *The Pittsburg Press,* November 22, 1900, 5.
15. Al. E. Gheny, "Utter Nonsense: Story that Writers Will Be Barred in 1901," *The Sporting News,* November 3, 1900, page 2.
16. *Ibid.*
17. Al. E. Gheny, "To Keep Williams: Dreyfus Will Not Trade Him for Doyle," page 3.
18. "Gossip of the Meeting," *The Pittsburg Press,* December 14, 1900, 5.
19. "Baseball Gossip," *The Pittsburg Press,* December 17, 1900, 5.
20. Cratty, "Pittsburg Points: Owners Pleased Over League Meeting Results," 9.
21. *Ibid.*
22. Pirate, "Proposed Trade: Kerr Offers Jesse Tannehill for Ed Scott," *The Sporting News,* December 29, 1900, 4.
23. "Baseball Gossip," *The Pittsburg Press,* December 28, 1900, 5.
24. "Off For Cuba! Twenty League Players Make the Trip," *Sporting Life,* November 3, 1900, 6.
25. Duquesne, "Dreyfus Hopeful: Pirates' President Confident of Holding His Job," *The Sporting News,* February 9, 1901, 4.
26. A. R. Cratty, "A Fall Bath: Pittsburg's Park Covered With a Flood Tide," *Sporting Life,* December 1, 1900, 6.
27. "Tanny's Troubles: The Pittsburg Club's Star Pitcher Caught for Over $1,000 in a Bank Failure," *Sporting Life,* December 1, 1900, 9.
28. "Baseball Gossip," *The Pittsburg Press,* December 26, 1900, 5.
29. "Star Players Are in Favor of Striking," *The Pittsburg Press,* December 28, 1900, 5.
30. A. R. Cratty, "Pittsburg Points: No Change in the Presidential Situation," *Sporting Life,* January 12, 1901, 8.
31. Duquesne, "Facts About the Deal: How Barney Dreyfus Beat Kerr and Auten," *The Sporting News,* March 2, 1901, 4.
32. *Ibid.*
33. "Baseball Magnates Still Have the Stage," *The Pittsburg Press,* January 19, 1901, 5.
34. "Dreyfuss' Deed: He Temporarily Blocks Pittsburg Club Election," *Sporting Life,* January 19, 1901, 7.
35. "Baseball Gossip," *The Pittsburg Press,* January 15, 1901, 5.
36. Francis Richter, "Doughty Dreyfuss: The Pittsburg President Scores Another Point," *Sporting Life,* January 26, 1901, 6.
37. "Baseball Gossip," *The Pittsburg Press,* January 16, 1901, 5.
38. A. R. Cratty, "Pittsburg Points: Pleasing Let-Up in the Pirate Directors' Squabble," *Sporting Life,* February 9, 1901, 8.
39. Francis C. Richter, "Dreyfuss Wins Out: Secures Control of Pittsburg Through Purchase," *Sporting Life,* February 23, 1901, 8.
40. *Ibid.*
41. *Ibid.*
42. "O'Brien No More: The Crack General Player of the Pittsburg Club Is Dead at Phoenix, Arizona," *Sporting Life,* February 9, 1901, 10.
43. *Ibid.*
44. "Baseball Gossip," *The Pittsburg Press,* March 21, 1901, 8.
45. "Honors for Fred Clarke: Chicago Man Says Manager Will Be Busy at the League Meeting," *The Pittsburg Press,* February 23, 1901, 6.
46. *Ibid.*
47. "Owners and Players Agree: Conference Between Zimmer and Magnates Result in Peace," *The Pittsburg Press,* February 27, 1901, 6.
48. *Ibid.*
49. Duquesne, "Pirates Prepared: Col. Dreyfus Signed Team in One Week," *The Sporting News,* March 16, 1901, 2.
50. "Suit Against Connie Mack: Pres. Dreyfuss of the Pittsburg Club To Bring Action for Alleged Breach of Contract," *Boston Daily Globe,* March 8, 1901, 3.
51. "Notes From the World of Sport," *Hamilton Daily Republican-News,* March 30, 1901, 8.
52. *Ibid.*
53. "Johnson Jots: The President Pays His Respects to Messrs. Murnane and Dreyfuss and Some of the Contract Jumpers," *Sporting Life,* April 6, 1901, 4.
54. "Notes From the World of Sport: Williams

Signs With the Baltimore Club," *Hamilton Daily Republican-News,* March 25, 1901, 7.

55. "Clarke's Men at the Springs: Pirates Arrive at Their Destination and Get Down To Work," *The Pittsburg Press,* April 1, 1901, 5.

56. "Notes From the World of Sport: Williams Signs With the Baltimore Club," 7.

57. Duquesne, "Is Saying Little: But Dreyfus Is Considering Jimmy Williams' Case," *The Sporting News,* April 6, 1901, 2.

58. *Ibid.*

59. "Clarke's Men at the Springs: Pirates Arrive at Their Destination and Get Down To Work," 5.

60. *Ibid.*

61. "Jimmy Williams Here: Will Not Talk Until He Consults His Attorney," *The Pittsburg Press,* April 3, 1901, 8.

62. "Baseball Gossip," *The Pittsburg Press,* April 5, 1901, 8.

63. "Jimmy Williams Here: Will Not Talk Until He Consults His Attorney," 8.

64. *Ibid.*

65. "Pittsburg Means To Sue: Courts To Be Asked To Compel Damages from Williams and the Baltimore Club," *Baltimore American,* April 2, 1901, 4.

66. "Jimmy Williams Is a Heartless Flirt: Dallies With Pittsburg's President, and McGraw Thinks of a Bunch of Advance Money," *Baltimore American,* April 5, 1901, 4.

67. *Ibid.*

68. "Clarke's Chaff: the Pirates' Young Leader Isn't Mourning Over Williams' Desertion and Jabs Relative Fraser," *Sporting Life,* April 27, 1901, 8.

69. Duquesne, "Pirates Pleased: No Training Point Equal To Hot Springs," *The Sporting News,* April 13, 1901, 5.

70. *Ibid.*

71. "Ritchey Off To Join Pirates: Second baseman Left Last Night With Col. Dreyfuss for Hot Springs," *The Pittsburg Press,* April 7, 1901, 16.

72. "Compares Two Local Teams: Manager Clarke Says New Club Is Stronger Than the 1900 Outfit," *The Pittsburg Press,* April 12, 1901, 8.

73. "Cool and Cloudy at Cincinnati: Pirates May Again Be Prevented From Meeting the Reds," *The Pittsburg Press,* April 19, 1901, 8.

74. "Pirates Start With a Victory: Bunched Hits Beat the Reds," *The Pittsburg Press,* April 21, 1901, 16.

75. "Bransfield Described: Jed Grillo Evidently Considers Newcomer a Fine Player," *The Pittsburg Press,* April 22, 1901, 8.

76. "Clarke Defends Rube Waddell: Bad Weather Affects Eddie As Much As Other Players," *The Pittsburg Press,* April 24, 1901, p .8.

77. "First Baseball Game of Season: It May Be Played at Exposition Park Tomorrow Afternoon," *The Pittsburg Press,* April 26, 1901, 8.

78. Alan H. Levy, *Rube Waddell: The Zany, Brilliant Life of a Strikeout Artist* (Jefferson, NC:McFarland, 2000), 76.

79. *Ibid.,* 76–77.

80. *Ibid.,* 77.

81. A. R. Cratty, "Pittsburg Points: Clarke's Men Split Even in First At-Home Series," *Sporting Life,* May 11, 1901, 8.

82. Duquesne, "Not Pennant Ball: The Brand That Pirates Have Been Playing," *The Sporting News,* May 11, 1901, 3.

83. Cratty, "Pittsburg Points: Clarke's Men Split Even in First At-Home Series," 8.

84. *Ibid.*

85. Duquesne, "Not Pennant Ball: The Brand That Pirates Have Been Playing," 3.

86. "Baseball Gossip," *The Pittsburg Press,* May 10, 1901, 8.

87. Duquesne, "Clarke Disabled: Pirates Feel the Loss of Their Leader," *The Sporting News,* May 18, 1901, 7.

88. "Features of Friday's Game," *The Pittsburg Press,* May 11, 1901, 8.

89. "Baseball Gossip," *The Pittsburg Press,* May 25, 1901, 8.

90. "Baseball Gossip," *The Pittsburg Press,* May 27, 1901, 8.

91. Duquesne, "Attacked Umpire: Cunningham's Close Call on Pittsburg Grounds," *The Sporting News,* June 8, 1901, 7.

92. "Umpire Chased by Angry Mob: Cunningham's Many Mistakes During Spirited Pittsburg-Cincinnati Game Yesterday Caused a Wild Scene at Exposition Park at the Finish," *The Pittsburg Press,* June 2, 1901, 1.

93. Duquesne, "Attacked Umpire: Cunningham's Close Call on Pittsburg Grounds," 7.

94. "Tommy Leach at Home," *The Pittsburg Press,* July 17, 1901, 8.

95. "Baseball Gossip," *The Pittsburg Press,* July 24, 1901, 8.

96. Dennis DeValeria and Jeanne Burke DeValeria, *Honus Wagner: A Biography* (New York: Henry Holt, 1995), 94.

97. "Ely Released, Doheny Signed: Pittsburg Club Parted With Its Veteran Short Stop," *The Pittsburg Press,* July 26, 1901, 8.

98. DeValeria, *Honus Wagner: A Biography,* 94.

99. *Ibid.*

100. Duquesne, "Americans Agent: Charge Of Disloyalty Made Against Ely," *The Sporting News,* August 3, 1901, 4.

101. "Baseball Notes," *Boston Daily Globe,* August 11, 1901, 4.

102. Duquesne, "Nothing To Fear: If the Pirates' Regulars Are on Duty," *The Sporting News,* August 31, 1901, 4.

103. "Wagner Scored Run That Won the Pen-

nant: Lefty Davis, Clarke, Beaumont and Bransfield Also Prominent in Rally That Ended the Long Struggle," *The Pittsburg Press,* September 28, 1901, 8.
104. *Ibid.*

Chapter 3

1. "Pennant Clinched: Pittsburg Wins the National League Bunting," *The Toledo Bee,* September 24, 1901, 6.
2. *Ibid.*
3. *Ibid.*
4. *Ibid.*
5. "R. R. Special Was on Time: Bad Weather Did Not Delay Cup Presentation to the Pirates," *The Pittsburg Press,* October 3, 1901, 8.
6. *Ibid.*
7. *Ibid.*
8. "Details of the Shooting: Latest Story of How President McKinley Was Wounded," *The Pittsburg Press,* September 7, 1901, 7.
9. "Baseball Gossip," *The Pittsburg Press,* September 12, 1901, 8.
10. "R. R. Special Was on Time: Bad Weather Did Not Delay Cup Presentation to the Pirates," 8.
11. Duquesne, "Royally Treated: Pirates Richly Rewarded by President Dreyfus," *The Sporting News,* October 19, 1901, 3.
12. *Ibid.*
13. *Ibid.*
14. "Ely Released, Doheny Signed: Pittsburg Club Parted With Its Veteran Short Stop," *The Pittsburg Press,* July 26, 1901, 8.
15. "Base Ball Caught on the Fly," *The Sporting News,* August 15, 1903, 5.
16. *Ibid.*
17. "Base Ball Caught on the Fly," *The Sporting News,* October 12, 1901, 5.
18. "Baseball Gossip," *The Pittsburg Press,* October 15, 1901, 8.
19. "Said By the Magnates," *The Sporting News,* October 19, 1901, 2.
20. "Pirates Dined at the Schenley: Final Celebration of Pennant Victory Took Place Last Night," *The Pittsburg Press,* October 16, 1901, 8.
21. "Baseball Gossip," *The Pittsburg Press,* October 17, 1901, 8.
22. "Base Ball Caught on the Fly," *The Sporting News,* October 26, 1901, 5.
23. "Conroy Loyal: New Shortstop Says He Will Stick to Pittsburg," *The Pittsburg Press,* October 22, 1901, 8.
24. *Ibid.*
25. "Baseball Gossip," *The Pittsburg Press,* October 31, 1901, 8.
26. "Base Ball Caught on the Fly," *The Sporting News,* November 9, 1901, 5.
27. *Ibid.*

28. Duquesne, "Were Approached: American Made Overtures to the Pirates," *The Sporting News,* November 2, 1901, 4.
29. *Ibid.*
30. *Ibid.*
31. Dennis DeValeria and Jeanne Burke DeValeria, *Honus Wagner: A Biography* (New York: Harry Holt, 1995), 89.
32. "Baseball Gossip," *The Pittsburg Press,* November 7, 1901, 8.
33. Duquesne, "Can't Get Grounds: No Chance of Opposition in New York," *The Sporting News,* November 16, 1901, 3.
34. "Baseball Gossip," *The Pittsburg Press,* November 25, 1901, 8.
35. "Baseball Gossip," *The Pittsburg Press,* November 14, 1901, 8.
36. "Ban Johnson's New Revelation: Peace Negotiation Spoiled by Blunder of John T. Brush," *The Pittsburg Press,* November 16, 1901, 3.
37. *Ibid.*
38. "Said By the Magnates," *The Sporting News,* December 14, 1901, 2.
39. "Captain Kerr Sent for Hough: Baseball Secrets of Last Summer Exposed by Johnson," *The Pittsburg Press,* November 30, 1901, 8.
40. *Ibid.*
41. "Baseball Gossip," *The Pittsburg Press,* November 30, 1901, 8.
42. Duquesne, "Outlined a Plan: National League Meeting Will Be Mere Formality," *The Sporting News,* December 7, 1901, 1.
43. *Ibid.*
44. Duquesne, "Went With Brush: Dreyfus Traveled to New York With John T.," *The Sporting News,* December 14, 1901, 2.
45. "Between Sessions: Baseball Talk Heard in Corridors of Fifth Avenue Hotel," *The Pittsburg Press,* December 11, 1901, 8.
46. *Ibid.*
47. *Ibid.*
48. "Freedman Won With a Threat: Got Boston's Vote by Talking of Deserting the League," *The Pittsburg Press,* December 13, 1901, 8.
49. "May Be Conference: American League Magnates Will Be in New York," *The Pittsburg Press,* December 13, 1901, 8.
50. "Freedman Won With a Threat: Got Boston's Vote by Talking of Deserting the League," 8.
51. "Pittsburg May Leave the National League and Join the American: Barney Dreyfus Is Angry at the Action of Freedman and Brush," *The Youngstown Daily Vindicator,* December 13, 1901, 11.
52. "Brush Scheming Since the Fall of 1900," *The Pittsburg Press,* December 13, 1901, 8.
53. *Ibid.*
54. *Ibid.*

55. "Big League Is in Bad Way: One Faction Bolts and the Other Elects Spalding President," *The Pittsburg Press*, December 14, 1901, 8.
56. *Ibid.*
57. *Ibid.*
58. "Was Spalding or Baseball Trust: Dreyfuss Preferred the New Leader and Made a Successful Fight for Him," *The Pittsburg Press*, December 15, 1901, 22.
59. "Baseball Case in Court Today: Judge Scott, of New York, Listening to Arguments of Magnates," *The Pittsburg Press*, December 20, 1901, 8.
60. "Bolters Walked Into a Trap: In Trying to Catch Spalding, They Tied Themselves Up," *The Pittsburg Press*, December 21, 1901, 8.
61. "A.G. Spalding Will Obey Order of New York Court: League Clubs Notified That While Case Is Tied Up, Each Must Take Care of Itself—Bolters Left in Bad Shape," *The Pittsburg Press*, December 23, 1901, 8.
62. "Baseball Gossip," *The Pittsburg Press*, December 16, 1901, 8.
63. "Politics' Part in Baseball War: New Administration in New York Will Be Unfriendly to Freedman," *The Pittsburg Press*, December 29, 1901, 18.
64. "Baseball Gossip," *The Pittsburg Press*, December 30, 1901, 10.
65. "J. T. Brush Did Propose Trust: Promised Report of League Meeting Cannot Alter the Fact," *The Pittsburg Press*, January 20, 1902, 10.
66. *Ibid.*
67. Duquesne, "Bluff Did Not Go: Tactics J. T. Brush Used With Dreyfus," *The Sporting News*, December 21, 1901, 1.
68. *Ibid.*
69. *Ibid.*
70. "J. T. Brush Did Propose Trust: Promised Report of League Meeting Cannot Alter the Fact," 10.
71. "Twelve-Club League Coming: Latest Guess Upon the Plans of Spalding and Johnson," *The Pittsburg Press*, January 17, 1902, 12.
72. "Big Leagues Will Stand Together: Decision Reached by Johnson, Spalding, Hart and Dreyfuss," *The Pittsburg Press*, January 19, 1902, 18.
73. "J. T. Brush Did Propose Trust: Promised Report of League Meeting Cannot Alter the Fact," 10.
74. "Col. Dreyfus Is Away for Purpose: President of Pittsburg Club To Remain at Louisville Until War Ends," *The Pittsburg Press*, January 12, 1902, 18.
75. "Fred Clarke Visits Chicago: Pirates' Manager Sees James A. Hart and Ban Johnson," *The Pittsburg Press*, December 26, 1901, 8.
76. *Ibid.*
77. "Wagner Turned Somers' Offer: Bookmaker Fay Tells How Hans Signed Latest Contract," *The Pittsburg Press*, January 23, 1902, 12.
78. *Ibid.*
79. "Brush Must Have a Trust: Will Not Return to Game Under any Other Condition," *The Pittsburg Press*, January 27, 1902, 10.
80. Duquesne, "No Trust for Him: Barney Dreyfus Prefers a Four-Club Circuit," *The Sporting News*, February 8, 1902, 3.
81. *Ibid.*
82. *Ibid.*
83. W. H. Locke, "Is For Spalding: W. C. Temple Is Dreyfus' Second Choice," *The Sporting News*, March 8, 1902, 3.
84. "Big Four True to Leader: Pittsburg, Philadelphia, Brooklyn and Chicago Decline to Accept Resignation of A. G. Spalding," *The Pittsburg Press*, February 23, 1902, 18.
85. "Col. Dreyfuss for President: Hart, of Chicago, Seems To Be for Pittsburg Magnate," *The Pittsburg Press*, March 3, 1902, 10.
86. *Ibid.*
87. "Busy Week for Baseball Men: Argument of the National League Injunction Case Was Postponed," *The Pittsburg Press*, March 2, 1902, 22.
88. "Freedman Won Legal Fight: Justice Truax Has Decided Against Spaldingites in Preliminary Bout," *The Pittsburg Press*, March 30, 1902, 20.
89. "Slate Makers Meet This Week: Pulliam May Be Sole Representative of the Pittsburg Club," *The Pittsburg Press*, March 30, 1902, 20.
90. "Peace Reigns in National: Magnates Invite W. C. Temple To Accept the Presidency," *The Pittsburg Press*, April 3, 1902, p, 12.
91. *Ibid.*
92. Duquesne, "Blow To Dreyfus: Temple's Refusal To Accept the Presidency," *The Sporting News*, April 12, 1902, 3.
93. *Ibid.*
94. "League Raises Fund To Raid the American: National Ready To Spend $100,000 To Get Back Players Stolen by Ban Johnson's Organization—Freedman's Plan Is Adopted," *The Pittsburg Press*, April 4, 1902, 16.
95. "Baseball Gossip," *The Pittsburg Press*, March 11, 1902, 12.
96. *Ibid.*

Chapter 4

1. "Magnates Meet; Truce Respected: Nick Young Presides and Three Schedules Are Discussed," *The New York World*, April 2, 1902, 5.
2. "Pirates Wanted by American: Even at This Late Day Room Can Be Made for Pittsburg Club," *The Pittsburg Press*, March 21, 1902, 20.
3. *Ibid.*
4. Frederick G. Lieb, *The Pittsburgh Pirates*

(Carbondale: Southern Illinois University Press, 2003), 87.

5. "Around the Sporting World: Record of Happenings for Those Interested in Athletics To Read," *New Castle News,* January 22, 1902, 7.

6. Ibid.

7. Duquesne, "Is Not Wavering: Barney Dreyfus With Spalding to the End," *The Sporting News,* January 18, 1902, 3.

8. "Clarke Fooled Waddell: Reduced Rube's Speed by Discussing Fall Hunting Trip," *The Pittsburg Press,* January 3, 1902, 12.

9. Duquesne, "Sure of Success: Dreyfus' Faith in Spalding Is Not Shaken," *The Sporting News,* February 1, 1902, 3.

10. "Baseball Gossip," *The Pittsburg Press,* February 5, 1902, 10.

11. Duquesne, "Sure of Success: Dreyfus' Faith in Spalding Is Not Shaken," 3.

12. "Baseball Gossip," *The Pittsburg Press,* February 4, 1902, 12.

13. "Clarke Played Hockey: Leader of the Pirates Made Hit in the Winter Sport," *The Pittsburg Press,* February 7, 1902, 12.

14. "Hockey and Skating," *The Pittsburg Press,* February 7, 1902, 12.

15. "Hockey and Skating," *The Pittsburg Press,* February 20, 1902, 12.

16. "Hockey and Skating," *The Pittsburg Press,* February 21, 1902, 12.

17. Duquesne, "Sure of Success: Dreyfus' Faith in Spalding Is Not Shaken," 3.

18. "Latest Baseball Gossip," *The Pittsburg Press,* February 9, 1902, 18.

19. "Gossip of the Players," *The Sporting News,* February 22, 1901, 2.

20. "Baseball Gossip," *The Pittsburg Press,* February 10, 1902, 10.

21. "Baseball Gossip," *The Pittsburg Press,* March 11, 1902, 12.

22. "Baseball Gossip," *The Pittsburg Press,* March 20, 1902, 12.

23. "Baseball Gossip," *The Pittsburg Press,* March 19, 1902, 12.

24. Duquesne, "Suspects a Trick: Dreyfus Wants All Magnates at Meeting," *The Sporting News,* March 29, 1902, 4.

25. "Baseball Gossip," *The Pittsburg Press,* March 19, 1902, 12.

26. Duquesne, "True To Spalding: Four Clubs Are With Him to a Finish," *The Sporting News,* March 1, 1902, 3.

27. "Baseball Gossip," *The Pittsburg Press,* February 14, 1902, 12.

28. "Beaumont Happy: Pirate Starts to Training and Has Confidence in Dreyfuss," *The Pittsburg Press,* February 16, 1902, 18.

29. "Tips by the Managers," *The Sporting News,* March 8, 1902, 2.

30. "Pirates Start Tonight for Training Place: Fifteen Players Will Board the Hot Springs Special at 7 O'Clock—Deacon Phillippe Will Have Charge of the Excursion," *The Pittsburg Press,* March 29, 1902, 12.

31. Ibid.

32. "Thirteen is the Pirates' Hoodoo: Starting With Jonahed Numbers Locals Have Much Trouble," *The Pittsburg Press,* March 31, 1902, 12.

33. "Pittsburg Points: Pennant Boys Have Landed in Arkansaw," *Sporting Life,* April 5, 1902, 9.

34. "Thirteen Is the Pirates' Hoodoo: Starting With Jonahed Number, Locals Have Much Trouble," 12.

35. Ibid.

36. Ibid.

37. "Pirates Pay Usual Penalty: Stiff and Sore After Yesterday's Exercise on the Diamond," *The Pittsburg Press,* April 2, 1902, 10.

38. Ibid.

39. Ibid.

40. "Pirates Keep Early Hours: Clarke Schedule Calls for Practice at 9:30 in the Morning," *The Pittsburg Press,* April 6, 1902, 20.

41. "Good Week for Clarke's Crew: Pirates Have Made Much Progress in Their Training," *The Pittsburg Press,* April 5, 1902, 16.

42. "Prof. Sam Leever Reports to Clarke," *The Pittsburg Press,* April 6, 1902, 20.

43. "Catcher Smith May Be a Jumper: Rumor Reaches Hot Springs That American League Has Taken Him," *The Pittsburg Press,* April 4, 1902, 16.

44. "All Pirates at Hot Springs: Pulliam, Smith and Tommy Leach Arrived There Today," *The Pittsburg Press,* April 7, 1902, 10.

45. "Good Practice for Clarke's Champions: Little Rock Defeated, But Gave the Pirates a Scare While Skopec Pitched," *The Pittsburg Press,* April 8, 1902, 12.

46. "Baseball Gossip," *The Pittsburg Press,* April 11, 1902, 16.

47. "Baseball Gossip," *The Pittsburg Press,* April 9, 1902, 10.

48. "Baseball Gossip," *The Pittsburg Press,* February 25, 1902, 10.

49. "Leever To Work on Opening Day: Schoolmaster Is in Better Shape Than the Other Twirlers," *The Pittsburg Press,* April 9, 1902, 10.

50. Duquesne, "Has the Managers: National League Teams Will Be Well Handled," *The Pittsburg Press,* April 19, 1902, 3.

51. Ibid.

52. "Lefty Davis Out of the Game: Speedy Rightfielder Injured on Hard Field at Hot Springs," *The Pittsburg Press,* April 10, 1902, 12.

53. "Baseball Gossip," *The Pittsburg Press,* April 11, 1902, 16.

54. "Little Rock Team Not Allowed to Score," *The Pittsburg Press,* April 12, 1902, 16.

55. "Rain Prevented Exhibition Game: Pirates Left Little Rock Without Playing the Half-

Holiday Match," *The Pittsburg Press,* April 13, 1902, 22.
56. *Ibid.*
57. *Ibid.*
58. "Great Pitching by Phillippe and Tanny: Pirates Shut Out St. Joe and Allowed That Team Only One Hit," *The Pittsburg Press,* April 14, 1902, 10.
59. "Tommy Leach Made a Great Double Play: Brilliant Fielding of the Sprinter Helped Pirates To Win a Close Game," *The Pittsburg Press,* April 15, 1902, 12.
60. "Baseball Gossip," *The Pittsburg Press,* April 15, 1902, 12.
61. "Tommy Leach Made a Great Double Play: Brilliant Fielding of the Sprinter Helped Pirates To Win a Close Game," 12.
62. "Baseball Gossip," *The Pittsburg Press,* April 15, 1902, 12.
63. "Brief Sporting Items," *New Castle News,* April 2, 1902, 15.
64. "Practice Ends This Evening: The Pirates Will Not Make the Side Trip to Des Moines," *The Pittsburg Press,* April 15, 1902, 12.
65. "Baseball Gossip," *The Pittsburg Press,* April 16, 1902, 10.
66. "Pirates Close Their Exhibition Series: Final Match at St. Joseph Shows Real Strength of the League Pennant Winners," *The Pittsburg Press,* April 16, 1902, 10.
67. "Practice Ends This Evening: The Pirates Will Not Make Their Side Trip to Des Moines," 12.
68. *Ibid.*
69. "Base Ball Caught on the Fly," *The Sporting News,* April 26, 1902, 5.
70. *Ibid.*
71. H. W. Lanigan, "Fred Clarke Not a Prophet: Boss of the Pirates Declines To Make Predictions," *The Pittsburg Press,* April 17, 1902, 12.
72. *Ibid.*
73. "Many Surprises for Ball Fans on Opening Day: Pittsburg's Champions Won From Donovan's New St. Louis Club, But Small Score Unexpected," *The Pittsburg Press,* April 18, 1902, 16.
74. *Ibid.*
75. "St. Louis Fans Are Stirred Up: They Believe New Cardinals Can Win From the Champions," *The Pittsburg Press,* April 19, 1902, 16.
76. H. W. Lanigan, "Pirates Capture Bad Game of Ball: Cardinals Suffer From Serious Attack of Rattles in Presence of Big Crowd," *The Pittsburg Press,* April 20, 1902, 22.
77. "Pirates Made a Clean Sweep: Nothing Left of Cardinals When Champions Started Home," *The Pittsburg Press,* April 21, 1902, 16.
78. *Ibid.*
79. "Baseball Gossip," *The Pittsburg Press,* April 21, 1902, 16.
80. *Ibid.*
81. "Hard Work Promised for Fred Clarke's Crew," *The Pittsburg Press,* April 19, 1902, 16.
82. Duquesne, "In Superb Shape: Pirates' St. Louis Victories Not a Surprise," *The Sporting News,* April 26, 1902, 3.
83. "Opening Day To Be Greatest on Record Here: Men of Prominence Will Be Present Tuesday To Help the Club Owners Celebrate," *The Pittsburg Press,* April 20, 1902, 21.
84. "Big Crowds Saw Players in Parade: People Lined the Street and Cheered the Champions As Well As Cincinnati Reds," *The Pittsburg Press,* April 22, 1902, 1.
85. "Pennant Day Exceeded All Expectations: Game, Weather and Patronage Combined To Make Event Greatest in History of Baseball Here," *The Pittsburg Press,* April 23, 1902, 12.
86. "Baseball Gossip," *The Pittsburg Press,* April 23, 1902, 12.
87. "Pennant Day Exceeded All Expectations: Game, Weather and Patronage Combined To Make Event Greatest in History Of Baseball Here," 12.
88. *Ibid.*
89. "Deacon Phil Downed Reds: Pittsburg Pitcher Was Team in Himself in Yesterday's Game," *The Pittsburg Press,* April 24, 1902, 12.
90. *Ibid.*
91. "Brief Comments Upon Pirates' First Defeat," *The Pittsburg Press,* April 25, 1902, 16.
92. "Pittsburg Out of First Place: Chicago's New Team Pushed Pennant Winners to Second Place," *The Pittsburg Press,* April 26, 1902, 8.
93. "Pirates Will Lose Games," *The Pittsburg Press,* April 26, 1902, 8.

Chapter 5

1. "Selee's New Team Will Get Rousing Welcome," *The Pittsburg Press,* April 27, 1902, 21.
2. *Ibid.*
3. "Pirates Again Lead the League: Regain First Place by Shutting Out the Ambitious Recruits From Windy City," *The Pittsburg Press,* April 27, 1902, 22.
4. *Ibid.*
5. Duquesne, "Faster This Year: Pirates Play Better Ball Than in 1901," *The Sporting News,* May 3, 1902, 3.
6. "Pirates Play at Windy City Today: Game Will Close Series That Has Attracted Attention All Over the Country," *The Pittsburg Press,* April 27, 1902, 21.
7. "Recruits Shut Out Once Again: Deacon Phillippe Applied the Whitewash Brush Artistically," *The Pittsburg Press,* April 28, 1902, 10.
8. "Comments of the Day in the Realm of the Rooter," *The Pittsburg Press,* April 30, 1902, 10.

Notes—Chapter 5

9. "Pirates Play at Windy City Today: Game Will Close Series That Has Attracted Attention All Over the Country," 21.
10. "Pittsburg's Champions: If They Win Another Flag May Go Around the World," *The Pittsburg Press*, April 28, 1902, 10.
11. "National League: How They Stand," *The Sporting News*, May 3, 1902, 2.
12. "Frost Pains the Jumpers: Heidrick Admits Antipathy of St. Louis Fans Is a Surprise," *The Pittsburg Press*, April 30, 1902, 10.
13. *Ibid*.
14. "Lefty Davis Wanted Dinner: He Shortened Yesterday's Game by Robbing Donovan of Long Hit," *The Pittsburg Press*, May 1, 1902, 12.
15. *Ibid*.
16. A. R. Cratty, "Pittsburg Points: Champions Have Lost None of Their Old Friends," *Sporting Life*, May 3, 1902, 13.
17. "Between the Innings," *The Pittsburg Press*, May 2, 1902, 16.
18. "Donovan's Men Took a Brace: Champions Had To Hustle To Win Yesterday's Game," *The Pittsburg Press*, May 3, 1902, 10.
19. *Ibid*.
20. Duquesne, "Proud of Pirates: Pittsburg Patrons Flock To the Games," *The Sporting News*, May 10, 1902, 6.
21. "Champions Won But Had To Fight: Brilliant Baseball Played in Closing Game of Series with St. Louis," *The Pittsburg Press*, May 4, 1902, 22.
22. *Ibid*.
23. *Ibid*.
24. *Ibid*.
25. "Comments of the Day in the Realm of the Rooter," *The Pittsburg Press*, May 1, 1902, 12.
26. "Reds No Match for Champions: Pittsburg Won As It Pleased Before Large Cincinnati Crowd," *The Pittsburg Press*, May 5, 1902, 10.
27. *Ibid*.
28. *Ibid*.
29. "Baseball Gossip," *The Pittsburg Press*, May 6, 1902, 12.
30. "Another Game for Pirates: Reds Unable To Check Advance of National League Champions," *The Pittsburg Press*, May 6, 1902, 12.
31. "Pirates Won in the Ninth: Bransfield's Triple and Ritchey's Homer Settled the Reds," *The Pittsburg Press*, May 7, 1902, 16.
32. *Ibid*.
33. "Comments of the Day in the Realm of the Rooter," *The Pittsburg Press*, May 9, 1902, 20.
34. *Ibid*.
35. "Doctor Newton Was Generous: Brooklyn Pitcher's Bases on Balls Gave Champions a Game," *The Pittsburg Press*, May 8, 1902, 16.
36. "Hanlon's Trio Made Great Hit: Sheckard, Dahlen and Kitson, Stars in Baseball Performance," *The Pittsburg Press*, May 9, 1902, 20.
37. "Comments of the Day in the Realm of the Rooter," *The Pittsburg Press*, May 10, 1902, 12.
38. "Donovan Paid for Kitson's Fun: Champions Got More Than Even for Defeat of Thursday," *The Pittsburg Press*, May 10, 1902, 12.
39. *Ibid*.
40. *Ibid*.
41. "Steady Playing by the Champions: Won Closing Game of Brooklyn Series by Giving Chesbro Fine Support," *The Pittsburg Press*, May 11, 1902, 22.
42. *Ibid*.
43. "Beaneaters Next on List: Buckenberger's Team Begins Four-Game Series Tomorrow," *The Pittsburg Press*, May 11, 1902, 21.
44. "Comments of the Day in the Realm of the Rooter," *The Pittsburg Press*, May 12, 1902, 12.
45. *Ibid*.
46. "Torture for John T. Brush: Owner of Reds Saw His Club Slaughtered by Champions," *The Pittsburg Press*, May 12, 1902, 12.
47. "Beaneaters Next on List: Buckenberger's Team Begins Four-Game Series Tomorrow," 21.
48. Duquesne, "No Limit in 1902: Pittsburg Will Not Part With Its Players," *The Sporting News*, May 17, 1902, 4.
49. *Ibid*.
50. *Ibid*.
51. *Ibid*.
52. *Ibid*.
53. "Tannehill Saved the Day: Southpaw Took Leever's Place and Outpitched Willis," *The Pittsburg Press*, May 13, 1902, 12.
54. "National League: How They Stand," *The Sporting News*, May 17, 1902, 2.
55. "Wild Pitching Beat Pirates: Chesbro's Lack of Control Gave Boston Six Runs at the Start," *The Pittsburg Press*, May 15, 1902, 8.
56. "Baseball and a Fist Fight: Pittsburgh Won Event No. 1 But Other Was a Draw," *The Pittsburg Press*, May 16, 1902, 20.
57. "In the Field of Sport: Clarke and Tenney Fight," *The Newark Advocate*, May 16, 1902, 7.
58. "Baseball and a Fist Fight: Pittsburgh Won Event No. 1 But Other Was a Draw," 20.
59. A. R. Cratty, "Pittsburg Points: Capt. Clarke Feels the Executive Board's Solid Hand," *Sporting Life*, May 24, 1902, 25.
60. "In the Field of Sport: Clarke and Tenney Fight," 7.
61. Cratty, "Pittsburg Points: Capt. Clarke Feels the Executive Board's Solid Hand," 25.
62. "In the Field of Sport: Clarke and Tenney Fight," 7.
63. Cratty, "Pittsburg Points: Capt. Clarke Feels the Executive Board's Solid Hand," 25.
64. "Comments of the Day in the Realm of the Rooter," *The Pittsburg Press*, May 16, 1902, 20.

65. Duquesne, "Fast and Daring: Pirates' Base Running Dazes Opponents," *The Sporting News,* May 24, 1902, 6.
66. "Good Day for Bransfield: Big Firstbaseman Batted in Five of Pittsburg's Six Runs," *The Pittsburg Press,* May 17, 1902, 10.
67. "Comments of the Day in the Realm of the Rooter," *The Pittsburg Press,* May 17, 1902, 10.
68. "Timely Drives Downed Quakers: Bransfield, Beaumont and Wagner Made Long Hits That Won for Leaders," *The Pittsburg Press,* May 18, 1902, 23.
69. "Champions at Chicago Today: They Will Be Home Tomorrow To Meet the Phillies Again," *The Pittsburg Press,* May 18, 1902, 20.
70. "Pirates Drew Great Crowd: Champions Crushed Chicago Cubs in Presence of 15,000 Persons," *The Pittsburg Press,* May 19, 1902, 10.
71. *Ibid.*
72. *Ibid.*
73. "President Will Speak at Pittsburg on July Fourth: How the Smoky City Is Going To Prepare for the Biggest Kind of Celebration," *The Newark Advocate,* May 19, 1902, 1.
74. *Ibid.*
75. *Ibid.*
76. "Conroy Scored Pirates' Runs: His Ninth Inning Triple Produced the Winning Tally," *The Pittsburg Press,* May 20, 1902, 12.
77. "Fine Finish by the Pirates: Tied Score in the Eighth and Won in Closing Inning," *The Pittsburg Press,* May 21, 1902, 12.
78. "New York Won First Round: Giants Held The Champions Down To Four Basehits," *The Pittsburg Press,* May 22, 1902, 12.
79. *Ibid.*
80. "Deacon Phil the Whole Show: Held the New York Club Down To Two Scratch Basehits," *The Pittsburg Press,* May 23, 1902, 20.
81. "Comments of the Day in the Realm of the Rooter," *The Pittsburg Press,* May 23, 1902, 20.
82. "Winning Run in the Ninth: Beaumont Earned the Tally That Decided a Well Pitched Game," *The Pittsburg Press,* May 24, 1902, 10.
83. *Ibid.*
84. "Eleven Batsmen Out on Strikes: Algy Chesbro Established New Record for Season in Final Game With Giants," *The Pittsburg Press,* May 25, 1902, 21.
85. *Ibid.*

Chapter 6

1. Duquesne, "Take To the Road: Pirates Have One Home Series in June," *The Sporting News,* May 31, 1902, 4.
2. *Ibid.*
3. Duquesne, "Fast and Daring: Pirates' Base Running Dazes Opponents," *The Sporting News,* May 24, 1902, 6.
4. "Comments of the Day in the Realm of the Rooter," *The Pittsburg Press,* May 24, 1902, 10.
5. *Ibid.*
6. "National League: How They Stand," *The Sporting News,* May 31, 1902, 2.
7. "Ned Hanlon Threatens To Crowd Champions," *The Pittsburg Press,* May 26, 1902, 12.
8. *Ibid.*
9. "Tanny Scored Winning Run: He Pitched Splendidly and Made Timely Three-Bagger," *The Pittsburg Press,* May 29, 1902, 12.
10. "Comments of the Day in the Realm of the Rooter," *The Pittsburg Press,* May 24, 1902, 10.
11. "Tanny Scored Winning Run: He Pitched Splendidly and Made Timely Three-Bagger," 12.
12. *Ibid.*
13. "Baseball Gossip," *The Pittsburg Press,* May 29, 1902, 12.
14. *Ibid.*
15. "First Shutout for Pirates: Menefee Pitched Chicago To Victory Before Big Crowd," *The Pittsburg Press,* May 31, 1902, 10.
16. *Ibid.*
17. "Colts Led When Game Was Called: Score 2 to 0 in Chicago's Favor When Darkness Stopped Scrapping Match," *The Pittsburg Press,* June 1, 1902, 20.
18. A.R. Cratty, "Pittsburg Points: Wind-Up of the Long Home Series of the Champs," *Sporting Life,* June 7, 1902, 5.
19. "Colts Led When Game Was Called: Score 2 to 0 in Chicago's Favor When Darkness Stopped Scrapping Match," 20.
20. Cratty, "Pittsburg Points: Wind-Up of the Long Home Series of the Champs," 5.
21. "Colts Led When Game Was Called: Score 2 to 0 in Chicago's Favor When Darkness Stopped Scrapping Match," 20.
22. *Ibid.*
23. *Ibid.*
24. Cratty, "Pittsburg Points: Wind-Up of the Long Home Series of the Champs," 5.
25. "Colts Led When Game Was Called: Score 2 to 0 in Chicago's Favor When Darkness Stopped Scrapping Match," 20.
26. *Ibid.*
27. "National League: The Official Record of the 1902 Pennant Race," *Sporting Life,* June 7, 1902, 11.
28. "Champions Fail When They Fight Umpires: Clarke Lost His Temper While Wrangling Over a Decision," *The Pittsburg Press,* June 1, 1902, 20.
29. Duquesne, "Lost One a Week: Pittsburg's Great Record at Exposition Park" *The Sporting News,* June 7, 1902, 6.
30. "National League: How They Stand," *The Sporting News,* June 7, 1902, 2.

31. Duquesne, "Lost One a Week: Pittsburg's Great Record at Exposition Park," 6.
32. "Comments of the Day in the Realm of the Rooter," *The Pittsburg Press,* June 3, 1902, 12.
33. "Harry Pulliam Will Attend League Meeting," *The Pittsburg Press,* June 2, 1902, 10.
34. "'All's Well,' Says Brush, But Gives No Details," *The Pittsburg Press,* June 4, 1902, 12.
35. *Ibid.*
36. *Ibid.*
37. "Col. Dreyfuss Captures a Star: Maloney of St. Louis Reported To Be Signed for Next Season," *The Pittsburg Press,* June 4, 1902, 12.
38. "Dr. Harry White Fooled Pirates: Phillies' Southpaw Allowed Champions Only Four Basehits," *The Pittsburg Press,* June 4, 1902, 12.
39. "Dreyfuss Will Back Team Against Pick of Country," *The Pittsburg Press,* June 4, 1902, 12.
40. "In the Field of Sport: Dreyfuss Will Back Pirates," *The Newark Advocate,* June 5, 1902, 7.
41. "Some Fun Ahead: That Square Sport, Barney Dreyfuss, Stirs Things Up," *Sporting Life,* June 14, 1902, 3.
42. *Ibid.*
43. "Pirates Won in the Windup: In Eighth and Ninth Innings the Necessary Runs Were Scored," *The Pittsburg Press,* June 5, 1902, 12.
44. "Champions Did the Old Trick: Hammered Out Enough Runs To Win in the Ninth," *The Pittsburg Press,* June 6, 1902, 20.
45. *Ibid.*
46. *Ibid.*
47. "Triple Play Saved the Day: Ritchey and Wagner Retired Giants in a Sensational Way in the Ninth," *The Pittsburg Press,* June 7, 1902, 10.
48. *Ibid.*
49. "Only One Giant Reached Second: Phillippe Gave Grand Exhibition of Pitching Before a Half Holiday Crowd," *The Pittsburg Press,* June 8, 1902, 22.
50. "Pittsburg Rooters Happy: They Sang Popular Ditty To Champions and Had Strong Chorus," *The Pittsburg Press,* June 8, 1902, 22.
51. Cratty, "Pittsburg Points: Wind-Up of the Long Home Series of the Champs," 5.
52. "Won Exhibition Game: Pirates Played Poorly at Newark, But Got Necessary Runs," *The Pittsburg Press,* June 9, 1902, 10.
53. A. R. Cratty, "Pittsburg Points: Champs Have Not Been Worried in the East," *Sporting Life,* June 14, 1902, 6.
54. *Ibid.*
55. "New York Team Won by Bunching Its Hits: Jesse Tannehill Pitched As Well As Sparks, But Was Not As Lucky," *The Pittsburg Press,* June 10, 1902, 12.
56. "Baseball Gossip," *The Pittsburg Press,* June 10, 1902, 12.
57. "New York Team Won by Bunching Its Hits: Jesse Tannehill Pitched As Well As Sparks, But Was Not As Lucky," 12.
58. "Baseball Gossip," *The Pittsburg Press,* June 12, 1902, 12.
59. "Comments of the Day in the Realm of the Rooter," *The Pittsburg Press,* June 11, 1902, 12.
60. "Brooklyn Won With Five Hits: Doheny's Clever Pitching Could Not Save the Champions," *The Pittsburg Press,* June 11, 1902, 12.
61. *Ibid.*
62. "National League: How They Stand," *The Sporting News,* June 21, 1902, 3.
63. "Pirates Say Story Is False: O'Connor and Wagner Deny That They Have Jumped to Outlaws," *The Pittsburg Press,* June 12, 1902, 12.
64. *Ibid.*
65. "Raid on Pittsburg: Reported That Wagner and Jack O'Connor Will Join the St. Louis Browns Soon," *Boston Daily Globe,* June 12, 1902, 5.
66. "Pirates Say Story Is False: O'Connor and Wagner Deny That They Have Jumped to Outlaws," 12.
67. Duquesne, "Looking Forward: Dreyfus Is Signing Players for Next Season," *The Sporting News,* June 14, 1902, 4.
68. *Ibid.*
69. "Sweet Revenge for Pirates: Hanlon's Ambitious Team Was Given a Coat of Whitewash," *The Pittsburg Press,* June 13, 1902, 16.
70. "Baseball Gossip," *The Pittsburg Press,* June 14, 1902, 10.
71. "Rain Spoiled Game Scheduled at Boston," *The Pittsburg Press,* June 14, 1902, 10.
72. "President Dreyfuss Expects Hot Finish: Says Champions Have Not Played Their Game and Will Start August 1," *The Pittsburg Press,* June 15, 1902, 20.
73. *Ibid.*
74. "Solitary Hit for Champions: Pittenger Made Magnificent Record Against the Pennant Winners," *The Pittsburg Press,* June 15, 1902, 20.
75. "President Dreyfuss Expects Hot Finish: Says Champions Have Not Played Their Game and Will Start August 1," 20.
76. *Ibid.*
77. "Frugal Ball Players," *The Salt Lake Tribune,* June 15, 1902, 20.
78. "Forfeited to the Champions: Boston Did Baby-Act in the Fifth Inning Yesterday," *The Pittsburg Press,* June 17, 1902, 12.
79. *Ibid.*
80. "Merritt Made a Three-Run Hit: Former Pirate Beat Champions at Worcester Yesterday," *The Pittsburg Press,* June 18, 1902, 12.
81. "Pirates Won at Wilmington: Struck Clever Pitcher But Managed To Get the Runs," *The Pittsburg Press,* June 19, 1902, 12.
82. "Comments of the Day in the Realm of the Rooter," *The Pittsburg Press,* June 17, 1902, 12.
83. "Comments of the Day in the Realm of

the Rooter," *The Pittsburg Press,* June 18, 1902, 12.
84. "Base Ball Caught on the Fly," *The Sporting News,* June 21, 1902, 5.
85. "Leaders Lost to Cardinals: Donovan's Men Gave O'Neill Brothers Perfect Support," *The Pittsburg Press,* June 20, 1902, 20.
86. A. R. Cratty, "Pittsburg Points: Champs Are Not Batting and Have a Downcast Look," *Sporting Life,* June 28, 1902, 6.
87. Duquesne, "Censured Clarke: Many of the Regular Patrons at Pittsburg," *The Sporting News,* June 28, 1902, 5.
88. *Ibid.*
89. Cratty, "Pittsburg Points: Champs Are Not Batting and Have a Downcast Look," 6.
90. *Ibid.*
91. Duquesne, "Not Appreciated: Pirates Are Belittled by Caption's Critics," *The Sporting News,* June 21, 1902, 7.
92. "Comments of the Day in the Realm of the Rooter," *The Pittsburg Press,* June 21, 1902, 10.
93. "Two More Games for the Pirates: Donovan Insisted on Playing a Double-Header and Was Made To Suffer," *The Pittsburg Press,* June 22, 1902, 20.
94. *Ibid.*
95. *Ibid.*
96. *Ibid.*
97. "Chicago Won in Nineteenth: Selee's Team Successful in Remarkable Game With the Champions," *The Pittsburg Press,* June 23, 1902, 10.
98. *Ibid.*

Chapter 7

1. Duquesne, "Are in Fine Shape: Pirates Will Run Away From Their Rivals," *The Sporting News,* July 5, 1902, 4.
2. "Fist Fight at Chicago Game: Conroy and Tinker Suspended for Scrapping, Pirates Won," *The Pittsburg Press,* June 24, 1902, 12.
3. *Ibid.*
4. *Ibid.*
5. "Comments of the Day in the Realm of the Rooter," *The Pittsburg Press,* June 24, 1902, 12.
6. "Frank Selee Will Not Quit: Plucky Manager Hustling To Reinforce Chicago Team," *The Pittsburg Press,* June 26, 1902, 8.
7. Duquesne, "Are in Fine Shape: Pirates Will Run Away From Their Rivals," 4.
8. *Ibid.*
9. *Ibid.*
10. "Base Ball Caught on the Fly," *The Sporting News,* July 5, 1902, 5.
11. *Ibid.*
12. "Tinker's Sub Was a Bungler: Kling's Short Stopping Helped Pittsburg To Win the Game," *The Pittsburg Press,* June 25, 1902, 12.
13. *Ibid.*
14. "Frank Selee Will Not Quit: Plucky Manager Hustling To Reinforce Chicago Team," 8.
15. "Great Playing by the Pirates: Clarke's Team Showed Its Full Strength at Chicago," *The Pittsburg Press,* June 27, 1902, 20.
16. *Ibid.*
17. "Baseball Gossip," *The Pittsburg Press,* June 28, 1902, 12.
18. "Heavy Rain at Cincinnati: Pirate-Red Half-Holiday Game Declared Off at Three O'Clock," *The Pittsburg Press,* June 29, 1902, 22.
19. Duquesne, "Are in Fine Shape: Pirates Will Run Away From Their Rivals," 4.
20. "Heavy Rain at Cincinnati: Pirate-Red Half-Holiday Game Declared Off at Three O'clock," 22.
21. *Ibid.*
22. *Ibid.*
23. "Baseball Gossip," *The Pittsburg Press,* June 30, 1902, 10.
24. "Conroy Found Guilty," *The Pittsburg Press,* June 30, 1902, 10.
25. "Shut Out for the Cincinnatis: Prof. Sam Leever Made Brush's Team Look Cheap," *The Pittsburg Press,* June 30, 1902, 10.
26. "National League: How They Stand," *The Sporting News,* July 5, 1902, 2.
27. "Great Bunting by the Pirates: Beaumont, Bransfield and Wagner Caught the Reds Off Their Guard," *The Pittsburg Press,* July 2, 1902, 12.
28. *Ibid.*
29. *Ibid.*
30. A. R. Cratty, "Pittsburg Points: Champs Home Again for a Long String of Games," *Sporting Life,* July 5, 1902, 6.
31. "Ten Games From Cincinnati's: Champions Added To Suffering of Brush by Beating Reds Again," *The Pittsburg Press,* July 3, 1902, 12.
32. *Ibid.*
33. *Ibid.*
34. Duquesne, "Scheme of Brush: Increase of Circuit Would Benefit Cincinnati," *The Sporting News,* July 12, 1902, 4.
35. *Ibid.*
36. "National League: How They Stand," *The Sporting News,* July 12, 1902, 2.
37. John H. Gruber, "Remarkable Games: Waistdeep in Water," *The Sporting News,* December 28, 1916, 4.
38. "Great Day for the Champions: Administered Two Doses of Whitewash To Hanlon's Team," *The Pittsburg Press,* July 5, 1902, 10.
39. Gruber, "Remarkable Games: Waistdeep in Water," 4.
40. "Great Day for the Champions: Administered Two Doses of Whitewash To Hanlon's Team," 10.

41. Gruber, "Remarkable Games: Waistdeep in Water," 4.
42. Ibid.
43. "Great Day for the Champions: Administered Two Doses of Whitewash To Hanlon's Team," 10.
44. "Flying Trip for Pirates: Champions Jump To Chicago To Play Today and Return Tomorrow," *The Pittsburg Press,* July 6, 1902, 21.
45. "Lefty Davis the Champion: Pittsburg Outfielder Best Base Runner In The Country," *The Pittsburg Press,* July 8, 1902, 12.
46. "Flying Trip for Pirates: Champions Jump To Chicago To Play Today and Return Tomorrow," 21.
47. "Taylor Downed the Champions: Chicago's Star Twirler Scored Another Victory Over Pirates," *The Pittsburg Press,* July 7, 1902, 10.
48. Ibid.
49. "Pirates Won in the Eighth: Once More Clarke's Men Resorted To Bunting with Good Results," *The Pittsburg Press,* July 8, 1902, 12.
50. Ibid.
51. "Pirate Pair Beat Phillies: Wagner and Chesbro Played Star Engagement at Expo Park," *The Pittsburg Press,* July 9, 1902, 10.
52. Ibid.
53. "Comments of the Day in the Realm of the Rooter," *The Pittsburg Press,* July 9, 1902, 10.
54. "No Fight in Quaker Team: Phillies Beaten Yesterday Before the Game With Champions Begun," *The Pittsburg Press,* July 10, 1902, 12.
55. "Manager Mugsy M'Graw Failed To Report Here: Started for Pittsburg From Baltimore Last Night But Must Have Been Side-Tracked—Saw Kelley, Seymour and Robinson," *The Pittsburg Press,* July 11, 1902, 12.
56. Ibid.
57. Ibid.
58. "Giants Earned Neat Victory: Freedman's Men Backed Up Roy Evans in Fine Style," *The Pittsburg Press,* July 11, 1902, 12.
59. "Paid Dearly for a Victory: Pirates Won Yesterday's Game But Lost Lefty Davis," *The Pittsburg Press,* July 12, 1902, 8.
60. Ibid.
61. Ibid.
62. "National League: The Official Record of the 1902 Pennant Race," *Sporting Life,* July 9, 1902, 8.
63. "Paid Dearly for a Victory: Pirates Won Yesterday's Game But Lost Lefty Davis," 8.
64. Duquesne, "Badly Crippled: Many of the Champions Unfit for Duty," *The Sporting News,* July 19, 1902, 5.
65. Ibid.
66. "Another Shutout by Jack Chesbro: New York the Third Club in Succession To Suffer at Pirates' Hands," *The Pittsburg Press,* July 13, 1902, 20.
67. "Sensational Record of Happy Jack Chesbro: Not a Run Has Been Scored Against Him in the Last Thirty-Five Innings He Has Pitched," *The Pittsburg Press,* July 13, 1902, 20.
68. "Beau's Bunt Paved the Way: Gentle Top Started a Mild Spurt That Won the Game," *The Pittsburg Press,* July 14, 1902, 10.
69. Duquesne, "Badly Crippled: Many of the Champions Unfit for Duty," 5.
70. Ibid.
71. "Fine Fielding by the Leaders: Pittsburg and Boston Gave Large Monday Crowd a Treat," *The Pittsburg Press,* July 15, 1902, 12.
72. "Boston Didn't Reach Second: Not One of the Visitors Advanced Beyond First Base," *The Pittsburg Press,* July 16, 1902, 10.
73. Ibid.
74. "Base Ball Caught on the Fly," *The Sporting News,* July 26, 1902, 5.
75. Ibid.
76. "Boston Got Solitary Run: Succeeded in Breaking Chesbro's String of Shut-Outs," *The Pittsburg Press,* July 17, 1902, 12.
77. "Clean Sweep by Champions: Took Entire Series from Manager Buckenberger's Boston Team," *The Pittsburg Press,* July 18, 1902, 15.
78. Ibid.
79. "Jack Taylor Did It Again: Defeated the Champions for the Third Time This Season," *The Pittsburg Press,* July 19, 1902, 7.
80. "Great Pitching by Jack Chesbro: Whitewashed Chicago, Making His Fourth Shutout Game of the Month at Exposition Park," *The Pittsburg Press,* July 20, 1902, 22.
81. Ibid.
82. "Long Trip for Pirates: Champions Will Not Play at Home Until August 26," *The Pittsburg Press,* July 20, 1902, 21.
83. Ibid.
84. A. R. Cratty, "Pittsburg Points: Champions on the Road for a Four Weeks Trip," *Sporting Life,* July 26, 1902, 5.
85. "Fine Comedy at Chicago: Twenty-Two Tosses Mixed Up in a Funny Play in Eleventh Inning," *The Pittsburg Press,* July 21, 1902, 12.
86. Ibid.
87. Ibid.
88. Ibid.
89. "Odds and Ends of Sport," *The Semi-Weekly Cedar Falls Gazette,* July 25, 1902, 3.
90. "Pittsburg Holds Key to Baseball Situation: Could Disrupt the National League by Joining the American at Close of Present Series—Only One Chance for Johnson," *The Pittsburg Press,* July 21, 1902, 7.
91. Ibid.
92. Duquesne, "Something Doing: Dreyfus Likes Many of the American's Methods," *The Sporting News,* July 26, 1902, 6.

Chapter 8

1. "Comments of the Day in the Realm of the Rooter," *The Pittsburg Press,* July 23, 1902, 10.
2. *Ibid.*
3. "Patched Team Had a Picnic: Pirates Won at St Louis Without Three of Their Star Players," *The Pittsburg Press,* July 23, 1902, 10.
4. *Ibid.*
5. "Bad Day for the Pirates: Patsy Donovan's Sluggers Sent Champions Down to Defeat," *The Pittsburg Press,* July 24, 1902, 12.
6. "Ten-Club Circuit Next Year: Pres. Ban Johnson Thinks New York and Pittsburg Would Fit in Nicely—Is on His way to Boston," *Boston Daily Globe,* July 24, 1902, 5.
7. *Ibid.*
8. "Champions Will Stick: No American League for Pittsburg, So Pulliam Says," *The Pittsburg Press,* July 24, 1902, 12.
9. *Ibid.*
10. "Barney Dreyfuss Balks: Says He Will Not Pay Any Share of Money Used To Wreck the Baltimore Club," *Baltimore American,* July 24, 1902, 10.
11. *Ibid.*
12. "Comments of the Day in the Realm of the Rooter," *The Pittsburg Press,* July 26, 1902, 8.
13. *Ibid.*
14. "Second Fall for Pirates: Donovan's Team Equaled the Record of Chicago Against Champions," *The Pittsburg Press,* July 25, 1902, 12.
15. *Ibid.*
16. A. R. Cratty, "Pittsburg Points: Champs Undergoing a Big Spell of Hard Luck," *Sporting Life,* August 2, 1902, 5.
17. "To Freeze out Dreyfuss: National Leaguers May Yet Drive the Pittsburgh Magnate into American League," *Baltimore American,* July 26, 1902, 2.
18. "American League Stands Fair Chance of Capturing Pittsburg from National: Pirate Fans Are Sore," *The Youngstown Daily Vindicator,* July 28, 1902, 8.
19. *Ibid.*
20. "Mass Meeting of Rooters: Loyal Supporters of Champions May Ask Dreyfuss To Join the American," *The Pittsburg Press,* July 27, 1902, 18.
21. Duquesne, "Prefer American: Pittsburg Patrons Sore on National League," *The Sporting News,* August 2, 1902, 6.
22. *Ibid.*
23. "Revenge for Sam Leever: Schoolmaster Gave Cardinals' Batting Average a Rude Jolt," *The Pittsburg Press,* July 27, 1902, 18.
24. "Fine Showing by Cardinals: Won Final Game of Series of Five with the Pittsburg Champions," *The Pittsburg Press,* July 28, 1902, 10.
25. *Ibid.*
26. "Poor Return for Kindness: St. Louis Magnate and His Manager Guilty of Ingratitude," *The Pittsburg Press,* July 29, 1902, 12.
27. "Comments of the Day in the Realm of the Rooter," *The Pittsburg Press,* August 4, 1902, 8.
28. "Poor Return for Kindness: St. Louis Magnate and His Manager Guilty of Ingratitude," 12.
29. "Beaumont's Record Clean: Accuser Takes Back a Silly Charge of Attempt at Spiking," *The Pittsburg Press,* July 28, 1902, 10.
30. *Ibid.*
31. "Pirates Have the Coin: Players Have All Got Stacks of the Necessary," *The Salt Lake Tribune,* July 27, 1902, 29.
32. *Ibid.*
33. *Ibid.*
34. *Ibid.*
35. *Ibid.*
36. "Chairman Brush Apologizes to Pittsburg Club: Boss of Executive Board Says Brown Filed False Testimony in the Wagner Case," *The Pittsburg Press,* July 30, 1902, 10.
37. *Ibid.*
38. "Pirates Were in Real Form: Played Like Champions of the World in First Game at Brooklyn," *The Pittsburg Press,* July 30, 1902, p .10.
39. "Bad Inning Beat Pirates: Tannehill and Two Infielders Tripped Up in the Sixth," *The Pittsburg Press,* July 31, 1902, 10.
40. "Just As Easy for Chesbro: For the Third Time This Season He Shut Out Brooklyn," *The Pittsburg Press,* August 1, 1902, 12.
41. *Ibid.*
42. "Kitty's Toss Was Costly: Bad Throw by Bransfield Gave the Brooklyns Three Runs," *The Pittsburg Press,* August 2, 1902, 8.
43. "Baseball Gossip," *The Pittsburg Press,* August 2, 1902, 8.
44. "Kitty's Toss Was Costly: Bad Throw by Bransfield Gave the Brooklyns Three Runs," 8.
45. Duquesne, "Cunning Silence: Brush Notified Dreyfus To Send in a Claim List," *The Sporting News,* August 9, 1902, 4.
46. *Ibid.*
47. *Ibid.*
48. *Ibid.*
49. A. R. Cratty, "Pittsburg Points: Champions Fare Fine on the Eastern Jaunt," *Sporting Life,* August 9, 1902, 4.
50. *Ibid.*
51. "The Champion Pittsburgs: Team Work Their Recipe for Success," *The Fort Wayne News,* August 1, 1902, 7.
52. "Double Plays Beat Giants: Sensational Fielding of the Champions Too Much for M'Graw's Team," *The Pittsburg Press,* August 3, 1902, 20.
53. *Ibid.*
54. "Baseball Gossip," *The Pittsburg Press,* August 4, 1902, 8.

55. "Pirates at Albany: South Side Boy Will Pitch Against Them Today," *The Pittsburg Press,* August 3, 1902, 20.
56. "Baseball Gossip," *The Pittsburg Press,* August 4, 1902, 8.
57. "Fred Clarke Won the Game: Boss Pirate Almost Whole Show at Polo Grounds Yesterday," *The Pittsburg Press,* August 5, 1902, 10.
58. *Ibid.*
59. "Baseball Gossip," *The Pittsburg Press,* August 5, 1902, 10.
60. "Record for Tannehill: First Nineteen Batsmen in Yesterday's Game Were Put Out," *The Pittsburg Press,* August 6, 1902, 10.
61. *Ibid.*
62. "Chesbro Did Trick Again: This Time New York Received the Coat of Whitewash," *The Pittsburg Press,* August 7, 1902, 12.
63. *Ibid.*
64. "Franchise Not Offered to President Dreyfuss," *The Pittsburg Press,* August 6, 1902, 10.
65. *Ibid.*
66. "Bad Finish for Pirates: Sam Leever Weakened in Ninth and Phillies Won the Game," *The Pittsburg Press,* August 8, 1902, 12.
67. *Ibid.*
68. "Pirates Even with Quakers: Phillies Pay Up for Being So Gay in Thursday's Game," *The Pittsburg Press,* August 9, 1902, 8.
69. "Baseball Gossip," *The Pittsburg Press,* August 9, 1902, 8.
70. "Pirates Even with Quakers: Phillies Pay Up for Being So Gay in Thursday's Game," 8.
71. "Battle of Tossers Won by Chesbro: Champion Pitcher of League Whitewashed Philadelphia in a Bitter Struggle," *The Pittsburg Press,* August 10, 1902, 18.
72. "Baseball Gossip," *The Pittsburg Press,* August 11, 1902, 8.
73. "National News," *Sporting Life,* August 16, 1902, 9.
74. A. R. Cratty, "Pittsburg Points: Defeats Abroad Arouse Home Patrons of Champs," *Sporting Life,* August 16, 1902, 3.
75. *Ibid.*
76. "Comments of the Day in the Realm of the Rooter," *The Pittsburg Press,* August 12, 1902, 10.
77. "John T. Brush Is Ambitious: Indianapolis Man Wants To Be President of the National League," *The Pittsburg Press,* August 11, 1902, 8.
78. Duquesne, "May Be President: Brush Must 'Show' Dreyfuss and Others," *The Sporting News,* August 16, 1902, 5.
79. "John T. Brush Is Ambitious: Indianapolis Man Wants To Be President of the National League," 8.
80. "Poole To Face the Pirates: Trapper Will Pitch Against Old Team at Cincinnati Next Sunday," *The Pittsburg Press,* August 12, 1902, 10.
81. *Ibid.*
82. "Pittinger at His Best: Shut Out National League Champions in Poor Game at Boston," *The Pittsburg Press,* August 13, 1902, 8.
83. "Comments of the Day in the Realm of the Rooter," *The Pittsburg Press,* August 13, 1902, 8.
84. "Even Break at Beantown: Jack Chesbro's Delivery Was Soaked Hard in First Game," *The Pittsburg Press,* August 14, 1902, 8.
85. *Ibid.*
86. "Baseball Gossip," *The Pittsburg Press,* August 15, 1902, 12.
87. "Brush Is the Boss of the Giants: Succeeds Freedman as Director of the New York Baseball Club," *The Pittsburg Press,* August 13, 1902, 8.
88. *Ibid.*
89. "New Record for Tom Leach: Midget Made Three Hits for Total of Eleven Bases," *The Pittsburg Press,* August 15, 1902, 12.
90. "Baseball Gossip," *The Pittsburg Press,* August 15, 1902, 12.
91. "Pirates Enjoyed Day with Friends at Shore," *The Pittsburg Press,* August 16, 1902, 8.
92. "Not a Pirate Was Captured by the Enemy: President Dreyfuss Rescued All Prominent Pirates from Clutches of American League Agents," *The Pittsburg Press,* August 16, 1902, 8.
93. "National News," *Sporting Life,* August 23, 1902, 9.
94. "Not a Pirate Was Captured by the Enemy: President Dreyfuss Rescued All Prominent Pirates from the Clutches of American League Agents," 8.
95. *Ibid.*
96. *Ibid.*
97. *Ibid.*

Chapter 9

1. "Chesbro Receives Big Offer," *North Adams Transcript,* August 20, 1902, 2.
2. "Baseball Notes," *Daily Kennebec Journal,* August 21, 1902, 3.
3. Duquesne, "Leach and Wagner: Two Pirates Whom Comiskey Is After," *The Sporting News,* August 23, 1902, 5.
4. "Champions Win Two Games to Celebrate Their Return: Quakers Were Outclassed," *The Pittsburg Press,* August 17, 1902, 16.
5. "Side Shows at the Games: Incidents to Double Bill at Exposition Park Were out of Ordinary," *The Pittsburg Press,* August 17, 1902, 16.
6. "Champions Win Two Games to Celebrate Their Return: Quakers Were Outclassed," 16.
7. "Side Shows at the Games: Incidents to Double Bill at Exposition Park Were out of Ordinary," 16.
8. *Ibid.*

9. "National News," *Sporting Life,* August 23, 1902, 9.
10. "Side Shows at the Games: Incidents to Double Bill at Exposition Park Were out of Ordinary," 16.
11. "Reds Win from Champions: Pitcher Eddie Poole Had Honor of Taking First Game," *The Pittsburg Press,* August 18, 1902, 8.
12. "Tommy Leach Whole Show: He Played Third with More Frills Than Ever Seen Here Before," *The Pittsburg Press,* August 19, 1902, 10.
13. *Ibid.*
14. "Base Ball," *The Mansfield News,* August 18, 1902, 3.
15. "New Stars for Pirates: Merritt and Sebring Will Report at Close of Eastern League's Race," *The Pittsburg Press,* August 19, 1902, 10.
16. "Wagner's Hit Won the Game: Timely Single Sent Two Runs Across Plate in the Ninth," *The Pittsburg Press,* August 20, 1902, 8.
17. *Ibid.*
18. "Comiskey's Proposition: Provided His White Sox Win the American Pennant He Wants To Play Pirates a Series of Three," *Boston Daily Globe,* August 20, 1902, 5.
19. "Jack O'Connor: Accused of Being an Agent for the American League," *The Daily Youngstown Vindicator,* August 21, 1902, 8.
20. "National League: How They Stand," *The Sporting News,* August 30, 1902, 2.
21. "Wagner Rejects Fortune: Star Turns Down Double the Amount That O'Connor Receives for Becoming a Traitor," *The Pittsburg Press,* August 21, 1902, 10.
22. *Ibid.*
23. *Ibid.*
24. "Dreyfuss Exposes Plot: Describes Secret Mission of Somers and Johnson to Pittsburg—Suspends O'Connor for Aiding Them," *Boston Daily Globe,* August 21, 1902, 3.
25. "Wagner Rejects Fortune: Star Turns Down Double the Amount That O'Connor Receives for Becoming a Traitor," 10.
26. *Ibid.*
27. "Comments of the Day in the Realm of the Rooter," *The Pittsburg Press,* August 21, 1902, 10.
28. *Ibid.*
29. "The Attempted Raid: President Dreyfuss Uncovers a Plot of American Leaguers and Suspends Catcher O'Connor as an Accomplice," *Sporting Life,* August 30, 1902, 4.
30. A. R. Cratty, "Pittsburg Points: Still Sneak by Johnson and Somers Awakens the Monotony in Pittsburg," *Sporting Life,* August 30, 1902, 4.
31. *Ibid.*
32. "American League Begins War Upon Colonel Barney Dreyfuss: Catcher O'Connor Released by the Pirate Manager, Charged with Acting As a Stool Pigeon in Attempt To Wreck Club—An Opposition Team Is Planned," *Syracuse Post Standard,* August 24, 1902, 3.
33. Dennis DeValeria and Jeanne Burke DeValeria, *Honus Wagner: A Biography* (New York: Henry Holt, 1995), 104.
34. Duquesne, "To Jump in 1903: Two Pitchers Leave Pittsburg with O'Connor," *The Sporting News,* August 30, 1902, 1.
35. "Comments of the Day in the Realm of the Rooter," *The Pittsburg Press,* August 22, 1902, 12.
36. Duquesne, "To Jump in 1903: Two Pitchers Leave Pittsburg with O'Connor," 1.
37. "Baseball Gossip," *The Pittsburg Press,* August 22, 1902, 12.
38. Duquesne, "To Jump in 1903: Two Pitchers Leave Pittsburg with O'Connor," 1.
39. "The Attempted Raid: President Dreyfuss Uncovers a Plot of American Leaguers and Suspends Catcher O'Connor as an Accomplice," 4.
40. Cratty, "Pittsburg Points: Still Sneak by Johnson and Somers Awakens the Monotony in Pittsburg," 4.
41. *Ibid.*
42. "Dreyfuss' Discovery: The Singular Manner in Which the Pittsburg President Discovered the Conspiracy in His Own Team," *Sporting Life,* November 29, 1902, 9.
43. *Ibid.*
44. *Ibid.*
45. DeValeria, *Honus Wagner: A Biography,* 103.
46. "Dreyfuss' Discovery: The Singular Manner in Which the Pittsburg President Discovered the Conspiracy in His Own Team," 9.
47. "The Accused Retort: Johnson and Somers Admit Their Attempted Raid and Hint at Pittsburg Invasion," *Sporting Life,* August 30, 1902, 4.
48. "Planning To Place Team To Oppose the Pirates," *Syracuse Post Standard,* August 24, 1902, 3.
49. "The Accused Retort: Johnson and Somers Admit Their Attempted Raid and Hint at Pittsburg Invasion," 4.
50. *Ibid.*
51. "Won the First Lost Second: Pittsburg Broke Even with New York in Yesterday's Doubleheader," *The Pittsburg Press,* August 22, 1902, 12.
52. *Ibid.*
53. "Baseball Gossip," *The Pittsburg Press,* August 23, 1902, 8.
54. "Seven Players Are Injured: Hospital List of the Pittsburg Club Is Growing Rapidly," *The Pittsburg Press,* August 23, 1902, 8.
55. "Two Games for Champions: Pittsburg Had a Pleasant Afternoon with Its Old Rival, Brooklyn," *The Pittsburg Press,* August 23, 1902, 8.
56. *Ibid.*

57. *Ibid.*
58. "Brooklyn Batted out a Victory: Sixteen Hits, Netting Thirty Bases Was Result of Afternoon's Work," *The Pittsburg Press,* August 24, 1902, 18.
59. *Ibid.*
60. "Two Games for Pirates: Cushman, of Millvale, May Be Pressed into Service Today," *The Pittsburg Press,* August 24, 1902, 18.
61. *Ibid.*
62. "Baseball Gossip," *The Pittsburg Press,* August 23, 1902, 8.
63. "O'Connor Deserves Sentence: Dreyfuss Commended for Having Courage To Punish the Offender," *The Pittsburg Press,* August 24, 1902, 16.
64. *Ibid.*
65. Duquesne, "Revenge on Mack: Dreyfus' Motive in Signing Burke and Conroy," *The Sporting News,* September 6, 1902, 5.
66. "American League Started the Trouble: First Violation of Agreement Occurred When Connie Mack Took Harry Smith After Selling His Release to Pittsburg Club," *The Pittsburg Press,* August 25, 1902, 8.
67. *Ibid.*
68. Duquesne, "Revenge on Mack: Dreyfus' Motive in Signing Burke and Conroy," 5.
69. "Cushman Took an Ascension: Millvale's Clever Pitcher Had One Bad Inning in Second Game," *The Pittsburg Press,* August 25, 1902, 8.
70. *Ibid.*
71. "American Made the First Raid: Dreyfuss and John T. Brush Tell Some Base Ball History," *The Pittsburg Press,* August 26, 1902, 10.
72. *Ibid.*
73. "Hanlon's Men Have Off Day: In Absence of Their Manager Superbas Play Everything but Baseball," *The Pittsburg Press,* August 26, 1902, 10.
74. "Baseball Notes," *Boston Daily Globe,* August 24, 1902, 5.
75. "Only One Run for Boston: Beaneaters Scored in First Game and Were Shutout in Second," *The Pittsburg Press,* August 27, 1902, 10.
76. *Ibid.*
77. "Senator Grady Offers Gold to Ball Players," *The Pittsburg Press,* August 27, 1902, 10.
78. "Not a Game for Boston: Pittsburg Made It Three Straight by Winning Yesterday," *The Pittsburg Press,* August 28, 1902, 10.
79. *Ibid.*
80. "A Great Grab for Players: Agents Here To Take up Job at Which Ban Johnson Failed," *The Pittsburg Press,* August 28, 1902, 10.
81. "Pirates Even with Taylor: Batting Matinee the Reward of Long-Suffering Champions," *The Pittsburg Press,* August 29, 1902, 12.
82. "Poor Support for Young Men: Cushman and Fohl Didn't Get Much Help from the Pirates," *The Pittsburg Press,* August 30, 1902, 8.
83. "Baseball Situation Remains Unchanged," *The Pittsburg Press,* August 30, 1902, 8.
84. "Game Won in Twelfth by Pirates: Chicago's Infield Weakened After Playing Good Ball for Two Hours," *The Pittsburg Press,* August 31, 1902, 18.
85. *Ibid.*
86. "Dreyfuss Will Not Play: Pittsburg Manager Refuses to Meet Champion American Team," *The Trenton Times,* August 30, 1902, 11.

Chapter 10

1. "Game Won in Twelfth by Pirates: Chicago's Infield Weakened After Playing Good Ball for Two Hours," *The Pittsburg Press,* August 31, 1902, 18.
2. "Pittsburg Will Have a Strong Team: President Dreyfuss Says He Will Have a Championship Team," *The Pittsburg Press,* August 31, 1902, 18.
3. *Ibid.*
4. "Johnson Tempter: American League President Said To Have Gone in Person To Worcester To Take Bransfield from Pittsburg," *Sporting Life,* September 6, 1902, 6.
5. *Ibid.*
6. A. R. Cratty, "Pittsburg Points: Americans' Raid Seems to be More Than a Pipe Dream," *Sporting Life,* September 6, 1902, 4.
7. *Ibid.*
8. "Comments of the Day in the Realm of the Rooter," *The Pittsburg Press,* September 1, 1902, 10.
9. Cratty, "Pittsburg Points: Americans' Raid Seems to be More Than a Pipe Dream," 4.
10. *Ibid.*
11. *Ibid.*
12. *Ibid.*
13. *Ibid.*
14. "National News," *Sporting Life,* September 6, 1902, 9.
15. "Tour Begins with Doublet: Pirates and Superbas Will Clash Twice at Brooklyn Today," *The Pittsburg Press,* September 1, 1902, 10.
16. "Champions Celebrated: Labor Day Brought Two More Games to the Pirates," *The Pittsburg Press,* September 2, 1902, 10.
17. *Ibid.*
18. *Ibid.*
19. "The Race Is Now Decided: By Losing First Game the Superbas Gave Pirates the Cinch," *The Pittsburg Press,* September 3, 1902, 10.
20. *Ibid.*
21. "Comments of the Day in the Realm of the Rooter," *The Pittsburg Press,* September 3, 1902, 10.
22. *Ibid.*
23. "Winning Hurting Pirates: Fans Consider Them Easy Winners and Attendance Is Small," *The Pittsburg Press,* September 4, 1902, 10.

24. "The Race Is Now Decided: By Losing First Game the Superbas Gave Pirates the Cinch," 10.
25. "Winning Hurting Pirates: Fans Consider Them Easy Winners and Attendance Is Small," 10.
26. "Bostonites Sensational: Fielding Brilliant Throughout Both Games," *The Pittsburg Press,* September 5, 1902, 12.
27. *Ibid.*
28. "Champions in New York: Ended Beantown Series by Winning First and Losing Second," *The Pittsburg Press,* September 6, 1902, 8.
29. "Champions Won Easily from Giants: Mathewson Pitched a Poor Game and Team Fielded Miserably Behind Him," *The Pittsburg Press,* September 7, 1902, 18.
30. "Clarke Left Team Today: Will Be Absent for a Week, Wagner Is Manager Pro Tem," *The Pittsburg Press,* September 7, 1902, 18.
31. "Champions Beat Utica: Blanked the Eastern Team and Scored But One Run," *The Pittsburg Press,* September 8, 1902, 10.
32. "Two Games Were Lost: Champions Downed by the Giants in the Double-Header," *The Pittsburg Press,* September 9, 1902, 10.
33. A. R. Cratty, "Pittsburg Points: Several Champions Playing Better Than Was Their Wont," *Sporting Life,* September 13, 1902, 2.
34. *Ibid.*
35. *Ibid.*
36. *Ibid.*
37. *Ibid.*
38. A. R. Cratty, "Pittsburg Points: Champions Sure To Scoop in Century of Games," *Sporting Life,* September 27, 1902, 3.
39. "American Affairs," *Sporting Life,* September 13, 1902, 11.
40. "National News," *Sporting Life,* September 13, 1902, 9.
41. A. R. Cratty, "Champion Chaff: Latest Reports as to Prospective Sliders," *Sporting Life,* September 20, 1902, 3.
42. *Ibid.*
43. "National News," *Sporting Life,* September 13, 1902, 9.
44. Cratty, "Pittsburg Points: Several Champions Playing Better Than Was Their Wont," 2.
45. "Pittsburg Invasion: Another Visit to the Smoky City by Johnson and Somers," *Sporting Life,* September 13, 1902, 4.
46. *Ibid.*
47. Duquesne, "Great Advantage: Dreyfus Has Best Pittsburgh Parks under Lease," *The Sporting News,* September 13, 1902, 6.
48. "Dickering for Grounds: American Syndicate Scheming for a Park in New York," *The Pittsburg Press,* September 10, 1902, 12.
49. *Ibid.*
50. "Dreyfuss Having Trouble: Pittsburg Pitchers Want Big Salaries for Next Year," *The Trenton Times,* September 10, 1902, 9.
51. *Ibid.*
52. "Dickering for Grounds: American Syndicate Scheming for a Park in New York," 12.
53. "Dreyfuss Having Trouble: Pittsburg Pitchers Want Big Salaries for Next Year," 9.
54. "Dickering for Grounds: American Syndicate Scheming for a Park in New York," 12.
55. "Dreyfuss Having Trouble: Pittsburg Pitchers Want Big Salaries for Next Year," 9.
56. "Dickering for Grounds: American Syndicate Scheming for a Park in New York," 12.
57. "Champions Victorious: A Small Crowd Saw Good Game at Philadelphia Yesterday," *The Pittsburg Press,* September 11, 1902, 12.
58. *Ibid.*
59. "Baseball Gossip," *The Pittsburg Press,* September 12, 1902, 16.
60. *Ibid.*
61. "Both Games Were Easy: Champions Now Going After That One Hundred Wins," *The Pittsburg Press,* September 12, 1902, 16.
62. "Baseball Gossip," *The Pittsburg Press,* September 12, 1902, 16.
63. "Four Games for Pirates: Capt. Wagner's Men Made Clean Sweep at Philadelphia," *The Pittsburg Press,* September 13, 1902, 8.
64. *Ibid.*
65. "Champions Come Home to Play Cincinnati Reds: All the Men Wanted by Manager Fred Clarke Have Signed To Play with the Pirates Another Season," *The Pittsburg Press,* September 13, 1902, 8.
66. "Pittsburg Points: The Situation in the Smoky City Becoming Placid," *Sporting Life,* September 20, 1902, 3.
67. Cratty, "Champion Chaff: Latest Reports as to Prospective Sliders," 3.
68. B. Wright, "St. Louis Sayings: The Local League Team Completed," *Sporting Life,* September 20, 1902, 9.
69. "National News," *Sporting Life,* September 6, 1902, 9.
70. Wright, "St. Louis Sayings: The Local League Team Completed," 9.
71. "Tannehill Called Down: Pitcher Did Not Obey Orders in Ninth Inning Yesterday," *The Pittsburg Press,* September 14, 1902, 22.
72. *Ibid.*
73. "Ed Poole Played in Great Luck: Donlin's Fielding and Beckley's Batting Enabled Him To Defeat Champions," *The Pittsburg Press,* September 14, 1902, 22.
74. *Ibid.*
75. Duquesne, "Superb Southpaw: But Tannehill Is in Bad at Pittsburg," *The Sporting News,* September 20, 1902, 6.
76. *Ibid.*
77. *Ibid.*
78. "Tannehill Called Down: Pitcher Did

Not Obey Orders in Ninth Inning Yesterday," 22.

79. "New Pitcher Won Another: McLaughlin, Poorly Supported, Was Too Much for St. Louis," *The Pittsburg Press,* September 15, 1902, 10.

80. "Pirates Won Final Round: Closed Their St. Louis Engagement by Scoring an Easy Victory," *The Pittsburg Press,* September 16, 1902, 12.

81. "New Pirates Are Praised: Critics and Players at St. Louis Compliment Sebring and Eddie Phelps," *The Pittsburg Press,* September 18, 1902, 12.

82. *Ibid.*

83. "New York Invasion: Barney Dreyfuss Makes Some Discoveries Anent the Alleged Plans of the Invading American League," *Sporting Life,* September 20, 1902, 5.

84. *Ibid.*

85. *Ibid.*

86. "Peace Talk is Going on: Mysterious Agent of American League with the National Magnates," *The Pittsburg Press,* September 16, 1902, 12.

87. *Ibid.*

88. "Champs Need Four Games: Record of One Hundred Victories Is Almost a Certainty Now," *The Pittsburg Press,* September 18, 1902, 12.

89. "Fred's Catch Saved Game: Captain Clarke Kept Donovan off Bases in Tenth Inning," *The Pittsburg Press,* September 19, 1902, 20.

90. *Ibid.*

91. "Easy for Champions: With Cushman Pitching, Pirates Had Snap at Homestead," *The Pittsburg Press,* September 20, 1902, 8.

92. "Fast Ball Played by Pirates: Aroused by Stubborn Fight of Cardinals, Clarke's Men Did Work Worth Seeing," *The Pittsburg Press,* September 21, 1902, 18.

Chapter 11

1. "Baseball Gossip," *The Pittsburg Press,* September 22, 1902, 10.

2. "Base Ball Caught on the Fly," *The Sporting News,* September 27, 1902, 5.

3. *Ibid.*

4. "Base Ball," *The Mansfield News,* September 24, 1902, 7.

5. *Ibid.*

6. "Even Hundred for Pirates: Double Victory at Chicago Yesterday Gave Them Coveted Record," *The Pittsburg Press,* September 22, 1902, 10.

7. "Seymour Presses Beaumont: Red Outfielder is Only Three Points Behind Pittsburgs' Best Slugger," *The Pittsburg Press,* September 22, 1902, 10.

8. "Timely Topics from the World of Sports and Athletes: New Possible Record—100 Games," *Biloxi Daily Herald,* October 1, 1902, 5.

9. "Even Hundred for Pirates: Double Victory at Chicago Yesterday Gave Them Coveted Record,"

10. *Ibid.*

11. "Class Told at Buffalo: Pirates Almost Whitewashed Stallings' Second Place Team," *The Pittsburg Press,* September 23, 1902, 12.

12. "Toronto Made Stubborn Fight: Eastern League Champions Ahead of Pirates for Six Innings," *The Pittsburg Press,* September 24, 1902, 12.

13. *Ibid.*

14. "Great Fielding by Champions: Montreal Fans Enthusiastic over Work of the Pittsburg Infield," *The Pittsburg Press,* September 25, 1902, 12.

15. "Davis Released, Tannehill Held," *The Pittsburg Press,* September 24, 1902, 12.

16. *Ibid.*

17. "Comments of the Day in the Realm of the Rooter," *The Pittsburg Press,* September 25, 1902, 12.

18. *Ibid.*

19. "Ban Johnson Failed To Get Pittsburg Stars," *The Pittsburg Press,* September 26, 1902, 20.

20. "New Pitcher Worth Having: Falkenberg Does a Clever Stunt Against League Champions," *The Pittsburg Press,* September 26, 1902, 20.

21. "First Bad Weather at Jack Chesbro's Town," *The Pittsburg Press,* September 27, 1902, 16.

22. "Sporting News: New York Americans—Kennedy Will Be Manager Only Under Certain Conditions—Pittsburg-All-American Series," *The Trenton Times,* September 27, 1902, 11.

23. *Ibid.*

24. Duquesne, "Hart Protested: Objects to Pirates Playing at Comiskey's Park," *The Sporting News,* October 4, 1902, 4.

25. "Sporting News: New York Americans—Kennedy Will Be Manager Only Under Certain Conditions—Pittsburg-All-American Series," 11.

26. "News and Gossip for Baseball Fans: Tips and Topics on the National Game," *Webster City Tribune,* September 26, 1902, 5.

27. "National News," *Sporting Life,* October 4, 1902, 6.

28. *Ibid.*

29. Duquesne, "Hart Protested: Objects to Pirates Playing at Comiskey's Park," 4.

30. "National News," *Sporting Life,* October 4, 1902, 6.

31. "Nineteen Basehits the Record: Champions Did Heavy Batting Against Rube Vickers, Cincinnati's Twirler," *The Pittsburg Press,* September 28, 1902, 19.

32. "World's Championship Games are in Demand: Hart and Bancroft Ask for Series that Pi-

rates Will Play with All-Americans," *The Pittsburg Press*, September 28, 1902, 20.
33. "Wild Scenes at Sunday Games: Reds Won but Cincinnati Crowd Mobbed Umpire Hank O'Day," *The Pittsburg Press*, September 29, 1902, 10.
34. "Base Ball Caught on the Fly," *The Sporting News*, October 4, 1902, 5.
35. "Wild Scenes at Sunday Games: Reds Won but Cincinnati Crowd Mobbed Umpire Hank O'Day," 10.
36. "Baseball Gossip," *The Pittsburg Press*, September 29, 1902, 10.
37. "World's Championship Games are in Demand: Hart and Bancroft Ask for Series that Pirates Will Play with All-Americans," 20.
38. "Base Ball," *The Mansfield News*, October 2, 1902, 7.
39. "Retirement of Freedman Will Help the National," *The Pittsburg Press*, September 30, 1902, 12.
40. "Chesbro's Estimate Too High," *The Pittsburg Press*, September 30, 1902, 12.
41. "Comments of the Day in the Realm of the Rooter," *The Pittsburg Press*, October 1, 1902, 16.
42. *Ibid.*
43. "Pirates Play to Even Score: Rochester Tie with Champions at End of the Eleventh Inning," *The Pittsburg Press*, October 2, 1902, 16.
44. "Reds Outplayed the Champions: Sam Leever's Pitching to Liking of Men from Porktown," *The Pittsburg Press*, October 3, 1902, 20.
45. "Serious Split in the Ranks of Kelley's Team: Fight Between Thielman and Seymour Costs Club the Services of Both Men," *The Pittsburg Press*, October 3, 1902, 20.
46. "Chesbro Helped by the Fielders: The Reds Scored Only One Run on Thirteen Basehits," *The Pittsburg Press*, October 4, 1902, 16.
47. *Ibid.*
48. Ren Mulford, Jr., "Red Gift Show: Farcical End of the Pirates Series," *Sporting Life*, October 11, 1902, 5.
49. "Reds Made Farce out of Finish: Beckley, Pitcher, and Vickers, Catcher, at Beginning of Final Game," *The Pittsburg Press*, October 5, 1902, 18.
50. *Ibid.*
51. *Ibid.*
52. *Ibid.*
53. *Ibid.*
54. "Reds Should be Censured: Conduct of the Players at Pittsburg Saturday Cannot be Overlooked," *The Pittsburg Press*, October 7, 1902, 12.
55. "Baseball Gossip," *The Pittsburg Press*, October 8, 1902, 16.
56. "Comments of the Day in the Realm of the Rooter," *The Pittsburg Press*, October 6, 1902, 10.
57. "Base Ball," *The Mansfield News*, October 10, 1902, 3.
58. Duquesne, "Saved his Stars: Dreyfus Gives List of his 1903 Players," *The Sporting News*, October 11, 1902, 5.
59. *Ibid.*
60. *Ibid.*
61. "Base Ball," *The Mansfield News*, October 6, 1902, 7.
62. Duquesne, "Saved his Stars: Dreyfus Gives List of his 1903 Players," 5.
63. *Ibid.*
64. "Inside Playing Won for Pirates: Science of National League Champions Too Much for All-Americans in First Game," *The Pittsburg Press*, October 8, 1902, 16.
65. *Ibid.*
66. "Grand Pitching by Mr. Phillippe: Deacon Whitewashed the All-Americans and Allowed Them Only Three Little Basehits in Nine Innings," *The Pittsburg Press*, October 9, 1902, 16.
67. *Ibid.*
68. "Comments of the Day in the Realm of the Rooter," *The Pittsburg Press*, October 11, 1902, 12.
69. A. R. Cratty, "Pittsburg Points: Incidents of the Series Between the Champions and the All-Americans," *Sporting Life*, October 18, 1902, 7.
70. "Comments of the Day in the Realm of the Rooter," *The Pittsburg Press*, October 11, 1902, 12.
71. Cratty, "Pittsburg Points: Incidents of the Series Between the Champions and the All-Americans," 7.
72. "In the Field of Sport: Chesbro Leaves Pittsburg," *The Newark Advocate*, October 10, 1902, 3.
73. "National League News," *Sporting Life*, October 25, 1902, 4.
74. "Champions Won Game: Charleroi the Shoot," *The Pittsburg Press*, October 10, 1902, 24.
75. "May Take Tannehill: Cincinnati Club Will Try To Get Even with the American," *The Pittsburg Press*, October 10, 1902, 24.
76. "Pirates Capture the Title: Leaguers Clinch World Championship by Making Third Game a Tie," *The Pittsburg Press*, October 11, 1902, 12.
77. *Ibid.*
78. "Champions Were Shut Out by American League Stars in a Sensational Game: Fumble by Tommy Leach Gave Lajoie's Team the Only Run Scored in Final Game of Championship Series," *The Pittsburg Press*, October 12, 1902, 18.
79. Duquesne, "Beat the Pirates: Wallace's Great Fielding and Fine Batting," *The Sporting News*, October 18, 1902, 4.
80. *Ibid.*
81. "Baseball Gossip," *The Pittsburg Press*, October 13, 1902, 10.

82. "National League News," *Sporting Life*, October 25, 1902, 4.
83. "Baseball Gossip," *The Pittsburg Press*, October 17, 1902, 24.
84. "Dreyfuss Didn't Block the Tannehill Deal: Southpaw Pitcher had Signed with American League Long Before Cincinnati Club Opened Negotiations with Him," *The Pittsburg Press*, October 22, 1902, 12.
85. "Baseball Gossip," *The Pittsburg Press*, October 23, 1902, 16.
86. Duquesne, "Leach's Loyalty: Says Dreyfuss Can Count on Him for 1903," *The Sporting News*, November 8, 1902, 6.
87. A. R. Cratty, "Pittsburg Points: Americans Expected To Have Plans Ready Soon," *Sporting Life*, November 29, 1902, 2.
88. Duquesne, "Leach's Loyalty: Says Dreyfuss Can Count on Him for 1903," 6.
89. *Ibid.*
90. *Ibid.*
91. "American League Affairs," *Sporting Life*, November 29, 1902, 3.
92. "National League News," *Sporting Life*, November 1, 1902, 3.
93. Duquesne, "Leach's Loyalty: Says Dreyfuss Can Count on Him for 1903," 6.
94. *Ibid.*
95. "National League Has Surprise for Trust," *The Pittsburg Press*, October 28, 1902, 16.
96. "Wild Rumor Denied: President Dreyfuss Has No Intention of Selling Pittsburg Club," *The Pittsburg Press*, October 29, 1902, 12.
97. Duquesne, "Traced to Somers: Advance Money Leach Secured from Johnson," *The Sporting News*, November 15, 1902, 2.
98. *Ibid.*
99. *Ibid.*
100. "Leach the Leader: Ban Johnson Says the Pittsburg Third Baseman Acted As the Agent of the American League," *Sporting Life*, November 22, 1902, 6.

Chapter 12

1. John B. Foster, "Brooklyn Bulletin: The Case of Pitcher Donovan Settled," *Sporting Life*, November 29, 1902, 8.
2. A. R. Cratty, "Pittsburg Points: Rumors about Americans Keep the Situation Well Stirred Up," *Sporting Life*, December 6, 1902, 7.
3. Duquesne, "Can Get Grounds: American League Has Option on Pittsburg Site," *The Sporting News*, December 6, 1902, 2.
4. Cratty, "Pittsburg Points: Rumors about Americans Keep the Situation Well Stirred Up," 7.
5. "Pittsburg Team Has Advantage: With Champions Money and Support of Lovers of Fair Play It Is Prepared To Meet Opposition of Baseball Trust," *The Pittsburg Press*, November 19, 1902, 12.
6. "Johnson's Denial Given for What It Is Worth," *The Pittsburg Press*, November 21, 1902, 20.
7. "President Johnson Talks: Tells of Plans for American League Club in New York," *Portsmouth Herald*, November 7, 1902, 4.
8. "Agent for No One: O'Connor Did Not Represent Ban Johnson," *The Sporting News*, November 15, 1902, 4.
9. *Ibid.*
10. *Ibid.*
11. Duquesne, "National Leader: Presidency Will be Tendered to W.C. Temple," *The Sporting News*, November 29, 1902, 7.
12. "Chesbro Paid Two Salaries: American League and Pittsburg Were the Contributors," *The Pittsburg Press*, November 9, 1902, 22.
13. "Syndicate Baseball Is Not Popular Here," *The Pittsburg Press*, November 3, 1902, 10.
14. "Baseball History Is Being Made: Leaders of Two Leagues Making Important Moves in New York City," *The Pittsburg Press*, November 16, 1902, 21.
15. "May Welcome Jim Kennedy: The American League Finds New York Invasion a Serious Matter," *The Pittsburg Press*, November 30, 1902, 20.
16. "National May Retain Committee: If W. C. Temple Does Not Accept Presidency Board Will be Re-Elected," *The Pittsburg Press*, November 30, 1902, 20.
17. "W. C. Temple Named for President: Pittsburger Reported To Be the Choice of National League Magnates," *The Pittsburg Press*, November 16, 1902, 20.
18. "National May Retain Committee: If W. C. Temple Does Not Accept Presidency Board Will be Re-Elected," 20.
19. "Comments of the Day in the Realm of the Rooter," *The Pittsburg Press*, December 3, 1902, 12.
20. "Barney Dreyfuss Has No Candidate: Prefers President to Board, But Since W. C. Temple Declined, Magnate Has No One to Support," *The Pittsburg Press*, December 5, 1902, 20.
21. "One Candidate for President: James A. Hart, of Chicago, Is for W. C. Temple and No Second Choice for League Leader," *The Pittsburg Press*, December 8, 1902, 10.
22. "League Ignores Johnson's Plea: American Baseball Trust's Request for a Compromise Turned Down by National at Early Conference," *The Pittsburg Press*, December 9, 1902, 16.
23. *Ibid.*
24. "Syndicate First to Seek Peace: Negotiations Between National League and American To End Baseball War Have Been on for Weeks," *The Pittsburg Press*, December 12, 1902, 20.

25. "Told Out of the Meeting: Gossip Heard While Baseball Magnates Were Behind Closed Doors," *The Pittsburg Press,* December 10, 1902, 16.
26. "Dreyfuss Favors Ward for League President," *The Pittsburg Press,* December 10, 1902, 16.
27. "Col. Dreyfuss Is Happy: League Adopts His Schedule and the Pirates Get Choice Dates—Gossip of Sensational Baseball Meeting," *The Pittsburg Press,* December 11, 1902, 16.
28. "Wise Move Made by the National: Selected Able Leader When It Made H. C. Pulliam President, Secretary and Treasurer by a Unanimous Vote," *The Pittsburg Press,* December 13, 1902, 10.
29. *Ibid.*
30. A. R. Cratty, "Pittsburg Points: Champs Will Miss the Sagacity of Col. Harry Pulliam," *Sporting Life,* December 20, 1902, 7.
31. "Dreyfuss Silent: Will Allow Conference Committee To Do the Talking," *The Pittsburg Press,* December 14, 1902, 20.
32. Cratty, "Pittsburg Points: Champs Will Miss the Sagacity of Col. Harry Pulliam," 7.
33. *Ibid.*
34. Duquesne, "Pulliam's Policy: Fair To and Firm with All Parties," *The Sporting News,* December 20, 1902, 4.
35. "Pulliam Will Sell Pittsburg Stock," *The Pittsburg Press,* December 13, 1902, 10.
36. "Diamond Doings," *The Mansfield News,* December 27, 1902, 11.
37. "Splendid Park for Amusements: Company with Capital of $500, 000 Will Have Baseball Grounds and High Grade Sports at Point Breeze," *The Pittsburg Press,* December 10, 1902, 16.
38. "Dreyfuss Doings: The Pittsburg Club May Have a Palatial New Ball Park in the Very Near Future," *Sporting Life,* December 20, 1902, 9.
39. "Col. Dreyfuss Is Happy: League Adopts His Schedule and the Pirates Get Choice Dates," 16.
40. "Pittsburgers Were Ignored: Application for a Franchise Not Even Considered by American League Syndicate Yesterday," *The Pittsburg Press,* December 23, 1902, 12.
41. "Baseball Gossip," *The Pittsburg Press,* December 23, 1902, 12.
42. "Leach Case Now Closed: American League Admits It Has No Claim to His Services," *The Pittsburg Press,* December 17, 1902, 12.
43. "Johnson Says Peace Will Come: American League President Repudiates Platforms Made by the Soreheads," *The Pittsburg Press,* December 14, 1902, 20.
44. "Dreyfuss Silent: Will Allow Conference Committee To Do the Talking," 20.
45. Francis C. Richter, "Settlement Secured; Peace Proclaimed!: The Popular Double League System Scores a Splendid Triumph," *Sporting Life,* January 17, 1903, 4.
46. "Pulliam Goes to Conference: President of League Was Summoned to Meeting Yesterday," *The Pittsburg Press,* January 9, 1903, 12.
47. Richter, "Settlement Secured; Peace Proclaimed! The Popular Double League System Scores a Splendid Triumph," 20.
48. *Ibid.*
49. "League Magnates Kick: John T. Brush, Col. Rogers and Ned Hanlon of the National Find Fault with Peace Agreement," *The Pittsburg Press,* January 12, 1903, 10.
50. "Brooklyn Club Has Team Signed: Absence of List in Peace Agreement Due to Kick Over the Loss of Keeler and Donovan," *The Pittsburg Press,* January 12, 1903, 10.
51. Frederick G. Lieb, *The Pittsburgh Pirates* (Carbondale: Southern Illinois University Press, 2003), 95.
52. "An Early Hearing in the Brush Case: New York Club's Injunction Which Prevents Ratification of Peace Plan Will Be Argued at Once," *The Pittsburg Press,* January 17, 1902, 10.
53. Francis C. Richter, "Peace Proclaimed; Disruption Averted: The Peace Proponents of the National League Triumphant," *Sporting Life,* January 31, 1903, 4.
54. *Ibid.*
55. "Baseball Notes," *The Pittsburg Press,* January 26, 1903, 10.
56. "Dreyfuss Has Prior Claim: Pittsburg Magnate Establishes His Right to Sebring's Services," *The Pittsburg Press,* January 14, 1903, 12.
57. *Ibid.*
58. "Comments of the Day in the Realm of the Rooter," *The Pittsburg Press,* February 9, 1903, 10.
59. "Pirate Chief's Pitchers Good: Fred Clarke Talks at Redville Concerning the New-Comers on His Staff of Twirlers," *The Pittsburg Press,* April 17, 1903, 22.
60. "Lefty Davis Has Been Forgotten: Jimmy Sebring's Spectacular Performance Makes the Record Of His Predecessor Appear Obscure," *The Pittsburg Press,* April 24, 1903, 18.
61. "Old Records Were Smashed: Pittsburg Whitewashed Boston and Scored Fourth Successive Shutout," *The Pittsburg Press,* June 6, 1903, 10.
62. Ralph S. Davis, "Pirates Blanked Bostons: World's Record Established by Five Successive Shutouts by Champions," *The Pittsburg Press,* June 7, 1903, 20.
63. "Runs Scored by Phillies: Zimmer's Men Really Succeeded in Crossing Pittsburg Home Plate," *The Pittsburg Press,* June 10, 1903, 14.
64. "M'Graw's Team is Outclassed: Eddie Doheny Pitched Rings Around Iron Man McGinnity," *The Pittsburg Press,* May 19, 1903, 14.

65. *Ibid.*
66. A. R. Cratty, "Pittsburg Points: Pitcher Doheny's Desertion of the Team a Singular Move— New England Twirler Is a Sensitive Man," *Sporting Life,* August 8, 1903, 6.
67. "No Rest Now for Clarke: Pirate Leader is Busily Looking for Men to Fill Holes on Crippled Team," *The Pittsburg Press,* July 29, 1903, 12.
68. Cratty, "Pittsburg Points: Pitcher Doheny's Desertion of the Team a Singular Move— New England Twirler Is a Sensitive Man," 6.
69. *Ibid.*
70. "Doheny Will Rejoin Team: Physician Writes Manager Clarke about the Famous Pitcher's Condition," *The Pittsburg Press,* August 9, 1903, 19.
71. "Doheny Has Joined Team: Clever Southpaw Again Returned to the Pirate Fold," *The Pittsburg Press,* August 16, 1903, 18.
72. "Kennedy Knew It," *The Pittsburg Press,* August 3, 1903, 10.
73. *Ibid.*
74. "A World's Series Has at Last Been Definitely Settled Upon," *Sporting Life,* September 26, 1903, 3.
75. "Pirates Win the Pennant: By Taking Two Games from Boston, the Champions Clinch Flag," *The Pittsburg Press,* September 19, 1903, 8.
76. Ralph S. Davis, "Pittsburgh Pride: Phillippe's Good Pitching in World's Series," *The Sporting News,* October 17, 1903, 1.
77. Louis Masur, *Autumn Glory: Baseball's First World Series* (New York: Hill And Wang, 2003), 148–149.
78. *Ibid.,* 205.
79. Andy Dabilis and Nick Tsiotos, *The 1903 World Series: The Boston Americans, The Pittsburg Pirates, And The "First Championship Of The United States"* (Jefferson, NC: McFarland, 2004), 140.
80. Masur, *Autumn Glory: Baseball's First World Series,* 205.
81. Dabilis and Tsiotos, *The 1903 World Series: The Boston Americans, The Pittsburg Pirates, And The "First Championship Of The United States,"* 138.
82. *Ibid.*
83. "Doings of Doheny: His Mad Outbreak the Result of Pittsburgh's Defeat by Boston—The Patient Certain to Recover His Reason," *Sporting Life,* October 24, 1903, 12.
84. *Ibid.*
85. Dabilis and Tsiotos, *The 1903 World Series: The Boston Americans, The Pittsburg Pirates, And The "First Championship Of The United States,"* 147.
86. "President Dreyfuss Shocked," *Sporting Life,* October 17, 1903, 6.
87. Ralph S. Davis, "Are Unbeatable: Pirates Won Six Straight Shut Out Games," *The Sporting News,* June 13, 1903, 1.
88. "O'Connor Dropped: But the Catcher Has Tight Contract with the Invaders," *The Pittsburg Press,* September 26, 1903, 10.

Bibliography

Books

Dabilis, Andy, and Nick Tsiotos. *The 1903 World Series: The Boston Americans, the Pittsburg Pirates, And The 'First Championship of the United States.'* Jefferson, NC: McFarland, 2004.

DeValeria, Dennis, and Jeanne Burke DeValeria. *Honus Wagner: A Biography.* New York: Henry Holt, 1995.

Finoli, David, and Bill Ranier. *The Pittsburgh Pirates Encyclopedia.* Urbana, IL: Sports Publishing, 2003.

Fleitz, David L. *More Ghosts in the Gallery: Another Sixteen Little-Known Greats at Cooperstown.* Jefferson, NC: McFarland, 2007.

Freese, Mel R. *Charmed Circle: Twenty-Game-Winning Pitchers in Baseball's 20th Century.* Jefferson, NC: McFarland, 1997.

Hittner, Arthur D. *Honus Wagner: The Life of Baseball's "Flying Dutchman."* Jefferson, NC: McFarland, 2003.

Koppett, Leonard. *Koppett's Concise History of Major League Baseball.* Philadelphia: Temple University, 1998. Reprint, New York: Carroll & Graf, 2004.

Lieb, Frederick G. *The Pittsburgh Pirates.* New York: Putnam's, 1948. Reprint, Carbondale: Southern Illinois University, 2003.

Levy, Alan H. *Rube Waddell: The Zany, Brilliant Life of a Strikeout Artist.* Jefferson, NC: McFarland, 2000.

Masur, Louis P. *Autumn Glory: Baseball's First World Series.* New York: Hill and Wang, 2003.

Neyer, Rob, and Eddie Epstein. *Baseball Dynasties: The Greatest Teams of All Time.* New York: W.W. Norton, 2000.

Pajot, Dennis. *Baseball's Heartland War 1902–1903: The Western League and American Association Vie for Turf, Players and Profits.* Jefferson, NC: McFarland, 2011.

Peterson, Richard, ed. *The Pirates Reader.* Pittsburgh: University of Pittsburgh, 2003.

Ritter, Lawrence S. *The Glory Of Their Times: The Story of the Early Days of Baseball Told By the Men Who Played It.* New York: Macmillan, 1966. Reprint, New York: William Morrow, 1984.

_____. *Lost Ballparks: A Celebration of Baseball's Legendary Fields.* New York: Penguin Books, 1992.

Waldo, Ronald T. *Fred Clarke: A Biography of the Baseball Hall of Fame Player-Manager.* Jefferson, NC: McFarland, 2011.

Wiggins, Robert Peyton. *The Deacon and the Schoolmaster: Phillippe and Leever, Pittsburgh's Great Turn-Of-The-Century Pitchers.* Jefferson, NC: McFarland, 2011.

Newspapers and Magazines

Anaconda Standard (Butte, MT)
The Atlanta Constitution
Baltimore American
Baltimore Sunday Herald
Biloxi Daily Herald (Biloxi, MS)
Boston Daily Globe
Chicago Daily American
Chicago Journal
Chicago Record-Herald
Cincinnati Enquirer
Commercial-Tribune (Cincinnati, OH)
Daily Kennebec Journal (Kennebec, ME)
The Decatur Daily Review (Decatur, IL)
Denver Post
Detroit Free Press
Elkhart Weekly Truth (Elkhart, IN)
Evening Telegram (Providence, RI)
The Fort Wayne News

The Fort Wayne Sentinel
Hamilton Daily Republican-News (Hamilton, OH)
The Indiana Progress (Indiana, PA)
The Mail and Express (Toronto, Ontario)
The Mansfield News (Mansfield, OH)
Moberly Daily Monitor (Moberly, MO)
The Newark Advocate (Newark, OH)
New Castle News (New Castle, PA)
The News-Democrat (Uhrichsville, OH)
New York Evening Telegram
New York Press
The New York Times
New York World
North Adams Transcript (North Adams, MA)
Oshkosh Daily Northwestern (Oshkosh, WI)
The Piqua Leader-Dispatch (Piqua, OH)
Pittsburgh Post-Gazette
The Pittsburgh Press
Portsmouth Herald (Portsmouth, NH)
Portsmouth Times (Portsmouth, OH)
St. Louis Star
The Salt Lake Tribune
The Semi-Weekly Cedar Falls Gazette (Cedar Falls, IA)
Sporting Life
The Sporting News
Syracuse Post Standard
Titusville Herald (Titusville, PA)
The Trenton Times
The Toledo Bee
Webster City Tribune (Webster City, IA)
The Youngstown Daily Vindicator

Websites

Baseball Almanac, http://www.baseball-almanac.com.
Baseball-Reference.com, http://www.baseball-reference.com.
LA84 Foundation, http://www.la84.org.
Retrosheet, http://www.retrosheet.org.
SABR, http://www.sabr.org.

Index

Numbers in ***bold italics*** indicate pages with photographs.

Abbaticchio, Ed 251
Albany, New York 161
Albany Senators 161
All-Americans 224–227
All-Nationals 226, 228
Allegheny City, Pennsylvania 2, 28, 35–36, 42, 85, 91, 175–176, 179, 199, 205, 214, 217, 231–232
Andover, Massachusetts 247–248, 250
Angus, Sam F. 207, 224, 233, 237, 243
Ashton, South Dakota 156
Atlantic City, New Jersey 9, 31–32, 164, 167, 179, 183, 214
Auburn Maroons 38
Auten, Phil L. 7–9, 11, 24–27, 30–33, 61, 233

Balliett, Frank 24–25, 30
Baltimore, Maryland 1, 36, 38, 93, 140, 148, 150, 211
Baltimore Orioles 5, 11, 35–38, 51, 54, 62, 110, 139, 149, 151–153, 159, 201–202, 211
Bancroft, Frank 221–222
Bankers team 71
Barclay, George 84, 92, 126, 150, 154
Bean, Joe 106, 117
Beaumont, Clarence "Ginger" 9, 14–15, 34, 43–45, 50, 53, 73–75, *77*, 78–80, 82–84, 87–89, 92, 94, 96–97, 100, 102, 104–105, 107, 109–113, 115–116, 118, 120–121, 126–128, 131, 134, 137–138, 140–147, 150–151, 155–158, 160–163, 170, 172–174, 177, 182–183, 186–189, 195–196, 198, 202–203, 205–206, 211–213, 217, 221, 223–224, 249, 251–252
Beaumont, Norma Olive (Vaughn) 53
Beck, Erve 94–95
Beckley, Jake 86, 94, 130, 134, 205, 213, 220–221
Bedford Springs, Pennsylvania 160, 192
Bellevue, Kentucky 30

Benham, J.A. 176
Bernhard, Bill 35, 226
Berry, Shad 138
Birmingham Barons 218
Boone, Daniel 156
Boston, Massachusetts 121, 123, 125, 164, 167, 172, 180, 195, 197, 247
Boston Americans 2–3, 62–64, 194, 224, 248–252
Boston Beaneaters 5, 16, 18, 28, 34–35, 41, 44, 48, 56–59, 66, 69, 98, 100–102, 121–123, 142–145, 165–166, 186–187, 190, 195–197, 213, 218, 222, 243, 246, 248
Boston Doves 251
Bowerman, Frank 107, 140, 173, 247
Bradford, Pennsylvania 10
Bradley, Bill 216
Bransfield, William Edward "Kitty" 33, 39, 42, 45, 50, 70, 72, 74, 77, 80, 83, 86, 91–92, 94–95, 98, 102, 104–107, 109, 116–118, 122–123, 127, 131, 133–135, 137–140, 142–144, 156, 158, 160, 162–164, 166–167, 170, 177, 182, ***191***, 195–197, 202–203, 208, 211, 214–215, 217–221, 223–224, 251
Brashear, Roy 92, 125, 127, 150
Brodie, Steve 140
Brooklyn, New York 61, 193
Brooklyn Superbas 5, 18, 20–23, 25–26, 29, 35, 42–44, 46, 50, 56–60, 62, 64–65, 96–98, 105, 110, 120–122, 127, 135–137, 141, 145, 157–161, 164, 167, 172, 182–183, 186, 188, 190, 193–195, 198, 222, 242–243, 245
Brown, Tom 112, 150, 152–153, 157
Browne, George 102, 115, 173
Brush, John T. 6, 29, 54, 56–62, 64–65, 67–69, 99–100, 102, 114, 130, 132, 135, 148, 151–153, 157, 159–160, 165–166, 185, 218, 237–238, 242–243
Buckenberger, Al 102, 144

285

Bucknell College 244
Budd, C.W. 80
Buffalo, New York 30, 48, 193, 213
Buffalo Bisons 213
Burke, Jimmy 45, 72, 74–75, 95–96, 105, 107, 114, 141–142, 147, 150, 154, 156, 162, 167, 170, 177–179, 181, 184–185, 194–198, 202, 206, 214, 217, 224, 251
Burkett, Jesse 52

Calhoun, Red 208
Cambridge Springs, Pennsylvania 17–18, 42
Camden, New Jersey 156
Campbell, Joe 13–15
Cantillon, Joe 82–83, 89, 123, 226, 228–229
Canton, Ohio 34
Carey, George "Scoops" 224
Carnegie, Andrew 2, 201
Carnegie, Pennsylvania 10, 50, 53, 70–71, 156, 200
Carney, Pat 144, 187
Carr, Lew 43
Casper, Wyoming 49
Cassatt, Mary 2
Chadwick Park 161
Chance, Frank 104, 113
Charleroi, Pennsylvania 218, 226
Chesbro, Jack "Happy Jack" 3, 8, 11–12, 28, 39–40, 42, 50, 71, 74, 78–79, 83, 86–87, 91, 94–96, 98, 100–102, 105, 107–108, 111–113, 116–117, 121, 123, 126, 131, 135–136, 138, 141–142, 144–145, 152, 156, 158, 162, 164–165, 169–170, 173–174, 177–179, 182, 186, 192–193, 196, 198, 201–202, 204, 208, 211–213, 215–218, 220, 223, *225*, 226–230, 236, 244–246, 252
Chicago, Illinois 10, 15, 18, 24, 41, 49, 51, 61–63, 89–90, 114, 127, 130–132, 137, 146, 150, 162, 166, 174, 180, 193, 214, 216, 228, 234
Chicago Cubs 86–89, 99, 104, 106, 109, 111–113, 118–120, 122, 127–132, 134, 137–138, 142, 145–147, 174, 188–190, 210–212, 216, 222, 238–239, 243, 246–247, 251–252
Chicago Orphans 7, 12, 15, 17–19, 24–26, 33, 35, 40–41, 44, 51–52, 56–58, 62, 64–66, 69
Chicago White Sox 53, 62, 104, 132, 169, 174, 185, 188, 194, 216–217
Childs, Cupid 138
Childs, Pete 115
Cincinnati, Ohio 30, 38–39, 53, 62–63, 68, 96, 98–100, 114, 119, 132–133, 135, 142, 147, 172, 183, 217–218, 226, 228, 230, 241–242, 244, 247, 249
Cincinnati Reds 6, 21, 28–29, 39, 41–44, 54, 56–58, 61, 69, 85–86, 93–95, 98–99, 110–111, 130, 132–135, 142, 145, 152, 159, 165, 172, 183, 185, 190, 204, 210, 213, 216–222, 226, 228, 239, 243–244
Clark, Roy 140
Clarke, Annette 8, 197
Clarke, Fred 2–3, 7–18, *19*, 20–24, 26–27, 29, 32–34, 36–50, 52, 55, 63, 70–86, 88, 89, 90–96, 98–102, *103*, 104–122, 125–126, 128–129, 131–132, 134–135, 137–146, 150, 152–155, 158, 160–167, 169–173, 175, 177–178, 181–182, 185–190, 192–193, 195–199, 204, 206, 208–215, 218–221, 223–229, 234–235, 244–252
Clarke, Helen 8
Clarke, Lucy 197
Clarke, William 197
Cleveland, Pres. Grover 53
Cleveland, Ohio 1, 63, 71, 148, 156, 176, 178–180, 216–217, 226–227, 230
Cleveland Blues 44, 62
Cleveland Broncos 84, 162, 216, 224, 226, 237
Cleveland Spiders 5, 11
Collins, Justice Gilbert 31–32
Collins, Jimmy 35
Columbia College 207
Columbus, Ohio 219
Comiskey, Charles 132, 169, 174, 217
Congalton, Bunk 87, 113, 128
Conroy, Dr. Edward C. 247, 249
Conroy, Wid 51–52, 63, 74–77, 79, 89, 92–97, 104–105, 113–115, 119, 126–131, 133, 135, 140–141, 143–145, 150, 152–153, 156, 158, 161–163, 165–167, 177–179, 181–186, 188–189, 192–196, 202–203, 206, 208, 210–212, 219, 224, 227, 229–230, 242, 252
Cooley, Duff "Dick" 15–16, 18, 143
Corcoran, Tommy 94–95
Courtney, Ernie 143–144
Coyle, James 72
Crane, Sam 139
Cratty, A.R. 178–179, 191–192, 198
Crawford, Sam 95, 205, 213, 220
Crolius, Fred 186
Cross, Lave 35
Cross, Monte 216, 224
Cunningham, Ellsworth Elmer "Bert" 8, 12, 42
Currie, Clarence 150
Cushman, Harvey 183, 185, 188, 195, 197, 209, 219
Czolgosz, Leon 48–49

Dahlen, Bill 137, 160, 194
Davis, Alfonzo "Lefty" 3, 43–45, 50, 74, 76–80, 82–84, 86–89, 91–98, 104–105, 110–111, 113, 116, 116–120, 126, 131–132,

134, 137–143, 146, 150, 156, 164, 169–170, 177–178, 182, 189, 193, 198–200, 204, 211, 214–215, 217, 219, 244, 252
Davis, Harry 216, 224
Davis, Gov. Jeff 78
Dayton, Kentucky 156
DeMontreville, Gene 143, 196
Denver, Colorado 36
Des Moines, Iowa 32, 150, 155, 197, 204
Des Moines Midgets 80
Detroit, Michigan 35, 211, 216
Detroit Tigers 15, 54, 62, 186, 207, 211, 215, 224, 233–234, 237, 243, 251
Dexter, Charlie 87, 112–113, 187
Diehl, Mayor William J. 23
Dillon, Frank "Pop" 14–15
Dobbs, Frank 142
Dr. Dickson 140
Dr. Jekyll 159
Doheny, Eddie 43, 50, 74–76, 96, 98, 101, 105, 107, 111–112, 117, 120, 134–135, 139, 142, 145, 150, 154, 156, 160–161, 165, 172, 177, 182, 186, 196–197, 218, 223, 244–251
Dolan, Patrick "Cozy" 45, 137, 159, 194
Donahue, Jiggs 41
Donlin, Mike 35–36, 218
Donovan, Bill 97, 137, 242
Donovan, Patsy 10–11, 15, 39, 52, 82–83, 90–91, 93, 122, 125–126, 150, 154, 182, 208–209
Dooin, Red 117, 139, 163
Douglass, Klondike 105, 170
Doyle, Jack 28, 106–107, 110–111, 117
Dreyfuss, Barney 1–2, 6–13, 15–19, 21, 23–27, 30–38, 40–43, 48–49, 51–61, *62*, 63–70, 72–73, 75, 84, 90, 99, 107, 110–111, 115–116, 120–122, 124–125, 130, 132–133, 135, 139, 141, 143–144, 147–149, 151–153, 155, 157, 159–160, 162–163, 165–169, 172–181, 183–185, 188–193, 195, 198–207, 212, 214–217, 220–244, 248–252
Dryden, Charley 124
Duffy, Hugh 35
Duggleby, Bill 163, 203
Dun and Bradstreet 155
Duquesne Gardens 71
Duquesne University 39
Dwyer, Frank 186, 243

Eason, Mal 87, 123, 143, 187, 196
Ebbets, Charles H. 62, 65, 68, 242
Egan, Pat 198, 204
Elliott, J.R. 80
Ely, Fred "Bones" 14–15, 28, 43–44, 55, 71, 185, 223, 230
Emlenton, Pennsylvania 74, 156, 193, 202

Emslie, Bob 95, 106, 162, 247
Evans, Roy 118, 158
Ewing, Bob 94
Ewing, Buck 18–19
Exposition Park 2, 18–22, 36, 39–44, 48–49, 51, 64, 71–72, 85–87, 89–90, 92–93, 96–98, 100–101, 104–107, 110–115, 119–121, 125–126, 128–129, 133–135, *136*, 139–140, 142, 145–146, 167, 169–170, *171*, 172–173, 178, 182, 186, 188, 190, 193, 199, 205–207, 211, 213–214, 216–218, 220–221, 223–224, 240, 244, 246, 248

Falkenberg, Fred "Cy" 215, 223, 244–245
Fanning, Jack 80
Farrell, Duke 45
Farrell, John 82–83
Father McDermott 39
Fay, Johnny 63
Finn, Mickey 79
Flaherty, Patsy 8
Flood, Tim 96
Fogel, Horace 108, 140
Fohl, Lee 183
Foster, John B. 183, 232
Fox, George 8, 11
Francis, David E. 7
Fraser, Chick 35, 117, 138, 203
Freedman, Andrew 54, 56–60, 64–66, 68–69, 99, 114–115, 139, 149, 151–152, 159, 166, 207, 218
French, Aaron 240
French Lick, Indiana 6
Friel, Bill 206–207

Gheny, Al. E. 14
Gilbert, Fred 80
Glenn, Ed 133
Goshen, Ohio 156
Grady, New York State Senator Thomas F. 187
Greene, Paddy 203
Gremminger, Ed 143
Griffith, Clark 35, 53, 111, 188, 252
Grillo, J. Ed 39, 87, 123, 228, 244–245
Gruber, John 129, 137, 144

Hackett, Jim 208–209
Hahn, Frank "Noodles" 29, 134, 142, 217
Hale, Ray "Dad" 144
Hallman, Bill 105
Hamilton, Billy 122
Hanlon, Ned 10, 20–22, 26, 110–111, 135, 158–159, 182, 186, 242
Hardy & Haynes 22
Harley, Dick 227
Harper, Jack 52

Hart, James A. 24, 33, 52, 60, 62–63, 65–67, 69, 130, 174, 216, 238–239, 241
Hartford City, Indiana 74
Hartman, Fred 83, 92, 138, 152
Havana, Cuba 29
Hazleton, Doc 82–83
Hearne, Hughie 121
Hedges, Robert 121
Heidrick, Emmet 52, 90
Heinz, H.J. 2
Heismann, Crese 95
Held, Anna 23
Herrmann, Garry 165, 185, 228, 239, 241
Hershman, Oliver S. 32, 239
Heyman, D.I. 31
Hoffer, Bill 11
Homestead, Pennsylvania 200, 209
Honey Creek, Wisconsin 53
Hot Springs, Arkansas 34–36, 64, 67, 71–76, 78, 81, 112, 198, 200
Hough, Frank 52–53, 55
Howarth, Oberlin 249–250
Hoy, Dummy 86
Hughes, Jim 98, 195
Hughes, Tom 252
Hulswitt, Rudy 105, 116, 163
Hurley, Pat 243
Hurst, Tim 22, 192

Iburg, Herman "Ham" 138, 170
Indianapolis, Indiana 58, 219
Indianapolis Hoosiers 11
Irwin, Charlie 45, 96, 98, 158

Jacobs, Mike 145–147
James, Jesse 80
Jefferson, Thomas 53
Jennings, Hughie 26–27, 138–139, 163–164, 172
Jersey City, New Jersey 239, 243
Johnson, Ban B. 35, 52, 54–55, 57, 62–63, 68, 84, 115, 120–121, 132, 148–151, 153, 159, 162, 168, 173–181, 183–186, 188–189, 191–192, 194, 196, 199–202, 207–208, 211, 214–216, 224, 226, 229–234, 236–238, 240–242
Jones, Davy 112–114, 130
Jones, Fielder 35
Jones, Jim 107, 160, 162
Jones & Laughlin 233
Joss, Addie 224

Kahoe, Mike 131
Kansas City, Kansas 229
Kansas City, Missouri 79
Keeler, Willie 97–98, 137, 182, 194, 242
Kelley, Joe 22–23, 139, 159, 173, 220–222

Kelley, Mike 8, 11
Kelly, King 123
Kennedy, Bill 244–245, 248
Kerr, William W. 1, 6–11, 16, 24–27, 29–33, 55, 61, 233
Kilfoyl, John F. 162, 237
Killilea, Henry J. 248
Kitson, Frank 45, 96, 158–159, 182, 186
Kling, Johnny 87, 128, 130, 146–147
Knowles, Fred 139
Krueger, Otto 83, 150
Krug, Henry 203

Lajoie, Nap 35, 39, 80, 84, 216, 219, 226–227, 229
Lanigan, Harold 81–82, 84, 207, 222
Latham, Arlie 203
Latimer, Tacks 8
Latrobe, Pennsylvania 251
Lauder, Bill 160
Leach, Nelson 74
Leach, Tommy 2, 8–9, 13, 20, 22, 38, 42–43, 50, 71, 74, 76, 79–86, 89, 92–97, 100, 104–105, 109, 112, 116–118, 124, 126–128, 131–132, 136–138, 142–147, 150, 156–158, 160, 162–166, 169–170, 172–175, 177, 179, 181–183, 187–189, 192–196, 202–204, 206, 208–211, 216–219, 223–224, 227, 229–232, 240, *241*, 242, 251–252
League Park, Cincinnati 15, 39
League Park, St. Louis 15, 82–83, 150, 152, 154, 206
Leever, Sam 9, 11–12, 15, 19, 22–23, 39, 44, 50, 70, 74, 76–80, 82, 86, 88, 92, 94–96, 100, 105, 114, 126, 133, 142, 144, 150, 154, 156, 163, 170, 177, 181–183, 187, 193, 196, 198, 203, 206, 209, 211, *212*, 217, 219, 223–224, 244–246, 249, 251
Leonard, Frank 243
Little Rock, Arkansas 79
Little Rock Travelers 76–79
Locke, William Henry 243, 247
Loftus, Tom 40–41
Long, Herman 28, 101, 123, 196
Los Angeles, California 229
Louisville, Kentucky 1, 6, 25, 50–51, 53, 61–62, 70, 132, 149, 241
Louisville Colonels 1–2, 5–12, 27, 32, 38, 42, 50, 132, 187, 199
Low, Seth 60, 207
Lowe, Bobby 128
Lundgren, Carl 131, 189, 212
Lush, Billy 196

Mack, Connie 16, 34–35, 44, 51–52, 55, 84, 116, 185
Madison, Art 8, 11

Index

Magee, Bill 105
Magoon, George 111, 134
Malarkey, John 196
Maloney, Bill 115, 121
Manhattan Field 57, 60, 114–115
Manning, Jim 54
Manor, Pennsylvania 227
Massillon, Ohio 156
Mathewson, Christy 106, 161, 181, 244
McAleer, Jimmy 72, 80, 91
McCreery, Tom 21, 96–97, 120, 223
McDonald, Pennsylvania 71
McFarland, Ed 19
McGann, Dan 160
McGinnity, Joe 22–23, 35, 159, 181, 198
McGraw, John 35–37, 52, 139–141, 149, 160–162, 173, 197, 200–201, 238, 245–246, 251
McGuire, Jim "Deacon Jim" 188
McKinley, Pres. William 48–49
McLaughlin, Warren 198, 202–203, 206, 209, 214, 223
McPhee, Bid 94
McQuiston, Frank 240
McRoy, R.B. 191
Menefee, Jock 104, 112, 189
Mercer, Win 224
Merritt, George 63, 74, 123, 173, 177, 215, 217, 223, 244
Mertes, Sam 35
Miller, Bill 182–183
Miller, Dusty 112–113, 145–147
Miller, Roscoe 173–174
Mills, A.G. 58
Millvale, Pennsylvania 185
Milwaukee, Wisconsin 51, 62, 73
Milwaukee Brewers 16, 34, 44, 51, 155, 181
Minneapolis, Minnesota 72, 156
Mr. Hyde 159
Montreal, Quebec 214
Montreal Royals 214
Morse, J.C. 52–53
Mt. Clemens, Michigan 71, 73
Mrs. Doheny 247, 249–250
Mulford, Ren, Jr. 53, 98, 115
Murnane, Tim 126, 129
Murphy, Ed 126
Murphy, John 72

Nashville, Tennessee 146
National League Park 115, 164
New Castle, Pennsylvania 128
New London Whalers 198
New York, New York 25–28, 31, 33–34, 53, 55–57, 59–62, 66, 68, 84, 90, 98, 114, 117, 120, 124, 139, 151, 165–166, 174, 178, 180, 183, 187, 191, 197, 202, 205, 207–208, 211, 215, 218, 226–234, 237–238, 240, 242
New York Giants 3, 7, 11, 18–19, 26, 28–29, 42–44, 50, 54, 56–58, 60, 93, 98–99, 102, 106–110, 114–115, 117–120, 139–141, 149, 152, 158–162, 166, 173–174, 181–182, 190, 197–198, 200–201, 207, 218, 222, 238, 242–243, 245–248, 251–252
New York Highlanders 252
Newark Sailors 119
Newton, Doc 42, 121, 195
Nichols, Art 150, 152, 155
Nicoll, DeLancey 59
North Adams, Massachusetts 156, 215
Northfield, Vermont 156

Oakland, Pennsylvania 233
O'Brien, John 8, 11
O'Brien, Tom 11–12, 18, 22, 29, 33
O'Connor, Jack "Rowdy Jack" 3, 16–17, 22, 34–36, 41, 49, 72, 74, 79, 82–83, 92–94, 98, 100–101, 104–105, 107, 109, 113–114, 117–121, 123, 126, 130, 132, 140, 143, 145–146, 152, 154, 156, 158, 163, 170, 173, 174–179, *180*, 181–185, 200, 204, 207, 211, 219, 223, 227, 230–231, 234–236, 244, 252
O'Day, Hank 22, 97–98, 101, 120–121, 130, 134, 152, 160, 163, 170, 189, 196–197, 213, 218, 221, 246
O'Neill, Jack 152
O'Neill, Mike 125

Padden, Dick 52
Palace of the Fans 93, 99, 132, 172
Pastorius, Jim 161
Paterson Silk Weavers 50
Pearson, Alexander 208
Peitz, Heinie 130, 185, 204
Pensacola, Florida 74
Phelps, Eddie 195, 202–203, 206–207, 210, 217, 224, 244
Philadelphia, Pennsylvania 42, 44, 53, 61, 84, 114, 130, 163, 165, 174, 180, 202, 237, 239
Philadelphia Athletics 34, 44, 55, 62, 80, 84, 116, 174, 181, 194, 202, 237, 249
Philadelphia Phillies 11, 15, 19–20, 26, 35, 42, 44, 46, 48, 56–58, 60, 62, 64–65, 84, 102, 104–105, 114–117, 138–139, 141, 145, 163–164, 169–170, 172, 190, 202–203, 216, 219, 222, 228–229, 242–243, 246, 251
Phillippe, Deacon 2, 7–8, 22–23, 34, 45, 50, 70–74, 79–80, 82, 86, 89, 93, 96, 104, 106–107, 115, 117–118, 122, *127*, 128, 134, 137–138, 140, 143, 150, 154, 156, 158, 161, 163, 166, 172–174, 177, 181, 183, 185, 188,

194, 196, 211–213, 215, 217, 221, 223–225, 227, 244–246, 249, 251
Phillips, Bill 94–95, 133, 185, 219
Phipps, Henry 2
Phoenix, Arizona 33
Pittinger, Togie 122, 144, 165, 196
Pittsburgh, Pennsylvania 1–2, 6–7, 9, 11, 16–17, 19, 23, 25–27, 30–31, 35–37, 39, 42–43, 49, 51, 55, 57, 59–61, 63–66, 68–69, 71–74, 76, 84–85, 88, 91–93, 98–99, 104–105, 113–114, 133–135, 140–142, 144, 146–147, 160–161, 164–165, 167, 169, 172–174, 176, 178–184, 186, 188, 192, 197, 199–200, 203–209, 211–216, 219, 223, 226, 229–230, 232–234, 236, 238–240, 242, 248
Pittsburgh College 39–40
Plano, Pennsylvania 35
Point Breeze, Pennsylvania 240
Polo Grounds 60, 114, 117–119, 161–162, 184, 197, 201, 246
Poole, Ed 74, 76, 96, 98, 101, 119, 123, 156, 165, 172
Power, Charley 112–113, 130, 158
Powers, Pat 62
Probst, Frank 178
Prospect, Pennsylvania 40
Pulliam, Harry 6, 8–9, 13, 15, 18, 22, 24–26, 30–31, 33, 35, 39, 49–51, 53, 55–56, 65–66, 70, 73, 76, 78, 80, 85, 90, 99, 112, 114, 120, 124, 126, 132, 135, 139, 143, 148, 151, 155, 157, 159, 175, 177–178, 181, 184, 191, 195, 199, 212, 215, 218, 226, 229, 231, 234–243
Punxsutawney, Pennsylvania 16

Quaker City team 71

Raymer, Fred 41
Recreation Park 60
Reese, Bonesetter 192
Rhoads, Bob "Dusty" 88–89, 145
Richmond Bluebirds 28
Rinehart, Mary Roberts 2
Risher, Howard 209
Ritchey, Claude "Little All Right" 8–9, 14–15, 36, 42, 50, 72, 74–76, 79–80, 82–84, 92, 94–95, 98, 104, 106, 113–114, 117, *118*, 126–127, 131, 134, 139–140, 142–144, 147, 150, 156, 158, 162, 164, 166, 170, 177, 182, 186–188, 193, 196–197, 202, 209–210, 217–220, 224, 251
Ritchey, Sophie (Boyer) 193
Robinson, Gen. George 2
Robinson, Wilbert 139
Robison 238
Robison, Frank de Haas 17, 57, 60, 64, 68, 90, 154–155, 241

Rochester, Pennsylvania 218–219
Rochester, Wisconsin 156
Rockefeller, John D. 156
Rockford, Illinois 131
Rogers, John I. 56, 58, 65, 114, 242
Roosevelt, Pres. Theodore 27, 48, 104–105, 135
Rowe, Judge Norman 31–32
Ryan, Jack 150

Saginaw, Michigan 176
St. Joseph, Missouri 78–80, 91
St. Joseph Saints 78–80
St. Louis, Missouri 35, 39, 49, 52, 54, 62, 74, 79–81, 84–85, 120, 123, 132–133, 146–148, 154, 156, 178, 180, 185, 204, 206–207, 222, 234
St. Louis Browns 72, 80, 90, 115, 120–121, 124, 147, 178, 184, 188, 194, 204, 206
St. Louis Cardinals 11, 15–17, 21, 35, 39–40, 42–43, 52, 57–58, 77, 81–83, 85–86, 90–93, 122, 125–127, 145, 147, 150, 152, 154–155, 157, 190, 206–209, 211, 222, 243–245, 251–252
St. Vrain, Jimmy 89
Schaefer, Germany 146
Schoepf, W. Kelsey 32–33, 239
Schriver, Bill "Pop" 13, 17
Scott, Ed 29
Scott, Judge Francis 59
Sebring, Jimmy 173, 177, 186, 197–199, 202–203, 206–209, 212, 215, 217, 221, 224, 227, 243–244, **245**
Selee, Frank 28, 88, 127, 133, 245
Seymour, Cy 139, 213, 219, 221
Sharon, Pennsylvania 227
Sheckard, Jimmy 96
Shibe, Ben 237
Slagle, Jimmy 131, 145
Smith, George "Heinie" 106–107, 117, 140
Smith, Harry 34–35, 51, 63, 74, 76, 92, 97, 109, 112, 116, 119, 126–127, 130–131, 140, 146, 156, 160, 163, 172–173, 177, 181–182, 184–187, 189, 194, 198, 204, 211, 223, 227, 229–230, 242, 251
Smoot, Homer 150, 206, 209
Soden, Arthur 56–60, 64, 66–67, 69, 218
Somers, Charles W. "Charley" 63, 174–179, 181, 183–184, 189, 192, 199–200, 204, 211, 227, 230–231, 234, 238
South End Grounds 121, 123
South Field 207
South Side Park 104
Spalding, Albert G. 56–60, 62–63, 65–66

Sparks, Frank "Tully" 11, 107, 119
Stallings, George 213
Steinfeldt, Harry 94, 111, 134, 219
Sudhoff, Willie 52

Tannehill, Jesse "Tanny" 3, 9, 18–19, 22–23, 28, *29*, 40–41, 44, 50, 53–54, 71–74, 76, 78–79, 83, 87, 91, 94, 96–97, 100, 102, 106, 109, 111, 116, 119–120, 122–123, 125, 131, 135, 138, 140–142, 147, 150, 154, 156, 158, 161–164, 166–167, 169–170, 175, 177, 179, 182–183, 185–186, 188–189, 192, 194–196, 198–199, 201–202, 204–206, 208–209, 211, 214, 216–218, 223, 226–228, 230–231, 244–245, 252
Tannehill, Lee 53–54, 216
Taylor, Dummy 106
Taylor, Harry 30
Taylor, Jack 113, 127–128, 137–138, 145, 188
Taylor, Dr. R.T. 7
Tebeau, George 132
Temple, William C. 66, 237–238
Tenney, Fred 101–102, 114
Thielman, Henry 111, 133, 219
Thomas, Roy 105, 116, 203
Thomasville, Georgia 12–13
Thornton, Captain James 85–86
Tinker, Joe 89, 104, 128–130, 133, 145, 152, 189
Topeka, Kansas 229
Toronto, Ontario 213
Toronto Maple Leafs 213
Trenton, New Jersey 31, 33
Truax, Justice Charles H. 65–66

Utica, New York 193, 197–198
Utica Pent-Ups 193, 198

Van Haltren, George 106–107, 140
Van Wyck, Robert Anderson 60
Veil, Fred "Bucky" 244–245
Verona, Pennsylvania 33
Vickers, Rube 217, 220–221

Waddell, Florence 41
Waddell, George Edward "Rube" 7–10, 16, 22–23, 28, 34–35, 39–41, 216
Waddell, John 40
Wagner, Charley 140–141
Wagner, Hans 49
Wagner, John Peter "Honus" 2, 7–10, 14–15, 21–22, 42–45, 50–51, 53, 55, 63–64, 69– 72, 74–80, 82–83, 86, 89, 92–98, 102, 104–107, 109, 112, 115–118, 120–124, 126– 127, 131–132, 134, 137–140, 142–147, 150, 152–153, 156, *157*, 158–162, 164, 166, 169–175, 177–178, 181–183, 186–189, 194– 195, 197, 203–205, 208–214, 217–220, 223–224, 227, 235, 251–252
Wagner, Katheryn 21
Wall, Berry 124
Wallace, Roderick "Bobby" 52, 188, 227
Ward, John Montgomery 238
Washington, D.C. 1, 104, 150–151
Washington Nationals 5, 11
Washington Park 120–121, 158
Washington Senators 44, 54, 62
Watkins, W.H. 6, 57
Weaver, Art 209
Weber, Lois 2
West Side Grounds 41, 89, 104, 114, 127, 130, 132, 137, 146, 216
White, Doc 102, 105, 115, 139, 164, 172
Whittington Park 75–78
Wicker, Bob 92, 207
Wilhelm, Irvin "Kaiser" 218, 223, 244–246
Williams, Art 131
Williams, Jimmy 9, 14–15, 19–22, 27–28, 35–38, 51–52, 200
Williams, Nan Lee (Smith) 28, 35–36
Willis, Vic 100, 143
Wilmington, Delaware 122–123
Wilmington Sailors 123
Winfield, Kansas 8–9, 70, 72, 74, 228
Wolverton, Harry 19
Woods, Walt 8
Woodside, S.P. 48–49
Worcester, Massachusetts 122–123, 156, 167, 191, 196
Worcester Farmers 33
Worcester Hustlers 123, 173, 207, 215, 243– 244

Yeager, George 63
Yerkes, Stan 82
Young, Cy 15, 216, 224, 227
Young, Nick 57–59, 68–69
Youngstown, Ohio 74, 192

Zimmer, Charles "Chief" 8, 15, 17, 34, 41– 42, 74–75, 83, 86, 113, 131, 146–147, 156, 170, 173, 177, 182, 186, 202–203, 209, 217, 221, 223, 228, 251
Zuber, Charley 95, 119

 www.ingramcontent.com/pod-product-compliance
Ingram Content Group UK Ltd.
Pitfield, Milton Keynes, MK11 3LW, UK
UKHW041927140426
5217IPUK00014B/350